First World War
and Army of Occupation
War Diary
France, Belgium and Germany

61 DIVISION
183 Infantry Brigade
Northumberland Fusiliers
9th Battalion
1 June 1918 - 3 November 1919

WO95/3062/1

The Naval & Military Press Ltd
www.nmarchive.com
Published in association with The National Archives

Published by

The Naval & Military Press Ltd

Unit 10 Ridgewood Industrial Park,

Uckfield, East Sussex,

TN22 5QE England

Tel: +44 (0) 1825 749494

www.naval-military-press.com

www.nmarchive.com

This diary has been reprinted in facsimile from the original. Any imperfections are inevitably reproduced and the quality may fall short of modern type and cartographic standards.

© Crown Copyright
Images reproduced by permission of The National Archives, London, England, 2015.

Contents

Document type	Place/Title	Date From	Date To
Heading	WO95/3062-1		
Heading	61st Division 183rd Infy Bde 9th Bn North'D Fusiliers Jun 1918-Aug 1919		
Miscellaneous	Cover For Branch Memoranda.		
Miscellaneous	9th North Fusiliers		
War Diary	La Lacque (Hazebrouck 5A F5)	01/06/1918	01/06/1918
War Diary	Ham-En-Artois	02/06/1918	08/06/1918
War Diary	Hamet Billet (Hazebrouck 5A G5)	09/06/1918	13/06/1918
War Diary	Bn Nd G5 P11a6.9 (36A)	14/06/1918	21/06/1918
War Diary	Hamet Billet (Hazebrouck 5A G5)	22/06/1918	26/06/1918
War Diary	Bn. Hd Qrs P5c2.9 (36A)	27/06/1918	30/06/1918
Miscellaneous	Appendices to War Diary June 1918		
Operation(al) Order(s)	61 Division Order No. 164	27/05/1918	27/05/1918
Miscellaneous	To 9th North'd Fus 184 Inf Bde	01/06/1918	01/06/1918
Operation(al) Order(s)	183 Inf. Bde Order No.213	01/06/1918	01/06/1918
Miscellaneous	March Table		
Operation(al) Order(s)	183rd Infantry Brigade Order No.215	10/06/1918	10/06/1918
Miscellaneous	C Form Messages And Signals		
Miscellaneous	9th North'd Fus	19/06/1918	19/06/1918
Operation(al) Order(s)	183rd Infantry Brigade Order No.217	19/06/1918	19/06/1918
Operation(al) Order(s)	183 Infantry Brigade Order No.213	23/06/1918	23/06/1918
Operation(al) Order(s)	Operation Orders No.40 9th (Northd Hussers) Bn Northumberland Fusrs		
Miscellaneous	War Diary		
Operation(al) Order(s)	Operation Orders No.41 9th (Northd Hussers) Bn Northumberland Fusrs		
Operation(al) Order(s)	Operation Orders No.42 9th (Northd Hussers) Bn Northumberland Fusrs	12/06/1918	12/06/1918
Operation(al) Order(s)	Operation Orders No.43 9th (Northd Hussers) Bn Northumberland Fusrs	16/06/1918	16/06/1918
Operation(al) Order(s)	Operation Orders No.43A 9th (Northd Hussers) Bn Northumberland Fusiliers	20/06/1918	20/06/1918
Miscellaneous	War Diary		
Operation(al) Order(s)	Operation Orders No.44 9th (North Hussers) Bttn Northumberland Fusiliers	24/06/1918	24/06/1918
Miscellaneous	War Diary		
Miscellaneous	Special Order Of The Day By Field-Marshal Sir Douglas Haig K.T. G.C.B. G.C.V.O. K.C.I.E. Commander-In-Chief British Armies in France	09/06/1918	09/06/1918
Miscellaneous	QM		
Miscellaneous	Special Order Of The Day By Field-Marshal Sir Douglas Haig K.T. G.C.B. G.C.V.O. K.C.I.E. Commander-In-Chief British Armies in France	13/06/1918	13/06/1918
Miscellaneous	Special Order Of The Day By Field-Marshal Sir Douglas Haig K.T. G.C.B. G.C.V.O. K.C.I.E. Commander-In-Chief British Armies in France	24/06/1918	24/06/1918
Miscellaneous	Officer Commanding 9th Bn. Northd. Fus	04/06/1918	04/06/1918
Miscellaneous	Battalion Orders By Lieut. Colonel W.A. Vignoles D.S.O.	07/05/1918	07/05/1918

Miscellaneous	Battalion Orders By Lieut. Colonel W.A. Vignoles D.S.O.	16/06/1918	16/06/1918
Miscellaneous	Battalion Orders By Lieut. Colonel W.A. Vignoles D.S.O.	19/06/1918	19/06/1918
Miscellaneous	War Diary		
Map	Map		
Map	France		
Miscellaneous	App "A"		
Heading	9 N.F Vol 35		
Miscellaneous	9th (N.H.) Bn. Northumberland Fusiliers July 1918		
War Diary	In The Line	01/07/1918	31/07/1918
Miscellaneous	Strength Of Battalion At The Beginning Of Month		
Miscellaneous	Kings Birthday Honours		
Map	Map		
Heading	War Diary 9th North'd Fus Appendix A Vieille Chapelle 1/20,000		
Operation(al) Order(s)	Operation Orders No.45 9th (Northumberland Hussers) Bttn Northumberland Fusiliers	30/06/1918	30/06/1918
Operation(al) Order(s)	Operation Orders No.46 9th (Northumberland Hussers) Bttn Northumberland Fusrs	03/07/1918	03/07/1918
Operation(al) Order(s)	Operation Orders No.47 9th (Northd Hussers) Bn Northumberland Fusrs	09/07/1918	09/07/1918
Miscellaneous	Report On Raid Carried Out By 9th (N.H) Bn Northumberland Fusiliers	07/07/1918	07/07/1918
Operation(al) Order(s)	Operation Order No.48 9th (Northd Hussers) Bn Northumberland Fusrs	16/07/1918	16/07/1918
Miscellaneous	War Diary		
Operation(al) Order(s)	Operation Orders No.49 9th (Northd Hussers) Bn Northumberland Fusrs	22/07/1918	22/07/1918
Miscellaneous	War Diary		
Operation(al) Order(s)	Operation Orders No.50 9th (Northd Hussers) Bn Northumberland Fusrs	31/07/1918	31/07/1918
Miscellaneous	War Diary		
Miscellaneous	9th (Northd Hussers) Bn Northumberland Fusiliers Defence Instructions	27/07/1918	27/07/1918
Operation(al) Order(s)	183rd Infantry Brigade Order No.322	06/07/1918	06/07/1918
Miscellaneous	Operation Orders 9th (Northd Hussers) Bn Northd Fusiliers	06/07/1918	06/07/1918
Miscellaneous	9th (Northumberland Hussars) Battn. Northumberland Fusiliers Syllabus Of Training	27/07/1918	27/07/1918
Miscellaneous	9th (Northumberland Hussars) Battn. Northumberland Fusiliers Syllabus Of Training	03/08/1918	03/08/1918
Heading	9 N Bn Vol 36		
Miscellaneous	9th (Northd Hussars) Battn Northumberland Fusiliers		
War Diary	Fontes	01/08/1918	06/08/1918
War Diary	Arcade Camp	07/08/1918	09/08/1918
War Diary	Caudescure Station	10/08/1918	10/08/1918
War Diary	Arcade Camp	11/08/1918	14/08/1918
War Diary	Front Line	15/08/1918	19/08/1918
War Diary	Chapelle Boom	20/08/1918	21/08/1918
War Diary	H.Q. Sachet Farm	22/08/1918	23/08/1918
War Diary	HQ Factory Merville	24/08/1918	24/08/1918
War Diary	HQ. Bourre River	25/08/1918	25/08/1918
War Diary	HQ Casa Doss	26/08/1918	31/08/1918
Miscellaneous	Strength Of Battalion At Beginning Of Month		
Map	Map		

Miscellaneous	App A		
Operation(al) Order(s)	183rd Infantry Brigade Order No.232	13/08/1918	13/08/1918
Miscellaneous	Appendix "B" 183 Infantry Bde Orders		
Miscellaneous	Table "A" Issued With 183rd Infantry Bde Order No.232		
Miscellaneous	Table "B" Issued With 183rd Infantry Brigade Order No.232		
Operation(al) Order(s)	183rd Infantry Brigade Order No.233	16/08/1918	16/08/1918
Miscellaneous	9th North'd Fus	19/08/1918	19/08/1918
Operation(al) Order(s)	183 Infantry Brigade Order No.235	21/08/1918	21/08/1918
Operation(al) Order(s)	183rd Infantry Brigade Order No.236	21/08/1918	21/08/1918
Miscellaneous	H.S. Rowe		
Operation(al) Order(s)	183rd Infantry Brigade Order No.237	23/08/1918	23/08/1918
Operation(al) Order(s)	183rd Infantry Brigade Order No.238	24/08/1918	24/08/1918
Miscellaneous	Movement Table Issued With 183 Inf Bde Order No.238		
Miscellaneous	Headquarters 183rd Infantry Brigade	28/08/1918	28/08/1918
Miscellaneous	183rd Infantry Brigade	19/08/1918	19/08/1918
Miscellaneous	Messages And Signals		
Miscellaneous	Appendix G Special Orders of The Day		
Miscellaneous	Special Order Of The Day By Field Marshal Sir Douglas Haig K.T. G.C.B. G.C.V.O. K.C.I.E. Commander-In-Chief British Armies in France	04/08/1918	04/08/1918
Miscellaneous	Special Order Of The Day By Field Marshal Sir Douglas Haig K.T. G.C.B. G.C.V.O. K.C.I.E. Commander-In-Chief British Armies in France	01/08/1918	01/08/1918
Miscellaneous	Special Order Of The Day By Field Marshal Sir Douglas Haig K.T. G.C.B. G.C.V.O. K.C.I.E. Commander-In-Chief British Armies in France	30/06/1918	30/06/1918
Miscellaneous	Special Order Of The Day By Field Marshal Sir Douglas Haig K.T. G.C.B. G.C.V.O. K.C.I.E. Commander-In-Chief British Armies in France	14/08/1918	14/08/1918
Miscellaneous	Special Order Of The Day By Field Marshal Sir Douglas Haig K.T. G.C.B. G.C.V.O. K.C.I.E. Commander-In-Chief British Armies in France	12/08/1918	12/08/1918
Miscellaneous	Special Order Of The Day By Field Marshal Sir Douglas Haig K.T. G.C.B. G.C.V.O. K.C.I.E. Commander-In-Chief British Armies in France	17/08/1918	17/08/1918
Miscellaneous	Special Order Of The Day By Field Marshal Sir Douglas Haig K.T. G.C.B. G.C.V.O. K.C.I.E. Commander-In-Chief British Armies in France	21/08/1918	21/08/1918
Miscellaneous	A Form Messages And Signals		
Miscellaneous	C Form Messages And Signals		
Miscellaneous	A Form Messages And Signals		
Miscellaneous	From Brigade Major	21/08/1918	21/08/1918
Miscellaneous	A Form Messages And Signals		
Miscellaneous	Messages And Signals		
Miscellaneous	A Form Messages And Signals		
Miscellaneous	Appendix "C" 184 Infantry Bde Operation Orders		
Operation(al) Order(s)	184th Infantry Brigade Order No. 215 By Brigadier-General A.W. Pagan D.S.O.	31/08/1918	31/08/1918
Miscellaneous	O.C.9th. Northumberland Fusiliers.	31/08/1918	31/08/1918
Operation(al) Order(s)	184th. Infantry Brigade Order No. 216 By Brigadier-General A.W. Pagan D.S.O.	31/08/1918	31/08/1918
Operation(al) Order(s)	184th. Infantry Brigade Order No. 217 By Brigadier-General A.W. Pagan D.S.O.	01/09/1918	01/09/1918

Type	Description	Date 1	Date 2
Miscellaneous	On Completion of relief Coys will recently following areas	25/08/1918	25/08/1918
Operation(al) Order(s)	Operation Orders No.60 9th (Northd Hussers) Bn Northumberland Fusiliers	31/08/1918	31/08/1918
Miscellaneous			
Miscellaneous	Appendix D 9th (N.H) Battn Northd Fusiliers Operation Orders		
Operation(al) Order(s)	Operation Orders No.50 9th (Northd Hussers) Bn Northumberland Fusiliers	31/07/1918	31/07/1918
Miscellaneous			
Operation(al) Order(s)	Operation Orders No.51 9th (Northd Hussers) Bn Northumberland Fusiliers	01/08/1918	01/08/1918
Miscellaneous	Attack by 2 Coys of 9th North'd Fus	09/08/1918	09/08/1918
Operation(al) Order(s)	Operation Orders No.52 9th (Northd Hussers) Bn Northumberland Fusiliers	13/08/1918	13/08/1918
Miscellaneous	Table Of Guides		
Miscellaneous	Patrol Operation	07/08/1918	07/08/1918
Miscellaneous	9th (N H) Bn Northumberland Fusiliers Guide Table	18/08/1918	18/08/1918
Operation(al) Order(s)	Operation Orders No.53 9th (Northd Hussers) Bn Northumberland Fusiliers	18/08/1918	18/08/1918
Operation(al) Order(s)	Operation Orders No.58 9th (Northd Hussers) Bn Northd Fusrs	23/08/1918	23/08/1918
Operation(al) Order(s)	Operation Orders No.59 9th (Northd Hussers) Bn Northd Fusiliers		
Miscellaneous	Appendix "E" Operation Orders 11th Suffolks Regt 2/6 Royal Warwicks 2/4 Royal Berks		
Miscellaneous	1/6th Bn. Royal Warwickshire Regiment Order No.160	14/08/1918	14/08/1918
Operation(al) Order(s)	11th Suffolks Order No.53	18/08/1918	18/08/1918
Operation(al) Order(s)	2/4th Bn. Royal Berkshire Regt Operation Order No.40	24/08/1918	24/08/1918
Heading	9th (Northd Hussars) Batn Northumberland Fusiliers		
War Diary	Sacret Farm	01/09/1918	01/09/1918
War Diary	Speziano Camp	02/09/1918	05/09/1918
War Diary	Rebermetz	06/09/1918	06/09/1918
War Diary	Neuf-Berquin	07/09/1918	07/09/1918
War Diary	Batn H.Q. G9d2.1	08/09/1918	11/09/1918
War Diary	Yam Farm	12/09/1918	20/09/1918
War Diary	Battn H.Q Gailly Bac St Maur Road	21/09/1918	28/09/1918
War Diary	Yam Farm	29/09/1918	30/09/1918
Miscellaneous	Strength At The Beginning Of Month		
Miscellaneous	Appendix "A" Orders 183 Infy Brigade		
Miscellaneous	All Recipients of 183 Inf. Bde. Order No.239	01/09/1918	01/09/1918
Operation(al) Order(s)	183rd Infantry Brigade Order No. 243	02/09/1918	02/09/1918
Operation(al) Order(s)	183 Infantry Brigade Order No.242	03/09/1918	03/09/1918
Operation(al) Order(s)	183rd Infantry Brigade Order No.246	11/09/1918	11/09/1918
Operation(al) Order(s)	183 Infantry Brigade Order No.245	10/09/1918	10/09/1918
Miscellaneous	Relief Table Issued With 183rd Inf. Bde. Order No.245		
Operation(al) Order(s)	183rd Infantry Brigade Order No.244	10/09/1918	10/09/1918
Operation(al) Order(s)	183rd Infantry Brigade Order No.243	09/09/1918	09/09/1918
Miscellaneous	C Form Messages And Signals		
Operation(al) Order(s)	183rd Infantry Brigade Order No. 249	24/09/1918	24/09/1918
Miscellaneous	Appendix "B" Orders 9th (N.H) Battn Northumberland Fusiliers		
Operation(al) Order(s)	9th (N H) Battn Northumberland Fusiliers Order No.71	27/09/1918	27/09/1918
Operation(al) Order(s)	9th (N H) Battn Northumberland Fusiliers Order No.70	27/09/1918	27/09/1918
Operation(al) Order(s)	9th (Northd Hussars) Battn Northd Fusiliers Order No.62	01/09/1918	01/09/1918

Type	Description	Date From	Date To
Miscellaneous	A Form Messages And Signals		
Miscellaneous	Appendix "C"		
Operation(al) Order(s)	9th (Northd Hussars) Battn Northumberland Fusiliers Order No.68	19/09/1918	19/09/1918
Operation(al) Order(s)	9th (Northd Hussars) Battn Northumberland Fusiliers Order No.69	27/09/1918	27/09/1918
Miscellaneous	War Diary		
Operation(al) Order(s)	9th Battn (N.H) Northumberland Fusiliers Order No.67	12/09/1918	12/09/1918
Miscellaneous	War Diary		
Operation(al) Order(s)	9th (N H) Battn Northumberland Fusiliers Order No.64	05/09/1918	05/09/1918
Operation(al) Order(s)	9th (N.H) Battn Northumberland Fus Order No.65	07/09/1918	07/09/1918
Operation(al) Order(s)	9th (N H) Battn Northumberland Fusiliers Order No.66	11/09/1918	11/09/1918
Operation(al) Order(s)	9th (Northumberland Hussars) Battn Northumberland Fusiliers Order No.63	05/09/1918	05/09/1918
Miscellaneous	Appendix "D" Special Order of the Day		
Miscellaneous	Special Order Of The Day By Field-Marshal Sir Douglas Haig K.T. G.C.B. G.C.V.O. K.C.I.E. Commander-In-Chief British Armies in France	26/09/1918	26/09/1918
Operation(al) Order(s)	9th Battalion The Royal Warwickshire Regiment Order No.37	20/09/1918	20/09/1918
Operation(al) Order(s)	2/4th Battalion, Royal Berkshire Regiment Operation Order No.4 By Lieut-Col. C.R.C. Boyle D.S.O. Cmdg	10/09/1918	10/09/1918
Miscellaneous	1st Bn R Lancashire Regt O.O. No. P 38		
Heading	Appendix I Training Programmes Sept 1918		
Miscellaneous	9th (Northd Hussars) Battn Northumberland Fusiliers	07/09/1918	07/09/1918
Miscellaneous	9th (Northd Hussars) Battn Northumberland Fusiliers	15/09/1918	15/09/1918
Miscellaneous	9th (N H) Battn Northumberland Fusiliers	18/09/1918	18/09/1918
Miscellaneous	Cover For Branch Memoranda.		
Miscellaneous	9th (Northd Hussars) Battn Northumberland Fusiliers		
War Diary	Yam Farm	01/10/1918	02/10/1918
War Diary	Les Gseaux	03/10/1918	06/10/1918
War Diary	Pommera	07/10/1918	09/10/1918
War Diary	Bivouacs (E27b7040)	10/10/1918	11/10/1918
War Diary	Bivouacs (L.3.c.2.5)	12/10/1918	18/10/1918
War Diary	Billets (H.Q. A &b 85 B)	19/10/1918	19/10/1918
War Diary	Avesnes Les-Aubert	20/10/1918	23/10/1918
War Diary	Battn H.Q. (Maison Druoa)	24/10/1918	24/10/1918
War Diary	St Martin	25/10/1918	25/10/1918
War Diary	La Folie	26/10/1918	27/10/1918
War Diary	Sepmeries	27/10/1918	27/10/1918
War Diary	La Folie	28/10/1918	30/10/1918
War Diary	Sepmeries	31/10/1918	31/10/1918
Miscellaneous	Strength At The Beginning Of The Month		
Operation(al) Order(s)	183rd Infantry Brigade Order No.254	01/10/1918	01/10/1918
Miscellaneous	March Table Issued With 183rd Infantry Brigade Order No.254	01/10/1918	01/10/1918
Operation(al) Order(s)	183rd Infantry Brigade Order No.255	04/10/1918	04/10/1918
Miscellaneous	March and Entraining Table Issued With 183rd Infantry Brigade Order No.255	04/10/1918	04/10/1918
Miscellaneous	Addendum To 183rd Infantry Brigade Administrative Instructions Issued In Connection With Move By Rail	04/10/1918	04/10/1918
Miscellaneous	183rd. Infantry Brigade Administrative Instructions Issued In Connection With Move By Rail No.2	04/10/1918	04/10/1918
Miscellaneous	Table "A" Supply Grouping 183rd Brigade Group		
Miscellaneous	183rd. Infantry Brigade Administrative Instructions Issued In Connection With Move By Rail. No.3	04/10/1918	04/10/1918

Type	Description	Date	Date
Operation(al) Order(s)	183rd Infantry Brigade Order No.253	07/10/1918	07/10/1918
Miscellaneous	Table "A" (Move Of Transport) Issued With 183rd Infantry Brigade Order No 256	07/10/1918	07/10/1918
Miscellaneous	Table "A" Entraining Table		
Miscellaneous	Table "B" Composition Of Transport Train		
Miscellaneous	183rd Infantry Brigade Administrative Instructions Issued In Connection With Brigade Order No. 256	07/10/1918	07/10/1918
Operation(al) Order(s)	9th (Northd Hussars) Battalion Northumberland Fusiliers Order No.72	02/10/1918	02/10/1918
Operation(al) Order(s)	9th (Northd Hussars) Battalion Northumberland Fusiliers Order No.73	04/10/1918	04/10/1918
Miscellaneous	Administrative Instructions To Battalion Northd Fusiliers Order No.73	05/10/1918	05/10/1918
Operation(al) Order(s)	9th (Northd Hussars) Battn. Northumberland Fusiliers Order No.74	08/10/1918	08/10/1918
Miscellaneous	9th (N.H) Battn. Northd Fusiliers Order No.T1	14/10/1918	14/10/1918
Operation(al) Order(s)	9th (Northd Hussars) Battn. Northd Fusiliers Order No.75	17/10/1918	17/10/1918
Miscellaneous	9th (Northd Hussars) Battn. Northd Fusiliers Order No.T.2	21/10/1918	21/10/1918
Miscellaneous	War Diary		
Operation(al) Order(s)	9th (Northumberland Hussars) Battn Northumberland Fusiliers Order No.76	22/10/1918	22/10/1918
Miscellaneous	File		
Operation(al) Order(s)	9th (Northd Hussars) Battn. Northumberland Fusiliers Order No.77	23/10/1918	23/10/1918
Miscellaneous	9th (N H) Battn. Northumberland Fusiliers Order No.77		
Miscellaneous	War Diary		
Miscellaneous	Special Order Of The Day By Field Marshal Sir Douglas Haig K.T. G.C.B. G.C.V.O. K.C.I.E. Commander-In-Chief British Armies in France	13/10/1918	13/10/1918
Miscellaneous	Special Order Of The Day By Field Marshal Sir Douglas Haig K.T. G.C.B. G.C.V.O. K.C.I.E. Commander-In-Chief British Armies in France	11/10/1918	11/10/1918
Miscellaneous	Special Order Of The Day By Field Marshal Sir Douglas Haig K.T. G.C.B. G.C.V.O. K.C.I.E. Commander-In-Chief British Armies in France	05/10/1918	05/10/1918
Miscellaneous	Special Order Of The Day By Field Marshal Sir Douglas Haig K.T. G.C.B. G.C.V.O. K.C.I.E. Commander-In-Chief British Armies in France	14/10/1918	14/10/1918
Miscellaneous	Special Order Of The Day By Field Marshal Sir Douglas Haig K.T. G.C.B. G.C.V.O. K.C.I.E. Commander-In-Chief British Armies in France	25/10/1918	25/10/1918
Miscellaneous	Special Order Of The Day By Field Marshal Sir Douglas Haig K.T. G.C.B. G.C.V.O. K.C.I.E. Commander-In-Chief British Armies in France	26/10/1918	26/10/1918
Miscellaneous	Special Order Of The Day By Field Marshal Sir Douglas Haig K.T. G.C.B. G.C.V.O. K.C.I.E. Commander-In-Chief British Armies in France	28/10/1918	28/10/1918
Miscellaneous	183rd Infantry Brigade Administrative Instructions Issued In Connection With Brigade Order No. 258 Of Today	17/10/1918	17/10/1918
Miscellaneous	Administrative Instructions Issued In Connection With Move	01/10/1918	01/10/1918
Miscellaneous	To All Recipients 183rd Infantry Brigade Order No.25	04/10/1918	04/10/1918

Miscellaneous	183rd Infantry Brigade Administrative Instructions Issued In Connection With Move By Rail	03/10/1918	03/10/1918
Miscellaneous	Entraining Steenbecque		
Miscellaneous	Table "B" Issued With 183rd Infantry Brigade Order No.258	07/10/1918	07/10/1918
Operation(al) Order(s)	183rd Infantry Brigade Order No.257	10/10/1918	10/10/1918
Map	Map		
Operation(al) Order(s)	183rd Infantry Brigade Order No.258		
Miscellaneous	Movement Table Issued With 183rd Infantry Brigade Order No.258		
Operation(al) Order(s)	183rd Infantry Brigade Order No.259	19/10/1918	19/10/1918
Miscellaneous	March Table "A" Dismounted Personnel		
Miscellaneous	March Table "B"		
Miscellaneous	183rd Infantry Brigade Administrative Instructions Issued In Connection With Brigade Order No. 259	18/10/1918	18/10/1918
Miscellaneous	9th. Northd Fus	19/10/1918	19/10/1918
Miscellaneous	C Form Messages And Signals		
Operation(al) Order(s)	183 Inf. Bde Order No.262	25/10/1918	25/10/1918
Heading	Novr 1918 9th (Northd Hussars) Bn. Northumberland Fusiliers War Diary		
Miscellaneous	9th (Northd Hussars) Bn. Northumberland Fus.	30/11/1918	30/11/1918
War Diary	Sepmeries	01/11/1918	01/11/1918
War Diary	La Folie	02/11/1918	02/11/1918
War Diary	Sommaing	03/11/1918	03/11/1918
War Diary	Avesnes Les-Aubert	04/11/1918	08/11/1918
War Diary	Bermerain	09/11/1918	14/11/1918
War Diary	St. Aubert	15/11/1918	15/11/1918
War Diary	Cambrai	16/11/1918	25/11/1918
War Diary	Longvillers	26/11/1918	30/11/1918
Miscellaneous	Strength At The Beginning Of Month		
Heading	War Diary November 1918 Appendix B		
Operation(al) Order(s)	9th (N H) Bn Northd Fusiliers Order No.81	02/11/1918	02/11/1918
Operation(al) Order(s)	9th (Northd Hussars) Battn Northd Fusiliers Order No.82	07/11/1918	07/11/1918
Miscellaneous	9th (Northd Hussars) Battn Northumberland Fusiliers Order No. T.2	10/11/1918	10/11/1918
Miscellaneous	9th (Northd Hussars) Battn Northumberland Fusiliers Order No. T.3	10/11/1918	10/11/1918
Miscellaneous	Space		
Operation(al) Order(s)	9th (Northd Hussars) Battn. Northd Fusiliers Order No.83	14/11/1918	14/11/1918
Operation(al) Order(s)	9th (N H) Battn. Northd Fus Order No.84	14/11/1918	14/11/1918
Operation(al) Order(s)	9th (Northd Hussars) Bn. Northumberland Fusr Order No.85	23/11/1918	23/11/1918
Miscellaneous	Amendment To 9th (Northd. Hussars) Bn. Northumberland Fusr Order No.85	24/11/1918	24/11/1918
Miscellaneous	War Diary		
Miscellaneous	9th (Northumberland Hussars) Battalion Northumberland Fusiliers		
War Diary	Longvillers	01/12/1918	08/12/1918
War Diary	Vauchelles Les-Quesnoy	09/12/1918	31/12/1918
Miscellaneous	Strength At Beginning Of Month		
Miscellaneous	Appendix 'B' Training Programmes 9th (N.H) Bn. Northd Fus		

Miscellaneous	Special Order Of The Day By Field Marshal Sir Douglas Haig K.T. G.C.B. G.C.V.O. K.C.I.E. Commander-In-Chief British Armies in France	26/11/1918	26/11/1918
Miscellaneous	Special Order Of The Day By Field Marshal Sir Douglas Haig K.T. G.C.B. G.C.V.O. K.C.I.E. Commander-In-Chief British Armies in France	27/11/1918	27/11/1918
Miscellaneous	Special Order Of The Day By Field Marshal Sir Douglas Haig K.T. G.C.B. G.C.V.O. K.C.I.E. Commander-In-Chief British Armies in France	29/11/1918	29/11/1918
Miscellaneous	Special Order Of The Day By Field Marshal Sir Douglas Haig K.T. G.C.B. G.C.V.O. K.C.I.E. Commander-In-Chief British Armies in France	01/12/1918	01/12/1918
Miscellaneous	Special Order Of The Day By Field Marshal Sir Douglas Haig K.T. G.C.B. G.C.V.O. K.C.I.E. Commander-In-Chief British Armies in France	02/12/1918	02/12/1918
Miscellaneous	Special Order Of The Day By Field Marshal Sir Douglas Haig K.T. G.C.B. G.C.V.O. K.C.I.E. Commander-In-Chief British Armies in France	04/12/1918	04/12/1918
Miscellaneous	Special Order Of The Day By Field Marshal Sir Douglas Haig K.T. G.C.B. G.C.V.O. K.C.I.E. Commander-In-Chief British Armies in France	05/12/1918	05/12/1918
Miscellaneous	War Diary		
Miscellaneous	Special Order Of The Day By Field Marshal Sir Douglas Haig K.T. G.C.B. G.C.V.O. K.C.I.E. Commander-In-Chief British Armies in France	09/12/1918	09/12/1918
Miscellaneous	Special Order Of The Day By Field Marshal Sir Douglas Haig K.T. G.C.B. G.C.V.O. K.C.I.E. Commander-In-Chief British Armies in France	10/12/1918	10/12/1918
Miscellaneous	Special Order Of The Day By Field Marshal Sir Douglas Haig K.T. G.C.B. G.C.V.O. K.C.I.E. Commander-In-Chief British Armies in France	14/12/1918	14/12/1918
Miscellaneous	Special Order Of The Day By Field Marshal Sir Douglas Haig K.T. G.C.B. G.C.V.O. K.C.I.E. Commander-In-Chief British Armies in France	16/12/1918	16/12/1918
Miscellaneous	Special Order Of The Day By Field Marshal Sir Douglas Haig K.T. G.C.B. G.C.V.O. K.C.I.E. Commander-In-Chief British Armies in France	20/12/1918	20/12/1918
Miscellaneous	Special Order Of The Day By Field Marshal Sir Douglas Haig K.T. G.C.B. G.C.V.O. K.C.I.E. Commander-In-Chief British Armies in France	23/12/1918	23/12/1918
Miscellaneous	Special Order Of The Day By Field Marshal Sir Douglas Haig K.T. G.C.B. G.C.V.O. K.C.I.E. Commander-In-Chief British Armies in France	26/12/1918	26/12/1918
Miscellaneous	Special Order Of The Day By Field Marshal Sir Douglas Haig K.T. G.C.B. G.C.V.O. K.C.I.E. Commander-In-Chief British Armies in France	31/12/1918	31/12/1918
Miscellaneous	Special Order Of The Day By Field Marshal Sir Douglas Haig K.T. G.C.B. G.C.V.O. K.C.I.E. Commander-In-Chief British Armies in France	03/01/1919	03/01/1919
Miscellaneous	Special Order Of The Day By Field Marshal Sir Douglas Haig K.T. G.C.B. G.C.V.O. K.C.I.E. Commander-In-Chief British Armies in France	04/01/1919	04/01/1919
Miscellaneous	Special Order Of The Day By Field Marshal Sir Douglas Haig K.T. G.C.B. G.C.V.O. K.C.I.E. Commander-In-Chief British Armies in France	09/01/1919	09/01/1919

Miscellaneous	Training Programme For Week Commencing 2nd December 1918	30/11/1918	30/11/1918
Miscellaneous	Training Programme	14/12/1918	14/12/1918
Miscellaneous	Training Programme		
Miscellaneous	Training Programme For The Period 25/12/18 28/12/18	23/12/1918	23/12/1918
Miscellaneous	183rd Infantry Brigade Training Programme For Period	30/12/1918	30/12/1918
Miscellaneous	Appendix "C" Special Orders of The Day		
Miscellaneous	9th (Northumberland Hussar) Battalion. Northumberland Fusiliers		
War Diary	Vauchelles-Les-Quesnoy	01/01/1919	31/01/1919
Miscellaneous	Strength At The Beginning Of Month		
Miscellaneous	9th (Northd Hussars) Battalion Northumberland Fusiliers Training Programme	04/01/1919	04/01/1919
Miscellaneous	9th (Northd Hussars) Battalion Northumberland Fusiliers Training Programme	11/01/1919	11/01/1919
Miscellaneous	9th (Northd Hussars) Battalion Northumberland Fusiliers Training Programme	12/01/1919	12/01/1919
Miscellaneous	9th (Northd Hussars) Battalion Northumberland Fusiliers Training Programme	25/01/1919	25/01/1919
Miscellaneous	9th (Northd Hussars) Battalion Northumberland Fusiliers Training Programme	01/02/1919	01/02/1919
Miscellaneous	O.C. Coy		
Miscellaneous	9th (Northumberland Hussars) Battalion Northumberland Fusiliers		
War Diary	Vauchelles-Les-Quesnoy	01/02/1919	15/02/1919
War Diary	St. Martin Eglise	16/02/1919	28/02/1919
Operation(al) Order(s)	183rd Infantry Brigade Order No.274	13/02/1919	13/02/1919
Miscellaneous	Operation Orders 9th (N.H.) Bn. Northumberland Fusiliers	13/02/1919	13/02/1919
Miscellaneous	9th (Northd Hussars) Battalion Northumberland Fusiliers. Training Programme	08/02/1919	08/02/1919
Miscellaneous	9th (Northumberland Hussars) Battn. Northumberland Fusiliers		
War Diary	St. Martin Eglise	01/03/1919	31/03/1919
Miscellaneous	9th (Northumberland Hussars) Battn. Northumberland Fusiliers		
War Diary	St. Martin Eglise	01/04/1919	30/04/1919
Miscellaneous	9th. (Northumberland Hussars) Battn Northumberland Fusiliers Educational Programme	19/04/1919	19/04/1919
Miscellaneous	9th. (Northumberland Hussars) Battn. Northumberland Fusiliers. Educational Programme	26/04/1919	26/04/1919
Miscellaneous	9th. (Northumberland Hussars) Battn. Northumberland Fusiliers. Educational Programme	03/05/1919	03/05/1919
Miscellaneous	9th. (Northumberland Hussars) Battn Northumberland Fusiliers. Training Programme	12/04/1919	12/04/1919
Miscellaneous	9th. (N.H.) Battn Northumberland Fusiliers. Training Programme	19/04/1919	19/04/1919
Miscellaneous	9th. (Northumberland Hussars) Battn Northumberland Fusiliers. Training Programme	26/04/1919	26/04/1919
Miscellaneous	9th. (N.H.) Battn Northumberland Fusiliers. Training Programme	03/05/1919	03/05/1919
Miscellaneous	9th. (Northumberland Hussars) Battn Northumberland Fusiliers		
War Diary	Martin Eglise	01/05/1919	31/05/1919
Miscellaneous	9th. (Northumberland Hussars) Battn. Northumberland Fusiliers. Educational Programme	03/05/1919	03/05/1919

Type	Description	Date From	Date To
Miscellaneous	9th. (Northumberland Hussars) Battn. Northumberland Fusiliers. Educational Programme	10/05/1919	10/05/1919
Miscellaneous	9th. (Northumberland Hussars) Battn. Northumberland Fusiliers. Educational Programme	17/05/1919	17/05/1919
Miscellaneous	9th. (Northumberland Hussars) Battn. Northumberland Fusiliers. Educational Programme	24/05/1919	24/05/1919
Miscellaneous	9th. (Northumberland Hussars) Battn. Northumberland Fusiliers. Educational Programme	31/05/1919	31/05/1919
Miscellaneous	9th. (N.H.) Battn. Northumberland Fusiliers. Training Programme	03/05/1919	03/05/1919
Miscellaneous			
Miscellaneous	9th. (Northumberland Hussars) Battn. Northumberland Fusiliers. Training Programme	10/05/1919	10/05/1919
Miscellaneous	O.C.C. Coy		
Miscellaneous	9th (Northumberland Hussars) Battn. Northumberland Fusiliers Training Programme	17/05/1919	17/05/1919
Miscellaneous	9th (Northumberland Hussars) Battn. Northumberland Fusiliers Training Programme	24/05/1919	24/05/1919
Miscellaneous	9th (Northumberland Hussars) Battn. Northumberland Fusiliers Training Programme	31/05/1919	31/05/1919
Miscellaneous	Brigade Major 182nd Infantry Brigade	03/07/1919	03/07/1919
Miscellaneous	9th (Northumberland Hussars) Battn. Northumberland Fusiliers		
War Diary	Martin Eglise	01/06/1919	30/06/1919
Miscellaneous	9th. (Northumberland Hussars) Battn. Northumberland Fusiliers Educational Programme	28/06/1919	28/06/1919
Miscellaneous	9th. (Northumberland Hussars) Battn. Northumberland Fusiliers Educational Programme	21/06/1919	21/06/1919
Miscellaneous	9th. (Northumberland Hussars) Battn. Northumberland Fusiliers Educational Programme	14/06/1919	14/06/1919
Miscellaneous	9th. (Northumberland Hussars) Battn. Northumberland Fusiliers Educational Programme	07/06/1919	07/06/1919
Miscellaneous	9th. (Northumberland Hussars) Battn. Northumberland Fusiliers Training Programme	28/06/1919	28/06/1919
Miscellaneous	9th. (Northumberland Hussars) Battn. Northumberland Fusiliers Training Programme	13/06/1919	13/06/1919
Miscellaneous	9th. (Northumberland Hussars) Battn. Northumberland Fusiliers Training Programme	06/06/1919	06/06/1919
Miscellaneous	9th. (Northumberland Hussars) Battn. Northumberland Fusiliers Training Programme	31/05/1919	31/05/1919
Miscellaneous	9th (Northumberland Hussars) Battn. Northumberland Fusiliers		
War Diary	Martin Eglise	01/07/1919	31/07/1919
Miscellaneous	9th (Northumberland Hussars) Battn. Northumberland Fusiliers Training Programme	24/07/1919	24/07/1919
Miscellaneous	9th (Northumberland Hussars) Battn. Northumberland Fusiliers Training Programme	26/07/1919	26/07/1919
Miscellaneous	9th (Northumberland Hussars) Battn. Northumberland Fusiliers Training Programme	11/07/1919	11/07/1919
Miscellaneous	9th (Northumberland Hussars) Battn. Northumberland Fusiliers Training Programme	12/07/1919	12/07/1919
Miscellaneous	9th (Northumberland Hussars) Battn. Northumberland Fusiliers Training Programme	27/06/1919	27/06/1919
Miscellaneous	9th (Northumberland Hussars) Battn. Northumberland Fusiliers Educational Programme	26/07/1919	26/07/1919

Type	Description	Start	End
Miscellaneous	9th (Northumberland Hussars) Battn. Northumberland Fusiliers Educational Programme	20/07/1919	20/07/1919
Miscellaneous	9th (Northumberland Hussars) Battn. Northumberland Fusiliers Educational Programme	12/07/1919	12/07/1919
Miscellaneous	9th (Northumberland Hussars) Battn. Northumberland Fusiliers Educational Programme	04/07/1919	04/07/1919
Miscellaneous	9th (Northumberland Hussars) Battn. Northumberland Fusiliers Educational Programme	29/06/1919	29/06/1919
Miscellaneous	Commg Officer		
Miscellaneous	9th (Northumberland Hussars) Battn. Northumberland Fusiliers		
War Diary	Martin Eglise	01/08/1919	31/08/1919
Miscellaneous	9th. (Northumberland Hussars) Battn. Northumberland Fusiliers Training Programme	21/08/1919	21/08/1919
Miscellaneous	9th. (Northumberland Hussars) Battn. Northumberland Fusiliers Training Programme	14/08/1919	14/08/1919
Miscellaneous	9th. (Northumberland Hussars) Battn. Northumberland Fusiliers Training Programme	07/08/1919	07/08/1919
Miscellaneous	9th. (Northumberland Hussars) Battn. Northumberland Fusiliers Training Programme	31/07/1919	31/07/1919
Miscellaneous	9th. (Northumberland Hussars) Battn. Northumberland Fusiliers Educational Programme	24/08/1919	24/08/1919
Miscellaneous	9th. (Northumberland Hussars) Battn. Northumberland Fusiliers Educational Programme	16/08/1919	16/08/1919
Miscellaneous	9th. (Northumberland Hussars) Battn. Northumberland Fusiliers Educational Programme	11/08/1919	11/08/1919
Miscellaneous	9th. (Northumberland Hussars) Battn. Northumberland Fusiliers Educational Programme	02/08/1919	02/08/1919
War Diary	Martin Eglise	01/09/1919	16/09/1919
War Diary	Rouxmesnil	17/09/1919	03/11/1919

2962 (1)

61ST DIVISION
183RD INFY BDE

9TH BN NORTH'D FUSILIERS

JUN 1918-AUG 1919

FROM 34 DIV. 103 BDE

32a

App A-D

183/61

COVER
FOR
BRANCH MEMORANDA.

Unregistered.

Referred to	Date	Referred to	Date
9th RHus	June – ~~Sep~~ 1918		

June '18
Aug '19

WAR DIARY
or
INTELLIGENCE SUMMARY

Army Form C. 2118

9th North'd Fusiliers

JUNE 1918.   32^a

Place	Date	Hour	Summary of Events and Information	Remarks and references to Appendices

Strength of Battalion at beginning of month - 43 Officers   905 OR
" " " end of " - 40 "   932 OR

Casualties Wounded Commission Evacuation Posted Base
Accidentally Wounded   9   4   43   2   = 61.
Struck off   1
Died   1   22   32   = 88
Week ending 8th = 14
              15th = 33
              22nd = 32
              29th = 19

Draft Officers Strangers to RGC
Joined
Lieut J.C. Kenrick 19th.   Captain W.D. Drysdale 13th.
Lieut H. Ansell 19th.   Lieut C. Bentley 16th
                                     Lieut L. Taylor 14th.

Decorations.
Bar to D.S.O.
Lt Colonel W A Vignoles D.S.O.

Military Cross
Captain R.C. Massal. (R.A.M.C.)
Lieut J.G.C. Brady
Lieut E.R.L. Piggott
Lieut D.M. Coates
"   J.L. Baxter

Bar to Military Cross
Capt W.J. Allan M.C
Lieut G.A. Howe M.C.
Lieut L. Hatcher M.C.

Wounded
Lieut J.C. Rogers M.C 18th
Lieut C.A. Murray 21st.

Distinguished Conduct Medal
18905 COM (MSM) A Richardson
46727 Cpl D Lowley
24/492 Sgt R Meakin
20995 Cpl E.G. Harrison
Bar to D.C.M.
41142 Sgt Hardman L D.C.M.

Military Medal
12940 Sgt Dixon J.E
22436 A/Sgt Cain J.
15939 " Beresford J.E
11244 " Bell G.H.
14302 Pte Wood R.J.
44389 " Bell J.J.
29998 " Garrard J
16289 " Taylor J

Bar to Military Medal.
41223 CSM Petchell R. M.M.
13/5147 Pte Petrey W. M.M.

Cards of Honour
23401 Pte O.D. Barber.   H8539 Pte A Tabbit
44372 " D Dancey.   235401 Pte J Anstey
41122 " G. Boyd   27213 Pte J Edgeworth
54998 " C. Boyd   316403 " B Dipper
14781 Sgt J B Sney   133354 9454 D Monty
29205 Pte R Greenwood   39907 Pte J Jury
12339 " J Headlam
235145 Cpl M Allyon   Sick in Hosp Ambulances Dept
39385 Cpl J Donelow
38354 Mgr R Holliday   Sgt E Wilkinson
16260 Pte R Willmott   Bdr L H C Clay
599Y3 Pte C Coad   Lieut G S Bootle
18084 " J Covell   Lieut G.A. Bennett
10143 " J. Bitlman   Lieut J E Croyford
12/18954 " D Dickinson Lieut J B Forsyth
                        Capt G W Collinson

Army Form C. 2118.

WAR DIARY
of 9th (Nortld Hussars) Bn. THE NORTHD FUS.
INTELLIGENCE SUMMARY
(Erase heading not required.)

Page 1

Instructions regarding War Diaries and Intelligence Summaries are contained in F.S. Regs, Part II. and the Staff Manual respectively. Title pages will be prepared in manuscript.

Place	Date	Hour	Summary of Events and Information	Remarks and references to Appendices
IN THE FIELD JUNE 1918				
LA CRECHE (HAZEBROUCK Sh F.5)	1st		Training was carried out. The Bn. paraded at 8.30 am Marching Order dress was worn at O.i.c. Inf. App. Dress worn during day. 183 Inf. Bde O No 213 received giving details of move of Bde Group to/from (2nd inst)	App.
HAMMIN-ARTOIS (do)	2nd		Church parades were held with the morning service. At 4.30 pm the Bn paraded & marched into billets at Hamin-Artois, where being reported complete about 6 pm.	O. No 40 App.
	3rd to 7th		Training under Company arrangements also specialist classes were carried out. The weather remained exceptionally fine. Bn Ord 6 inst. 183 Inf. Bde Order No 214 was received. This was to effect that 157 & 83 Inf. Bdes would relieve 182 Inf. Bde in in left sectn of the Divisional Front on the night of the 9/10. The Bn was inspected at 8.30 am by Brig-Genl A.H. Spooner CMG DSO who presented 16 Cards of Honour awarded for gallantry in the field in addition to duty during recent operations.	App.
HAMET BILLET (HAZEBROUCK Sh 6C)	9th		Church parades were held during the morning. Later Bde relief ordered in 183 Inf. Bde order No 214 was carried out. The Bn relieving the 2/7 Bn R Warwickshire Regt in Bde Reserve in Hamet Billet. Personnel detailed as a nucleus left for Div Reception Camp by march route during the afternoon.	
	10th to 13th		A quiet period was experienced. Training as per as position allowed was carried out. 183 Inf. Bde ord. No 215 was received on 13/10th ordering the Bn to relieve the 1st Batt. Lancashire Regt. in the front line 9 the 183rd Bde front. on the night of the 13/14 inst.	
Bn H.Q.D. 14th PN a 6.9 (Sh.9)	14th		Relief was completed without incident. Dispositions as follows: "A" "B" Coys Right and Left forward respectively. "C" Coy in Support. "D" Coy in Reserve.	

Army Form C. 2118.

Page VII

WAR DIARY
or
INTELLIGENCE SUMMARY.
(Erase heading not required.)

Place	Date	Hour	Summary of Events and Information	Remarks and references to Appendices
In the Line	15th to 21st		Throughout the period enemy attitude was fairly quiet although certain localities received attention from his Artillery regularly. Hostile machine gun fire was spasmodic. Trench mortars h.c. enemy aircraft were not in activity. Our Artillery, Trench Mortars, Machine Guns fired usual Programmes & engaged Special Targets reported by Patrols. The enemy Infantry showed little inclination to challenge our supremacy "in front" & appeared to rely on the alertness of the garrisons of his posts who were to prevent our patrols securing encounter. Our Patrols were very active, frequently entering & searching enemy posts. Our M.G.s became heavily engaged than rifle & machine gun fire. Hostile movement was on the whole slight. A certain amount (?) defence work was accomplished by the enemy. Visibility fair, afford The aititude. The enemy pointed towards a certain interference Thrice nightly as from Stations. On the night of The 17/18th with A Coy. reliefs were carried out, C Coy relieving A Coy & The 115th & D Coy taking over from B Coy on the left. A & B then withdrew to support & reserve positions respectively. On the 19th inst. 183rd Infy Bde Order No 217 was received ordering relief of the Bn. on the night of 21st/22nd by the 11th Suffolks. This was duly carried out without casualties. The Bn. withdrew into Bde Reserve being located in HAMEL BILLET.	app. app.
HAMEL BILLET (HAZEBROUCK SA (GS) 26.6	22 to 26		Parades under Coy. arrangements v bathing. 183rd Infy Bde Order No 218 received on 23rd list forth effect that the Bn. would relieve the 1st Bn. East Lancashire Regt. in the left Section of the Bde Front on the night 26th/27th inst.	app.

WAR DIARY
or
INTELLIGENCE SUMMARY

(Erase heading not required.)

Army Form C. 2118

Page III

Place	Date	Hour	Summary of Events and Information	Remarks and references to Appendices
Bn. Hd Qrs. P.S.C. 2.9 (36 A)	27.12. to 30.12.		Relief was completed satisfactorily. Dispositions as follows:- "B" Coy.= Right front, "A" Coy.= Left front, "D" Coy.= Support, "C" Coy.= Reserve. Up to the end of the period under review the enemy attitude generally remained normal. The noticeable features of his policy was lack of retaliation from artillery, programmes, absence of trench mortars, a continued tendency on his part to permit our patrols to have matters more or less as they liked. It would appear that the enemy has an erratic habit of holding his posts various of trench line. Hostile snipers are shown an increased activity with little success. Throughout however he is been exceptionally fine weather. Visibility has been good but nature of the country prevents full advantage being taken of this.	

[signature] Capt.
for O.C. 2/5 (Northumberland Fusiliers) Batt.
Northumberland Fusiliers.

APPENDICES TO
WAR DIARY
JUNE 1918.

A   Brigade Operation Orders.

B   Battalion Operation Orders

C   Special Orders of the Day.

D   Routine & Battalion Orders, showing Honours & Awards.

appendix A

SECRET.

Copy No. 35

61 DIVISION ORDER No. 164.

27th May, 1918.

1. G.O.C., 182nd Inf. Bde. will assume command of 183rd Inf. Bde. front at 6 p.m. 28th May, at which hour 183rd Inf. Bde. (less 183rd Inf. Bde. H.Q.) will pass to command of G.O.C., 182nd Inf. Bde.

2. 183rd Inf. Bde. H.Q. on completion of handing over will move to LA LACQUE and G.O.C., 183rd Inf. Bde. will assume command of :-

    9th (North'd Hussars) Northumberland Fusiliers.
    11th Suffolk Regt.
    1st East Lancashire Regt.

3. G.O.C., 183rd Inf. Bde. will continue to administer troops of 183rd Inf. Bde. which have passed to command of G.O.C., 182nd Inf. Bde., until further orders.

4. (a) At 6 p.m., 28th May, G.O.C., 182nd Inf. Bde. will assume tactical command of all Machine Guns now in position in 182nd Inf. Bde. area and 183rd Inf. Bde. area as far West as the AMUSOIRES - HAVERSKERQUE Line inclusive.

   (b) At 6 p.m. 28th May, G.O.C., 184th Inf. Bde. will assume tactical command of all Machine Guns now in position in 184th Inf. Bde. area as far West as the AMUSOIRES - HAVERSKERQUE Line inclusive.

5. ACKNOWLEDGE. ✓

Issued at 7.45 p.m.

A. Anderson Major
for Lieut. Col.,
G.S., 61 Division.

DISTRIBUTION.

Copy No. 1 - A.D.C. for G.O.C.	19 - D.G.O.
2 - 61 Signal Coy.	20 - G.
3-4 - 16 Div. Art.	21-22 - War Diary.
5 - C.R.E.	23-28 - Spare.
6 - 61 Bn. M.G.C.	29 - XI Corps.
7 - 1/5 D.C.L.I.	30 - 4th Div.
8 - 182 Inf. Bde.	31 - 5th Div.
9 - 183 Inf. Bde.	32 - 3rd Canadian Div.
10 - 184 Inf. Bde.	33 - 8th Canadian Inf. Bde. (through 3rd Can. Div.).
11 - A.D.M.S.	
12 - D.A.D.V.S.	34 - 28th Bde., R.G.A.
13 - D.A.D.O.S.	35 - 9th (North'd Hussars) Northumberland Fus.
14 - A.P.M.	
15-16 - 61 Div. Train.	36 - 11th Suffolk Regt.
17 - Camp Commandant.	37 - 1st East Lancashire Regt.
18 - "Q"	38 - 34th Div.
	39 - 42nd Squadron, R.A.F.

SECRET

To: 9th North'd Fus   184 Inf Bde   B.M. 27
    11th Suffolks   2/3 Field Amb
    1st E Lancs   3 Coy Div Train
    Staff Captain   Camp Cmdt
    61st Div G   War Diary
    182nd Inf Bde   File

1. Tomorrow, 2nd June 1918, 183rd Inf Bde (less 1st E/Lancs) will move to HAM-EN-ARTOIS — GUARBECQUE area.

2. On completion of moves, dispositions of the Brigade will be as follows:—
   183rd Bde H.Qrs   — HAM-EN-ARTOIS
   9th North'd Fus   — Ditto
   11th Suffolks   — GUARBECQUE
   1st E Lancs.   — LA MIQUELERIE
   Rear Bde H.Q, Batt'n
   Q.M Stores & Transport } — BERGUETTE
   Lines

3. Orders as to times & routes will be issued later.

4. Billeting parties will be sent tomorrow morning to take over from Batt'ns of 8th Can. Inf Bde, & arrange Billets for their respective incoming Units.

ACKNOWLEDGE   J.R. Holm?? Capt
1/6/18   A/Bde Major 183 Inf Bde

Copy No. 5

183 Inf. Bde Order No. 213 - 1-6-18
Reference B.127 dated 1st June 1918.
Ref Map sheet 36A. 1/20,000.

1. 2/9th Northumberland Fusiliers and 11th Suffolks will march from LA CLIQUE Camp to Billets in HAM-EN-ARTOIS and GUARBECQUE respectively on the evening of the 2nd June, in accordance with attached table.

2. A distance of 500 yards will be maintained between Battalions.

3. Transport and Cookers will proceed in advance. The Staff Captain will notify transport arrangements.

4. Billeting parties as already detailed should report to the Staff Captain at BERGUETTE before proceeding to the Billeting Areas.

   Brigade H.Q. will close at LA CLIQUE Camp at 4 p.m. and re-open at HAM-EN-ARTOIS, O.27.c.5.4. at the same hour.

J.R. Tolson
Captain,
Staff Captain, 183 Inf. Bde.

March Table.

Serial No.	Units	Starting Point	Time	Route
1.	9th Northumberland Fus.	Drawbridge W. exit of LA CLAQUE CAMP.	5 pm	X Roads N.6.d.5.5 MOLINGHEM — O.20.a. and b — Road junc to O.21.c.1.8.
2.	11th Suffolks.	ditto.	5.30 pm	CANAL LOCK — X Roads I.32.d.3.2 — O.36. — O.10.a, b. and d.

Remarks. Transport of 11th Suffolks via ISBERGUES.

Copy No. 1. War Diary.   Copy No. 6. 11th Suffolks.
      "   2. File.   (to acknowledge)
      "   3. Staff Captain.   "   7. 1st R. Lancs.
      "   4. Bde Sgnal Officer.   "   8. A.D. Medical
      "   5. 9th North. Fusiliers.   "   9. 61 Division G.

SECRET   Copy No 5

103rd INFANTRY BRIGADE ORDER I.O. 215.   10/6/18.

Ref: Map, Sheets 36A.
          36A.N.E.
          36A.S.E.

1.   The 9th Northumberland Fusiliers will relieve 1st East Lancs
     Regt. in the Right Section of the Brigade Front on the night of
     the 13th/14th instant.
        On relief 1st East Lancs. Regt. will withdraw to HAMET
     BILLET and be in Brigade Reserve.
        All arrangements in connection with the Relief, and for
     reconnaissances of the line prior to relief, will be made
     direct by O's.C. concerned.

2.   1 Officer per Company, 1 N.C.O. per Platoon, No. 1's of
     Lewis Gun Teams and a proportion of Signallers and Runners will
     go into the line on the night 12th/13th instant.
        All Liaison duties at present found by East Lancs Regt. will
     be taken over by 9th Northumberland Fusiliers.

3.   All Aeroplane Photos, Paper Maps, Gas and Trench Stores will
     be handed over on relief, and a list of articles so handed over
     will be forwarded to this H.Q. within 24 hours of relief.
        Work in hand and projected will be carefully explained to
     incoming Unit.

4.   Completion of relief, and arrival of Battalion in HAMET
     BILLET will be notified to this H.Q. by code words "NO FURTHER
     GRENADES REQUIRED".

5.   No movement in connection with relief will take place before
     10 p.m.

6.   ACKNOWLEDGE. ✓

                                                          Captain,
     Issued at 2-30 p.m.   Brigade Major, 103rd Infantry Bde.

     Copy 1 - War Diary   Copy 7 - 1 E.Lancs   Copy 13 - 473 Fld Co
          2 - File   8 - 103 T.M.B.   14 - 473 Fld Co
          3 - S.C.   9 - Loft Group MGC.   15 - 104 Inf. Bde
          4 - B.S.O.   10 - Liaison Officer   16 - 95 Inf. Bde
          5 - 9th N.F.   11 - 177 Bde. RFA.   17 - 61 Div. G.
          6 - 11 Suffolks   12 - 180 Bde. RFA.

"C" Form.
MESSAGES AND SIGNALS.

Army Form C. 2123
(In books of 100.)
No. of Message 7

Prefix .... Code CK Words 34
From TUQU
By Hood

Office Stamp
DOFI
19/6/18

Handed in at TUQU .... Office 3.50 p.m. Received 4.30 p.m.

TO .... DOFI

*Sender's Number	Day of Month	In reply to Number	AAA
BM23	19		

BM730 of todays date aaa Para 3 is cancelled aaa Verbal instruction given you on this matter by Brigade Commander this morning will be carried out

FROM TIME & PLACE: TUQU 3.35 pm

SECRET.

B.M.30

To:
    9th North'd Fus.
    1st E.Lancs Regt.
    183 L.T.M.B.
    11th Suffolks
    Left Group M.G.Bn.)
    D.T.O.   ) for inf.
    S.C.   )
    476 Field Coy.
    478 Field Coy.

1.   Tomorrow, 20th instant, 5th Division is carrying out an offensive operation to advance at certain points the line now held by them.

2.   61st Divisional Artillery is assisting this operation by:
   (a) Continuing the Artillery Barrage as far South as the line Q.1.b.90.50 to Q.2.b.50.40.
   (b) Placing a Smoke Screen across the Front of CALONNE-sur-la-LYS.

   The firing of this Barrage will commence from the normal S.O.S. Lines advancing in lifts of 100 yards. Firing will cease at Zero plus 30.

3.   In order to prevent casualties from any hostile retaliation in answer to the above barrage, Battalions in Line will thin out the Garrisons of Front and Support Lines tonight 19/20th instant. Posts so vacated will be reoccupied on the night 20th/21st instant. Battalion Commanders will use their discretion with regard to the number of Platoons or Sections that are withdrawn. The Garrisons withdrawn may be accommodated in the AMUSOIRES System.
   It is suggested that the withdrawal of 1 Platoon from each Company front, and a temporary redistribution of the remaining 3 Platoons will answer the purpose.

4.   Any orders with regard to working parties and Zero hour will be notified later.

5.   Two Battalions in Line to acknowledge.

BHQ.
19/3/18.

                      Captain,
          Brigade Major, 183rd Infantry Bde.,

SECRET   Copy No... 5

183rd INFANTRY BRIGADE ORDER NO. 217.   19/3/18.

Ref: Map - Sheets 36A.
             36A.N.E.
             36A.S.E.

1. The 11th Suffolks will relieve 9th Northumberland Fusiliers in the Right Section of the Brigade Front on the night of the 21st/22nd instant.
   On relief 9th North'd Fus. will withdraw to HAMET BILLET and be in Brigade Reserve.
   All arrangements in connection with the Relief, and for reconnaissances of the line prior to relief, will be made direct by O's.C. concerned.

2. 1 Officer per Company, 1 N.C.O. per Platoon, No.1's of Lewis Gun Teams, and a proportion of Signallers and Runners will go into the line on the night 20th/21st instant.

3. All Aeroplane Photos, Paper Maps, etc, will be handed over on relief.
   List of Trench Stores handed over will be forwarded direct to Staff Captain.
   Work in hand and projected will be carefully explained to incoming Unit.

4. Completion of relief, and arrival of Battalion in HAMET BILLET will be notified to this H.Q. by code-words "COURSE CANCELLED".

5. No movement in connection with relief will take place before 10 p.m.

6. ACKNOWLEDGE.

                                                    Captain.
Issued at 7-30 p.m.   Brigade Major, 183rd Inf.Brigade.

Copy 1 - War Diary   Copy 7 - 1st E.Lancs   Copy 13 - 476 Fd.Co
     2 - File   8 - 183 T.M.B.   14 - 478 Fd.Co
     3 - S.O.   9 - Loft Group MGC.   15 - 184 Bde.
     4 - D.S.O.   10 - Liaison Officer   16 - 15 Bde.
     5 - 9th N.F.   11 - 177 Bde. RFA.   17 - 31 Div. "G"
     6 - 11th Suffolks.   12 - 180 Bde. RFA.   18 - Bde Supply Off

SECRET

COPY NO.
33/3/16.

183 INFANTRY BRIGADE ORDER NO.218.

1. The 9th. NORTHD. FUSILIERS will relieve the 1st. EAST LANCS. REGT. in the Left Section of the Brigade Front on the night 26/27th.inst.
   On relief the 1st. EAST LANCS. REGT. will withdraw to HAMET BILLET and be in Brigade Reserve.

2. One Officer per Company, 1 N.C.O. per Platoon, No. 1's of Lewis Gun teams and a proportion of Signallers and Runners will go into the Line on the night 25/26th. inst.

3. All Photos, Paper Maps, etc. will be handed over on relief.
   List of Trench Stores handed over, will be forwarded direct to Staff Captain.
   Work in hand, and projected, will be carefully explained to incoming Unit.

4. Completion of relief and arrival of Battalion in HAMET BILLET will be notified to this H.Q. by Code words " 50 SHOVELS "

5. No movement in connection with relief before 10.0pm.

   Acknowledge. —Done

   Issued at 7.30 p.m.

   Roland Le Fanu
   Captain,
   Brigade Major,183 Inf.Bde.

```
Copy 1 - War Diary        Copy 7 - 1st. E.Lancs.    Copy 13- 478 Fd.Coy.
     2 - File                  8 - 183 T.M.B.            14- 473 Fd.Coy.
     3 - S.C.                  9 - Left Gr. MGC          15- 184 Bde.
     4 - D.S.O.               10 - Liason Off.           16- 15 Bde.
     5 - 9th. N.F.            11 - 177 Bde.R.F.A.        17- 61st.Div."G"
     6 - 11th. Suffolks.      12 - 190 Bde.R.F.A.        18- Bde.Supply Off.
```

SECRET   APPENDIX B   **COPY NO 1**
OPERATION ORDERS No 40.

9th (North'd Hussars) Batt. Northumberland Fusiliers.

1. MOVE.	The Battalion will move from LACQUE Camp to billets in HAM-EN-ARTOIS, today.
2. TRANSPORT.	Transport and cookers will proceed in advance at 3.0 p.m.
3. PARADE.	4.30 p.m. In field opposite Drawbridge, on South side of canal, in close column of companies. Head of column will pass the Drawbridge at 5.0 p.m.
4. ORDER OF MARCH.	"C" Coy, Band, Battn. Hd. Qrs. Company, "D", "B" & "A" Coys. The Quarter Guard will march in rear of column. A distance of 500 yards will be observed between Companies.
5. DRESS.	MARCHING ORDER.
6. OFFICERS MESS KIT & VALISES.	Valises to be ready at Q.M. Stores by 12.30 p.m. Officers Mess kit will be packed in cookers opposite the Orderly Room by 2.0 p.m.
7. OFFICERS CHARGERS.	Will be on the parade field at 4.45 p.m.
8. L.G. LIMBERS & COOKERS.	Teams will be sent for these at 2.30 p.m.
9. ROUTE.	X Roads N6 d 5.8 — MOLLINGHEM — O 20 a. and b. — Road Junction O 21. C 1.8.
10. BILLETING PARTY.	Lieut A.W. Freshwater and 1 N.C.O. per Coy will proceed on bicycles at 11.0 a.m. to report to Staff Captain, BERGUETTE and thence to billeting area. O.C. Coys. will detail 1 man per platoon to proceed with cookers at 3.0 p.m. to report to Lieut. Freshwater on arrival. Company Officers mess cooks should go with this party.
11. BILLETS.	Company Commanders are responsible that billets are left scrupulously clean and in a sanitary condition. The Orderly Officer will remain with a rear party consisting of Sanitary Corpl. and 1 sanitary man detailed each by A & B Coys. and will obtain a certificate of cleanliness from the Camp Commandant before following on.
12. MARCHING OUT STATES	Will be rendered to Orderly Room by 4.0 p.m.

ACKNOWLEDGE.

Copies to —
No 1. War Diary
2. Retained
3. Army Officer
4. Second in Command
5. 8. Coys unit
7. Quartermaster
10. Transport Officer
11. Medical Officer
12. R.S.M.
13. Master Cook.

DATED. 2.6.18

A.W. Milburn, Lieut
for Captain & Adjutant.
9th (N.H.) Bn. Northumberland Fus.

War Diary

SECRET   COPY No. 1

OPERATION ORDERS No. 4.

1. RELIEF
The 143rd Infantry Brigade will relieve the 182nd Infantry Brigade on the night 5th/6th June 1916.
The 9th (North [Staffs]) [&] 1st Royal Fus[iliers] will relieve the 2/7th Bn Warwicks in Brigade Reserve at HAMEL BILLETS.

2. ORDER OF RELIEF
GUARD (1) O.C. A Coy will take over from opposite numbers Companies. & 3 men at road junction O.12.b.3.a. to relieve guard now mounted by 182nd [Brigade]
(2) O.C. B Coy will provide [a] guard of 1 NCO & 3 men to relieve guard of the 2/7th Warwicks at BRIDGE, I.33.d.3.3. at 6.0 p.m. [not]

3. PARADE
Coys will parade on Coy parade ground, & will march in following order:— A.B.C.D. H.Qrs. Coys. Head of Column passing X Roads O.28.c.20.50 at 6.15 [pm]. Intervals 200 yards between Companies.

4. DRESS
Marching Order. Officers may take trenches [kits.] These will be got ready for collection by the Transport Officer at 8 p.m. outside Coys Hd Qrs.

5. GUIDES
The Coys and Hd Qrs N.C.Os sent on with advance party will meet Battalion at X Roads at P.19.d.3.3. and will guide Coys to Billets.

6. TRANSPORT
The Transport Officer will arrange for [serving] [out] limbers & field kitchens; also tool limber maltese, water cart & mess cart for Hd Qrs. Also [extra ?] officers trench kits. All transport will march together.
Officers mess kit will be placed on cookers.

7. ROUTE
X Roads O.28.c.20.50 — O.28.d.0.0 — O.24.b.6.6 — Road & track through O.24.c.0.5 — O.24.d — O.24.c — O.30.a — O.24.d — [to ?] track from point P.19.b.3.0 to [village] at P.13.b.2.4. (Coy) Transport via Bridge in [I.24?]

8. OFFICERS HOUSES
Will be dumped at Coy & Bn Hd Qrs for collection at 7.0 p.m. & storage at Q.M. Stores.

9. BILLETS
Company Commanders will ensure that all billets are left in a clean & sanitary condition. A small party should go round billets after them. The Bn Orderly Officer will remain with a rear party consisting of sanitary [men ?] & 1 sanitary man per Company, and will obtain a certificate of cleanliness from the [Town] [Commandant] before following the Battalion.

OPERATION ORDER No. ...

10. PROPOSED OPERNS	Anticipate the completion of a Bypass Bridge, Gas & Petrol dumps & commence to install flares this afternoon. A report will be taken to morrow morning into the of when will be received by Orderly Room at 9-0 am 10/6/18.
11. RELIEF CASUALTIES	Will be advised to Bn Hd Qrs using code words "VICKORY NOT REQUIRED" followed by name of Company Commander.
12. ADVANCE PARTY	As already detailed
13. DETAILS	Will proceed by march route to Div Reception camp at CINQ CAUES on the 9th inst under Capt Wm Roberts. Lorries to be notified
14. MARCHING OUT STATES	To be rendered to Orderly Room by 4.0 pm.

ACKNOWLEDGE
Dated 8th June 1918

Copies
No 1. Hd Qrs Army
2. received
...

R. Ross Lieut
Adjutant

SECRET.   COPY No. 2
MAP REF.
36.P.S.E.   OPERATION ORDERS. No. 142.
                         9th (Northᵈ Hussars) Bn. Northumberland Fusᵣˢ.

1. RELIEF. The Battalion will relieve the 1st East Lancashire Regt. as the Right Battalion of the Left Brigade on the night of the 13/14th inst. in the following order.
"B" Coy relieves "A" Coy 1st East Lancs. Left Forward Coy.
"A"   "   "C"   "   "   "   Right Forward Coy.
"C"   "   "D"   "   "   "   Support Coy.
"D"   "   "B"   "   "   "   Reserve Coy.

2. GUIDES. At the rate of 4 per Coy & 1 for Battn H.Qrs. will be at the road junction P.14.b.9.4 at 10.0 p.m. On reaching the front line Coy H.Qrs. 1 guide per post will be provided. 300 yds interval to be maintained between platoons.

3. DISTRIBUTION IN POSTS. Coys will tell off their Coy. to posts in accordance with table issued to each Coy. before leaving HAMET BILLET. Every man must know the No. of his post & location of Coy. (e.g. No.5 post Right Forward Coy). After getting into the line every man is to reconnoitre the posts on either flank of the one he is in.

4. ADVANCE PARTY. 1 officer per Coy, 1 N.C.O. per platoon, Nos. 1 of all Lewis Guns teams, 1 runner and 1 orderly per Coy. R.S.M. and 2 runners for Battn H.Qrs., will go into the line on the night of 12/13th inst., leaving HAMET BILLET not before 9.30 p.m. and moving in small parties. Guides will be provided at Battn H.Qrs. at P.14.a.9.2.

5. LIAISON All liaison duties to be taken over.

6. TRENCH STORES. Advance parties will take over:—
(A) Aeroplane photos, defence schemes, Special maps, reserve ammunition, bombs, hot food containers, gas & trench stores, and fire recipes. Copy of list signed to be handed in to Battn H.Qrs. before dawn on 14th inst.
(B) Details of work in hand.

7. TRANSPORT. T.O. will provide 5 limbers for water, any officers mess kit not required and mess carts for Battn H.Qrs. to be at Bn H.Qrs. at 8.0 p.m. Any extra magazines required by Companies beyond 4 per man will be carried on the limbers. These will be handed over to D Coy. who will provide a guard and be responsible for magazines reaching the respective Coys.

8. WATER. All water bottles will be filled before leaving and men warned that they may not get a further supply for 24 hours. If petrol tins are available, a tin per post will be sent to Coy H.Qrs. each night for front line & support coys — empty tins (except for first night) must be handed over in exchange for full ones. A receipt will be given for full and empty tins respectively. One water cart nightly will be sent up for Battn H.Qrs. and Reserve Coy.

9. RATIONS. For 14th inst will be carried on the men. On subsequent nights rations will be carried to Coy or Platoon H.Qrs by Reserve Coy under guidance of an N.C.O. of Coy. who will report at Bn. H.Qrs at 10.0 p.m.

OPERATION ORDERS. No 42. Contd.

10. COOKING — All rations will be sent up cooked, except for Battn H. Qrs. Tommy Cookers will be issued to the three forward Coys for making tea. Sergeant Cook will arrange for D Coy to take Camp Kettles for making tea, these to be handed over to Coy in relieved by another Coy. Q.M. and Sergt. Cook will arrange for Soup at night.

11. BILLETS — Will be taken over by 1st East Lancs Regt. Coy Commdrs will obtain usual certificates of cleanliness.

12. TOOLS — 200 Shovels will be taken over by the Battn in accordance with BM 30 dated 11-6-18.

13. COOKS — Sergt. Cook will arrange for distribution of Cooks between Transport Lines and forward area as required, reporting arrangements made to the Adjutant.

14. Completion of relief will be notified by Code.
- A. Coy. OK for cave — ONE
- B " do — TWO
- C " do — NINE
- D " do — FOUR

15. ACKNOWLEDGE.
dated 12th June 1918.

Copies:—
- No 1 War Diary
- 2 Retained
- 3 Comdg Officer
- 4/8 OC. Coys.
- 9 OC. 1st East Lancs Regt.
- 10 Q.M.
- 11 T.O.
- 12 R.S.M.
- 13 Master Cook.

H. S. Root, Lieut
for Capt & Adjt
9th (Northumberland Hussars) Battn
Northumberland Fusiliers

SECRET   COPY NO. 3

OPERATION ORDERS No. 43
9th (N'ld Hussars) Bn. Northumberland Fus'rs.

1. RELIEF — An inter-company relief will be carried out on the night 17/18th June. Present Support & Reserve Companies relieving forward Coys in the following order:—

"C" Coy relieves A Coy right forward Coy
  D Coy   "   B Coy left forward Coy.

& vice-versa. Relief to commence as soon as Rations have arrived <u>C & A. Coys RELIEF</u>. This will be carried out 1 platoon at a time, second platoon of C Coy moving forward when first platoon of A Coy is in Support line. Details to be arranged between Coy Commanders concerned.

2. GUIDES — at the rate of 1 per post will be provided by OC A & B Coys to meet the incoming Coys at respective forward Coy Head Qrs.

3. DISTRIBUTION IN POSTS — OC C & D Coys will tell off their Coys in Posts in accordance with table issued herewith. Every man must know the No of his post & location of

OPERATION ORDERS — No 43 — Contd.

Coy (eg No. 3 post right forward Coy)
After getting into the Line, every man
is to reconnoitre the posts on either
flank of the one he is in.

4. ADVANCE PARTY — 1 Officer per Coy, 1 NCO per platoon
+ 1 runner will be detailed by O's C.
Companies to go into the Line tonight
for purpose of taking over all stores,
tools etc, and gaining all information
possible as to dispositions of own and
neighbouring Coys — also state of wire,
work in hand and contemplated.

5. WATER RATIONS — Water at the rate of 1 tin per
Post, and Rations will be dumped at
Support & Reserve Coy H.Qrs at Dusk.
C & D Coy. will take their water &
rations in with them. A & B Coys
will find theirs at H.Qrs of Support
and Reserve respectively. A & B Coys.
Advance parties will take charge of
these until Coys arrive.

6. WORK — All work will be carried on
until relief takes place; After relief
is complete, will be continued on
as far as possible.

OPERATION ORDERS No. 43 — Contd.

Completion of relief will be notified by Code —

"A" Coy	Very lights in possession			1½ boxes
B "	"	"	"	2½ "
C "	"	"	"	3 "
D "	"	"	"	4½ "

ACKNOWLEDGE.
dated 16th June 1918.

A.P. Roul. Lieut & A/Adjt.
9th (N.H.) Bn. North'd Fus"

Copies to —
No 1 OC A Coy
   2 OC B "
   3 OC C "
   4 OC D "
   5 Retained

SECRET   Copy No 1

OPERATION ORDERS No 43A
9th (North'd Hussars) Batt. North'd Fusiliers

1 RELIEF	The Batt. will be relieved by the 11th Batt. Suffolk Regiment on the night of the 21/22 inst. in the following order:—
	B Coy 11th Suffolks will relieve C Coy Right forward Coy
	D " " " " " D " Left forward Coy
	A " " " " " A " Support Coy
	C " " " " " B " Reserve Coy
2 GUIDES	Guides at the rate of 1 per Platoon and 1 from Batt. H.Qrs. will report at 11th Suffolks Regt H.Qrs at HAMET BILLET (P.14.a.0.2) at 9.45 am on the 21st inst. These guides will be provided from the Reserve Coy.
	Guides at the rate of 1 per Post will report to Lieut RWood at junction of path to Kent Line and Road near Batt. H.Qrs.
3 BILLETS	On completion of relief the Batt. will take over Reserve Billets at HAMET BILLET. Companies taking over same billets as previously occupied by them, reporting to Batt. H.Qrs. when in same
4 RATIONS	Arrangements will be made with reference to these direct with the Quartermaster
	Aeroplane Photos, maps, defence schemes, works in hand etc etc to be handed over and receipts for same to be sent in to Batt. H.Qrs. by 9.0 am on 22nd inst.
	Company Commanders will ensure that the trenches and all posts are left in a clean and sanitary condition
	Completion of Relief in forward Area will be wired to Batt. H.Qrs. using the following code:—
	A Coy — Bombs not required
	B Coy — One cook required
	C Coy — No NCO available
	D Coy — Cancel last indent

ACKNOWLEDGE
Dated 20 June 1918

Copies to
No 1 War Diary
2 Retained
3 Coming Officer
4/8 OC Coys
9 OC 11th Suffolk
10 QM
11 TO
12 RSM
13 Mr to Cook

2/Lieut
for Capt & Adjt

War Diary

SECRET COPY NO. 1

MAP REF:
Sheet 36A

OPERATION ORDERS No. 44

4th (North'd Hussars) Batt'n Northumberland Fusiliers

1. RELIEF
The Batt'n will relieve the 1st East Lancashire Regiment in the Left Sub-sector of Brigade Front on night 25/26th inst.
"A" Coy will relieve left front Coy. East Lancs.
"B" " " " right front " " "
"D" " " " Support " " "
"C" " " " Reserve " " "

2. GUIDES
At the rate of 1 per platoon + 1 for Bn. H.Qrs. will be at road junction F.14.b.9.4 at 10 p.m. On reaching front line Coy H.Qrs., 1 guide per post will be provided. 200 yards interval will be maintained between platoons.

3. ADVANCE PARTY
One officer per Coy, 1 N.C.O. per platoon, No. 1 of the L.G. Teams, 1 runner + 1 Signaller per Coy, RSM + 2 runners from Bn H.Qrs, will go into line on night of 25/26th.
They will leave HAMEL BILLET at 9.30 p.m. and will proceed in small parties. Guides will be provided at Bn H.Qrs. at P.5.c.1.9.

4. DISTRIBUTION
Coy. Officers with advance party will arrange as to which posts platoons will man, and will instruct the guides accordingly.

5. LIAISON
Any Liaison duties will be taken over.

6. TRENCH STORES
Advance party will take over ALL trench stores, aeroplane photos, paper maps etc. details of work in hand, and work projected.

7. TRANSPORT
T.O. will provide 4 limbers for water and officers kits, and mess cart for Battn H.Qrs, to be at Bn H.Qrs. at 6.0 p.m.
Any extra magazines required by Companies over and above 5 per man will be carried on the limbers.

8. WATER
O.C. Coys are responsible that all water bottles are filled before leaving. Certificates that this has been done will be rendered to Orderly Room by 7.30 p.m. on the 26th.

9. RATIONS
For 24th inst. will be carried on the man.
Arrangements for cooking will be made later.

10. BILLETS
O.C. Coys. are responsible that Billets are left in a scrupulously clean + sanitary condition and will obtain certificates to that effect from the incoming unit.

11. CODE
Completion of relief will be notified by following code word:-
A Coy — NONE AVAILABLE
B " — NOT YET RECEIVED
C " — THIRTY TWO
D " — ONE ONLY

No movement before 10 p.m.

ACKNOWLEDGE.
dated 24th June 1918.

A.W. Freshwater Lieut & Adjt.
4th (North'd Hussars) B'n North'd Fus.

Cpts. No 1 War Diary
2 Retained
3 Orderly Officer
4/8 O.C. Coys.
9 O.C. 1st East Lancs. Regt.
10 Q.M.
11 M.O.
12 R.S.M.
13 T' water Cart.

War Diary

APPENDIX "C"

SPECIAL ORDER OF THE DAY
By FIELD-MARSHAL SIR DOUGLAS HAIG
K.T., G.C.B., G.C.V.O., K.C.I.E
Commander-in-Chief, British Armies in France.

The following telegrams are published for the information of all ranks:—

To FIELD-MARSHAL SIR DOUGLAS HAIG FROM THE SUPERINTENDENT, TEACHERS AND SCHOLARS ROATH ROAD WESLEYAN SUNDAY SCHOOL, CARDIFF.

4-6-18.

Teachers and Scholars, Roath Road Wesleyan Sunday School, Cardiff, send you and brave men fighting for us the following message:—

"We thank you. We trust you. We pray for you. 420 young men already joined the colours from this Sunday School."

FROM FIELD-MARSHAL SIR DOUGLAS HAIG TO THE SUPERINTENDENT, TEACHERS AND SCHOLARS ROATH ROAD WESLEYAN SUNDAY SCHOOL, CARDIFF.

7-6-18.

All ranks under my command send their best thanks to the Teachers and Scholars of the Wesleyan Sunday School for their friendly message. I congratulate you warmly on the very satisfactory number of young men who have joined the Army from your school.

D. Haig, F.M.

General Headquarters,
June 9th, 1918.

*Commander-in-Chief,
British Armies in France.*

SPECIAL ORDER OF THE DAY
By FIELD-MARSHAL SIR DOUGLAS HAIG
K.T., G.C.B., G.C.V.O., K.C.I.E
Commander-in-Chief, British Armies in France.

The following messages are published for the information of all ranks:—

To FIELD-MARSHAL SIR DOUGLAS HAIG FROM GOVERNOR GENERAL, SOUTH AFRICA (THROUGH WAR OFFICE, LONDON).

6-6-18.

Resolution passed at a public meeting at Harrismith, Orange Free State, on 6th April and forwarded by the Governor General of S. Africa:—

"We the citizens of Harrismith in Orange Free State assembled at a public meeting held for the purpose desire to express to Field-Marshal Sir Douglas Haig, and the Forces under his command, our deep sense of the valour and tenacity shown by them in the great battle now in progress. We are proud to think that our brother South Africans have quitted themselves like men in the desperate struggle. We fervently pray that the Almighty may grant complete success to the Arms of Britain and her brave Allies, and we earnestly hope that the issue may lead to the establishment of a general and lasting peace among the nations of the World."

FROM FIELD-MARSHAL SIR DOUGLAS HAIG TO GOVERNOR GENERAL, SOUTH AFRICA.

11-6-18.

The encouraging message you have sent us from the citizens of Harrismith, Orange Free State, has given universal pleasure. Please convey to them on behalf of myself and all ranks, especially on behalf of the South Africans fighting so gallantly in France for all we hold most dear, our warmest appreciation and grateful thanks.

To FIELD-MARSHAL SIR DOUGLAS HAIG FROM THE EXECUTIVE COUNCIL, GREAT WAR VETERANS' ASSOCIATION OF CANADA, VANCOUVER, B.C.

6-5-18.

With you and yours in this glorious hour of defence, would that we could still be with you.

May the laurels of victory soon crown the efforts of the Allied Armies.

From FIELD-MARSHAL SIR DOUGLAS HAIG to THE EXECUTIVE COUNCIL, GREAT WAR VETERANS' ASSOCIATION OF CANADA, VANCOUVER, B.C.

11-6-18.

Cordial thanks to you all from the British Army in France for your inspiriting message.

To FIELD-MARSHAL SIR DOUGLAS HAIG from THE SECRETARY, BELPER TOWN AND TRADE ASSOCIATION, NR. DERBY.

3-6-18.

At a general meeting of the above Association held recently, it was unanimously proposed and carried that a message be sent, asking you to kindly convey to the men serving at the front especially those of the Sherwood Foresters connected with Belper and also to those serving in the Air Service, the hearty appreciation of their gallant conduct in the war and to assure them of our continued interest in their doings.

From FIELD-MARSHAL SIR DOUGLAS HAIG to THE SECRETARY, BELPER TOWN AND TRADE ASSOCIATION, NR. DERBY.

11-6-18.

On behalf of all ranks, and especially on behalf of the Sherwood Foresters and the Air Service, I beg you to convey to the Belper Town and Trade Association our warmest thanks for their welcome and encouraging message.

General Headquarters,
June 13th, 1918.

D. Haig, F.M.
Commander-in-Chief,
British Armies in France.

SPECIAL ORDER OF THE DAY
By FIELD-MARSHAL SIR DOUGLAS HAIG
K.T., G.C.B., G.C.V.O., K.C.I.E
Commander-in-Chief, British Armies in France.

The following messages are published for the information of all ranks:—

To FIELD-MARSHAL SIR DOUGLAS HAIG FROM THE GENERAL SECRETARY, THE SUNDAY SCHOOL UNION, 56 OLD BAILEY, LONDON, E.C. 4.

19-6-18.

I have the honour to send to you the message below which has just been unanimously and cordially adopted by Teachers and Scholars in Sunday Schools throughout the Kingdom: in most instances all standing while special intercession was offered.

Any acknowledgment that you may be able to make will be brought before the Sunday Schools of the land, and in sending it to the Superintendents, we propose asking them definitely to remember you, and the leaders of the War, in their public petitions from Sunday to Sunday.

MESSAGE.

"To the brave men fighting for us—
We thank you.
We trust you.
We pray for you."

FROM FIELD-MARSHAL SIR DOUGLAS HAIG TO THE GENERAL SECRETARY, THE SUNDAY SCHOOL UNION, 56 OLD BAILEY, LONDON, E.C. 4.

23-6-18.

All ranks of the British Army in France join with me in sending our heartiest thanks to the Teachers and Scholars of the Sunday Schools throughout the Kingdom for the friendly and encouraging message which they have been good enough to send us through you. We are all greatly touched by this mark of thoughtfulness and appreciation and send you all our very best wishes.

General Headquarters,
June 24th, 1918.

Commander-in-Chief,
British Armies in France.

APPENDIX "D"

34th Div. No. C.H./Card.

Officer Commanding,
9th Bn. Northd. Fus.

The enclosed Cards of Honour have been awarded to the undermentioned of the Battalion under your Command:-

23701 Pte. C.S. BARBER	59973 Pte. H. GLOVER
44312 Pte. W. DAUNCEY	16057 Pte. A. CONNELL
41122 Pte. C.A. BROWN.	10743 Pte. J. AITCHISON
59998 Pte. G. LEWIS.	12/18754 Pte. T. Dickenson.
14781 L/Cpl. R.B. SIREY	48539 Pte. A. TARBIT.
29/705 Pte. W. GREENWOOD.	235701 L/Cpl. F.G. ARMSTRONG.
12239 L/Cpl. J. HEADLAM.	27/213 Pte. J. ELDERBRANT.
235875 L/Sgt. M.J. ADAMSON.	315443 Pte. T. STAFFORD.
59385 Pte. J. DONOHOE.	13357 A/C.S.M. T. HORNBY.
38354 L/Cpl. R. HOLLIDAY.	37907 Pte. F. JERMY.
16260 L/Cpl. D. WILMOTT.	

4/6/18.

Lieut-Colonel,
A.A. & Q.M.G., 34th Division.

War Diary

BATTALION ORDERS   7-5-18
by
LIEUT. COLONEL W. A. VIGNOLES D.S.O.
Commg. 9th (Northd. Hussars) Battn. Northumberland Fusiliers

HONOURS and AWARDS

231. The following have been awarded the MILITARY MEDAL for gallantry in the Field on 21/22nd March 1918 in the operations near ST. LEDGER.

Number	Rank	Name
5226	Pte	Bradbury E.
19/1542	"	Reay G.
59840	"	Bastard R.J.V.
20/1668	"	Octon R.
41112	"	Brown C.A.
19427	Cpl	Coulson E.
235757	"	Watson A.E.
15347	L/C	Hallam W.
14454	"	Southworth J.
41179	Pte	Hall W.M.
41157	"	Davies G.
14787	Sgt	Stafford J.
41223	L/S	Schofield A.
801	Pte	Key G.
29/488	"	Cock T.E.
13357	A/CSM	Hornby T.
235551	Pte	Arkless M.G.
22182	"	Gibbons J.G.
13/5947	"	Ready W.

BAR TO MILITARY MEDAL

Number	Rank	Name
41132	Sgt	Bennett J.J.
59852	L/C	O,Neill J.

2nd Lieut. & A/Adjt.
9th (Northd. Hussars) Bn. Northd. Fusiliers

BATTALION ORDERS 16-6-18
by
LIEUT COLONEL W.A.VIGNOLES D.S.O.
Commanding 9th (Northumberland hussars) Battn. Northumberland Fusiliers.

HONOURS and AWARDS

329.
(Extract from 61st Divisional Routine Orders, No. 1855 dated 15th June 1918.) HONOURS AND AWARDS.

The following awards for gallantry and devotion to duty have beeen made :-

THE BAR TO THE DISTINGUISHED SERVICE ORDER
    Lieut. Colonel W.A.Vignoles D.S.O.

THE MILITARY CROSS
    Captain K.D.C.Macrae   R.A.M.C.

THE BAR TO THE DISTINGUISHED CONDUCT MEDAL.
    41172 Sergeant R.Hardman D.C.M.

THE DISTINGUISHED CONDUCT MEDAL.
    18700 C.S.M. (A/R.S.M.) A.Richardson M.M.
    46727 Sergeant W.Lumley
    27/492 S/Sergt. R.Madden

H.P. Rowe   Lieut. A/Adjt.
9th (Northd. Hussars) Northd. Fusiliers.

BATTALION ORDERS.   10-6-18.
by
LIEUT COLONEL W.A.VIGNOLES D.S.O.
Commanding 9th(Northumberland Hussars)Battn. Northumberland Fusiliers.

HONOURS AND AWARDS 330.

The Field Marshal Commanding-in-Chief has, under authority granted by His Majesty the KING awarded the following decorations :-

THE BAR TO THE MILITARY CROSS.
    a/Captain W.S.Allen M.C.
    Lieut H.S.Rowe M.C.
    2nd Lieut L.Fletcher M.C. M.M.

THE MILITARY CROSS.
    Captain I.G.C.Brady.
    Lieut E.B.L.Piggott.
    2nd Lieut W.H.Corner.
    2nd Lieut J.L.Baker.

The IX Corps Commander has, under authority granted by His Majesty the KING, awarded decorations as under.

THE BAR TO THE MILITARY MEDAL.
    41223 Cpl Schofield A. M.M.
    13/6947 Pte Ready W. M.M.

THE MILITARY MEDAL.
    12970 Sgt Stoker F.E.
    22736 " Oxlee A.J.
    15939 L/C Dawson J.W.
    11277 " Bell R.W.
    17382 Pte Hood R.J.
    44669 " Hill J.
    29796 " Pearson F.
    48545 " Taylor J.

The Army, Corps and Divisional Commanders send their congratulations to the recipients.

H.S.Rowe.
Lieut. A/Adjutant.
9th (Northd Hussars) Battn. Northd Fus.

War Diary

App "A"

Army Form C. 2118.

WAR DIARY
or
INTELLIGENCE SUMMARY.
(Erase heading not required.)

9th (N.H.) Bn. Northumberland Fusiliers.

JULY 1918.

APPENDICES.

A. MAP

B. OPERATION ORDERS.

C. ORDERS FOR AND REPORT ON RAID
(FOR MAP SEE A)

D. SYLLABUS OF TRAINING.

WAR DIARY
INTELLIGENCE SUMMARY.

5th Bn. NORTH'D FUS. — Army Form C. 2118. Page 1.

JULY 1918.

Place	Date JULY	Hour	Summary of Events and Information	Remarks and references to Appendices
In the line.	1st to 4th		Holding the line in the ST. FLORIS Sector. Inter Coy reliefs on the night of June 30/July 1st. Operation Order 45.	MAP appendix A. O.Os. appendix B.
	4/5th		Relieved this night by 11th Bn SUFFOLK REGT. Operation order 46. and became Bn. in Bgde Reserve in billet at HAMET BILLET.	
	5th		The above town was quiet, enemy activity being slight. A large working party supplied to work on defences this night.	
	6/7th		A, B and D Coys. A raid was carried out this night by a force consisting of 2 offs and 50 O.R.s divided into 5 patrols. Three patrols reached their objectives but no enemy was encountered and no identifications obtained. The other two patrols had not reached their objectives when what was taken to be the recall signal (a red Very light) was seen. This signal was either fired by enemy or by the Batn on the right. Orders and report attached.	Appendix C
	7th		Church parades.	
	7/8th		A working party at night from C and D Coys. 2 killed 6 wounded.	
	8th to 10th		Cleaning up and parades for training by Coys.	
	11th		Division relieved in the line by the 74th Div. Batn relieved at HAMET BILLET by the 24th Bn Welsh Regt. See O.O. 47.	
	12+13th		Parades by Coys for cleaning up, inspections, refitting.	

WAR DIARY

9th Bn NORTHᵈ FUS. Army Form C. 2118.

INTELLIGENCE SUMMARY. JULY 1918. page 2.

(Erase heading not required.)

Place	Date	Hour	Summary of Events and Information	Remarks and references to Appendices
Fifth Army	14th		Division in XI Corps, but held in G.H.Q. reserve. Church Parade attended by General Birdwood commanding Fifth Army.	
	15th 16th		Coy training.	
	17th		Moved by route march to LIETTRES	See appendix D
	18 to 20th		Coy training - in accordance with programme. Commanding officer and Coy Commanders reconnoitred the ground on the left of the XI Corps front North East end of the FORET DE NIEPPE with a view to operations in case of an enemy attack. Church Parades.	See O.O. No 48 Appendix B.
	21st		Division transferred to XV Corps Second Army. in G.H.Q. reserve	O.O. 49
	22nd		Division moved by route march to LA SABLONNERE South East of BLENDECQUES. Interfered with by heavy rain on several days.	
	23rd to 27th		Training as per programme. Bn & Coy Commanders reconnoitred positions in the "Army Line" near CAESTRE and assembly position with a view to any operations required in case of an enemy attack. Positions for Bn HQs selected. The Corps area generally was reconnoitred on another day.	
	28th		Church Parades. Reconnaissance by officers - in open warfare	
	29th		The Batt. carried out an attack practice on the high ground South of BLENDECQUES. 1 sect of M.G.C. and 2 guns from 93rd L.T.M. Battery took part in the operations.	

WAR DIARY
of
INTELLIGENCE SUMMARY.

9th Bn North'd Fus

JULY 1918.

Army Form C. 2118.

Page 3.

Place	Date July	Hour	Summary of Events and Information	Remarks and references to Appendices
	30th		Training Battn Drill and outpost scheme. In the afternoon all officers + N.C.O.s were formed into a Coy and carried out a Coy Attack under Batn Commander.	Programme D
	31st		Inspection of Batn by C.O. – Moved at night to NORRENT FONTES Division having been transferred to XI Corps Fifth Army. G.H.Q. Reserve.

During this period of training special attention was devoted to open warfare. Training was seriously interfered with by three moves, bad weather, and lack of suitable training grounds. Systematic training was very difficult as the period the Battn was to be "out" was unknown, and absence of Commanders on reconnaissance. Instructions were prepared as to the action of the Batn in case of active operations being resumed. See Defence instructions Appendix B.– An attack in this sector appears to have been expected, but owing to the success of the French counter offensive between the MARNE and the AISNE, the enemy seems to have moved a large part of his reserves in this sector to the South, and the anticipated attack did not take place. On the other hand the 9th Division recaptured METEREN and an Australian Division recaptured MERRIS without any very serious opposition. | |

Army Form C. 2118.

Page 4

WAR DIARY
or
INTELLIGENCE SUMMARY.   JULY 1918.

(Erase heading not required.)

Summary of Events and Information

Strength of Battalion at the beginning of month = W.O. Officers 932 O.R.
                     "   at the End of month = W.O. Officers 914 O.R.

Casualties.
Killed.   Acc. Wnd.   Wounded.   Evacuation.   Misfits   Struck off.   To Army 22nd   Transfers   Commissions
  2   1   13   51   2   14   2   4   3

                                                                                              TOTAL = 95

Drafts.   Week ending   6ᵗʰ   =   8
              "   "   13ᵗʰ   =   9
              "   "   20ᵗʰ   =   34
              "   "   27ᵗʰ   =   26
              "   "   31ˢᵗ   =
          To End of month   TOTAL 80

Officers.
Reinforcements.   Wounded.   Evacuation.   Transfer.
2ⁿᵈ Lieut A. Paw 29ᵗʰ   Capt R.H. Peters 17ᵗʰ   Capt G.W. Atkinson 13ᵗʰ   Lieut A.W. Wilkin 29ᵗʰ
Lieut J. Stewart 29ᵗʰ   Lieut A. Horn 11ᵗʰ   Capt J. McCloy 3ᵗʰ   Lieut E. Joliet 26ᵗʰ
Hon Lt J. Cook 25   Capt H. Babbitt 10ᵗʰ   Lieut J. L. Crayford 6ᵗʰ
Hon Lt H. Bobbitt 10ᵗʰ
Hon Lt J. Norman 17ᵗʰ
Lieut J.O. Younger 20ᵗʰ
Lieut J.H. Caco 20ᵗʰ

                                                        To Hospital in France
                                                        Officer = NIL

WAR DIARY
INTELLIGENCE SUMMARY.

5th Bn North'd Fus.   JULY 1918.

Army Form C. 2118.

Page 5

Kings Birthday Honours.
D.C.M. — 200995 Sgt. G. MATTHEWS.
M.S.M. — 18137 Sgt. T. CAMPBELL and 2/1702 Sgt T. SLATER.
Capt. J.M.F. CRAVEN, and 5124 L/Cpl. J. SHIELDS.

Mentions. Capt. J.M.F. CRAVEN.

Promotions. T/Capt. J.C.C. BRADY M.C. to be T/MAJOR April 18th 1918.
London Gazette July 18th 1918.

Note on method of holding line. — The diagram on MAP A. shows the general method of holding. — The front posts were isolated and there were no communication trenches. Posts and trenches were protected by breastworks, the country being flat and water level near the surface — It was possible to visit some of the forward posts (ST. FLORIS) R&LR sub/sector Coy HQs were in trenches — It was not possible to get some from view — In the day as there was a great deal of sniping. Movement by day was possible. right Batn. (LA HAYE) sub/sector. Men outside was killed by this. Coy. HQs were in large shell holes. This outside being shot at. Batn. at the end of (June) work was difficult as the nights being short very little time was available. The difficulty was increased on moonlight nights and the dropping of large parachute flights from aeroplanes on some nights. Sniping but on exposure against our front posts.

W.D.Signoles Lt Col.

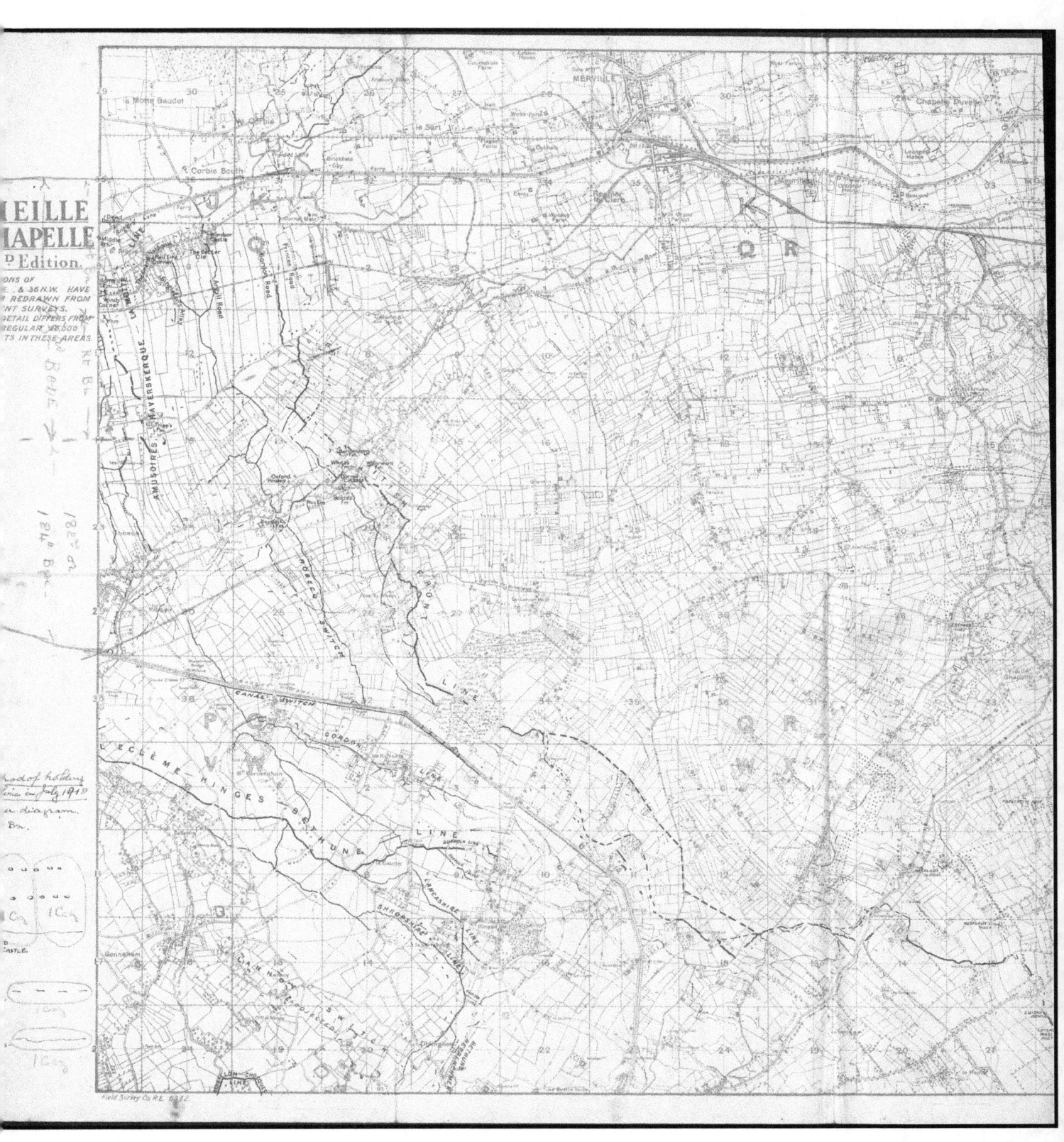

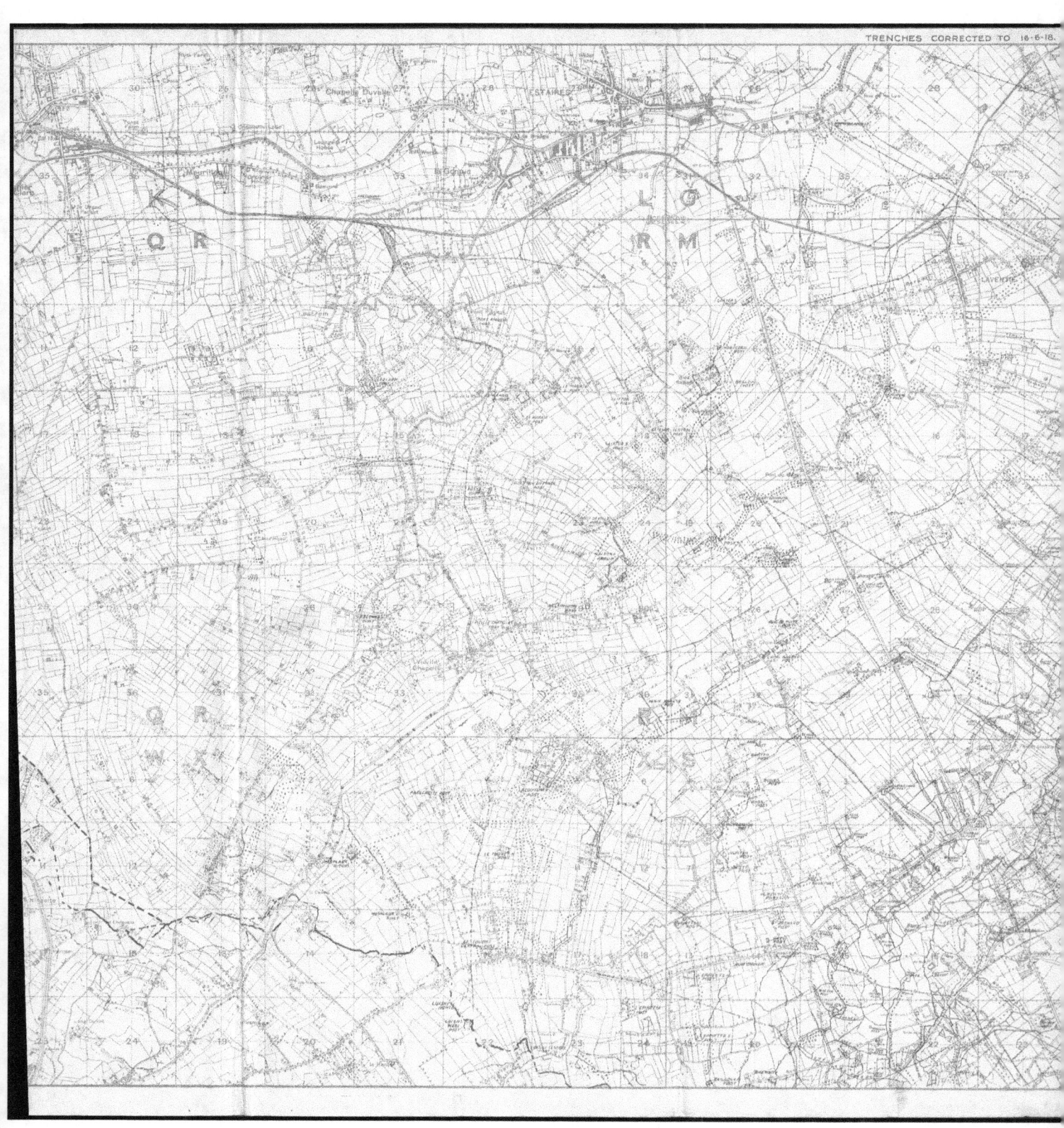

WAR DIARY
9th NORTH'd FUS'rs
APPENDIX A

VIEILLE
CHAPELLE.

1/20,000

SECRET   WAR DIARY. JULY 1918.   APPENDIX B   COPY No 13

OPERATION ORDERS No 45.

9th (Northumberland Hussars) Batn. Northumberland Fusiliers

1. An inter-Company relief will be carried out tonight 30th June/1st July 1918

ORDER OF RELIEF
"C" Coy relieves "A" Coy on left of Battn. Sector
"D" Coy " "B" " right of Battn Sector
and vice versa.

Relief will be carried out by half Companies, i.e. the last two platoons of "C" and "D" Coys will not move until the first two platoons of "A" and "B" Coy are in position. Details to be arranged between Company Commanders.

TIME
No movement to take place before 10.30 p.m.

GUIDES
O's C. Coys will detail 1 guide per post to report to respective opposite Coy Hd Qrs. at 10.45 p.m. for purpose of guiding Platoons to new positions.

RATIONS AND WATER
Will be dumped as follows
"C" and "D" Coys at Left and Right forward Coy H.Q. respectively.
"A" and "B" Coys at Left and Right Support Coy H.Q. respectively.

WORK CONTEMPLATED OR IN PROGRESS STORES ETC.
One Officer per Coy and 1 N.C.O. per Platoon will proceed to new positions on receipt of these orders for purpose of taking over all Stores etc and gaining all available information as to work in progress or contemplated, patrols and disposition of neighbouring Units.

DISPOSITION
On completion of relief OC Coys. will render a disposition return accompanied by sketch showing how their respective Companies are disposed and number of O.Rs in each post.

Completion of relief to be notified by code as follows.
"A" Coy ORs. for special leave 3
"B" " ORs for special leave 5
"C" " ORs for special leave 4
"D" " ORs for special leave 6.

ACKNOWLEDGE
Dated 30 June 1918.

Copies to:-
No 1 War Diary
2 Comdng. Officer
3 OC "A" Coy
4 OC "B" Coy
5 OC "C" Coy
6 OC "D" Coy
7 Quartermaster
8 Transport Officer.
9

H. L. Rowe   Lieut and Adjt.

SECRET.   Copy No. 1

OPERATION ORDERS No. 46.

9th (Northumberland Hussars) Battn. Northumberland Fus.

1. RELIEF. The 11th Bn. The Suffolk Regt. will relieve the 9th (N.H) Battn. Northumberland Fusiliers in the left sub-section of the Brigade front on the night of 5th July. On relief the Battn. will withdraw to HAMET BILLET and be in Brigade Reserve.

2. ORDER OF RELIEF.
"C" Coy (Left Front) will be relieved by "D" Coy 11th Bn Suffolk Regt.
"D" " (Right Front)   "   "   "B" "   "   "   "
"A" " (Left Support)   "   "   "C" "   "   "   "
"B" " (Right Support)   "   "   "A" "   "   "   "

Front line Coys. will march out by Posts.
Reserve & Support Line Coys. " " " by Platoons at 200 yds interval.

3. ROUTE. as before.

4. GUARD. O.C. "B" Coy will detail a Guard of 1 N.C.O. & 3 men to proceed to Battn. Bde. H.Qrs. to relieve guard at present found by 11th Bn. Suffolk Regt. by 6.30 p.m.

5. GUIDES. One per Post for Front Line and one per Platoon for Reserve & Support Lines. Guides to report to Lieut R.Wood at X Roads P5 c 5.2 at 10.30 p.m.

6. RATIONS. Q.M. will arrange for these to be dumped at respective Coy. H.Qrs in HAMET BILLET under care of C.Q.M.S's. The master cook will arrange to have tea and breakfast for men as before.

7. TRANSPORT. T.O. will arrange after having dumped rations at HAMET BILLET to send Mess Cart for H.Qrs., Maltese Cart for Aid Post & Limbers for Coys. to collect Officers Rolls - mess kit - camp kettles - water tins etc., from Battn. and Coy. H. Qrs., also Signalling Stores.

8. BILLETS. Coys will occupy same billets in HAMET BILLET as before, reporting to Bn. H.Qrs. when in camp.

9. STORES WORK IN PROGRESS &c. All aeroplane Photos - maps, stores etc. together with details of work in progress and contemplated will be handed over on relief.

10. TRENCHES POSTS, etc. Coy. Commanders will ensure that all Trenches, Posts and Quarters are left in a clean and sanitary condition and the usual certificate of cleanliness will be obtained.

11. COMPLETION OF RELIEF. The forward area will be notified to Bde. H.Qrs. using code words:
"A" Coy   "Rations quite good"
"B" Coy   "Rations OK"
"C" Coy   "Rations no complaints"
"D" Coy   "Rations Splendid"

ACKNOWLEDGE.
Dated 5th July 1918.

Copies to:
No 1 Machinery
   2 Rations
   3 Covering Officer
  4/8 O.C. Companies
      [illegible]
   9 T.O.
      [illegible]
  13 [illegible]
  14 Northumberland [illegible]

A.S. Rash, Lieut & Adjt.
9th (N.H.) Bn. North'd Fus.

SECRET.   COPY NO. 1

REF.
N/BF 1/40000
SHEET 36sw

OPERATION ORDERS No. 47
9th (North'd Fusrs) Bn. Northumberland Fuso.

1. RELIEF

The Division is being relieved by the 74th Division. On relief the Division will be in G.H.Q. Reserve.

The 231st Infantry Brigade will relieve the 183rd Infantry Brigade, in the ST. FLORIS SECTION on the night 10th/11th July 1918.

183rd Infantry Brigade, on completion of relief, will withdraw to the ST. HILAIRE – BOURECQ Area.

The 9th N.F. Bn. Northumberland Fusiliers will be relieved by the 24th Welsh Regt. tomorrow night 10th/11th inst.

On relief the Battalion will proceed by march route to ST. HILAIRE.

The following will remain behind until such time as their services will no longer be required. – 2 Officers + 2 N.C.Os – Battn. H.Qrs. 2 N.C.Os each Company.

ORDER OF MARCH.

Companies will march out independently, on being relieved and will rendezvous on the LA MIQUELLERIE – LA PIERRIERE ROAD, in order – A.B.C.D. Bn. H.Qrs. Head of Column to be on X roads at point O.30.c.20.55.

2. ROUTE.

Via Bridge P.13.d.3.6 – Track to P.19.6.3.9 – X roads LA PIERRIERE, thence through LA MIQUELLERIE – HAM en ARTOIS.

3. DISTANCES

EAST of AIRE CANAL. 100 yards between Platoons.
WEST of do. 100 do do Companies.

4. GUIDES.

Advanced party will meet Battalion at road junction T.6.c.5.6.

5. TRANSPORT.

Transport Officer will arrange for Lewis Gun Limbers, Mess Cart, Limbers for Camp Kettles, Company Mess Kit. Teams for Maltese Cart, Orderly Room Limber + Water Cart to be at Bn. H.Qrs at 5.0 pm. Cookers will be sent on in advance under Sergeant Cook. Gun limbers will march with Battalion; the remainder of Transport sent on in advance.

6. OFFICERS VALISES.

These will be ready for collection at 10 a.m. tomorrow morning 10th inst. A Lorry allotted to Battn. will be at rear Brigade H.Qrs, BERGUETTE at 1.30 pm 10th inst. to convey Stores etc., and may do two journeys. Q.M. will arrange for guide for above to report to Staff Captain at 1.30 pm.

OFFICERS CHA. BERS.

Will be at Battn. & Coy. H.Qrs by 10.30 p.m.

BILLETS

Coy Comdrs. will ensure that all Billets are left in a clean and sanitary condition & the usual certificate of Cleanliness obtained.

STORES

All stores etc. will be handed over to incoming unit. Tents & trench shelters will be handed to Bde Q.M. Serjt. by 12 noon 10th inst.

The Guard at P.33.d.3.3 will be relieved at 6 p.m.

7. MAPS.

All Documents, Top. & trench maps, including Secret Maps, Air Photos, excepting printed maps, scales 1/100,000, 1/40,000, 1/20,000 will be handed in to Orderly Room by 10.0 a.m. tomorrow 10th inst.

10. ADVANCE PARTY

Consisting of Signal NCO + 1 Serjt. Bn. H.Qrs + 1 NCO per Coy will parade at 8.0 am, under Capt. S.C. Wein, as detailed.

11. RELIEF COMPLETE

Will be notified to Bn. H.Qrs by runner.

ACKNOWLEDGE.
dated 9th July 1918.

Copies to:-
No 1 War Diary   No 10 183 Inf. Bde.
2 Retained   11 Q.M.
3 Comdg. Offr.   12 T.O.
4 (6 OC. Coys.   13 M.O.
9   14 Revd.
OC. 24th Welsh Regt.   15 Serjt. Cook.

R.S. Rowe, Lieut + Adjt.
9th N.F. Bn. North'd Fus.

REF.
VIEILLE
CHAPELLE
1/20,000

Report on Raid carried out by
9th (N.F.) Bn. Northumberland Fusiliers,
on the night 6th/7th July 1918.
under 183rd Infantry Brigade Order No. 222 dated 6/7/18.

APPENDIX C

Raiding force consisting of 2 officers + 50 O.Rs. was divided up into 5 Patrols, distributed along front of Raid zone.

Right Patrol of 10 O.Rs. under 2nd Lieut V. Curson.
Centre Patrols (3) each of 8 men under N.C.Os.
Left Patrol of 10 men under 2nd Lieut W. Bateson. M.M.

Men carried 10 pounds ammunition in pockets and 10 pounds in rifle, also 2 bombs each. Very Pistols were carried by Patrol Leaders in order to fire Red Light if prisoners captured. Box Respirators left in Front Line Posts. Four Duckboards were carried for purpose of bridging stream for Centre Patrols. Four Stretcher Bearers with 2 Stretchers followed in rear of Right & Left Centre Patrols with orders to remain on WEST bank of stream at bridges.

Arrangements were made with O.C. Left Battalion for supply of stretcher bearers from Front Line to Aid Post.

Tea + Rum provided for men before and after Raid.

Red Very Light (single) was the order to withdraw.

ZERO. 1 a.m.

Fire ceased at ZERO + 25 minutes.

Patrols were in position along our Front outside wire at ZERO - 5 minutes.

At ZERO Patrols proceeded direct to objective - (Enemy Trench immediately EAST of stream in Q.2.a)

Three Patrols reached objective but no enemy found. Remaining two Patrols had only reached stream when recall signal went up.

Right Patrol under 2nd Lieut V. Curson advanced through gap in enemy wire into two unoccupied Posts, 30 yards WEST of stream & approx 50 yards N. of Railway. While continuing on to stream 2 men were hit by M.G. fire coming almost directly from behind. This gun had apparently been brought up

/to

Railway after Patrol had passed as 3 flashes were seen on Railway in rear of Patrol and no fire had been encountered from this direction previously. Wounded men were sent to S.B's and remainder of Patrol crossing stream near Railway, entered enemy lines at junction of stream and Railway; (Q2 a 1.1) A Post with cubby hole was examined here but no enemy found. Track from this post leading back to enemy lines.

Patrol was continuing NORTH up enemy trench, when Red Very Light went up and they returned to our lines without finding anything that would give identification.

Centre Patrol. Sergt Whichelow & 8 men proceeded direct to objective crossing stream by means of duckboard bridge & entered enemy trench on EAST side of stream, without encountering enemy. One man was hit (shell fire) going out & again with bullet while being brought back.

Right Centre Patrol. L/Cpl Charlton & 8 ORs also reached objective. This Patrol encountered wire on EAST of stream which they cut through; patrol was fired on from Right Rear by M.G. This Patrol returned on Red Light going up.

Left Patrol. 2nd Lieut. W.Bateson. M.M. & 10 ORs proceeded through enemy wire on WEST side of stream, which they had some difficulty in crossing. An enemy Post (unoccupied) was found behind this wire, consisting of consolidated shell hole with cubby hole, but nothing in the way of identification was found. This Patrol were on the WEST bank of stream when the Red Very Light went up & thinking a prisoner must have been secured, they returned. No opposition was met with, excepting the wire.

Left Centre Patrol also only reached the EAST bank of stream.

The Red Very Light that was taken to

be the recall signal was sent up on Right Rear of Raiding force at 1.20 am and was either put up by enemy or Battalion on right flank, as no Flare was sent up by us.

Fortunately, 3 Patrols gained their objectives before this occurred.

(Sgd) D.R.Osborne
Major.
Comdg. 9th (N.H.) Bn. Northumberland Fus.

In the Field.
7.7.18.

SECRET
REF. 36ᴬ
Y/40000B

OPERATION ORDERS No 48

COPY No 1

9th (Northumberland Hussars) Bn. Northumberland Fus.

1. MOVE
The Brigade will move to the LINGHEM area tomorrow 17th July 1918 in relief of the 184th Infantry Brigade.
The Battalion will relieve the 2/4th Bn Oxford & Bucks Light Infantry at LIETTRES.

2. PARADE
The Battalion will parade in following order, Band, A B C D & H.Q. Coys and will proceed by route marked LIETTRES. Head of column to be on Cross roads at T5d 40 90 at 9.0 am, the 17th inst.
DRESS. Marching Order.

3. ROUTE
NORRENT FONTES — N29 c 80.05 — N.W. to ROMBLY — Cross Roads N19 c 60.90 — N.19.c.8.w. to LIETTRES.

4. DISTANCES
100 yards between Companies.
25 yards between sections of 6 vehicles.

5. GUIDES
Advance party will meet the Battalion at N19.c.9.4.

6. RATIONS
Coy Cooks will prepare Dinners at usual time at LIETTRES.

7. TRANSPORT
Transport Officer will arrange for 2 Lewis Gun Limbers and Cooker to march in rear of each Company. Remainder of Transport to march in rear of Battalion.
The day's Rations will be carried in the Cookers Dixies.
Camp Kettles will be carried in Cookers Crates.

8. OFFICERS VALISES
These will be packed ready for collecting at Coy Hd Qrs by Baggage Wagon at 7.30 am.

9. OFFICERS CHARGERS
Will be at Battalion and Coy Hd Qrs at 8.45 am.

10. BILLETS
Company Commanders, Quartermaster and Transport Officer will ensure that all billets are left in a clean and sanitary condition, and render a certificate to this effect to O.Room.

11. STORES
All documents relating to Training Areas and all Area Stores will be handed over. Quartermaster will arrange for guide to meet Supply Wagons at Dump. He will also arrange loading of Surplus kit to be sent to CLETY.

12. REAR PARTY
Capt. S.C. Wells and one sanitary man per Coy and Sanitary Corpl will remain behind to ensure all billets are clean. This Officer will obtain certificates of cleanliness from in-coming unit, also any claims made in by inhabitants, and a certificate from the Mairie that there are no outstanding claims. He will proceed to LIETTRES at 12 noon.
All men excused duty will parade under 2nd Lieut. J.A. Godfrey and an officer to be detailed by O.C. "C" Coy outside A Coys Hdqrs at 10 am. and marched to LIETTRES. The packs belonging to these men will be handed in to Q.M. Stores by 9 a.m.

13. MARCHING OUT STATES
Will be rendered to Orderly Room by 8.0 am.

ACKNOWLEDGE
Dated 16th July 1918.

Copies to:—
No 1. War Diary
  2. Retained
  3. Commanding Officer
  4. Second in Command
  5. 183 Infantry Bde.
  6-9 Coy Companies
  10. P. Company
  11. Transport Officer
  12. Quartermaster
  13. R.S.M.
  14. M.O.

H.S. Noel Lieut. & Adjutant
9th (N.H.) Bn. Northumberland Fus.

War Diary

SECRET.   COPY N°

OPERATION ORDERS N° 49.

9th (North'd Hussars) Bn. Northumberland Fus'rs.

1. MOVE. — The 61st Division is transferred to XV Corps.
The 183rd Infantry Bde, 2/3rd Field Arty, and No.3 Coy, Divisional Train, will march today 22nd inst., to the HERINGHEM-CAMPAGNE Area.
The Battalion less fatigue parties will parade at 10.0 a.m. in mass facing SOUTH on Battn Parade Ground and after inspection will move by route march in order Band, H.Qrs, A B C D Coys to HERINGHEM-CAMPAGNE Area. Head of column will pass Cross Roads EAST of S in LIETTRES at 11.0 am.
DRESS — Full Marching order.

2. ROUTE. — BLESSY — MARTHES — REBECQ.

3. GUIDES. — Will be at ECQUES church, from 1.30 pm to guide Battn to new billets.

4. TRANSPORT. — Will march with Battn.

5. FATIGUE PARTY — Each Coy will detail a fatigue party of 5 men, under the Orderly Officer, to ensure that Camp and billets are left in a clean and sanitary condition. This party will join their Companies by 10.45 a.m.
Capt S.C. Wells will remain until 2 pm to receive claims for damage. This officer will obtain certificates of cleanliness from area Commandant, also if possible, damage certificate to the effect that no outstanding claims exist from Mairie.

ACKNOWLEDGE.
dated 22nd July 1918

A. S. Rowe
Lieut a/Adjt.
9th (N.H.) Bn. North'd Fus'rs

Copies to:
No 1 War Diary
2 Returnee
3 Comdg Officer
4 2nd in Command
5
6
7 } O.C. Coys.
8
9
10 Transport Officer
11 Quartermaster
12 183rd Infy Bde.
13 Hdqrs
14 M.O.

Nan Dean

SECRET

OPERATION ORDERS No. 50.

Copy No. 1

9th (Northd Hussars) Bn Northumberland Fusiliers

1. MOVE.	The Division is transferred to XI Corps. The 183rd Infantry Brigade Group will march to FONTES-LINGHEM area tonight 31st July/1st Aug. The Battalion will proceed by Route march to billets at FONTES.
2. PARADES.	Battalion will parade on the LA SABLON – QUIESTEDE road in order B. C. D. A. + HdQrs. Head of Column at point B.22.d.1.2 (road junction) at 8.45 pm. Officers chargers to be ready at respective HdQrs. at 7.15 pm.
3. ROUTE.	QUIESTEDE – ECQUES – road junction G.11.6. – CRECQUES – BLESSY – WITTERNESSE – ROMBLY.
4. DISTANCES.	100 yards between Companies. 25 yards between sections of 6 vehicles. Rear Companies will put out connecting files to keep touch.
5. GUIDES.	Advance Party will provide 1 guide per Company to meet Battn. on track at N.29.a.10.20 (junction) at 1.0 am.
6. RATIONS.	Sergt. Cook will arrange for dinners to be ready at 6.30 pm and tea as soon as possible after arrival in new billets.
7. TRANSPORT.	Gun Limbers & Cookers to march with Companies, remainder of Transport in rear of Battalion.
8. OFFICERS VALISES.	To be dumped at Coy. HdQrs ready for collecting at 3.0 pm.
9. BILLETS.	To be left in a clean and sanitary condition and certificate to that effect obtained from Billet Warden by O.C. rear party.
10. STORES.	Coy Commanders will render list of all stores to be handed over to Orderly Room by 3.0 pm. Tents & French Shelters will be struck and dumped at Coy. HdQrs. by 2.30 pm.
11. ADVANCE PARTY.	Of 1 N.C.O. per Coy. Q.M. & Transport, under 2nd Lieut. R Woods will meet lorry at Brigade Hd Qrs. HEURINGHEM at 2.50 pm. to take over billets at FONTES.
12. REAR PARTY.	Of 1 sanitary man per Company under Orderly Officer will remain after Battalion has marched out to ensure Billets are in a clean condition & certificate to that effect obtained from Billet Warden, also "No damage" certificate from the MAIRE.
13. MARCHING OUT STATES.	will be rendered to Orderly Room by 7.0 pm.

ACKNOWLEDGE.

Dated 31st July 1918.

Copies to:—
No 1 War Diary
    2 Retained
    3 Commg Officer
    4 2nd in Command.
    5 183rd Infy Bde.
 6/10 O.C. Coys.
   11 Transport Officer
   12 Quartermaster
   13 Medical Officer
   14 R.S.M.
   15 Master Cook.

H. L. Root, Lieut &
A/Adjutant.
9th (N.H.) Bn North'd Fus'rs

9th (North'd Hussars) Bn. Northumberland Fusiliers

SECRET

DEFENCE INSTRUCTIONS

COPY No. 1

REF MAPS. 2nd Ed. 3. Belts 40000 + 27. 5.6. Eastern Half 1/20000

The Division now forms part of XV Corps, Second Army.
   (a) In the event of attack the Brigade as part of the Division will be prepared to assemble in area HONDEGHEM. Vu.
   (b) Occupy Army line from the CAESTRE — FLETRE road W.14.d.2-8 to R.3.a.9.9 (South of BOIS de PAILLE)
   (c) Operate on any portion of the XV Corps front. Corps Northern Boundary from EAST to WEST:—
      Sheet 27 S.E. (Eastern half) a line through. X.17.a.5.0 — X.11.a.5.0 — X.4 — X.3
                               R.32 — R.31; Q.36 — Q.35 — Q.34.
           " (Western half) . . . . . . Q.33 — Q.32 — Q.31;
                                 P.36; V.6 — V.5 — V.4 — V.3 — V.2.
      Southern Boundary:—
         Sheet 36.A. N.E. a line through K.4 — K.3 — K.2 — K.1;
                              J.3.
                                  D.30 — D.29 — D.28 — D.27 — D.26.d.

2. Reference 1(a) above.
   (a) On receipt of the order "MAN BATTLE STATIONS" Battn. will turn out and rendezvous on the road to LE BIBEROU through A.10 central. (Sheet 36.A), head of column at first house in LE BIBEROU facing N.W.
   (b) Order of March. A. B. C. D. H'dQrs.
   (c) Dress – Fighting Order.
   (d) Reports to Head of Column; leaving billets to be reported to Orderly Room by Cycle Orderly.
   (e) Destination. — Field V.f. 84.8, S.W. of HONDEGHEM.
   (f) Route. Battalion will march via LA HOCQUET, A.10.a.0.1, road junction A.11.c.1.8 — CAMPAGNE — RENESCURE — Road through T.15.c. and 6. road junction T.10.c.6.1, thence direct road to cross road:— V.1.c.95.05. to destination.
   (g) Brigade H.Q. at V.8.a.75.90, where Adjutant will report on arrival
   (h) Surplus personnel will remain behind in present billets and move to CAMPAGNE with Q.M. Stores.
   (i) Transport & Q.M. Stores.
      First line transport will proceed with Battalion and will act in accordance with orders laid down in Brigade Administrative Instructions S.C. 6973 dated 23.4.18.
      The Q.M. will be responsible for collecting Officers valises & spare mess kit not taken forward with Battalion.
   (j) Lieut. J.C. FENWICK will act as liaison officer between Bn. H.Q. and Q.M. Stores and Transport.
      4 Cycle Orderlies will be attached to Q.M. Stores — detailed by Coys. (1 per Coy)

3. Reference 1(b) above.
   (a) On command "OCCUPY POSITIONS" the Battalion will move and occupy the ARMY LINE, from CAESTRE – FLETRE road W.14.d.2-8 (inclusive) to junction of Trench and road Q.35.d.55.95 (exclusive)
   (b) Dispositions. Coys will be disposed in depth.
      "C" Coy. Right Coy from Bn. Boundary to W.14.b.7.9.
      "D" " Centre Coy. hence to Q.35.c.70.75.
      "B" " Left Coy. thence to Bn. Boundary, including defences of THIESHOUR. W of the THIESHOUR – FLETRE road.
      Coys will find their own support and arrange for piquets & standing patrols to occupy tactical points in front of their line.
      "A" Coy. Reserve in trench through Q.34 central.
      Bn. H.Q. Farm Q.34.c.5.3
   (c) "C" Coy will establish touch with 183rd Infy Brigade.
      "B" Coy will establish touch with 11th Suffolks.
      Coys H.Qs will be reported to Bn. H.Q.
   (d) Brigade H.Q. at Q.29.a.5.9
      Left Bn. H.Q. Q.35.d.5.9
      Support Bn. H.Q. Q.33.b. central

DEFENCE INSTRUCTIONS — CONT?   COPY No 1

(e). Signal communications will be established within the Brigade as follows:—

LINES.
Two lines, taking different routes, will run from Brigade H.Q. at Q.27.a.30.90 to the Support Battalion H.Q. at Q.33.b.Central. They will be continued, again taking different routes, to the Right Battalion H.Q. at Q.34.c.50.30. A buried route runs from the Right Battalion H.Q. to Farm at Q.34.b.30.40. Two lines will run on this route continuing from Farm at Q.34.b.30.40 as ground lines to Left Battalion H.Q. at Q.33.b.50.90.

A number of Brigade Linesmen and Orderlies will be attached to the Support Battalion H.Q. for maintenance of lines between Brigade H.Q. and the Right Battalion H.Q. 2 Brigade Linesmen will be attached to the Left Battalion H.Q. for maintenance of lines from Left Battalion to the buried route at Farm Q.34.b.30.40.

The number of lines to be used on the buried route will be allotted in due course.

VISUAL.
Visual communication will be maintained as follows:—
1. Between Brigade H.Q. and Support Battalion.
2. Between Brigade H.Q. and Right Battalion.
3. Between Brigade H.Q. and Left Battalion.

Direct communication can be obtained in each case. All stations will get into touch with one another immediately on arrival at the Battle H.Q.

PIGEONS.
Pigeons will be supplied to Brigade and Battalion H.Q. The Lofts are at WARDRECQUES and will be in telephonic communication with Adv. Divisional H.Q.

WIRELESS & POWER BUZZER
Arrangements will be notified later.

(f). TRANSPORT. A forward echelon will be formed in accordance with Brigade administrative Instructions.

(g). LEWIS GUNS & DRUMS. 2 A.A. Lewis guns will be sent to Transport lines. These will be manned by surplus personnel or band.
Not more than 32 Lewis gun drums per gun will be taken into action, remaining 12 drums per gun will be a reserve at transport lines.

ACKNOWLEDGE

Dated 27th July 1918.

Copies to:—
No 1. War Diary
2. Retained
3. Comm'g Officer
4. }
5. } O.C. Coys
6. }
7. A.O. Coys
8. 183rd Infy Bde
(not sent) → 9. Transport Officer
10. Quartermaster
11.
12. Medical Officer
13. R.S.M.

H. S. Rowe, Lieut & Adjutant
9th (N.I.) Bn North'n Fus'rs

SECRET.

183rd INFANTRY BRIGADE ORDER NO. 283.   1/7/18. Copy 5

Ref: VIEILLE CHAPELLE 1/20,000.

1. Tonight 6th/7th July, Fighting Patrols of 9th Battalion, The Northumberland Fusiliers, will raid enemy trenches South of CORNET MALO between the ST. FLORIS - CORNET MALO Road and the Railway and secure identifications.
    The objective and limit of advance will be the general line O.8.a.35.30 - O.2.c.15.50.

2. The Raid will be supported by Artillery - Trench Mortar, and Machine Gun fire as under:

    (a) <u>18 pounders.</u> At Zero 18-pounders will put down a box barrage as follows: O.1.d.90.90 - K.31.d.70.90 - K.32.c.10.90 - O.2.c.25.80. At Zero plus one minute the front and rear face of the box barrage will lift 100 yards.
    At Zero plus 2 minutes the front face of the barrage will lift 100 yards and remain on the line from which the rear face has lifted until Zero plus 5 minutes, when it will join the rear face of the box barrage.

    (b) <u>4.5" Howitzers.</u> From Zero to Zero plus 25 minutes 4.5" Hows. will engage the following targets:
      i. House O.2.c.55.75.
      ii. House K.31.d.70.20.
      iii. Track O.2.a.70.90 - O.2.c.45.90 - K.32.c.50.90.
      iv. The Railway in O.2.d.
    In addition 4.5" Hows. will put down a smoke screen if wind is favourable.   d - O.2.b.30.05

    (c) <u>Heavy Artillery</u> will fire on road O.2.b.90.95/ and in addition will neutralize Hostile Batteries if required.

    (d) <u>Trench Mortars.</u> <u>2" Mortons</u> will fire on road and Houses from O.2.a.70.35 to O.2.c.37.87.
    <u>Stokes Mortars</u> will fire on the Orchards in K.31.d.

    (e) <u>Machine Guns.</u> Machine Guns will fire on the following lines:

      1 Gun - O.2.c.25.35 - O.2.d.30.90.
      1 Gun - O.2.c.45.95 - O.2.b.90.90.
      1 Gun - On K.32.c.80.90.
      1 Gun - On K.32.c.94.10.

    (f) Right Group 31st Divisional Artillery will cooperate on the Right.
    All fire will cease at Zero plus 25 minutes.

3. Raiding Patrols will be formed up ready outside our wire at Zero minus 5 minutes. At Zero they will advance on the objective.

4. Patrols will wear Raid Identity Discs. All badges and identifications will be removed.

5. Zero hour will be 1 a.m.

6. Watches will be synchronised at Brigade Hdqrs at 9 p.m.

7. 11th Suffolks will arrange for an advanced dressing station and the evacuation of any casualties.

8. The signal for withdrawal will be Red Very Lights.

9. ACKNOWLEDGE.

                                  Captain,
Issued at 5 p.m.   Brigade Major, 183 Inf.Bd.

Copy 1 - War Diary	Copy 7 - 1 E.Lancs	Copy 13 - 478 Field Coy RE
2 - File	8 - 183 T.M.B.	14 - 182nd Inf.Bde.
3 - S.C.	9 - L.Grp.M.GC.	15 - 95th Inf.Bde.
4 - E.S.C.	10 - Liaison Off'r	16 - 61 Division
5 - 9th N.F.	11 - 330 Bde.RFA.	17 - 28 Bde.RGA.
6 - 11th Suffolks	12 - 331 Bde.RFA.	18 - CRA.

OPERATION ORDERS.

REF:
VIEILLE CHAPELLE
1/20000

9th (North^d Hussars) Bⁿ North^d Fusiliers

1. Tonight 6/7th July 1918, O.C. "B" Coy. will detail a fighting patrol of 50 O.Rs, under 2nd Lieut W.Bateson M.M. & 2nd Lieut V.Curzon to raid enemy trenches SOUTH of CORNET MALO between the ST FLORIS — CORNET MALO road and the Railway, to secure identification. Objective & limit of advance will be general line Q.2.a.25.00 — Q.2.a.15.50.

2. The raid will be supported by artillery, Trench Mortars and Machine Gun Fire.
   All fire will cease at ZERO plus 25 minutes.

3. Raiding force will be divided into 5 Patrols and will be formed up outside our wire at ZERO minus 5 minutes as follows.

   Right Patrol .. 10 O.Rs under 2nd Lieut V.Curzon.
   " Centre " ... 8 O.Rs " N.C.O.
   Centre Patrol 8 O.Rs " N.C.O.
   Left Centre " 8 O.Rs " N.C.O.
   Left Patrol 10 O.Rs " 2nd Lieut W.Bateson M.M.

   At ZERO patrols will advance on objective as speedily as possible.
   ZERO hour will be 1.0 a.m.

4. The Right & Left Centre Patrols will both arrange to carry one duckboard bridge for purpose of bridging stream. These will be drawn from Right Front Coy.
   DRESS. Soft Caps, no equipment, Box Respirators to be left in front line trench. 10 rounds ammunition in pockets – 10 rounds in rifle & 2 bombs per man will be carried.
   Each Patrol Leader will carry Very Pistol with 4 red light cartridges.
   Two stretcher bearers with stretchers will follow in rear of Right Centre and Left Centre Patrols respectively and will remain on WEST bank of stream at bridges.

5. On a Patrol capturing prisoner a Red Very light will be sent up by the Patrol Leader which will be the signal for all Patrols to withdraw.

6. Raiding party will rendezvous at 11.30 p.m. at WHITE HOUSE where arrangements will be made for supply of tea & rum.

7. A Forward Aid Post will be established at/
Right

7. contd.
Right Front Coy. Hd.Qrs. of Left Battalion. Arrangements will be made with O.C. Right Battalion for supply of Stretcher Bearers from Front Line to Forward Aid Post & thence to R.A.P.

H. S. Rowe
Lieut & Adjutant
9th (N.H.) Bn. North'd Fusrs.

Lillefield.
6-7-16.

9th (Northumberland Hussars) Battn. Northumberland Fusiliers.

SYLLABUS OF TRAINING.

APPENDIX D.

2nd WEEK.   Period:- July 22nd 1918 to July 27th 1918 (inclusive)

Date.	Day.	Time.	Nature of Training.	Place.
July 22nd	Monday	8.0 a.m. – 12.30 p.m.	B.C.D. Coys. Contact Scheme with Aeroplane. A. Coy. On Range.	High ground above LINGHEM N.20.b T.15.b.4.8
		5.0 p.m. – 6.30 p.m.	Lewis Gun, Rifle Grenadiers & Signallers etc., training with their own weapons, etc. Demonstration.	Grounds in vicinity of Camp – M.23.c
July 23rd	Tuesday	8.0 a.m – 2.0 p.m.	Battalion in Attack.– Attack from West into	M.32 & S.2.
July 24th	Wednesday	8.0 a.m. – 12.30 p.m	B. Coy. Range practices. Lewis Guns on Range. A.C & D. Coys.– Musketry, P.T. Coy Drill. Small Schemes by platoons. e.g. Platoon as "Point" to an advance guard.	Quarry N.21.a Quarry N.21.b Vicinity of Camp.
July 25th	Thursday	8.0 a.m. – 10.0 a.m.	A & B Coys., in attack. C & D Coys., Musketry, P.T. & Drill.	N.20.b Vicinity of Camp M.23.c
		10.0 a.m. – 12 noon.	A & B Coys, Musketry, P.T., Drill C & D, Coys. Coy in attack	do N.20.b
		5.0 p.m. – 6.30 p.m.	Scouting and Patrols. Lewis Gunners, etc.	N.23.c
July 26th	Friday	8.0 a.m. – 2.0 p.m.	Battalion Scheme and Route March C Coy on Range.	Ground to be notified later T.15.b.4.8
July 27th	Saturday	8.0 a.m. – 12.30 p.m.	Musketry, P.T., Drill. Small Schemes by Coys. Special Practices in writing reports and sending in information	Vicinity of Camp M.23.c
			Lectures and Talks by Officers.	

9th (Northumberland Hussars) Battn. Northumberland Fusiliers.

SYLLABUS OF TRAINING.

3rd WEEK.

Period:- July 29th 1918, to August 3rd 1918, (inclusive)

Date.	Day	Time.	Nature of Training.	Place.
July 29th	Monday	8.0a.m.– 2.0p.m.	Battalion Scheme.	"A" Ground.
July 30th	Tuesday	8.30a.m.–9.30a.m. 9.30a.m.–12.30p.m. 2.0p.m.–3.30p.m.	Battalion Drill. Battalion Outpost Scheme. Musketry, L.G. Drill, Rifle Grenade Practise and Special Classes.	A 16 & 22
July 31st	Wednesday	8.0a.m.–12.30p.m. 3.0p.m.–5.0p.m.	Advance Guard Scheme. Companies on Range.	From BELLE CROIX – QUESTEDE Road thro: BANDRINGHEM to LA CROIX. A.24a.6.0
August 1st	Thursday	8.0a.m.–2.0p.m.	Battalion Scheme.	"A" Ground.
August 2nd	Friday	8.0a.m.–12.30p.m. 2.0p.m.–3.30p.m.	Rear Guard holding LAYBOURNE RIVER. Musketry, L.G. drill and Special Classes.	From – G.9.b to A.29.a.
August 3rd	Saturday.	8.0a.m.–2.0p.m. Afternoon	Companies on Range "Y" Coys not on Range Musketry & Coy Drill. Games.	S.22.d.6.6.

Army Form C. 2118.

WAR DIARY
— OF —
INTELLIGENCE SUMMARY.
(Erase heading not required.)

9th (North Lancs) Battn Northumberland Fusiliers — August 1918

APPENDICIES

- A   MAPS
- B   183 Infantry Brigade Orders
- C   184 Infantry Brigade Orders
- D   9th (NH) Bn Northd. Fus Orders
- E   Operation Orders 1" Suffolk Regt
    2/6 Royal Warwick
    9th Royal Berks
- F   MISCELLANEOUS Orders & Messages & Reports
- G   Special Orders of the Day

9th Bn (N.F.) Pa. N.76 Fr.

Army Form C. 2118.

WAR DIARY
INTELLIGENCE SUMMARY.
(Erase heading not required.)

Aug. 1918

Place	Date	Hour	Summary of Events and Information	Remarks and references to Appendices
FONTES	Aug 1		Arrived at FONTES.	
FONTES	2		Battalion Drill. Companies practice Advance Guard schemes	
FONTES	3		Companies at the disposal of Company Commanders. "A" Coy on the range	
FONTES	4		Sunday. Battalion parade for Divine Service	
FONTES	5		Commanding Officers Inspection of Battalion.	
FONTES	6		Battalion moved to ARCADE CAMP in FORET DENIEPPE at 2.30 pm and arrived in camp at 9.30 pm	
ARCADE CAMP	7		Quiet day resting and cleaning up	
ARCADE CAMP	8		Battalion to be in readiness to move to forward area at about 2 hours notice. Battalion moved at 10 a.m. Orders to move received at 10 a.m. Companies placed in support trenches vicinity of CAUDESCURE STATION. "B" and "C" Coys are in Batt. H.Q. at near CAUDESCURE STATION Coy and a minor operation at about 12 mn tonight (9-10th)	
ARCADE CAMP	9		The operation of "B" and "C" Companies referred to above was postponed to 3.0 am. The intention was to cross the river PLATE BECQUE at K.16.b.2.2 and K.11.E.15. H.Q and secure a bridge head. At 3.0 am "C" Coy crossed the bridge which they had placed at K.11.E.15. H.Q and moved forward a short distance though K.11.E.50 and K.11.E.00. Heavy machine gun fire was opened on the Company apparently from H.Q. 50 and K.11.E.00. "B" Coy No. 5 & 8 Platoons attempted to cross but failed owing to heavy machine gun fire. At 5.30 am "C" Coy withdrew had to fall back to ARCADE CAMP at about 9.30 am. Green & pale arrived. The Battalion marched back to ARCADE CAMP at about 9.30 am	
CAUDESCURE STATION				

Army Form C. 2118.

WAR DIARY
or
INTELLIGENCE SUMMARY.
(Erase heading not required.)

Instructions regarding War Diaries and Intelligence Summaries are contained in F.S. Regs. Part II. and the Staff Manual respectively. Title pages will be prepared in manuscript.

Place	Date	Hour	Summary of Events and Information	Remarks and references to Appendices
ARCADE CAMP	11		SUNDAY Divine Service	
ARCADE CAMP	12		Company training special attention paid to musketry.	
ARCADE CAMP	13		Company training. Musketry. Orders received that Brigade would relieve the 8th Infantry Brigade in the front line tomorrow.	
ARCADE CAMP	14		Companies prepare to move into the front line. Battalion moved by train on light railway from CROWE to MEREDITH STATION. "A" Coy relieved 1 Coy of 2/3 Royal Berks. ¼ Royal Norwich Regt and B. C and D Coy relieve 9th ⅔ Royal Berks Regt (and 1 platoon ⅔ 1/3rd R Hardwick Regt) Battalion HQ Dro near CAUDESCURE STATION "A" Right Front Coy. B Left Front Coy. C Left Support Coy D Right Support Coy 1st East Lancashire Regt on our left.	
FRONT LINE	15		Heavy shelling by enemy, some casualties in A and C Coys. Major W. Bosworth M.C. (Second) in Command takes over temporary Command of the Battalion from Lieut. Colonel N.A. Vignoles D.S.O. who proceeded to 11th Corps Officers Rest Station	
FRONT LINE	16		Enemy shelled vicinity of Battalion Hd Qrs heavily about 6 a.m. Fairly quiet day during day.	
FRONT LINE	17		Fairly quiet. Our patrols report no practicable bridge over the PLATE BECQUE and enemy holding trench covering the broken bridge at K.16.8 & D. Enemy special 5 in H.D at 1 am.	O.C.
FRONT LINE	18		Explosion heard in MERVILLE and vicinity - not caused by shell fire. O.C. "A" and "C" Companies (front line) at 2.30 pm ordered to push out patrols as follows:	

WAR DIARY

INTELLIGENCE SUMMARY

Army Form C. 2118.

Place	Date	Hour	Summary of Events and Information	Remarks and references to Appendices
FRONT LINE	18		(as follows:-) "A" Coy to triangular enclosure on road in K.22.a and c. "B" Coy to cross the river at K.16.d.6.55 and afterwards to secure the known enemy trench from K.16.d.7.65 NORTHWARD to K.16.b.20.40 from the flank and rear. At about 3.30 pm O.C. "A" Coy (Capt A.V. Arenkals) reported that his patrols had entered his objective and captured 8 of the enemy with one machine gun. About 4.30 pm O.C. "B" Coy (Capt R.M.L. Lopes) reported that No. 5 Platoon commanded by Lieut J.L. Baker M.C. had successfully crossed the river. Later his officer was again in collision. RENNET FARM securing 38 prisoners and 4 machine guns. Two other platoons of "B" Company were then pushed across the river to reinforce No 5 Platoon. "A" Company advanced their posts to cover the ground taken on the frontage of "A" Coy took a wounded enemy N.C.O. and one machine gun about 12 M.N. The Battalion was to have been relieved by the 11th Suffolk Regt tonight (18/19th) but owing to the nature of the operations in progress the relief was cancelled.	
FRONT LINE	19.	9.33 am	Order received from Brigade to push forward patrols to the Road between RENNET FARM — SACHET FARM. At about 6.0 pm patrols were sent forward on to the M?ERVILLE — VIERHOUCK Road at K.17.b.60.00 and K.17.d.50.20. Orders were received about the same time that the	

WAR DIARY
INTELLIGENCE SUMMARY
(Erase heading not required.)

Army Form C. 2118.

Instructions regarding War Diaries and Intelligence Summaries are contained in F. S. Regs., Part II. and the Staff Manual respectively. Title pages will be prepared in manuscript.

Place	Date	Hour	Summary of Events and Information	Remarks and references to Appendices
FRONT LINE	19 (contd)		(contd) the Battalion was to be relieved by the 11th Suffolk Regt tonight. Arrangements were made and the Battalion was relieved by the Suffolks without a hitch. Our Companies moved back into the old British front line about 12 mn and Battalion HQrs moved to CHAPELLE BOOM about 12 midnight.	
CHAPELLE BOOM	20		A quiet day.	
CHAPELLE BOOM	21		The Battalion was ordered to place a Company at disposal of OC 11th Bn Suffolk Regt (183rd Infantry Brigade Advance Guard Commander) D Coy was detailed and moved off at about 11-45am also the Battalion was ordered to relieve the 11th Suffolk Regt on half of their frontage from about L.19 Central L.25 Central S.N.15 thence S.N.15 the canal. Batth HQrs moved to house near SACHET FARM. All Companies and HQ in position at 2.0am.	
HQ SACHET FARM	22		The Battalion was ordered to move forward at 8.0am "D" and "O" Coys in front line, "A" and "B" Companies in support. Considerable opposition was met with from hostile of SKELTER CROSS and MEURILLON. O Coy suffered many casualties and Companies dug in on the line originally held by the Battalion.	
HQ SACHET FARM	23		Companies remained in same place. Active patrolling to ensure touch being kept with the enemy. Enemy fast wiring in front of his positions SKELTER CROSS – LA CRINQUETTE LOTTE. Batth HQrs moved to factory in NEUVILLE arriving about 6.30pm.	

WAR DIARY
INTELLIGENCE SUMMARY.
(Erase heading not required.)

Army Form C. 2118.

Place	Date	Hour	Summary of Events and Information	Remarks and references to Appendices
H.Q. FACTORY MERVILLE	24th		Heavy gas shelling during night 23rd–24th. About 3 am a 5.9 inch enemy shell arrived in the cellars where the Commg. Officer and Adjutant were, but failed to explode and finished up on the bed on which the Adjutant was sitting but beyond bruises and scratches neither Commg. Officer or Adjutant were injured. During the day Captain H.S. Rowe M.C. (Adjutant) Lieut R. Noms (Intelligence Officer) and Lieut J.H. Hurson (Lewis Gun Officer) and about 15 Other Ranks went into Hospital gassed. Captain As. Freshwater took over the duties of Adjutant. On account of the gas in the factory the Headquarters moved out on to the banks of the Bourre River behind the factory.	
H.Q. BOURRE RIVER	25		Quiet day. Relieved by the 4th Bath. Royal Berk Regt. during night 25th–26th. "A" and "C" Coys moving back into the old British Front Line between K.25d 6.5.10 and K.22 a.70.98. "B" and "D" Companies and Batt. Head quarters at about K.13 C central (CASA DOSS)	
H.Q. CASA DOSS	26		Quiet day. Visited by Major General F.J. Duncan CMG. CB. DSO. (Divisional Commander) who expressed his appreciation of the good work done by the Battalion.	

Army Form C. 2118.

WAR DIARY
or
INTELLIGENCE SUMMARY.
(Erase heading not required.)

Instructions regarding War Diaries and Intelligence Summaries are contained in F. S. Regs., Part II. and the Staff Manual respectively. Title pages will be prepared in manuscript.

Place	Date	Hour	Summary of Events and Information	Remarks and references to Appendices
HQ Casa Dell	27		Quiet day. resting Salvage work	
HQ Casa Dell	28		Quiet day. Salvage work	
HQ Casa Dell	29		Quiet day. Salvage work	
HQ Casa Dell	30		Quiet day. Salvage work. Warned about 11.0 pm by the Brigadier that we were to be loaned to the 184th Infy Brigade in support for relay.	
HQ Casa Dell	31		Orders arrived at 5.30 am to move up in support of 184 Infy Brigade. 15 K.14 and 23. Headquarters at RENNET FARM, moved to be complete by 11.0 am. Moved off at 9.30 am and got into position. Obtained permission of 184 Infy Brigade to establish Batt HQrs at our old place, house at B.6.C. h.22 c 50.80. Batt HQ B.C.C. 184 Infy Brigade 15 h.22 c 50.80. Received orders from B.6.C. 184 Infy Brigade 15 - Care Cross - Robermetz. Own 1½ Companies to the line L.30 & 80.15 - Care Cross - Robermetz. Moved 'A' Coy and 2 Platoons 'C' Coy to that line at about 4 open.	

Army Form C. 2118.

WAR DIARY
or
INTELLIGENCE SUMMARY.
(Erase heading not required.)

AUGUST 1918.

Instructions regarding War Diaries and Intelligence Summaries are contained in F. S. Regs., Part II. and the Staff Manual respectively. Title pages will be prepared in manuscript.

Place	Date	Hour	Summary of Events and Information	Remarks and references to Appendices
			Strength of Battalion at beginning of month = 4 Officers 914 O.R.	
			" " " end of month = 32 Officers 837 O.R.	
			Strength	
			Casualties	
			Killed. D. of Wounds. Wounded. Missing Wounded (B.S.) Evacuate. Commun. To Base. Onerous Sickness Shrapnel	
			20 1 147 2 2 20 2 9 2 = 206	
			Drafts etc for week ending Aug 10 = 28 O.Rs	
			" 17 = 31	
			" 24 = 8	
			" 31 = 55 = 122	
			Officers.	
			Died of Wounds.	
			Lieut. F.G. McCormick 9/8.	Draft off. in Error. Lieut. B. Welsh 24/8
			Wounded	Transfers
			Lieut. W.L. Brown M.C. 11/8 2nd Lieut Pte. W. Patterson 1/8	Capt. W.R. Roberts 29/8
			Lieut. A. Ross 22/8 Lieut. W.J. Maddox 8/8	Lieut. E. Fitch 28/8
			Lieut. R.D. McQueen Capt. W.W. Thompson 14/8	Captain C.M. Goodall 2/8
			Capt. J.C. Wylie 23/8 Capt. W.H. Roberts 11/8	Lieut. T.R. Ainsworth 7/8
			Capt. A.J. Rose M.C. Capt. E.M. Jackson 20/8	Lieut. G.A. Peacock 15/8
			Lieut. R. Roberts	
			Lieut. H. Stewart	
			Lieut. J.A. Keegan	In hospital in France.
				2nd Colonel W.A. Vivian D.S.O.
				Lieut. C. Wilkinson
				Lieut. F.J. Porter

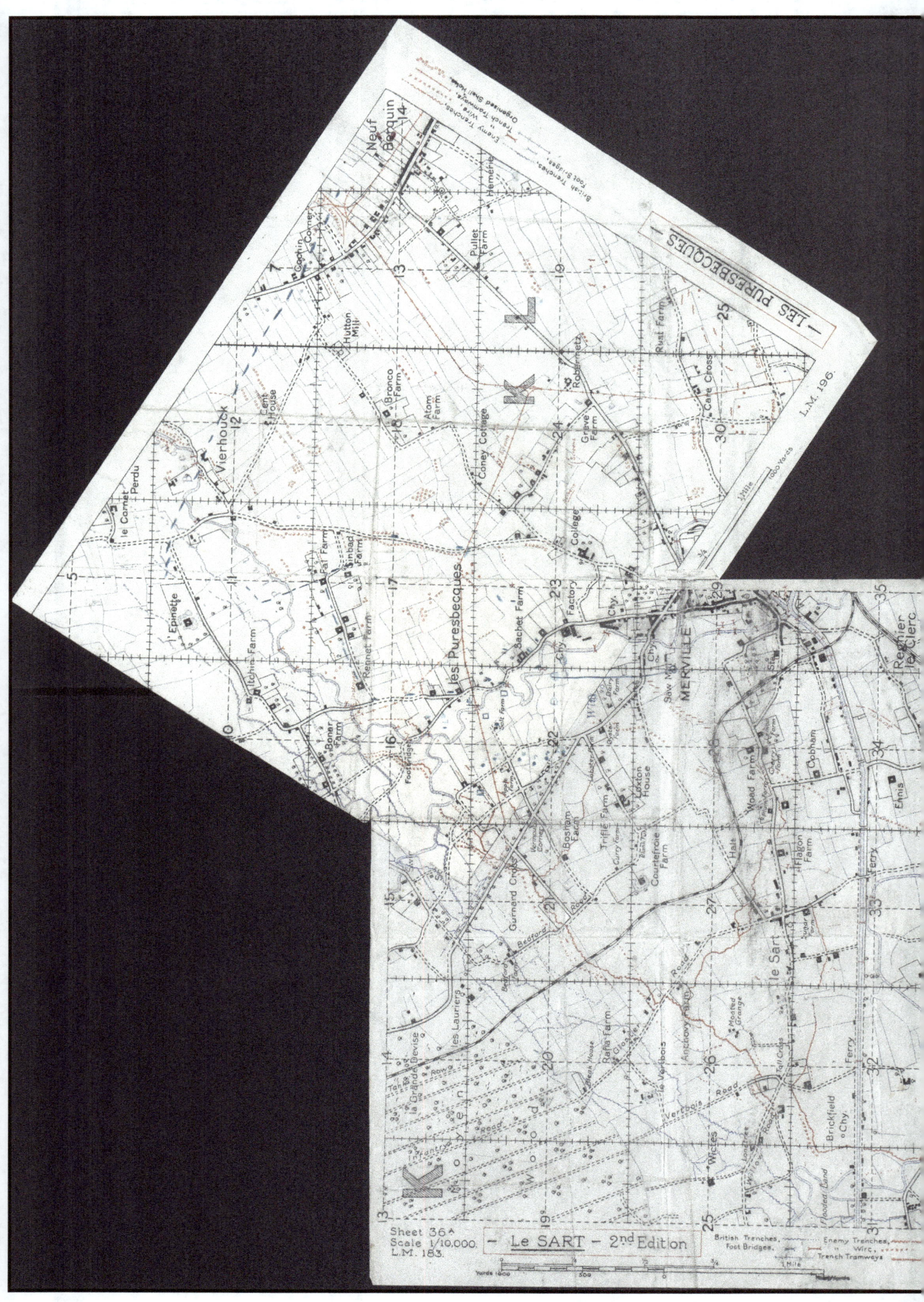

APP "A"

SECRET   Copy No. 8

183rd Infantry Brigade Order No. 23   12/5/18

Reference Maps
35A Hazebrouck
35A NE Vieux...

1. The 183rd Infantry Brigade will relieve 102nd Inf.
Bde. in the ARRÉWAGE Sector (left), and take over
the Line at present held by 182nd Infantry Brigade
as far south as LA MOTTE — MERVILLE Road
(exclusive) on the night 14th/15th August in
accordance with Table "A" attached.

2. 9th North'd Fus. and 1st East Lancs Regt will
entrain at CRUWE Station (J.14.b) in
accordance with Table "B" attached.

3. Details of relief will be arranged direct
between Commanding Officers concerned.

4. Defence Schemes, documents, and Maps in
connection with Sector, French Stores, S.O.S.
Grenades &c will be taken over and receipts
given. List of Stores taken over will be sent
to Brigade H.Q. by 6 p.m. on 15th instant.

5. Completion of relief will be reported by
Code Words as follows:—
    9th North'd Fus.   —   "50 foreign Pickets"
    11th Suffolks   —   "None required"
    1st East Lancs   —   "10 Coils"
    183rd C.T.M.B.   —   "25 Boxes"

6. Disposition sketches will be sent to Bde.
H.Q. by 10 a.m. on 15th inst.

7. Battalions will go into the line at the
strength laid down in this Office letter
B.M. 26/20 dated 3/5/18 vice B.5.9.

8. 183rd Bde H.Q. will close at STEENBECQUE
and reopen at J.4.c.7.5. at 6pm on 14th inst.

9. Command of Sector will pass to B.G.C.
183rd Inf. Bde on completion of relief.

10. ACKNOWLEDGE   Done JH

                                        John Hunter
Issued at 8.30 p.m.   for Bde Major
                                          Captain

Copy No 1 - File   Copy No 9 - 4th Suffolks   17 -
       2 - War Diary   10 - 1st E Lancs   18 -
       3 - G.O.C.   11 - 183 T.M.B.   19 -
       4 - B.C.   12 - 183 MG Coy.   20 -
       5 - Bde S.O.   13 -   21 -
       6 -   14 -   22 -
       7 - I.O.   15 - 1st Inf. Bde.   23 -
       8 - 9 North'd Fus   16 - 182   24 -

APPENDIX "B"

183 Infantry Bde
Orders.

Table "B" annexed with 182nd Infantry Brigade Order No 232

No	Details	Entraining Stations	Time Train Leaves	Detraining Station	Remarks
1	2 Coys 1/North'd Fus ½ Coy 1st G Gurwal ½ Coy Party of 16th Inf & 1/6th Rif Bn & Draws	CROWE Station J. 14.b.	8.30 am	MERION Station J.18.b.	Front Coy & Coy to travel by Friday trains
2	2 Coys 1/North'd Fus 2 Coy 1st G Gurwal Remainder of Batt HQ of Hund Bns & 1st & Draws	Ditto	9.4 A.M.	Do	

Note Nos 1 & 2 each consist of 14 trucks
Nos Officers will be appointed O.C. each train

SECRET.
Copy No. 7
16.8.18.

183rd. Infantry Brigade Order No.233.

(AE)

1. 11th. Battalion Suffolk Regt. will relieve 9th. Battalion Northumberland Fusiliers in the Right Subsection of the Brigade front on the night 18/19th. inst.
   On relief Northumberland Fusiliers will withdraw to position vacated by Suffolks.

2. All Photos Paper Maps, all trench stores and work in hand will be handed over.
   A list of Trench Stores taken over will be forwarded direct to Staff Captain.

3. Details of relief will be arranged by Commanding Officers concerned.

4. Completion of relief and arrival of Support Battalion in position will be reported to this Headquarters by Code word "ANDAMAN".

5. No movement in connection with relief until dusk.

   Acknowledge.

Issued at 9.0 p.m.

Captain,
Brigade Major, 183 Inf. Bde.

Copy 1.	War Diary.	Copy No.13.	61 Div. "G".
2.	File.	14.	184 Inf. Bde.
3.	Staff Captain.	15.	182 Inf. Bde.
4.	Bde.I.O.	16.	20 10? Inf. Bde.
5.	" Sig. Off.	17.	Left Gr. R.F.A.
6.	B.T.O.	18.	479 Field Coy.
7.	9th. N.F's.	19.	2/2 Field Amb
8.	11th. Suffs.	20.	3 Coy. Div. Train
9.	1st. E.L.	21.	C.R.A.
10.	183 L.T.M.B.	22.	C.R.E.
11.	"D" Coy. 61 M.G.C.	23.	Bde. Supply Off.
12.	61 Btn. M.G.C.		

To:

9th North'd Fus.	183nd Inf.Bde.	
11th Suffolks	184th Inf.Bde.	B.M.30
1st E.Lancs Regt.	120th Inf.Bde.	19/8/18
183rd L.T.M.B.	61st Division "G"	
"D" Coy 61 M.G.C.	C.R.A.	
479 Field Coy, R.E.	C.R.E.	
Left Group, R.F.A.		

1. At 10 a.m. Patrols of the Brigade had made good the following line:

   K.22.c.30.80 – K.16.c.80.20 – K.16.d.30.50 – K.16.b.50.20 – RENNET FARM, and thence North to the PLATE BECQUE.

2. Patrols of Units have been ordered, and will now make good, the following line:-

   SACHET FARM – thence along the Road LES PURESBECQUES – Road Junction K.16.b.50.20 – thence N.N.E. through RENNET FARM – FAL FARM – Point K.11.d.70.10, and then N to VIERHOUCK to the present left boundary of the Brigade.

   Junction between Patrols of Battalions will be RENNET FARM inclusive to 1st East Lancashire Regt.

3. 9th Northumberland Fusiliers will maintain close touch with 183nd Inf.Bde. on our right, and 1st E.Lancashire Regt. with the 120th Inf. Bde. on our left.

4. Battalions will report when the line in para. 2 has been reached, and beyond sending protective patrols forward of this line to the line given in para. 5, no advance East of it will be made, unless ordered by this Hdqrs.

5. The probable forecast of moves by Units in the event of the line in para. 2 having been reached is as follows:-

   (a) Patrols will advance to the line SACHET FARM (inclusive) N.E. to point (Road and Track junction) K.17.d.45.20 – thence N along the track to the present position of our left Flank at VIERHOUCK. Junction between Patrols of Units point K.17.b.60.00.

   (b) The four Companies of the two Battalions in front and immediate support lines, will cross the stream and consolidate the Lines of the roads given in para 2.

   (c) The four Companies in the Line of Retention will move to the lines at present held by the four front line Companies.

   (d) 11th Suffolks will move to the line of Retention from their present position.

6. The moves forecasted are dependent on many matters still obscure, and nothing will take place without orders from this H.Q.

7. All advances will be made slowly and methodically, and every single move will be _complete_ before another is contemplated.

8. 479 Field Coy have been ordered to bridge the PLATE in accordance with the requirements of the situation.

9. In the event of front line companies crossing the stream the 4 Machine Guns now forward of the Line of Retention will move with them, and come under the direct orders of O.C. Battalions concerned. Arrangements for this move will be made by O.C. "D" Coy, 61st Bn. M.G.C.

10. 183rd L.T.M.B. will arrange to attach 3 guns to each front line Battalion.

ACKNOWLEDGE.

BHQ.
19/8/18.

Captain,
Brigade Major, 183rd Infantry Bde.

SECRET   Received 10-40 PM   COPY No 5
                                                    NE

Reference   153 Infantry Brigade Order No. 235.   21.8.18
SHEET 36ANE
1/20000.

1.   The Brigade is on the general line COCHIN CORNER -
        BULLET FARM - L.19.c.y.2. which will now be consolidated
        and held.

2.   The left flank of 9th Division on the right
        is reported to be about K.36.b.1.5.
            The right flank of 31st Division on the left, is
        at GENT HOUSE.

3.   The following re-adjustments and reliefs will
        take place tonight 21st/22nd August and to be
        completed before 2.0 a.m.

    (a) 1st Battalion East Lancashire Regt. will extend South
        and take over the line at present held by 11th Suffolks
        as far as the track (exclusive) running immediately
        South of the centre grid line in K.14.

    (b) 9th Northumberland Fusiliers will relieve
        11th Suffolk Regt. from track below centre grid line
        in K.14 (inclusive) to the LYS CANAL.

    (c) Both Battalions on completion of relief will be
        disposed with 2 Companies in front and 2 Coys.
        in support.
            1st Battalion East Lancs. Regt. will continue to
        guard the left flank of the Brigade, and the
        2 Coys. in support will be echeloned for this
        purpose behind the left flank of that Unit.
            The Coys. in Support of 9th Northd. Fusiliers
        will be disposed at the discretion of the Battalion
        Commander.

    (d) 11th Suffolk Regt. will on completion of relief
        withdraw to Brigade Reserve and be disposed as
        under:-
            Headquarters - TANKARD FARM K.9.b.
            2 Coys. E. of the PLATE BECQUE in Squares K.1.b. and K.1.d.
            2 Coys. W. of the PLATE BECQUE in Squares K.1.c. K.1.a. K.1.b.

All details of relief to be arranged by commanding Officers concerned.

An adequate provision must be made for guides.

4. All localities that may be held in advance of the main line will be taken over by relieving units.

5. No advance beyond the line now being consolidated will be made without orders from this HQrs.

6. Brigade front will be protected by active patrolling during the night.

7. 9th North'd. Fus. will endeavour to obtain touch with 4th Division as soon as possible.

8. The Section of 18 pdrs., the Section of MGs, the Trench Mortars and the Section 179 Fd Coy at present under command of OC 11th Suffolks will pass to command of OC 9th North'd. Fus.

9. Completion of relief will be reported to this HQ by code word "CERTAINLY."

10. Acknowledge.

Done 10.40pm

Issued at 9.50pm.

M Cambke Sums
Captain
Brigade Major 183 Inf. Bde.

Copy No 1. War Diary.
" " 2. File
" " 3. GC
" " 4. BTO
" " 5. 9th North'd Fus
" " 6. 11th Suffolks
" " 7. 1st Cambs
" " 8. 183 LTMB
" " 9. B Coy 183 MGC
" " 10. 179 Field Coy
" " 11. 4/Sth Comp RAMC
" " 12. 182 Brigade
" " 13. 184 "
" " 14. 120 "
" " 15. G Div Q
" " 16. CRA
" " 17. CRE
" " 18. Gen Supply Officer GS Bde 61st Div

SECRET 183rd Infantry Brigade Order No 236 Copy No. 5

21.8.18

Reference 36A NE, 1/20000

1. The Brigade will continue the advance tomorrow 22nd August from the line now held.

2. The first objective to be gained will be the following line:—
LOUNGE HOUSE — CHAPELLE DUVELLE — thence along the Road running NNE to TROMPE BRIDGE — RUE MONTIGNY.

Units on arrival at the above objective will consolidate, and no advance beyond the line given will be made without orders from this Hdqrs.

3. The dividing line between Units will be the line K.19. Central — OBAS Cottage (inclusive to Right Battalion) to a point 500 yds S of TROMPE BRIDGE.

4. The advance will commence at 8 a.m.

5. Units will keep the closest touch during the advance.

6. Acknowledge.

A. Huttley Unwin
Captain
Bde Major 183rd Inf Bde

Issued at 12-15 am 22/8/18.

Copy No 1 — War Diary
2 — 2 i/c
3 — J.C.
4 — BSO
5 — 9 North'd Fus
6 — 11th Suffolks
7 — 1st S Lancs
8 — 183 TMB
9 — A Coy 61 MGC
10 — Left Group
11 — Left Bde Right Div
12 — 120th Bde

Ack'd A.M.
12.45 A.M.

H. S. Rowe.

H. S. Rowe.

SECRET.   Copy No 5

183rd Infantry Brigade Order No 237.   23/8/18

Refce Sheet 36A NE 1/20000

1. The line now held by 183rd Inf Bde is as follows:-
L.31.b.00.60 – L.25.b.20.00 – L.19. Central – L.14.d.10.50
– L.14.b.30.30.

2. 120th Inf Bde last night established the line COCHIN
CORNER – PONT RONDIN.

3. (a) At 4 p.m. today 23rd August 120th Inf Bde are
advancing to the line BISHOPS CORNER – BECKET
CORNER (F.26).
The right Boundary of the advance of this Brigade
is the line of the Road L.13.b.20.70 – RUE PROVOST.

(b) In conjunction with this advance by the
Brigade on our left, 183rd Inf Bde will advance
& make good the following line which will be
consolidated as soon as it has been reached:-
L.14.b.30.30 – along the Road & Track to
L.9.a.35.00 – thence Northward to BISHOPS
CORNER, where touch with 120th Inf Bde will
be established.

4. The advance to the line in para 3 (b) above
will be made by 1st Batt. The East Lancashire Regt.
Touch, during the advance, with the Brigade
on our left will be maintained on the line of the
Road COCHIN CORNER – RUE PROVOST.

5. At the conclusion of the above operation the line
held by the Brigade, and for which it will be
responsible will be the line from the present
boundary on the LYS CANAL to BISHOPS CORNER (L.3).

6. The line held by the Brigade at the conclusion of
today's operation will be consolidated as follows:-
(a) A line of dug-in posts will be established on the
line L.31.b.00.60 – L.25.b.20.00 – L.19. Central –
L.14.d.10.50 – L.14.b.30.30 – along road & track
to L.9.a.35.00. thence North to BISHOPS CORNER

1.

(b). <u>A line of Resistance</u> resting approximately on the following localities:—
K.36.b.90.25 — CARE CROSS — ROBERMETZ — PULLET FARM — Road junction L.13.b.95.10 — BOWERY COTTAGES — RUE PROVOST + L.2.d.10.80.

The line in (b) above will be developed in the first place on the system of defended and mutually supporting localities at or about the points given.
The linking up of these points is a matter for the future.

(c) O.C. Battalions in Line will be responsible for touch & mutual support with the Units on their flanks.

7. The Section of the Field Coy at present attached to each Battn. will generally supervise the development of the LINE of RESISTANCE.

8. <u>Machine Guns</u>. Machine Guns will be disposed in the Line of Resistance, & behind it, under arrangements which are now being made by O.C. M.G. Battn.

9. <u>Boundaries</u>. Boundaries of the Brigade will be readjusted as follows:—
<u>Southern Boundary</u> — As at present
<u>Northern Boundary</u> — The Grid Line K.11. Central — L.3. Central.
<u>Inter Battn Boundary</u> — The line RENNET FARM — ATON FARM — PULLET FARM — HENERIE CHAPEL — all inclusive to Right Battalion

10. The following readjustments & reliefs will take place tonight 23rd/24th August.
(a) 9th North'd Fusiliers will extend Northwards to the line PULLET FARM — HENERIE CHAPEL (inclusive).
(b) 11th Suffolks will relieve 1st Bn E Lancs Regt in the left subsection of the Brigade Front
(c) 1st Bn E Lancashire Regt. will withdraw to Brigade Reserve.
All details of relief will be arranged by O.C. concerned.
(d) 1st Bn E Lancs Regt on completion of relief will be

2.

disposed as under:-
1 Coy near BONAR FARM.
3 Coys East of the PLATE BECQUE and BOURRE RIVER on the line VIERHOUCK - SACHET FARM.

(c). Completion of relief and readjustment to be reported to this H.Q. by code words "HOLD FAST"

11. 1 Coy Cyclists, now under command of G.O.C. 183rd Inf. Bde will be disposed about L'EPINETTE.
A detachment of these Cyclists will be attached to 1st E. Lancs Regt under orders to be issued.
The primary duty of the Cyclist Coy will be inter-communication in accordance with orders issued by the Brigade.

NOTE - In the event of our advance to BISHOPS CORNER being interfered with by fire from the line G in MONTIGNY REGAL LODGE - PRINCE FARM, a barrage of shrapnel and smoke is ready to come down on the line T in MONTIGNY - L.G. Central - PRINCE FARM.
This barrage will open in response to a red light signal to be fired by the Infantry.

12. ACKNOWLEDGE

Issued at 12.15 pm

Roland Henry
Bde Major 183 Inf. Bde
Captain

R.P. 1-10 pm
Copy No 1 - War Diary
2 - File
3 - S.C
4 - B.S.O
5 - 9th North? Fus
6 - 11th Suffolks
7 - 1st E. Lancs
8 - 183 TMB
9 - 478 Field Coy

Copy 10 - "A" Coy 61 MG Bn
11 - Left Group RFA
12 - 61 Div "G"
13 - 182 Bde
14 - 154 Bde
15 - 120 Bde
16 - Left Bde Right Div
17 - CRA
18 - CRE

"SECRET"   Copy No.

Ref. Sheet 36 A NE 1/20000
               183rd Infantry Brigade Order No. 238   24. 8. 18

1. 183rd Infantry Brigade will be relieved by 184th Infantry Brigade in the Advance Guard Brigade area on the nights 24th/25th and 25th/26th August. Relief will take place in accordance with the Table issued with this order.

2. On completion of relief 183rd Infantry Brigade will be responsible for the defence of the Main Line of Retention.

3. Dispositions of Units of 183rd Inf Bde will be those now held by Units of 184 Inf Bde.

4. The following troops, now a part of the Advance Guard Brigade, will come under orders of OC 184th Infantry Brigade on completion of relief.

    2 Batteries RFA   2 Sections Field Coy RE
    1 Company 61st M.G.C   1 Company XI Corps Cyclists

5. All details in connection with relief will be arranged by C O's concerned.

6. All paper Maps and Trench Aerox, excepting S O S Rockets, Very Lights & Flares will be handed over.
   Work in hand will be carefully explained to incoming units.

7. Completion of all moves by units will be reported to this HQ by code words "ONE MORE STEP".

8. Command of Advance Guard Brigade Area, and Main Line of Retention, will pass respectively to GOC 184th Infantry Brigade & GOC 183rd Infantry Brigade on completion of relief.

9. Brigade Hdqrs will close at K.8.c.20.20, and reopen at J.4.c.70.60, at an hour to be notified.

10. Acknowledge.

Issued at 2.30 pm
                                              Roland Le Sueur
                                                    Captain
                                        Brigade Major 183 Inf Bde

Copy No 1 - War Diary   Copy No 12 - 61 Div "G"
       2 - File   13 - 182 Bde
       3 - SC   14 - 184 "
       4 - B.10   15 - 120 Bde
       5 - 9 North'd Fus   16 - Lys Bde Night Div
       6 - 11 Suffolks   17 - CRA
       7 - 1 5 Lancs   18 - CRE
       8 - 183 T M B   19 - OC Detachment XI Corps Cyclists
       9 - 476 Field Coy   20 - S Coy Div Train
      10 - A Coy 61 M.G.Bn   21 - 2/4 Oxford & Bucks L.I.
      11 - Left Group RFA   22 - 1/2 Field Amb

Movement Table issued with 183 Inf Bde. Order No 238.

Serial No	Date	Unit	From	To	Relieved by	Route	Remarks
1	24/25 Aug	11 A/Suff R	Left Subsection M.L.R.	Left Subsection M.L.R.	2/4 Oxford & Bucks L.I.	Any	2 Coys in Line, 2 Coys in Support about CHAPEL BCOM. Coys of 11th Suffolks in Support will be relieved of tomorrow 24th, & proceed direct to M.L.R.
2	Do	3 Guns LTM B.	Do.	Do	3 Guns 184th LTM Bty.	Any	Guns will be exchanged – Daylight relief.
3	25/26 Aug	1st E.L. Regt.	Reserve	Reserve at SPRESIANO Camp.	2/5 Gloucesters	By train from MEREDITH	Extra half will proceed by train arrivals bring up 2/5 Gloucesters.
4	Do.	3 Guns TMB.	Right Subsection M.L.R.	Left Subsection M.L.R.	3 Guns 184th LTM Bty.	Any	Guns will be exchanged – Daylight relief
5	Do	9 North Fus.	Right Subsection	Right Subsection M.L.R.	2/4 Royal Scots	Any	2 Coys in Line, 2 Coys Support in K 13 c & d, K 13 c 80 50. Coys of North D. Fus. will be relieved afternoon 25th & proceed direct to M.L.R.

N.T.E. – All movement during daylight by small parties only.
Left limit of 184 Inf Bde in Piave unreserve Guard Area will be under Command of SOC 183.
Bde until relief is complete.
The Boundary between Right & Left sections of M.L.R. is the MERVILLE – LANETTE Rd.
Right 183 Bde.

Headquarters,
183rd Infantry Brigade.   61st Division No. A.76/3.

"I should be very glad if you would tell your officers and men how pleased I am with the work they have done during the recent advance guard operations.

It must be a great satisfaction to you all to get away from the drudgery of Trench Warfare in to the open once more.

It is just four years since the old Army fought the battle of Le Cateau in the old open warfare style, and I hope that your Brigade will take them as its ideal and do their very best to fit themselves for the thrashing of the Germans in the open field.

D.H.Q.
27th August 1918.

(Sgd) F.J. DUNCAN, Major-Genl
Commanding 61st Division.

-2-

9th (N.H.) Bn. Northd. Fusiliers.
11th Bn. Suffolk Regt.
1st Bn. East Lancashire Regiment.
183rd L.T.M. Battery.

For information.

B.H.Q.(REAR).
28/8/18.

A/Staff Captain, 183rd Infantry Brigade.

Captain.

183 Infantry Brigade.

G.434.   19.8.18.

The following received from Fifth Army.

"Army Commander congratulates 61st. Division upon success yesterday   aaa   Addsd 61st Divn. reptd XI Cps.

(Sgd) E.S.BATES.Lt.
For G.S.61st.Divn.

_____

9th. Northd Fus
11th. Suffolks.
1st E.Lancs.
T.M.B.
Staff Captain.

For information.

Captain,
Brigade Major,183 Inf.Bde.

BHQ.
19.8.18.

MESSAGES AND SIGNALS.

TO Major Ebsworth and all Ranks of 9th North'd Fusiliers

Sender's Number: PK 95
Day of Month: 18
AAA

Congratulations from the 1st Bn East Lancashire Regiment

From 1st East Lancashire Regt

Appendix "G"

Special Orders
of the Day

SPECIAL ORDER OF THE DAY
By FIELD-MARSHAL SIR DOUGLAS HAIG
K.T., G.C.B., G.C.V.O., K.C.I.E
Commander-in-Chief, British Armies in France.

The conclusion of the fourth year of the war marks the passing of a period of crisis. We can now with added confidence look forward to the future.

The revolution in Russia set free large hostile forces on the Eastern front which were transferred to the West. It was the enemy's intention to use his great numbers thus created to gain a decisive victory, before the arrival of American troops should give superiority to the Allies.

The enemy has made his effort to obtain a decision on the Western front, and has failed. The steady stream of American troops arriving in France has already restored the balance.

The enemy's first and most powerful blows fell on the British; his superiority of force was nearly three to one. Although he succeeded in pressing back parts of the fronts attacked, the British line remained unbroken. After many days of heroic fighting the glory of which will live for all time in the history of our race, the enemy was held.

At the end of four years of war, the magnificent fighting qualities and spirit of our troops remain of the highest order. I thank them for the devoted bravery and unshaken resolution with which they responded to my appeal at the height of the struggle, and I know that they will show a like steadfastness and courage in whatever task they may yet be called upon to perform.

General Headquarters,
August 4th, 1918.

Commander-in-Chief,
British Armies in France.

SPECIAL ORDER OF THE DAY
By FIELD-MARSHAL SIR DOUGLAS HAIG
K.T., G.C.B., G.C.V.O., K.C.I.E
Commander-in-Chief, British Armies in France.

The following telegrams are published for the information of all ranks:—

To FIELD-MARSHAL SIR DOUGLAS HAIG, FROM LORD BUXTON, SOUTH AFRICA.

29-7-18.

A Public Meeting at UMTALI, July 22nd, carried with acclamation resolution reaffirming confidence in British and Allied Armies at this time of crisis.

BUXTON.

FROM FIELD-MARSHAL SIR DOUGLAS HAIG, TO LORD BUXTON, SOUTH AFRICA.

30-7-18.

All ranks of the British Armies under my Command have received with greatest appreciation this further mark of confidence and encouragement from the people of UMTALI. Will you be so good as to convey to them our hearty thanks.

General Headquarters,
August 1st, 1918.

D. Haig. F.M.
Commander-in-Chief,
British Armies in France.

PRINTED IN FRANCE BY ARMY PRINTING AND STATIONERY SERVICES.   PRESS A—8/18

SPECIAL ORDER OF THE DAY
By FIELD-MARSHAL SIR DOUGLAS HAIG
K.T., G.C.B., G.C.V.O., K.C.I.E
Commander-in-Chief, British Armies in France.

The following telegrams are published for the information of all ranks:—

FROM FIELD-MARSHAL SIR DOUGLAS HAIG TO GENERAL DIAZ, COMMANDO SUPREMO, ITALY.

27/6/18.

All ranks of the British Armies in France are watching with admiration the progress of the battle in Italy and rejoicing in the gallantry of the Italian Armies which have already secured such striking successes. We are proud to know that British Divisions from France are taking part in your victory. I beg you to accept from me my warmest personal congratulations and to convey to your troops the enthusiastic good wishes of their British comrades under my orders.

TO FIELD-MARSHAL SIR DOUGLAS HAIG FROM GENERAL DIAZ.
(TRANSLATION.)

29/6/18.

In the name of the Italian Army I offer to you and to all the brave British troops in France my most profound and heartfelt admiration.

It is a pleasure to me to assure you that we have reason to be proud in these days of burning struggle and of victory that the splendid British Divisions are by our side.

To you and to all troops under your command I repeat my warmest greetings and my most trusting hopes.

Commander-in-Chief,
British Armies in France.

General Headquarters,
June 30th, 1918.

PRINTED IN FRANCE BY ARMY PRINTING AND STATIONERY SERVICES.   PRESS A—6/18

SPECIAL ORDER OF THE DAY
By FIELD-MARSHAL SIR DOUGLAS HAIG
K.T., G.C.B., G.C.V.O., K.C.I.E
Commander-in-Chief, British Armies in France.

The following telegrams are published for the information of all ranks:—

FROM HIS MAJESTY THE KING OF THE BELGIANS TO FIELD-MARSHAL SIR DOUGLAS HAIG.

11-8-18.

I send you my warmest congratulations on the occasion of the splendid success won by the courage and dash of your gallant troops.

TO HIS MAJESTY THE KING OF THE BELGIANS FROM FIELD-MARSHAL SIR DOUGLAS HAIG.

12-8-18.

I beg to offer, on behalf of the British Army under my command, our warmest and respectful thanks for Your Majesty's gracious message of congratulations.

D. Haig. F.M.
Commander-in-Chief,
British Armies in France.

General Headquarters,
August 14th, 1918.

PRINTED IN FRANCE BY ARMY PRINTING AND STATIONERY SERVICES.   PRESS A—8/18.

SPECIAL ORDER OF THE DAY
By FIELD-MARSHAL SIR DOUGLAS HAIG
K.T., G.C.B., G.C.V.O., K.C.I.E
Commander-in-Chief, British Armies in France.

The following telegrams are published for the information of all ranks:—

To FIELD-MARSHAL SIR DOUGLAS HAIG FROM GENERAL ALLENBY, BRITISH EXPEDITIONARY FORCE, PALESTINE.
9-8-18.

Army in Palestine is delighted at your great success and sends congratulations to you all.

FROM FIELD-MARSHAL SIR DOUGLAS HAIG TO GENERAL ALLENBY, BRITISH EXPEDITIONARY FORCE, PALESTINE.
11-8-18.

Heartiest thanks for the kind message of congratulations which you have sent us from the Army in Palestine. I have communicated it to the troops.

To FIELD-MARSHAL SIR DOUGLAS HAIG FROM Rt. HON. THOMAS, UNITY HOUSE, EUSTON ROAD, LONDON.
9-8-18.

Hearty congratulations upon magnificent victory. It justifies confidence many of us had in you through good and ill times. We are proud of the valour of our fellow-countrymen, the Tommy, and equally proud of their brilliant leader.

FROM FIELD-MARSHAL SIR DOUGLAS HAIG TO Rt. HON THOMAS, UNITY HOUSE, EUSTON ROAD, LONDON.
11-8-18.

Your welcome message of congratulations written from Unity House has been greatly appreciated by all ranks. We soldiers know well how thoroughly we can always rely on the support of our brothers of the railways at home. May I add how much touched I am personally by your kind reference to myself.

To FIELD-MARSHAL SIR DOUGLAS HAIG FROM THE MANAGING DIRECTOR, THE BRITISH METAL AND TOY MANUFACTURERS, LTD., AUDREY HOUSE, ELY PLACE, LONDON.
8-8-18.

The Board and Employees of the British Metal and Toy Manufacturers, Ltd., Audrey House, Ely Place, London, E.C., take the occasion of the opening of their Welfare Rooms and Canteens, by Sir Charles A. Nicholson, to transmit to you and your brave troops their hearty congratulations on the splendid victories recently attained. Will you kindly accept and convey our gratitude to our boys, and tell them that our thoughts are with them in the midst of our pleasure.

From FIELD-MARSHAL SIR DOUGLAS HAIG to THE MANAGING DIRECTOR, THE BRITISH METAL AND TOY MANUFACTURERS, LTD., AUDREY HOUSE, ELY PLACE, LONDON.

11-8-18.

The encouraging wire you have been good enough to send us is very welcome to the whole Army. We appreciate very heartily your thinking of us on the occasion of the opening of your Welfare Rooms and Canteens.

D. Haig, F.M.

General Headquarters,
August 12th, 1918.

Commander-in-Chief,
British Armies in France.

SPECIAL ORDER OF THE DAY
By FIELD-MARSHAL SIR DOUGLAS HAIG
K.T., G.C.B., G.C.V.O., K.C.I.E
Commander-in-Chief, British Armies in France.

The following telegrams are published for the information of all ranks:—

To FIELD-MARSHAL SIR DOUGLAS HAIG FROM THE COMMANDER-IN-CHIEF, INDIA.
14-8-18.
   We congratulate you warmly on your most brilliant success in France.

FROM FIELD-MARSHAL SIR DOUGLAS HAIG TO THE COMMANDER-IN-CHIEF, INDIA.
16-8-18.
   I send you and the Army in India our heartiest thanks for your kind message of congratulations which I have communicated to the troops.

To FIELD-MARSHAL SIR DOUGLAS HAIG FROM THE SCOTTISH BRANCH OF THE COMRADES OF THE GREAT WAR, EDINBURGH.
13-8-18.
   Comrades of the Great War, Scottish Branch, congratulate you, and troops under your command, in conjunction with those of our Allies, on the splendid success of the recent offensive, and express unbounded admiration of all ranks. All have entire confidence in your leadership and in ultimate victory.

FROM FIELD-MARSHAL SIR DOUGLAS HAIG TO THE SCOTTISH BRANCH OF THE COMRADES OF THE GREAT WAR, EDINBURGH.
16-8-18.
   Heartiest thanks for the very kind wire you have sent to me and to the Army in France from the Scottish Branch Comrades of the Great War. We greatly appreciate your congratulations on the recent fighting, and your confidence in ultimate victory. I am much touched by your generous reference to myself.

D. Haig. F.M.

General Headquarters,
   August 17th, 1918.

Commander-in-Chief,
British Armies in France.

PRINTED IN FRANCE BY ARMY PRINTING AND STATIONERY SERVICES.   PRESS A—8/18.

SPECIAL ORDER OF THE DAY
By FIELD-MARSHAL SIR DOUGLAS HAIG
K.T., G.C.B., G.C.V.O., K.C.I.E
Commander-in-Chief, British Armies in France.

The following messages are published for the information of all ranks:—

To FIELD-MARSHAL SIR DOUGLAS HAIG FROM GENERAL DIAZ, COMMANDING-IN-CHIEF, ITALIAN ARMY.
17-8-18. *(Translation).*

In these joyful days for the Allies the Italian Army sends to its heroic British brothers in Arms the most sincere felicitations on the memorable victory won against the common enemy, and the warmest wishes for further successes.

FROM FIELD-MARSHAL SIR DOUGLAS HAIG TO GENERAL DIAZ, COMMANDING-IN-CHIEF, ITALIAN ARMY.
19-8-18.

I heartily thank you for the cordial message of congratulations which you have so kindly sent to the British Armies in France and myself on behalf of yourself and the gallant Army under your command. We watch with admiration and eager interest your continued successes, and we warmly reciprocate your wishes for further victories.

To FIELD-MARSHAL SIR DOUGLAS HAIG FROM THE LORD MAYOR, LONDON.
15-8-18.

The citizens of London send their warmest congratulations to you and the Allied Forces on the recent brilliant victories, and convey their grateful appreciation of services and sacrifices heroically rendered.

FROM FIELD-MARSHAL SIR DOUGLAS HAIG TO THE LORD MAYOR, LONDON.
19-8-18.

The congratulations which you have so kindly sent us from the citizens of our great Capital are very gratifying to the whole Army. We beg you to convey to them our heartfelt thanks. I am glad to tell you that London Regiments have won fresh laurels for themselves in the recent fighting.

To FIELD-MARSHAL SIR DOUGLAS HAIG FROM THE CHAIRMAN, URBAN DISTRICT COUNCIL, ALDERSHOT.
17-8-18.

Aldershot Council send sincerest congratulations on splendid achievement of yourself and gallant men in last great push. We follow your wonderful successes with the utmost pride.

From FIELD-MARSHAL SIR DOUGLAS HAIG to THE CHAIRMAN, URBAN DISTRICT COUNCIL, ALDERSHOT.

19-8-18.

Please convey to the Aldershot District Council, on behalf of myself and all ranks under my command, our hearty thanks for their kind message. We greatly appreciate their congratulations.

To FIELD-MARSHAL SIR DOUGLAS HAIG from THE HON. SEC., THE NATIONAL FEDERATION OF DISCHARGED AND DEMOBILISED SAILORS AND SOLDIERS, CROWLE.

15-8-18.

At a general meeting of the Crowle Branch of the above Federation held on the 14th inst., it was unanimously resolved to extend to you and all other ranks of the British Forces fighting in France, our sincerest thanks for the splendid results you have obtained during the last offensive, and also to wish you all a speedy and safe return to your "kith and kin."

From FIELD-MARSHAL SIR DOUGLAS HAIG to THE HON. SEC., THE NATIONAL FEDERATION OF DISCHARGED AND DEMOBILISED SAILORS AND SOLDIERS, CROWLE.

19-8-18.

Heartiest thanks from the British Army in France for your cordial message of congratulations which we all greatly appreciated.

General Headquarters,
August 21st, 1918.

D. Haig, F.M.
Commander-in-Chief,
British Armies in France.

"A" Form
MESSAGES AND SIGNALS.

Army Form C. 2121
(In pads of 100.)

No. of Message..........

Prefix....Code....m.	Words	Charge	*This message is on a/c of :*	Recd. at......m.
Office of Origin and Service Instructions				
	Sent		..................Service.	Date..........
SDR	At ......m.			From..........
	To		(Signature of "Franking Officer")	By..........
	By			

TO— { 9th Norfolk Fus&
11th Suffolks
1/6 E. Lancs Regt

| Sender's Number. | Day of Month. | In reply to Number. | AAA |
| 19M5-7 | 19 | | |

Bridges are in existence or will
be constructed tonight at the following places—

K 16 d 10·50
K 16 d 05·75
K 16 d 15·95
K 16 b 25·05
K 16 b 25·15
K 16 b 45·50
K 16 b 70·65
K 10 d 85·00
K 10 d 95·25
K 11 c 60·25
K 11 d 00·45
K 11 d 35·80

From 183rd I B
Place
Time 9.30 pm

The above may be forwarded as now corrected. (Z)

Censor. Signature of Addresser of person authorised to telegraph in his name
* This line should be erased if not required.

Order No. 1625. Wt. W3253/ P 511. 27/2. H. & K., Ltd. (E. 2634).

"C" Form.
MESSAGES AND SIGNALS.

Army Form C. 2123.
(In books of 100.)

No. of Message..................

Prefix **SD** Code **SAP** Words **43**

Received. From **RJ1FU** By **Pte Gibbs**

Sent, or sent out. At..........m. To.......... By..........

Office Stamp. **MOL 22/8/18**

Handed in at **RUFU PRIORITY** Office..........m. Received **6.20** m.

TO **MOL**

*Sender's Number	Day of Month	In reply to Number	AAA
BM74	22	—	

consolidate present line and hold it aaa no further advance without orders aaa section of NIGU in reserve will report VOFA forthwith and is at disposal of that unit aaa Acknowledge aaa addressed MOL VOFA repeated MOL

Time 6.20 p.m.

FROM TIME & PLACE: **RUFU 6 pm**

"C" Form.
MESSAGES AND SIGNALS.

Army Form C. 2123.
(In books of 100.)

No. of Message..........

Prefix. 915 Code. DHPM Words. 72

Received. From RUFU advd. By Pte Lowell G

Sent, or sent out. At.......m. To....... By.......

Office Stamp. MOLI 22/8/18

Charges to Collect

Service Instructions. RUFU PRIORITY

Handed in at............Office.......m. Received.......m.

TO MOLI

*Sender's Number: Br 73
Day of Month: 22
In reply to Number:
AAA

Situation 3 PM aaa Line runs as follows L25 B20.00 - L19 - L31 B0.6 central L14 A10.50 L14 B30.30 aaa Enemy offering strong resistance all along this line aaa Enemy MGs very active and Trench artillery active throughout the day aaa Touch with division on left at GENT HOUSE Touch with division on right is being established at K36 B00.50 aaa 1 Prisoner captured aaa addressed MGDO repeated flank Brigades and

FROM: Battalion RUFU
TIME & PLACE: 4.30 PM

*This line should be erased if not required.

"C" Form.
MESSAGES AND SIGNALS.

Army Form C. 2125.
(In books of 100.)

No. of Message 63

Prefix SB. Code D9/M Words 39 Received From MOU Sent, or sent out. At ... m Office Stamp HVC 19/8/18

Charges to Collect — By Brown To ... By ...

Service Instructions: Priority

Handed in at RUFU Office 4.35 p.m. Received 5.25 p.m.

TO HVC

*Sender's Number	Day of Month	In reply to Number	AAA
BM 53	19		
We	now	hold SNIPERS	HOUSES
HOUSES	SINBAD FARM	FALL	
FARM	aaa	progress	interfered
with	by	rifle	and
MG	fire	especially	from
K11b	and	K23V	aaa
otherwise	no	change	address
Msg	repeated	all	concerned

FROM RUFU
PLACE & TIME 4:30 pm

"A" Form.
MESSAGES AND SIGNALS.

Army Form C. 2121.
(In pads of 100.)

Prefix	Code	Words	Charge		This message is on a/c of:	Recd. at ...... m.
		78		Sent At ..... m.	9·45 pm RUFU Service	Date 21·8·18 From
Office of Origin and Service Instructions. RUFU Urgent Operation Priority				To By	(Signature of "Franking Officer.")	MOLI By

TO — MOLI

Sender's Number.	Day of Month.	In reply to Number.	
* BM69	21		AAA

Line held at 9 pm reported as follows aaa K31a 8·6 — RUST FARM thence through 19 Central to HEMERIE CHAPEL inclusive — cross roads K13D 6·6 to COCHIN CORNER aaa Touch on left with RUQE at GENT HOUSE aaa 7 prisoners 189 IR and 2 machine guns captured aaa Total captures to date 55 OR 7 machine guns aaa Considerable rifle and machine gun fire encountered during the day aaa addressed MEDO repeated all concerned

From RUFU
Place
Time 9·55 pm

From Brigade Major

21/8/15   6.20 pm

VOFA will extend
S. as far as light
Railway junction in
K.26.b. Central.

I take over Krubeek
along the line of the
light railway line
~~South~~ to the Brigade
Boundary.

The locality of CARE
CROSS and TENET
FARM has been badly
gassed.

2 Companies will
be in that line, one
of whom is already in
position. The remaining
2 Companies will be
Reserve about NORTH
of the line FROMRY
COLLEGE and GREIVE
FARM are areas and

"A" Form.
MESSAGES AND SIGNALS.

Recd. at 9.40 a.m.

TO: MOLI.

Sender's Number: W56
Day of Month: 19
AAA

Brigade Major speak.—

You will now make good by patrols the following line K22 b 70.60 – LES PURESBECQUE – ROAD JUNCTION K16 b 50.20 – RENNET FARM (to VIERHOUCK)

The next line will be SATCHET FARM inclusive to you aaa You will there join with the 182nd Brigade aaa. From SATCHET FARM N.E to the Road junction at K17 d 55.20 – N. to K17 b 60.00 where we join the East Lancs.

From Place: RUFU.
Time: 9.55 am

MESSAGES AND SIGNALS.

TO: MOLI

Sender's Number: W67
Day of Month: 19

Have arrived and am lying out 80 yds behind road; have my Lewis gun with me; about 50 yds in front is barbed wire aaa Everything OK aaa Not in touch with flank aaa Time 9.55 p.m.

From: HVB.
Time: 10.35 p.m.

"A" Form.
MESSAGES AND SIGNALS.

Army Form C. 2121.

TO: MOL1

Sender's Number: W58
Day of Month: 19
AAA

From Capt Trestrivaler

Positions are as follows:-

K22 a 30.70 H.Q.
Posts from right to left at
K22 c 75.90
K22 a 8.1
K22 a 75.25
K22 a 85.40
K22 b 25.75
K22 b 30.60

From: HVA
Place:
Time: 11.15 am

APPENDIX "C"

18+ Infantry Bde

Operation Orders

SECRET.   Copy No. 15

184TH. INFANTRY BRIGADE ORDER NO. 215.
by Brigadier-General A. W. PAGAN, D.S.O.

Reference Map:-
  Sheet 36A. and Sheet 36, 1/40,000.   31st. August, 1918.

1.   With reference to 184th.Inf.Brigade No. G.315/2 ("Provisional Instructions (No.2) in the event of enemy withdrawal') dated 30th. August 1918.

        The next bound will be :-

        Right Battalion to the line PT.DE LA LYS (L.54.b.6.7.) - L.29.a.0.9. - L.23.d.4.8. - G.19.b.8.8. (inclusive).

        Left Battalion to the line G.19.b.8.8. (exclusive) - G.13.b.9.5. - Road junction G.8.d.8.5. - G.2.b.7.0.;

        and not as stated in the above mentioned Brigade Instructions.

2.   Patrols are to be pushed forward on the whole front and are to keep in touch with enemy continuously and, wherever they are able, are to push straight on to the objective.
        Battalion Commanders are to use the Artillery and Trench Mortars at their disposal to this end.

3.   One Section "D" Coy. 61st.Battn.M.G.C. will reinforce that already at the disposal of O.C. 2/4 Royal Berkshire Regiment and will act under his orders immediately on receipt of this order.

4.   2/4 Oxf. & Bucks Lt. Inf. will be in the area L.13. by 10 A.M. today in support of 2/5 Gloucestershire Regiment.
        9th. Northumberland Fusiliers will be in the area K.17.c. and d, and K.23.a. and b. by 11 A.M. today in support of 2/4 Royal Berkshire Regiment.
        "C" Coy. 61st.Battn.M.G.C. will be in Reserve to the Brigade and will be in the area ITCHIN FARM (Sheet 36A.N.E. 1/20,000, Edition 7B.).

5.   Headquarters as under (Reference Map, Sheet 36A.N.E.1/20,000 Edition 7B.):-
        184th. Infantry Brigade.   - FACTORY (K.25.c.)
        2/4 Royal Berkshire Regt. - CARE CROSS (L.30.b.)
        2/5 Gloucestershire Regt. - COCHIN CORNER (L.7.d.)
        2/4 Oxf. & Bucks Lt. Inf. - HUTTON MILL (L.13.a.)
        9th.Northumberland Fus.   - REINET FARM (K.16.b.)
        "C" Coy.61st.Bn.M.G.C.   - ITCHIN FARM (K.10.d.)
6.   ACKNOWLEDGE.
Issued at 1.45 A.M.
                                                        R.K.Lindsay
                                                        Captain,
                                                        A/Brigade Major,
                                                        184th.Infantry Brigade.

Distribution:-
Copy No. 1 - 4 Brigade H.Q.   5. 2/5 Gloucester Regt.
             6 2/4.Oxf. & Bucks LI.   7. 2/4 Royal Berks Regt.
             8.184 L.T.M.B.   9. "D" Coy.61st.Bn.M.G.C.
            10. "C" Coy.61st.Bn.MGC.   11. 61st.Battn.M.G.C.
            12.O.C.Adv.Grd.Arty.   13. Brigade Sigs.Officer.
            14.183 Inf.Bde.   15. 9th.Northumberland Fus.
            16.61st.Div. "G".   17. O.C.Troop, K.E.H.
            18.177 Inf.Bde.   19. 121 Inf.Bde.
            20.O.R.A.61 Div.   21. C.R.E.61 Div.
                                       23 - 24. War Diary.

O.C. 9th Northumberland   SECRET.   G.346/A.
    Fusiliers.
Copy to 183rd. Infantry Brigade.

Reference Map:-
36A.N.E. 1/20,000, Edition 7B.

1.   You will move today, 31st August, 1918, to the area Squares K.17.c and d, and K. 23.a and b.

        Move to be completed by 11 a.m. today.

        Your Headquarters to be at RENNET FARM.

        Move to be carried out by Platoons, and completion of relief to be notified to these Headquarters by code word "HUMBER".

2.   ACKNOWLEDGE.

Issued at 2. am.

B.H.Q.
31/8/18.

                                              Captain,
                                              A/Brigade Major,
                                              184th Infantry Brigade.

SECRET.
                                                          Copy No. 6

           184TH. INFANTRY BRIGADE ORDER NO. 216.
           by Brigadier-General A. W. PAGAN, D.S.O.

                                                    31st.August,1918.

1.   If they have not reached the objective laid down in
   184th. Infantry Brigade Order No. 215 dated 31st.August 1918,
   tonight, the 2/4 Royal Berkshire Regiment and 2/5 Gloucestershire Regiment will push forward Patrols tomorrow morning
   1st. September 1918 until they reach those objectives and will,
   at all costs, keep in close touch with the enemy.

           9th. Northumberland Fusiliers will continue to hold
   the line K.36.b.7.8. - CARE CROSS - ROBERMETZ - PULLET FARM
   (exclusive) with one and a half Companies and will be prepared
   to hold the line - LOUNGE HOUSE to NEUF BERQUIN - ESTAIRES
   Road (inclusive) about L.21.a.3.8. with two Companies.

           2/4 Oxf. & Bucks Lt. Inf. will continue to hold the
   line - PULLET FARM (inclusive) to DENVER with two Companies
   and will be prepared to hold the line from Point L.21.a.3.8.
   (exclusive) to Point L.3.c.6.0. (inclusive) with two
   Companies.

2.   All Units to notify their present dispositions to
   Brigade H.Q. as soon as possible after the receipt of this
   Order.

3.   ACKNOWLEDGE.

                                                    Captain,
Issued at 7-15 P.M.   A/Brigade Major,
                                                    184th.Inf.Brigade.

Distribution:-
                Copy No. 1 - 2. Brigade H.Q.
                          3. 2/5 Gloucestershire Regt.
                          4. 2/4 Oxf. & Bucks Lt. Inf.
                          5. 2/4 Royal Berkshire Regt.
                          6. 9th.Northumberland Fus.
                          7. 61st.Div. "G".
                          8. 183 Inf. Bde.
                          9. O.C.Adv.Guard Arty.
                         10. "C" Coy.61st.Bn.M.G.C.
                    11 -12. War Diary.

SECRET. Copy No. 3

184TH. INFANTRY BRIGADE ORDER NO. 217.
By Brigadier-General A. W. PAGAN, D.S.O.

1st. September, 1918.

1. On receipt of these orders 9th. Battn. Northumberland Fusiliers will move forward and occupy area LOUNGE HOUSE – ESQUAIRES – NEUF BERQUIN Road (inclusive) about L.21.a.3.8. HEMERIE CHAPEL – SKELTER CROSS – CRINQUETTE LOTTE.

2. Line LOUNGE HOUSE – L.21.a.3.8. will be held by two Companies.

3. Battalion H.Q. will be K.30.b.5.3.
   9th. Northumberland Fusiliers will ensure that continuous communication is maintained during move with Brigade H.Q. A line already exists from new Battalion H.Q. to Brigade H.Q.

4. All movement will be by Platoons.

5. 9th. Northumberland Fusiliers will notify this office when the first Platoon moves off.

6. Completion of move and disposition sketch will be forwarded to Brigade H.Q. as soon as possible.

7. During the afternoon of today 1st. September 1918, 2/6 Battn. Royal Warwick Regt. will relieve 9th. Northumberland Fusiliers in area as in para 1.

8. 9th. Northumberland Fusiliers will send guides (1 per Platoon and 1 for Battn.H.Q.) for 2/6th. Battn. Royal Warwick Regt. to FACTORY K.23.c. at 3-30 P.M.

9. ACKNOWLEDGE.

Issued at 1-30 P.M.

Captain,
A/Brigade Major,
184th. Infantry Brigade.

Distribution:-

Copy No. 1 – 2. Brigade H.Q.
         3. 9th. Northumberland Fus.
         4. 2/4 Oxf. & Bucks L.I.) for
         5. 2/4 Royal Berks Regt.) information.
         6. 61st. Div. "G".
         7. 183 Inf. Bde.
         8. 182 Inf. Bde.
         9. Staff Captain.
        10 -11. War Diary.

Disposition. On completion of Relief Coys will occupy following areas.

'A' Coy. Old British front line trench from K31.d.25.35 NE to Ghosti Road (latter inclusive)

B Coy. Huts occupied by C Coy 7th Royal Berks. in KB

C Coy. Old British front line trench from (Ghost Road (exclusive) to the Railway inclusive K31.a.10.95

D Coy. Huts occupied by D Coy 7th Royal Berks. in K13

Batt. HQ will be established at K13.c.9.4

COMPLETION OF RELIEF will be notified to these HQ using Code Word.

ONE UP

Acknowledge
Codrid W. 8.18

Copies to: Lt (W14/Rm No the Form   Capt / Sgt A

No 1   War Diary
   2   OC 7th Royal Berks
   3   OC A Coy
   4   OC B Coy
   5   OC C Coy
   6   OC D Coy
   7   108 Bde
   8   To + A in
   9   Major LG @ Brady

SECRET.   Copy No. 8

Ref Map Sheet
LA NE. 1/20,000   OPERATION ORDERS No 60

                    9th (Works H. Coy.) Batt. North'd Fusiliers

1. INTENTION   The Battalion will move into support of the 9th
                    Batt. ROYAL BERKSHIRE REGT. of the 184th Infantry
                    Brigade.

2. MOVE.   The Battalion will move to Squares K 17 c and d
                    and K 23 a and b. in the following order.
                        "C" Coy   to   K. 17 d
                        B   "   to   K. 17 c
                        A   "   to   K. 23 b
                        D. "   to   K. 23 a.
                    movement will be by platoons

3. INTERVALS.   100 yards between platoons.

4. TIME.   All Companies will move at 9.30 a.m. They must
                    be in position by 11.0 a.m.

5. ROUTE.   "B" & "C" Coys will move by the light railway
                    from GURNARD CROSS.
                    A & D Coys will use the LA MOTTE - MERVILLE
                    ROAD as far as K 23 d 5.2 thence by track and
                    newly constructed bridge at K 23 c 60.60

6. DRESS.   Fighting Order with pack.   Greatcoats and
                    haversack will be collected under arrangements
                    to be made by Quartermaster.

7. LEWIS GUN   Will accompany their Companies as far as the
   LIMBERS   point at which they leave the LA MOTTE - MERVILLE Road
                    (This will not apply to C Coy who will carry their guns etc.)

8. RATIONS   The Transport Officer will arrange for dinners for
   WATER   today to be brought up in the field kitchens to
   COOKING   SATCHET FARM
                    All water bottles to be filled and all water tins
                    to be taken.

9. TOOLS.   Every man should be equipped with a P.S. shovel
                    if possible.

10. REPORTS.   Batt. Hd. Qrs. will be established at KENNETS
                    FARM in K.16.B. where completion of occupation of
                    positions assigned to Companies will be reported by
                    code word   "ANCHOVY"

                    ACKNOWLEDGE
                    DATED 31 Aug. 1918

                                                        (Sd) A.N. Freshwater.
                                                             Captain & Adjutant
                                                        9th (Works H. Coy.) Batt. North'd

Copies to:-
No. 1 Wai Diary
    2 Retained
    3 OC A Coy
    4 " B "
    5 " C "
    6 " D "
    7 " HQ "
    8 Comdg Officer
    9 184 Infy Bde
   10 T.O & Q.M.
   11 Sergt Cook

Coming
Office

APPENDIX D

9th (N.H.) Battn
Northd Fusiliers

OPERATION ORDERS

SECRET.

OPERATION ORDERS No. 50.

COPY No.

9th (North'd Hussars) Bn. Northumberland Fusiliers

1. MOVE. The Division is transferred to XI Corps.
The 183rd Infantry Brigade Group will march to FONTES-LINGHEM area tonight 31st July/1st Aug.
The Battalion will proceed by Route march to billets at FONTES.

2. PARADES. Battalion will parade on the LA SABLON – QUIESTÈDE road in order B. C. D. A. & H.Qrs. Head of Column at point A 22 d 1.2 (road junction) at 8.45 p.m. Officers chargers to be ready at respective Hd.Qrs. at 7.15 p.m.

3. ROUTE. QUIESTÈDE – ECQUES – road junction G14.b. – CRECQUES – BLESSY – WITTERNESSE – ROMBLY.

4. DISTANCES. 100 yards between Companies.
25 yards between sections of 6 vehicles.
Rear Companies will put out Connecting files to keep touch.

5. GUIDES. Advance Party will provide 1 guide per Company to meet Battn. on track at N.29.a.10.20 (junction) at 1.0 am

6. RATIONS. Sergt. Cook will arrange for dinners to be ready at 6.30 pm and tea as soon as possible after arrival in new billets.

7. TRANSPORT. Gun Limbers & Cookers to march with Companies, remainder of Transport in rear of Battalion.

8. OFFICERS. VALISES. To be dumped at Coy. Hd.Qrs ready for Collecting at 3.0 pm.

9. BILLETS. To be left in a clean and sanitary condition and certificate to that effect obtained from Billet Warden by O.C. rear party.

10. STORES. Coy Commanders will render list of all stores to be handed over to Orderly Room by 3.0 pm. Tents & French Shelters will be struck and dumped at Coy. Hd.Qrs. by 2.30 pm.

11. ADVANCE PARTY. 1 N.C.O. per Coy. Q.M. & Transport, under 2nd Lieut. R. Woods will meet lorry at Brigade Hd.Qrs. HEURINGHEM at 2.50 pm. to take over billets at FONTES.

12. REAR PARTY. 1 Sanitary man per Company, under Orderly Officer will remain after Battalion has marched out to ensure Billets are in a clean condition & certificate to that effect obtained from Billet Warden, also "No damage" certificate from the MAIRE.

13. MARCHING OUT STATES. Will be rendered to Orderly Room by 7.0 pm.

ACKNOWLEDGE.

Dated 31st July 1918.

Copies to:—
No 1 War Diary
2 Retained
3 Commanding Officer
4 2nd in Command
5 183rd Infy Bde.
6/10 O.C. Coys.
11 Transport Officer
12 Quartermaster
13 Medical Officer
14 R.S.M.
15 Master Cook.

H. S. Rowl. Lieut & A/Adjutant.
9th (N.H.) Bn. North'd Fus'rs.

July 18/10
J. G. Clues MC
Maj. April 4/916

Onikayanoma
206995 Capt J. Matthews
A.S.M.
13127 Sgt T Cambell
4/1702 Sgt T Stala
Montoro
Capt J.M. LCraven
5124 L/cpt J Shields

Spare

SECRET COPY No.

OPERATION ORDERS No. 61

9th (Works) Bn. Northumberland Fusiliers

1. MOVE
The 61st Division is relieving the 5th Division in the left sector of the X Corps Front.
The 183rd Infantry Brigade will be in Div'l Reserve.
The 9th Battalion Northumberland Fus. will proceed by march route to GODDE CAMP J.2.a & relieve the 7th Bn Warwicks Regt. on the night of 6/7th August 1918.

2. PARADE
The Battalion will parade, marching order at 4.50 p.m. in column of route. Head of column at cross roads N19.a.5.5 facing S.W. in order Bn HQrs. C. D. A. B. Coys.

3. ROUTE
LAMBRES (starting point, Road Junction N10.b.60.10 - time of passing 5.0 p.m.) - AIRE - BOESEGHEM - STEENBECQUE - where guides will meet the Battalion.

4. DISTANCES
100 yards between Coys. 25 yards between each section of 6 vehicles.

5. ADVANCE PARTY
1 N.C.O. each Company & Q.M. Stores & Transport as detailed, under 2nd Lieut R. Woods

6. TRANSPORT & Q.M. STORES
Will be permanently established at TANNEY and occupy billets & lines vacated by unit of 7th Infantry Bde. Q.M. Stores and Transport will proceed direct to TANNEY and establish themselves there, and not accompany Battalion.
Transport Officer to arrange for teams for S.A.A. limbers, also mess cart, maltese cart & signal stores etc, which will be with the Battalion.

7. OFFICERS VALISES
Will be dumped ready for collection at Coy H.Q. at 3 p.m.

8. OFFICERS CHARGERS
Will be at respective HQrs at 4.30 p.m.

9. BILLETS
Coy Comdrs. will ensure that all billets are left in a clean and sanitary condition. The Orderly Officer and 1 Sanitary man per Coy will be left behind and CLEAN BILLETS and NO DAMAGE Certificates to be obtained and forwarded to Orderly Room by the Rear Party on arrival to new Camp.

ACKNOWLEDGE.
6th August 1918.

Copies:-
No 1 War Diary
2 Retained
3 Orderly Room
4-7 O.C. Coys
8 O.C. Coys
9 183rd Inf. Bde.
10 T.O.
11 Q.M.
12 M.O.
13 R.Sm.
14

W. L. Rose, Captain &
Adjutant
9th (N.F.) Bn. North'd Fus.

O.O. 2.

To O.C. B Coy.

Attack by 2 Coys of 9th North'd Fus'rs.

Objective To form a bridge head from stream at K.16.b.70.65, East of RENNET F'm. thence to building K.16.d.3.5 to river at K.16.d.1.3.

B Coy will attack across bridge in K.16. Central & will secure the general line RENNET F'm to S.E.

C Coy. less 1 Platoon will support B & garrison present enemy trench on East bank of Stream K16 b+a.

One platoon of C Coy will cross stream at K.16.b.5.7 & assist B Coy in securing RENNET F'm and will establish post between RENNET F'm and River. R.E. will assist in bridging stream

BARRAGE Hows. will deal with farms in 16 b+d and 17 a.

Field guns will fire a creeping barrage in accordance with table. —
Between first Objective and ITCHIN F'm —
LES PURES BECQUES Rd. . ZERO to +5
Line of road. +5 to +8
Lift 100 yds at +8
" 100 yds at +11

(2)

BARRAGE contd—
  trench back up to +16.
  4 M.Gs will give covering fire in bursts on enclosures in K.16.d and 17.a from ZERO to +30

LTMS will fire on first objective, i.e. Enemy trench East of Stream from —5 mins to ZERO.

REPORTS. To advanced Bn. H.Qrs at K.15.a.90.45.

SIGNALS. A direct wire will be run forward from Advanced Bn. H.Qs. to Coy H.Qrs. of the Bn. holding the line at K.15.b.8.8 and will be carried forward into trench East of Stream in K.16 central as soon as situation permits.

CONSOLIDATION to be carried out with a series of small posts.

TOOLS Shovels to be carried.

FLARES to be used on final objective. Very lights by advanced parties as they push forward.

ZERO HOUR Notified later.

ACKNOWLEDGE.
9-8-18 1.20pm
                        H. R. Rowe
                        Capt. for Lieut-Col
                        Commg. 9th (D.L.I.) Bn North'd F.

SECRET.   COPY 2

OPERATION ORDERS No 52.

9th (Northd Hussars) Bn. Northumberland Fusiliers

1. RELIEF. The 183rd Infantry Brigade will relieve 184th Infantry Bde in the ARREWAGE Section (Left) and take over LINE at present held by 182nd Infy Bde, as far South as LA MOTTE – MERVILLE Rd (exclusive), on the night 14th/15th August 1918.

The 9th (N.H) Bn. Northd Fusiliers will relieve the 2/4th Bn. R. Berkshire Regt. in the Right subsection and Line held by 2/6th Bn. R. Warwicks Regt. as far South as LA MOTTE – MERVILLE Rd (exclusive) as follows:–

A Coy (3 Platoons) Right Front Coy in relief of 2/6th Bn R. Warwicks Regt + 1 Platoon in Support.
B Coy. Left Front Coy.   " "   " B" Coy 2/4th R. Berks Regt.
C Coy. Left Support Coy.   " "   " A + C Coys 2/4th R. Berks Regt.
D Coy. Right Support Coy.   " "   { D Coy 2/4th R. Berks Regt.
                                       { 1 Platoon 2/6 Bn R. Warwicks.

Order of Relief... B, A, C, D Coys.

No movement to take place East of NIEPPE FOREST until after dusk.

Companies will entrain at CROWE STATION J.14.b. and detrain at HERRON Station J.18.b. as follows:–

No 1 train.. B + A Coys entrain at 8.30 pm
No 2   "   .. C, D + H.Q.   "   9.0 pm.

O.C. B Coy. will appoint an officer to be O.C. No 1 train.
O.C. C Coy "   "   "   "   "   " O.C. No 2 train.

2. GUIDES. to be at MEREDITH Station as per attached Guide table.

3. ADVANCE PARTIES. As already detailed.

4. TRENCH STORES. Trench Stores, Water tins, S.O.S. Grenades and all Defence Schemes documents + maps in connection with sections, to be taken over and receipts given. List of Stores so taken over to be at Bn. H.Qrs by 12 noon 15th inst.

Company Commanders will render Disposition sketch to Bn. H. Qrs. by 7.30 am on 15th inst.

5. RATIONS. for 15th inst will be cooked and taken up by Companies. Quartermaster will arrange for Rations for following days to be sent up ready cooked to MEREDITH Station where Support Companies will provide carrying parties to convey to own + Front Coys, at dusk. Q.M. will also arrange for supply of Tommy's Cookers to be issued to each section.

WATER when available, to be obtained near Coy areas failing this, to be drawn from water point near Bn. H.Qrs. by Support Coy carrying parties at dusk.

6. SPARE MESS KIT. to be ready for collecting at Bn + Coy H.Qrs at 9.0 pm.

OFFICERS VALISES. to be dumped at Company H.Qrs for collecting at 6.0 pm

BILLETS. to be left in a clean and sanitary condition and certificate to that effect handed in at Orderly Room by Coys Commanders.

CODE. Completion of relief reported by following code:–
A Coy   "PICKETS NUMBER 12"
B "   "PICKETS NUMBER 10"
C "   "PICKETS NUMBER 13"
D "   "PICKETS NUMBER 15"

ACKNOWLEDGE.
dated 13th August 1918

                                            H. S. Rowe.
                                            Captain +
                                            Adjutant
                                            9th (N.H) Bn. Northd Fusrs.

Copies to. No 1 War Diary
           2   Retained
           3   Commg Officer
           4/8 O.C. Coys
           10   184th Inf Bde
           10   2/4th Bn R. Berks Regt.
           11   2/6th " R. Warwicks Regt.
           12   Q.M.
           13   T.O.
           14   M.O.
           15   R.S.M.
           16   Mess Cook

TABLE OF GUIDES

9th (N.I.) Bn. North'd Fusiliers	Relieved	Guides
"B" COY. Front Line, Right Company Forward Cross to River Coy HQ. K.21.b. 60.85	2/8 Warwicks. 3 Platoons of Left Forward Company	5 Guides, 1 per platoon and 1 for Coy H.Q. by 2/8 Warwicks.
"A" COY. Right Support Platoons K.15.c.Y.0 to Wicig Bridge. 2 Platoons K.15.c.2.4 to K.15 Central Coy. HQ. K.14.b. 65.45	2 Platoons of Support Coy (C) of 2/8 Warwicks 2 Platoons of "B" Coy 2/8 Berkshires	2 Guides by 2/8 Warwicks 2 Guides by Battalion
"C" COY. LEFT FORWARD Coy HQ. K.15.c. 05.95	B Coy Battalion	Guides by Battalion
"D" COY. LEFT SUPPORT Coy HQ. at K.15.a. 95.00	A.C. Company H/Q Battalion	Guides from H.Q. Coy by H.Q. Coy

ORDER OF MARCH "B" Coy, "A" Coy, "C" Coy, "D" Coy.

Secret   Patrol Operation   Copy No.
                              A.E. 1.

1. INTENTION. To reconnoitre enemy trench
                EAST of the river from K16 b 22.32
                to K16 d 15.60 and if unoccupied or
                held weakly to enter it and hold
                it with a view to establishing a
                bridge head.

2. STRENGTH.   2nd Lieut Porter and two
                sections of riflemen, 2 runners
                of No 6 and 2 of No 7 Platoons.
                RENDEZVOUS in the German line at
                K16 a 85.05

3. DRESS.   TRENCH ORDER. ie fighting
                order less the pack.

4. ROUTE OF   Leave the trench at K16 a 85.05
   APPROACH   at 12 Mn. and proceed to
   & TIME.   the ditch at K16 b 1.0. At this point
                Lieut Porter and two scouts will
                cross the bridge at K16 d 15.95. The
                remainder of the patrol & runners will
                then cross. The patrol will then move
                SOUTH and reconnoitre the SOUTHERN
                portion enemy trench. As the result
                of the reconnaissance of the SOUTHERN

(2)

patrol. A French Lieut Porter will determine whether to enter it, or proceed to reconnoitre the N portion.

5. SUPPORTS. No. 6 & 7 Platoons will be in readiness at K16 a 85.05 at 12 M.N. and will immediately move off to reinforce the Patrol when they enter the trench. The two runners of No 7 & 8 Platoons will bring the message and act as guides. DRESS. F.O. Packs. Rations on the man.

6. COY H.Q. Coy H.Qrs will be established at No 8 Platoon H.Qrs. at 11.0 pm

7. COMMUNICATIONS A line to be laid to advanced Coy H.Qrs by 10.30 pm.

8. PATROL RATIONS The rations for the patrols will be taken over by No 6. Platoon.

9. STRETCHER BEARERS. Coy S. Bearers will accompany No 6 & 7 Platoons. 2 S. Bearers of "C" Coy with stretcher will report to O.C. B Coy at 12 M.N.

③

10. REPORTS   Coy. Comm.r will send back by Telephone the Code word "ENTERED" if enemy trench is occupied.   If unsuccessful "WASHOUT".

11. SPECIAL   Lieut Porter is to clearly understand that his mission is to enter the trench only if unheld or weakly held.

ACKNOWLEDGE.

Copy No 1   War Diary   from   2nd Lieut for major
       2   O.C. B Coy   9th (N.F.) Bn.   North.d Fus.
       3   O.C. C Coy
       4   153rd Inf Bde.
       5   O.C. 1/7th E. Lancs
       6   O.C. A Coy.

In the field
17-8-18

9th (NH) Bn Northumberland Fusiliers

GUIDE TABLE

Ref Map 36A NE 1/20000

Coy Now	Relieved By	Guides
A Coy Right Front	B Coy 11th Suffolk	1 per Coy HQ & 1 per platoon to be at French & road junction at K15a 05.45 at 7.45 pm. 1 per post to be at K15d 75.25 at 8.30 pm
B Coy Left Front	A Coy 11th Suffolk	1 per Coy HQ & 1 per platoon to be at A Coy Suffolk HQ at 7.45 pm. 1 Guide per post to be at junction of trench with road at SWING BRIDGE at 8.30 pm
C Coy Left Support	D Coy 11th Suffolk	1 per Coy HQ & 1 per platoon to be at D Coy Suffolk HQ at K9a 80.05 at 7.45 pm
D Coy Right Support	C Coy 11th Suffolk	1 per Coy HQ & 1 per platoon to be on road 100 yards SE of HORSE SHOE DUMP at 7.45 pm

A.S. Rowe
Capt & Adjt
9th (Northumberland Hussars) Battn.
Northumberland Fusiliers.

18/8/18

SECRET　　　**OPERATION ORDERS No 53**　　　COPY No 2

9th (North'n Hussars) Bn. Northumberland Fus'rs.

RELIEF.	1. The 11th Bn. Suffolk Regt. will relieve 9th (N.H.) Bn. North'd Fusiliers in the Right Sub Section of the Brigade front tonight 18th August inst.
	2. "A" Coy of the Battn. will withdraw to position evacuated by "A" Coy 11th Bn Suffolk Regt.
	"B" Company will occupy positions vacated by opposite Company of the 11th Bn Suffolk Regt.
	Companies will move to new positions by platoon.
GUIDES.	3. One per Platoon & one per Coy H.Q. will be provided by Advance Party to meet Companies at a point to be notified by respective Coy Commdr.
	4. Guides for 11th Bn. Suffolk Regt as per guide table.
ADVANCE PARTY.	5. As already detailed.
RATIONS	6. Will be drawn from Bn. H.Qrs uncooked and will be cooked by Company Cooks who will be sent up tonight.
	WATER for drinking purposes to be drawn with Rations.
TRANSPORT.	7. Transport Officer to arrange for Mess Cart & Maltese Cart to be at Bn H.Qrs at dusk.
STORES etc	8. All Photos, paper maps, trench stores, work in hand and contemplated will be handed over & receipts obtained. Lists of trench stores taken over & handed over to be rendered to Orderly Room by 12 noon 19th inst.
	9. O.C. "B" Coy will detail a guard of 1 N.C.O. & 2 men to relieve guard at ÉTERPIGNY INN, at present found by 11th Bn Suffolks.
	10. O.C. D Coy will provide guard to relieve guard at Brigade H.Qrs, at present found by 11th Bn Suffolks.
RELIEF COMPLETE.	11. Completion of relief and arrival in new positions will be reported to Bn. H.Q. by code words as follows:-
	A Coy　　O.R.s for Leave 18.
	B Coy　　O.R.s for Leave 8.
	C Coy　　O.R.s for Leave 19.
	D Coy　　O.R.s for Leave 18.
	ACKNOWLEDGE.
	Dated 18th Aug 1918.

H. S. Rowe Capt & Adjutant
9th (N.H.) Bn North'd Fus'rs

Copy No 1　War Diary
　　　　2　Retained
　　　　3　Commdg Officer
　　　　4-8　All Coys.
　　　　9　150th Infy Bde
　　　　10　O.C. 11th Bn Suffolks
　　　　11　Q.M.
　　　　12　T.O.
　　　　13　M.O.
　　　　14　R.S.M.
　　　　15　Orderly Room

SECRET. OPERATION ORDERS No. 58   Copy No. 6
REF. MAP. 9th (N.H.) Bn. North'd Fus'rs.
36a N.E. 1/10000

1. **INTENTION.** In consequence of the operations of the Battalion on our left and the Brigade on its left this afternoon, the Battalion will take over the following additional frontage tonight 23/24th —
   From L19 Central to HEMERIE CHAPEL (inclusive).

2. **DISTRIBUTION.**
   D Coy — Right Front Coy.
   B " — Centre Coy.
   C " — Left Coy.
   A " — Close Support.

   D & B Coys will retain their present frontage and C Coy. will take over the new frontage from L19 Cent'l to HEMERIE CHAPEL (inclusive). The 3 front line Coys will rectify their line of posts as explained to Company Comm'rs today by the Comm'g. Officer on the line L31 a 90.90 — L25 b 20.00 — L19 Cent'l — HEMERIE CHAPEL.

   DIVISION BETWEEN Coys. Between D & B Coys, the horizontal line from K30 a 00.20 through CARE CROSS to L25 b 20.20 inclusive to D Coy.
   Division between B & C Coys. — The horizontal GRID line running through the centre — K23, K24 and L19 inclusive to C Coy.

   LEFT BATT'N BOUNDARY. — RENNET FARM, ATOM FARM, PULLET FARM, HEMERIE CHAPEL (all inclusive).

employed in holding the line of Posts will be withdrawn tonight at dusk and will dig in under the supervision of the RE at the following localities —

    D. Coy. K.36.b.90.90.
    B Coy CARE CROSS.
    C Coy PULLET FARM.
    A Coy. ROBERNETZ/in
                  Battn (Close Support)

This line will be developed in the first place on the system of defended and mutual supporting localities. The joining up of these points is a matter for the future.

4. COMPLETION. Completion of the occupation by C Coy of the new piece of line, the readjustment of the line of posts, the supporting platoons and of A Coy to be reported to these H.Qrs by using the code words "HOLD FAST"

ACKNOWLEDGE.

Issued at 7.45 p.m.
3rd August 1918.

Copy No. 1 O. A Coy.
       2   B "
       3   C "
       4   D "
       5 183rd Inf.Bde.
       6. War Diary.

Capt.
a/adjt
9th (H.) Bn. North'n Rgt.

Secret   Copy No.

OPERATION ORDERS No. 39
9th (Works) (Bn) Royal Welsh Fusiliers
Map Ref. Sheet
36 A NE /20000

1. **INTENTION** — The Battalion will be relieved in the right Sub-Sector by the 2/4th Royal Berkshire Regt. tomorrow 25th inst.

2. **RELIEF**
   D Coy Royal Berks will relieve D Coy
   B "   "   "   "   "   B "
   C "   "   "   "   "   A "
   A "   "   "   "   "   C "

3. **GUIDES** — 1 Guide for Coy HQ. and 1 per platoon to be at K.16.d.70.10 (Potard's Right Railway Junction) as follows:—
   Right Support Coy (A Coy) 4.0 pm
   Left   "   " (C ") 4.30 pm
   2 platoons & Coy HQ Right Front Coy (D Coy) 5.0 pm
   2 platoons & Coy HQ Left Front Coy (B Coy) 5.30 pm

   Platoons in Front Line
   1 Guide per platoon moving into the Front Line at the same places as follows
   Right Front Coy (D Coy) at 6.0 pm
   Left Front Coy (B ") at 6.30 pm

Guides (cont)   Post Guides.
            1 Guide for each post of
Right front (D) to be at BARE CROSS
(Rd & Railway junction) at 6.30 pm
            1 Guide for each post
Left front Coy (B) to be at Road &
Railway junction ROBERMETZ at
7.0 pm.
            1 Guide for Battn HQ to be
at K16D 70·10 at 6.0 pm.

4.
ROUTE   The 1/4 Rl Royal Berks will
be led in and our own companies
will move out by the light railway
leaving to GURNARDS CROSS

5.
HANDING OVER. All papers Maps & trench stores
    excepting S.O.S. Rockets, very lights
    flares will be handed over and
    receipt obtained.   Work in
    hand will be carefully explained
    to incoming unit.

6.
TAKING OVER   The Second in Command will
    detail a party to reconnoitre and
    take over from 1/4 Royal Berks

1

TRANSPORT Transport Officer will arrange for limbers to be at ROBERMETZ (Road Railway junction) at dusk.
    The Maltese cart & Mess cart and half limber to be at Batt. HQ at 8.0pm

LEWIS GUNS Reference above, para Coys will leave their Lewis Guns & Walker hues (in charge of an NCO) when passing ROBERMETZ. The NCO will see them loaded and will accompany the limber which will convey the Lewis Guns to new Coy HQ.

COOKERS Transport Officer will make arrangements for cookers to be at their Coy area.

INTERVAL BETWEEN UNITS East of GURNARD CROSS units will move by section.

GUIDES Coys will close at GURNARDS CROSS where guides from the details will meet them.

APPENDIX "E"

OPERATION ORDERS

11th SUFFOLKS REGT
2/6 ROYAL WARWICK
2/4 ROYAL BERKS.

1/8th. BN. ROYAL WARWICKSHIRE REGIMENT.   Copy No. 8

Order No. 1/3. Dated 14/8/18.

Reference Map:- Sheet 36.a. N.E. 1/20000

1. (a) The 143rd Infantry Brigade will relieve the 184th Infantry
      Brigade in the AVELUY Section on the night 14th/15th inst.

   (b) On the same night the inter-Brigade boundary will be altered
       to the following:-
          HENVILLE ROAD as far west as the house at K.14.b.1.5 –
          K.13.b.0.8 – K.17. central (all inclusive to the Right
          Brigade).

2. The Battalion boundaries will be altered as follows:-

      Northern Boundary:- Brigade Boundary (see para. 1.)
      Southern Boundary:- Road junction K.20.a.1.5 – GLOSTER
                           ROAD at K.27.a.4.5 – thence GLOSTER
                           ROAD (inclusive)

   Inter-company boundary will be altered as follows:-

          K.20.c.1.5 – K.21.c.4.5 – K.14.d.8.0.

3. The 9th Battalion Northumberland Fusiliers will relieve all
   troops of A. & D. Companies north of the HENVIEW – LA MOTTE
   road.

4. Five guides from A.Coy. and two guides from D.Coy. will report
   to the Intelligence Officer at junction of HENSEY ROAD and VIA
   DUMA, K.21.b.95.70. at 6.15 p.m., 14th inst.

5. A. & D. Companies will report completion of relief by the 9th
   Battalion Northumberland Fusiliers by the code words "One tin
   Chloride of Lime".

6. On completion of this relief:-

      A.Coy. will relieve all troops of B.Coy. north of the
      inter-company boundary and will be disposed as follows:-
          Two platoons in Outpost Line
          Two platoons in the old German Front Line.

      C.Coy. will relieve all troops of D.Coy. north of the
      inter-company boundary, and will be disposed as follows:-
          Three platoons in the old British Front Line
          One platoon in the old British Support Line.

7. Completion of relief will be reported by the code words "Five
   hundred sandbags".

8. On completion of this relief:-
      B.Coy. will relieve any troops of the 2/8th Battalion
   Worcestershire Regt. which may be north of the inter-battalion
   boundary and will be disposed as follows:-
          Two platoons in the Outpost Line.
          One platoon in local support, east of the old German
             Front Line.
          One platoon in the old German Front Line.

      D.Coy. will relieve any troops of the 2/8th Battalion
   Worcestershire Regt. which may be north of the inter-company
   Battalion boundary, and will be disposed as follows:-
          Two platoons in old British Front Line.
          Two platoons in old British Support Line.

9. B. & D. Companies will report completion by the code words
   "Pave boxes 1. & A" and will confirm by runner.

- 2 -

10. Details of relief will be arranged direct between company commanders concerned.

11. There will be no movement in connection with the relief east of NIEPPE FOREST before dark.

12. All trench stores, except petrol tins, Hot Food containers and tools in the areas being relieved (including inter-company reliefs) will be handed over and receipts obtained.
 Copies of receipts will be forwarded to Battalion H.Q. by first D.R. 13th inst.

13. ACKNOWLEDGE.

 J. Austin,
 Capt. & Adjt.
 for O.C. 2/8th R. Warwick. Regt.

Issued at .....2pm..... by runner.

DISTRIBUTION.
Copy No. 1 to O.C.
 2 to Adjutant,
 3 to A. Coy.
 4 to B. Coy.
 5 to C. Coy.
 6 to D. Coy.
 7 to H.Qrs.
 8 to 9th Northumberland Fusiliers,
 9 to 2/8th Worcester Regt.
 10 to Transport Officer, & Quartermaster,
 11 to Rear
 12 File

S.E.C.R.E.T.   Copy No. 12

11th SUFFOLKS ORDER No. 53.   18:8:18.

Reference Sheet 56.A. N.E.

1. The Battalion will relieve the 9th N.F. in the Right Subsection of the ARREWAGE Sector tonight 18/19th inst. –
    B.Coy. will relieve A.Coy. 9th N.F. and become Right Front Coy.
    A. "   "   "   B. "   "   "   "   Left Front Coy.
    C. "   "   "   D. "   "   "   "   Right Support Coy.
    D. "   "   "   C. "   "   "   "   Left Support Coy.
   Battalion H.Qs. will be at K.8.c.2.2.
   No movement in connection with relief until dusk.

2. All Photos, Papers, Maps, and Trench Stores, and Work in hand will be taken over.
   List of Trench Stores taken over will be sent to Battn. H.Qs. by 8 a.m. 19th inst.

3. Advance Parties from the 9th N.F. will report at respective Coy.HQs. this afternoon.

4. Guides from the 9th N.F. will report as under :-
   for Right Front Coy.   1 per platoon and 1 per Coy.H.Q. at Trench and Road junction K.15.a.05.45 at 7.45 p.m.
                          1 per Post (eight) at K.15.d.75.25 at 8.30 p.m.
   for Left Front Coy.   1 per Platoon and 1 per Coy. H.Q. at A.Coy. H.Q. at 7.45 p.m.
                          1 per Post (eight) on Road by SWINGBRIDGE (K.15.d) at 8.30 p.m.
   for Right Support Coy. 1 per Platoon and 1 per Coy. H.Q. on Road 100 yds. S.E. of HORSE SHOE DUMP (K.8.d.) at 7.45 p.m.
   for Left Support Coy. 1 per Platoon and 1 per Coy.H.Q. at D.Coy. H.Q. K.c.a.80.05 at 7.45 p.m.

5. Rations will come up cooked to MEREDITH STATION and then pushed to point where railway crosses canal for B. and C. Coys, and point where railway meets DENEEFARM Road for A. and D. Coys.
   Water for B. and C. Coys is obtained from Water Point near Bn.H.Qs. and for A. and D. Coys from CHINESE FARM.
   C. and D. Coys. will find these pushing and carrying parties.

6. On relief the Guard at Bde.H.Qs. furnished by A.Coy., the Guard at the STATION ESTAMINET furnished by B.Coy., and the two Signallers on the Power Buzzer Station will report to Right Bn.H.Qs. at K.8.c.2.2. for duty as Dump and Water Guards, etc. They will be rationed with Bn.H.Q.

7. Completion of relief will be notified to Battn.H.Qs. by the following codes :-
              A.Coy.   REAPING HOOKS REQUIRED.
              B. "   BILL HOOKS WANTED.
              C. "   CANNOT SAY.
              D. "   DO NOT REQUIRE ANY.

8. ACKNOWLEDGE.

                                              Captain and Adjutant,
                                        11th Battalion THE SUFFOLK REGT.

Copy No. 1   War Diary.
        2.   File.
        3 - 6 Companies.
        7.   Battn. H.Qs.
        8.   Intelligence Officer.
        9.   Quartermaster.
       10.   Transport Officer.
       11.   Medical Officer.
       12.   9th Bn. N.F.

SECRET   Copy No 11

2/4TH BN ROYAL BERKSHIRE REGT

Ref Map   OPERATION ORDER No 40   24 AUG 1918
Sheet 36a NE   BY MAJOR A G CAMERON. COMDG
1/20000

1. 184 INF BDE will relieve 183 INF BDE in Advanced Brigade Area on night 24th/25th and 25th/26th August 1918, as under :—

   (a) 2/4TH OXF & BUCKS LT INF will relieve 11TH BN SUFFOLK REGT on night 24th/25th and will come under orders of G O C 183 INF BDE until Brigade relief is complete.
   Similarly 11TH BN SUFFOLK REGT will withdraw to positions now held by 2/4TH OXF & BUCKS LT INF and will come under orders of Brigade Commander 184 INF BDE.

   (b) 2/4TH ROYAL BERKSHIRE REGT. will relieve 9TH BN NORTHUMBERLAND FUSILIERS on night 25th/26th August in Right Sector Advanced Brigade Front.

   (c) 2/5TH GLOUCESTER REGT will relieve 1st BN E LANCS REGT on night 25th/26th August in support.

2. This Battalion will relieve the 9th NORTHUMBERLAND FUS as under :—

   "D" Coy. 2/4 R BERKS will relieve D Coy 9th N F in the Right Front Section. Two platoons of this Coy will occupy 8 posts in the Line of Observation running approx from L 31 a 45 95 to L 25 d 05 60
   The remaining two platoons will occupy No 1 Defended Locality (in conjunction with Right Support Coy) at approximately K 36 b 90 90 to K 30 d 95 40.

   "B" Coy 2/4. R BERKS will relieve B Coy 9th N F in the Left Front Section. Two platoons of this Coy will occupy 8 posts in the Line of Observation running approximately along grid line from L 25 d 05 70 to L 19 Central

   The remaining two platoons of this Coy will occupy No 2 Defended Locality at CARR CROSS

(2)

'C' Coy 2/4 R BERKS will relieve 'A' Coy 9th NF as Right Support in No 1 Defended Locality

'A' Coy 2/4 R BERKS will relieve 'B' Coy 9d NF as Left Support in No 3 Defended Locality near ROBERMETZ

3. <u>Guides for Support Coys</u> - Rendezvous at K 16 d 70 10 Guides, one per platoon & one for Coy H.Q. will meet 'C' Coy at 4 p.m. & 'A' Coy at 4-30 p.m. at rendezvous. Sections will move at 100ˣ interval and in file. Connecting files will be used to keep touch. Guides for Front Coys, one per platoon & one for Coy H.Q. will be at rendezvous (K 16 d 70 10) as follows:—
For 'D' Coy at 9.30 p.m.   For 'B' Coy at 10 p.m.
Platoons holding posts in Line of Observation will meet Section guides as follows:—
'D' Coy at Cane Cross   'B' Coy at Robermetz (K 24 a 45 65)

4. Relief by Support Coys to be completed by 7 p.m.
All movement East of Main Line of Retention will be by sections.
Relief by Front Coys to be completed by dawn. No movement of these companies East of Main Line of Retention before 9 p.m.

5. All maps, documents, photos, etc relating to the Sector will be taken over on relief and receipted lists forwarded to Bn. H.Q. by 9 am. 26 August.

6. Completion of relief will be reported to Bn. H.Q. by Code Word "Trust Morris"

7. Disposition Sketches will be forwarded to Bn H.Q. by 9 am. 26 inst.

8. On completion Bn. H.Q. will close at K 13. c. 9 5 & reopen at K 23. c. 4 4.

9. Acknowledge.

<u>ISSUED AT 6-30 AM</u>

<u>DISTRIBUTION</u>

COPIES   1 - 4   O.C. COYS
         5   QM
         6   TO
         7   R.S.M.
         8   WAR DIARY
         9   FILE
        10   184 BDE
        11   9th NF   2/4 Royal Berks

WAR DIARY
INTELLIGENCE SUMMARY

September 1918

WR 37

9th (North'd Husrs) Bn. Northumberland Fusiliers

APPENDICES

A. 183 Infantry Bde Orders.
B. 9th (NH) Bn Northumberland Fusiliers
C. Operation Orders ⅔ Royal Berks Regt
   ⅔ Royal Norfolk
   1 East Lancs Regt
D. Special Orders of the Day.
F. Training Programme.

September 1918 Army Form C. 2118.

WAR DIARY
or
INTELLIGENCE SUMMARY.

9th (Northumberland Hussars) Batt^n
Northumberland Fusiliers

Place	Date	Hour	Summary of Events and Information	Remarks and references to Appendices
	SEPT			
SACKET FARM.	1		Received orders at 2.10 p.m. to move two companies to one LOUNGE HOUSE- L21a38 and two companies to line HEMERE CHAPEL- SHELTER CROSS- CRINQUETTE LOTTS. The same orders also gave the information that we were to be relieved that afternoon by 2/6 & Bath. Royal Warwick Regt. Moved D and B Coys to front line and A and C Coys in rear line. Arranged to guides and Royal Warwick came in about 6.30 p.m. Relief was complete about 8 p/m and all companies got in form Cooker near Bath at Dr. Muncks, crossed to MEREDITH STATION and light railway from back to CROWE STATION from which it was only 5 minutes walk back to SPEZANO Camp. The Battalion had completed 18 days in front line and supplies	0.6 APP. 3
SPEZIANO CAMP	2		Rested and cleaned up	
– do –	3	10.12.30 p.m	Battalion Route march of about 7 miles 9.30 – 12.30 p.m	

WAR DIARY
or
INTELLIGENCE SUMMARY.
(Erase heading not required.)

September 1918   Army Form C. 2118.

5th (Northumberland Hussars) Battn.
Northumberland Fusiliers

Instructions regarding War Diaries and Intelligence Summaries are contained in F.S. Regs., Part II. and the Staff Manual respectively. Title pages will be prepared in manuscript.

Place	Date	Hour	Summary of Events and Information	Remarks and references to Appendices
SPEZIANO CAMP	4		Progressive training for the Battalion	WD
— do —	5		Marched to CRONE STATION - trained to GUINANDS CROSS - marched from NEUF-BERQUIN and on arrival at billets left Bn at REBERS METZ.	WD 063 AOD B
THOERMETZ	6		Fine morning and about our Kings Battalios's numerals at 11 a.m. and bivouaced in ruins & farms at 1 RUE MONTIGNY. Bn. moved to NEUF-BERQUIN.	WD 064 Apx B OO B
NEUF-BERQUIN	7		Fair during morning. Battalion paraded at 5.30 p.m. and moved up to Support of 183 Infantry Brigade. 'B' Coy 8e 'A' Coy in T.K, D. Coy in 24 e, C Coy in 24 e & C (Cul G Square). Relief complete about 12 midnight. Bath. MD at Q 7 d 2.1.	WD 065 822 A
Bugar AID Post L21	8		Fairly quiet some gas shelling	WD OOB
— do —	9		Fairly quiet. 10/6 man No.2391 R. Jones B now 25749 Pte Pearson N Fj. D Company killed by shell fire. Moved Pt Coy back to Bathn HQ Dr.	WD

/ September 916   Army Form C. 2118.

WAR DIARY
or
INTELLIGENCE SUMMARY.

9th (Northumberland Hussars) Batt.
Northumberland Fusiliers

(Erase heading not required.)

Place	Date	Hour	Summary of Events and Information	Remarks and references to Appendices
BIVm Etc Sqd 2	10.		Fairly quiet day	mt
-do-	11.		Fairly quiet. Battalion relieved by 7th Batt. Royal Berks. Regt. Relief complete by 8.45 pm. Battalion moves back to YAM FARM. 12.2n S.8 1 Km N.E. Kemmel. Battalion in reserve to the Brigade who man the SOUTHERN SECTOR of the CORPS BATTLE Line	O.69 APP B mt
YAM FARM	12		During morning Companies at disposal of Company Commanders improving and repitting. During the afternoon the Battalion moved to its position on the Br.B Battle Line	M.967 App 3
YAM FARM	13		Coy training in morning. Company Officers and Coy Commanders made tactical surveys in afternoon under Brigadier	mt
YAM FARM	14		Coy training under Coy Commanders from 9 am to 1 of. lecture at Hdqrs for all Officers and NCO. during afternoon. Major A.E Leather M.C. proceeds for 3 day course at II Corps School and Captain N.H Thornton Assumes temporary Command of the Battalion	mt

WAR DIARY of INTELLIGENCE SUMMARY

Army Form C. 2118.

September 1918

9th (Northumberland Hussars) Battn. Northumberland Fusiliers.

Place	Date	Hour	Summary of Events and Information	Remarks and references to Appendices
YAM FARM	15		Sunday Divine Service	Out
YAM FARM	16		Training under Company Commanders as per training programme	Out
YAM FARM	17		During the day cleaning and fitting equipment etc. G.O.C. Division inspected the Battalion at 6.0 pm and congratulated the Battalion on its smart turn out	Out
YAM FARM	18		Companies at disposal of Company Commanders for the first hour (9.0 a.m. – 10.0 a.m.) afterwards a route march by Company Cops. of about ten miles each Coy route. 12.30 pm	Out
YAM FARM	19		Battalion paraded in heavy marching order Road junction L31.c.40.80 – THOMPE BRIDGE 915 – L.11 en Cal – Road junction R30a.20.21 – CAPE CROSS ROSERNETZ – R.24 junction W.13 95.05. at 9.5 toll sent Coy Commanders with to be given details of advance to be Coming out – @ Coy did not go on the route march but were put in position to represent enemy Order received to move next day to front end	N/F

WAR DIARY
or
INTELLIGENCE SUMMARY

September 1918 — Army Form C. 2118.

9th (Northumberland Hussars) Battn.
Northumberland Fusiliers

Place	Date	Hour	Summary of Events and Information	Remarks and references to Appendices
NAM FARM	20		Company paraded at 10.30 am for rifle inspection. Parties at 5.15 pm to proceed to front line trenches in relief of 17th Royal Warwick Regt. viz. B Coy (Left front Coy) @ C Coy (Centre front Coy), D Coy (Right front Coy) A Coy (Left Sup't Coy). It was a quiet relief with no casualty. Relief complete abt 2 a.m.	O.68 App. B WT
Potts Kill	21		Quiet day in the line with intermittent shelling. Lieut-Col W.E. Walsh M.C. was wounded during the afternoon whilst visiting front line posts (B Coy) and had about 7 pm to mourn to Lieut Colonel H Cook Brown D.S.O. found the Battalion and assumed command of the Battalion. B. Coy had 2 casualties (killed) & 1 wounded.	WT
— do —	22		Quiet day. Shelling on both sides. Our aeroplanes active. Lieut C.B.E Rupert Cran slightly wounded.	WT
— do —	23		Quiet day with intermittent shelling of back area. 6 rounds on Ainee Coy (B.C. v.B.) 1 killed 5 wounded.	WT
— do —	24		Quiet day. Enemy artillery active with Battalion on our left. Col. Coonville, N.F.	WT

WAR DIARY or INTELLIGENCE SUMMARY

Army Form C. 2118.

September 1918

9th (Northumberland Fusiliers) Battn.
Northumberland Fusiliers

Place	Date	Hour	Summary of Events and Information	Remarks and references to Appendices
BATT N HQ SANLY. BRG ST MAUR ROAD	Sept 25		Quiet day. Intermittent shelling on both sides during day, which increased towards night. A carrying party of "D" Coy suffered Casualties through shell fire on Bro St Maur Road Casualties 3 killed and 3 wounded. B Coy H Cronelle N line 2 killed and 3 wounded.	Nil
	26 26	10-00	The Battalion on our right 1 Bn Line Regt made an attack on Capture BARLETTE FARM and Junction Post and 8 prisoners were taken. Intelligence Officer of war came into our lines during the attack Enemy Counter Attacked 300 strong and retook objectives at 6pm night. During the day it was quiet not slight shelling on both sides.	Nil
	27		Quiet day in line. C Coy captured a prisoner (wounded) Orders received that Battn (none) be relieved by the 6th Royal Regt but O Company keep post forward during O/O 71 Regt but was Cancelled later. O Company keep post forward during O/O 71 app B to early morning (28th)	067[?] app 2
	28		Quiet day every artillery active during afternoon and right flank occurred through morning. Battn was to be relieved by the 6th Royal M to 6th Battn and 7th Bn Royal Marine Regt. Relief completed about 10pm. Battn had done 6 days in front lines.	067[?] app 3

WAR DIARY
INTELLIGENCE SUMMARY

Army Form C. 2118.

September 1918

4th (Northumberland Fusiliers) Battn. Northumberland Fusiliers

Place	Date	Hour	Summary of Events and Information	Remarks and references to Appendices
YAM FARM	29		Bath resting and cleaning up. 9/h Town in the line. Sunday voluntary church service.	AM
YAM FARM	30		Thorough cleaning up of Arms & equipment etc again in view economy under Coy. arrangements.	AM

WAR DIARY or INTELLIGENCE SUMMARY

Army Form C. 2118.

SEPTEMBER 1918.

Summary of Events and Information

Strength at the beginning of month — 32 Officers, 834 O.Rs.
"   " " end   "   "   — 40 Officers, 915 O.Rs.

INCREASE
Drafts etc for week ending Sept 7th = 118
"   "   "   "   "   14th = 21
"   "   "   "   "   21st = 22
"   "   "   "   "   28th = 11
                                    = 142

DECREASE
Killed   11
Wounded   30
Evacuation   49
Commissions   1
Transfers   3
                            = 94

OFFICERS

Killed
Capt/Lt-Colonel A. Elsworth M.C. 2/9/18.

Wounded
Lieut Rupert Rumm 20/9/18.

Transfers
Lieut Colonel W.A. Hyndside D.S.O. 26/9/18.
Major D.R. Nicholas 26/9/18.

Joined the Battalion
2/Lieut J. Pearson   } 8/9/18
Lieut G.O. Johnson   }
Lieut Rupert Rumm   }
Lieut R. Robinson   }
Lieut J.A. King   }
Lieut R.G. Harrison   } 11/9/18
2/Lieut H. Stewart   } 9/9/18
Lieut O.D. Maclean   9/9/18
Capt/Lt Colonel A. Elsworth M.C. 14/9/18
Captain M.L. Angus   16/9/18
Lieut C.H.K. Turpin   2/9/18
Lieut Colonel W. Cook Brown 21/9/18

In Hospital in France.
2/Lieut J.S. Porter.
Lieut C.W. Dunjon.
Other Ranks = 112.

WAR DIARY

Army Form C.
September 1918
5th (Northumberland Hussars) Bat.
Northumberland Fusiliers

INTELLIGENCE SUMMARY

(Erase heading not required.)

The undermentioned Honours and Awards have been
prom.td during the Month of September 1918.

BAR TO MILITARY CROSS

2Lieut L Baker M.C.

MILITARY MEDAL

23/4059	Pte R. Turnbull	D Coy
64737	Pte A Bowen	B Coy
64960	Pte T. Turner	B Coy
240118	Pte N Turnbull	B Coy

APPENDIX 'A'

ORDERS 183 Inf Brigade

To: All recipients of 183 Inf.Bde. Order No.239.

B.M.27
1/9/18

Reference Brigade Order No. 239 dated 30/8/18.

1. Battalions of 183rd Inf.Bde. will be relieved as follows and not as stated in the above order:-

   1st E.Lancashire Regt by 2/9th Worcester Regts
   11th Suffolk Regiment by 2/7th R.Warwick Regt.
   9th North'd Fusiliers (under orders of G.O.C. 184th Inf.Bde)
   by 2/8th R.Warwick Regt.

2. After relief Battalions will move as follows:-

   9th North'd Fusiliers - entrain at MEREDITH STATION for SPRESIANO CAMP.

   11th Suffolk Regt. - To VILLORBA CAMP by march route.

   1st E.Lancashire Regt - entrain at MEREDITH STATION for CROTH STATION - thence to ST.LUKE CAMP by march route.

3. 1 Officer per Unit entraining to be at MEREDITH STATION at 8 p.m. to take charge of trains and superintend entraining.

4. ACKNOWLEDGE.

Issued at 10.30 a.m.

John Hunter
Captain,
A/Brigade Major, 183rd Inf. Brigade.

DHQ.
1/9/18.

9th North'd Fus

SECRET.   Copy No... 6

183rd INFANTRY BRIGADE ORDER NO. 241.   5/9/18

1. The following moves will take place tomorrow morning 6th instant:-

   (a) 1st N.Lancs. Regt. to area C.14.a. - FROU BAYARD - D.M. FARM, starting at 8.30 a.m.

   (b) 11th Suffolk Regt. to area SELSEY FARM - COBALT COTTAGES starting at 8.30 a.m.

   (c) 8th Northumberland Fusiliers to area RUE DU CHIEN, starting at 6.0 a.m. *[handwritten: 11 am few taken instruction of B.G.C.]*

   Any route may be used.

2. Transport Lines will move to R.13.d. in accordance with Administrative Instructions dated 4/9/18.

3. Trench Shelters will be taken forward to new area.

4. Arrival in new area, and location of Headquarters will be notified to Brigade H.Q. immediately on arrival.

5. 1st N.Lancs. Regt. will go into the line on the right on the night 6th/7th September and remaining 2 Battalions and Brigade H.Q. on night 7th/8th September.

   Further particulars will be notified later.

6. ACKNOWLEDGE.
                                           [signature]
                                                         Captain,
Issued at 6-45 p.m.   for A/Brigade Major, 183rd Inf.Bde.

            Copy No. 1 - War Diary
                     2 - File
                     3 - Staff Captain.
                     4 - B.S.O.
                     5 - B.T.O.
                     6 - 8th North'd Fus.
                     7 - 11th Suffolks.
                     8 - 1st N.Lancs.Regt.
                     9 - 183 L.T.M.B.
                    10 - 2/2nd Field Ambulance.
                    11 - 61st Bn. M.G.C.
                    12 - 61st Division "G"
                    13 - 182nd Inf. Bde.
                    14 - 184th Inf. Bde.
                    15 - C.R.A.
                    16 - C.R.E.
                    17 - No. 3 Coy, Div. Train.
                    18 - 61st Div. Train, A.S.C.

8.   Location of new Brigade H.Q. and time of closing of old Brigade H.Q. will be notified later.

9.   Acknowledge.

✓ done

John Hunter
Captain,
A/Brigade Major, 183 Inf. Bde.

Issued at 6.30 a.m.

Copy No. 1 - War Diary.
       2. - File.
       3. - Staff Captain.
       4. - B.S.O.
       5. - B.I.O.
       6. - B.T.O.
       7. - 9th. Northd Fus.
       8. - 11th. Suffolks.
       9. - 1st. E.Lancs.
      10 - 183 L.T.M.B.
      11 - 2/2 Field Ambce.
      12 - 61st. Btn. M.G.C.
      13 - 61st. Division "G".
      14 - 182nd Inf. Bde.
      15 - 184th. Inf. Bde.
      16 - C.R.A.
      17 - C.I.A.
      18 - No.3 Coy. Div. Train.
      19 - 61st. Div. Train A.S.C.
      20 - No.4 Coy. Div. Train.

SECRET.   Copy No. 7
                                                                       6.9.18.

183 Infantry Brigade Order No.242.

Ref. Map Sheet
   36A NW 1/20000.
   36 NW 1/20000.

1.   183 Infantry Brigade will relieve 182 Infantry Bde.
        in the Advanced Guard Brigade Area on the night 6/7th.
        and 7/8th. insts. as follows :-

   (a) 1st. E.Lancs Regt. will relieve 2/8 WORCESTERS
        on the RIGHT on the night 6/7th and will come
        under the orders of G.O.C.182 Infantry Brigade
        until completion of relief on night 7/8th. inst.
            1 guide per Platoon and 1 guide for Battalion
        H.Q. of 2/8 WORCESTERS will be at PACK MULE BRIDGE
        at G.27.a.9.4. at 8.0 p.m. on 6th. inst.
            2/8th. WORCESTERS will move to area G.14.a.
        TROUBAYARD - DEAL FARM on completion of relief
        and come under orders of G.O.C. 183 Infantry Bde.
        until completion of Brigade relief on 7/8th. inst.
   (b) 11th. SUFFOLKS will relieve 2/7th. ROYAL WARWICK
        REGT. on the LEFT on the night 7/8th. inst.
            Reconnoitring parties will meet guides at Batt-
        alion H.Q. G.23.a.8.4. at 8.0a.m. tomorrow 6th. inst.
   (c) 9th. NORTHUMBERLAND FUSILIERS will relieve
        2/6th. ROYAL WARWICKSHIRE REGT. in Support on the
        night 7/8th. inst.
            Reconnoitring parties will meet guides at 182 Inf.
        Bde. H.Q. at G.14.a.2.1. at 10.0 a.m. tomorrow 6th. inst.
   (d) 183 L.T.M.B. will relieve personnel 182nd. L.T.M.B.
        on the 7/8th. inst. and exchange 4 guns in the line
        (2 attached to each front Battalion).
            Remaining 2 guns and personnel of 183rd L.T.M.B.
        will proceed to new Brigade H.Q. on the 7th. inst.
            Guide will be at 182nd Brigade H.Q. at 12.0 a.m. to
        meet O.C. 183rd. L.T.M.B.

2.   Further details of relief will be arranged between
        Commanding Officers concerned.

3.   Flares, S.O.S. Grenades, Shovels etc. will be taken
over.

4.   Dispositions will be sent to Brigade H.Q. by 10.0 a.m.
on 8th. inst.

5.   The following troops which form part of the Advanced
        Guard Brigade will come under the orders of G.O.C. 183rd.
        Infantry Brigade on completion of relief:-

            1 Brigade R.F.A.
            1 Field Coy. R.E.
            2 Companies 61st. Bn. M.G.C.
            1 Troop K.E.H.

6.   Units will notify completion of relief to Brigade H.Q.
        by the following code words :-

            1st East Lancs Regt.   -   ALICE
            11th. Suffolks.   -   WHEN
            9th. Northd. Fus.   -   ART
            183 L.T.M.B.   -   THOU

7.   Command of Advanced Guard will pass to G.O.C. 183rd
        Infantry Brigade on completion of relief.

1.

SECRET.   OPERATIONS FILE   Copy No. 4
                               11.8.18.
              183rd Infantry Brigade Order No.246.

Reference Map Sheet
  55 NW. 1/20000.

1.   On the morning of 12th inst the 2/4th. Oxford & Bucks
   L.I. will attack and capture JUNCTION POST and trenches in the
   vicinity and will establish posts at H.32.b.0.4., H.32.b.3.3.
   H.32.b.5.7., H.32.a.7.7. and H.25.d.10.05.

2.   After establishing these posts they will exploit their
   success by pushing up the old British trenches running N. as
   far as H.25.d.6.5. and H.25.a.65.60.
        The line of Resistance will then run along the road from
   H.19.c.40.90 to H.32.b.75.70 and thence back to the present line
   at H.31.d.90.80 with patrols pushed forward in advance.

3.   The jumping off places will be from the enclosures 6,7,
   H.31.b.99.05. to H.32.a.50.85 and approximately from H.32.c.
   to H.32.c.99.40.   ^

4.   The strength of the attacking force will be 2 Companies.

5.   The Artillery Programme is attached.(Issued to 2/4 O.B.L.I. only)
        If the weather is favorable, smoke will be used to screen
   the operations from observation on the North and East.

6.   Machine Guns will keep BARTLETT FARM and enclosures in
   H.26.a. under heavy fire and will also sweep the HUT DE QUESNE
   and the enclosures on the East side of it with heavy bursts of
   fire throughout the operations.
        All the guns of the 2 Companies with the Advanced Guard
   will be utilised for this purpose.

7.   The L.T.M's will cooperate by firing on the vicinity of
   BARTLETT FARM if this locality has not already been taken by us.

8.   The Left Battalion will create a diversion by rifle fire
   and Lewis gun fire on hostile posts on their front and by a lavish
   use of rifle grenades in the vicinity of ESQUINCHY.

9.   Zero hour will be   5.15 a.m.

10. Synchronisation.   A watch, after being synchronised with 307th
    Brigade R.F.A. at 4 p.m., will be sent to H.Q. 2/4th O. & B.L.I.
         M.G.Coys and L.T.M.B. will synchronise at H.Q. 2/4th O. &
    B.L.I. under arrangements to be made by O.C. 2/4th O. & B.L.I.

11.   ACKNOWLEDGE by wire.
                                        John Hunter
                                               Captain,
   Issued at 5 p.m.   A/Brigade Major, 183rd Infantry Bde.

             Copy No. 1 - War Diary.
                     2 - File.
                     3 - S.C.
                     4 - 8th North'd Fus.
                     5 - 11th Suffolks.
                     6 - 12? L.N.L.R.
                     7 - 2/4 O. & B.L.I.
                     8 - "A" Coy M.G.Bn.
                     9 - "D" Coy 61st M.G.Bn.
                    10 - 182nd Inf.Bde.
                    11 - 184th Inf.Bde.
                    12 - 173rd Inf.Bde.
                    13 - 110th Inf.Bde.
                    14 - 61st Division "G"
                    15 - 307th Brigade R.F.A.

SECRET.   OPERATIONS FILE   Copy No. 6
                                     10.3.18.

      183 Infantry Brigade Order No.245.

Ref. Map Sheet
36 N.W 1/20000.
36A N.W 1/20000.

1.   The 183rd. Infantry Brigade less 1st. E. Lancs Regt. will
        be relieved by the 184th. Infantry Brigade less 2/4 Oxford
        and Bucks Light Infantry as the Advanced Guard Brigade
        tomorrow night 11/12th. inst.

        Relief will take place in accordance with Table attached.

2.   Advanced parties of 184th. Infantry Brigade will be met
        tomorrow 11th. inst. as follows :-

           2/5th. GLOUCESTERS   at 11th. SUFFOLKS H.Q. at
           2/4th. R. BERKS.   at   9th. NORTHD. FUS. H.Q. at
           184th. L.T.M.B.   at 183 L.T.M.B. H.Q. at

3.   S.O.S. Grenades, Reserve S.A.A. and Grenades, flares
        and shovels will be handed over to relieving Units.

4.   All further details of relief will be arranged direct
        between Commanding Officers concerned.

5.   The following troops which form part of the Advanced
        Guard Brigade will come under the orders of G.O.C. 184th.
        Infantry Brigade on completion of relief :-

                1 Brigade R.F.A.
                1 Field Coy. R.E.
                2 Coys. 61st. Btn. M.G.C.
                1 Troop K.E.H.

6.   Command of the Advanced Guard will pass to G.O.C. 184th.
        Infantry Brigade on completion of relief, at which hour
        1st. E. LANCS. REGT. will revert to command of G.O.C. 183rd.
        Infantry Brigade and 2/4th. OXF OXF. & BUCKS L.I. to G.O.C.
        184th. Infantry Brigade.

7.   Completion of relief will be reported to Brigade H.Q.
        by Code words as follows :-

           9th. Northd Fus.   -   ANOTHER
           11th. Suffolks.   -   LITTLE
           183 L.T.M.B.   -   DRINK

        Units will also report arrival in new area and location
        of H.Q.

8.   On completion of relief the Brigade will be responsible
        for the defence of the Southern Subsection of the Corps
        Battle Line.

9.   Brigade H.Q. will close at G.14.a.2.1. and reopen at
        L.27.a.0.3. on completion of relief.

10.   Acknowledge.

Issued at   p.m.   Captain
                7.30.   A/Brigade Major, 183 Inf. Bde.
                                                      P.T.O.

Relief Table issued with 183rd Inf.Bde.Order No. 245.

Serial No.	Unit.	From	Relieved by	On relief to area	Remarks
1.	11 Suffolk R.	Left Subsection.	2/5th Gloucester R.	L.29b.0.4 - L.32.c.2.8. - L.28.d.5.0.	Take over Billets of 2/5th Gloucester Rgt.
2.	9 North. Fus.	Brigade Reserve	2/4th R. Berks R.	About VANFAR.	Take over Billets of 2/4 R.Berks.
3.	183 L.T.M.B.	2 Guns in each Subsection, 2 guns in reserv.	184th L.T.M.B.?	F Lf FdR. L.27.b.	Re'duce 4 guns in Line, Take over Billets of 184 L.T.B.

SECRET.   Copy no. 4

183rd INFANTRY BRIGADE ORDER NO. 244.   10/8/18.

Reference Map, 36 N.E. 1/20,000.
              36A.N.W. 1/20,000.

1. 1st E.Lancashire Regiment will be relieved by 2/4th Oxford & Bucks L.I. tonight 10th/11th instant in the right Subsection of the Advanced Guard Line.

2. On relief 1st E.Lancashire Regiment will withdraw to the area L.30.a.8.5 – L.24.a.9.0 – L.23.b.3.4 – L.29.b.0.4, and will come under the command of G.O.C. 184th Inf.Bde.

3. S.O.S. Grenades, Reserve S.A.A. and Grenades, Flares, and Shovels, will be handed over to relieving Battalion.

4. 2 Sections of "D" Coy 1st Bn. M.G.C. attached to 1st E. Lancs. Regt. will become attached to 2/4th Oxford & Bucks L.I. on relief.

5. O.C. 1st E.Lancashire Regt will arrange for 17 Guides (1 per Platoon and 1 for Battalion H.Q.) to be at NOUVEAU MONDE G.27.c.5.2 at 8 p.m.

6. Completion of relief will be reported by code word "TEN".
   Arrival in new area, and location of H.Q. will be reported to these H.Q. and to 184th Inf.Bde.

7. On completion of relief 1st E.Lancashire Regt. will come under the orders of G.O.C. 184th Inf.Bde.

8. 183rd Inf.Bde. less 1st E.Lancashire Regt, will be relieved by 184th Inf.Bde. less 2/4th Oxford & Bucks L.I. in the Advanced Guard line on the night 11th/12th instant.

9. ACKNOWLEDGE.

                                              John Hunter
                                                Captain,
Issued at 12-45 p.m.   A/Brigade Major, 183rd Inf. Bde.

                Copy No. 1 – War Diary
                        2 – File
                        3 – Staff Captain.
                        4 – 9th North'd Fus.
                        5 – 11th Suffolks.
                        6 – 1st E.Lancs Regt.
                        7 – 183rd L.T.M.B.
                        8 – 61st Division "G"
                        9 – 184th Inf.Bde.

SECRET.   Copy No 5

        183rd Infantry Brigade Order No. 243.   9/9/18.

Reference Map 36 N.W. 1/20,000.

1. The 1st E.Lancashire Regiment will attack with 1 Company tomorrow morning 10th instant at 5-30 a.m. JUNCTION POST and the enclosures in H.32.a. and will establish posts at H.32.b.0.4 - H.32.b.5.5 - H.32.b.3.8 - H.32.a.7.7 and H.26.d.10.05.

2. After the above posts have been established the 1st E.Lancashire Regt. will exploit their success along the trenches running N.W. through:

    (a) H.26.c. and ~~~~~~~
    (b) H.32.b. a ~~~~~~~

3. Two Trench Mortars and 8 Machine Guns are already at the disposal of C.O. 1st E.Lancashire Regt. and will cooperate under arrangements made by him.

4. Artillery Programme will be issued later.

5. In the event of patrols establishing the above posts (mentioned in para. 1) during the night, C.O. 1st E. Lancashire Regt. will notify Brigade H.Q. at once so that the Artillery programme can be cancelled.

6. Acknowledge.

                                                                         Captain,
Issued at 7 p.m.   A/Brigade Major, 183rd Inf.Brigade.

        Copy No. 1 - War Diary.
               2 - File.
               3 - S.C.
               4 - B.S.O.
               5 - 9th North'd Fus.
               6 - 11th Suffolk Regt.
               7 - 1st E.Lancashire Regt.
               8 - 183rd L.T.M.B.
               9 - "B" Coy 31st Bn.M.G.C.
             10 - "C" Coy   do
             11 - Adv. Guard Artillery Group.
             12 - 176th Inf.Bde.
             13 - 119th Inf.Bde.

"C" Form.
MESSAGES AND SIGNALS.

Army Form C. 2123
(In books of 100.)

No. of Message ....

Prefix **GM** Code **KSP** Words **13**

Received. From **RUFU** By **Cpl Edmonds**

Sent, or sent out. At .... m. To .... By ....

Office Stamp **MOLI** **18-8-18**

Charges to Collect £ s d

Service Instructions **RUFU**

Handed in at **183 Bde** Office **9.57** m. Received **10.22** m.

TO **MOLI**

*Sender's Number	Day of Month	In reply to Number	AAA
BM44	18		

Brigade order 233 postponed addressed 174 DO repeated all concerned

FROM **RUFU**
TIME & PLACE **9.50 PM**

"C" Form.
MESSAGES AND SIGNALS.

Army Form C. 2123
(In books of 100.)

No. of Message..........

| Prefix | Code | Words | Received From Rufa By West | Sent, or sent out. At ... m. To ... By ... | Office Stamp MOLI 19·8·18 |

Handed in at .... Rufa Road .... Office 6·7 m. Received 6·8 m.

TO — MOLI

*Sender's Number	Day of Month	In reply to Number	AAA
BM 54	19		

Brigade order dated 16th To 233 will be carried out tonight aaa acknowledge addressed LOOI MOLI repeated all concerned

FROM TIME & PLACE — Rufa 5·50 p.

*This line should be erased if not required.

SECRET   Copy No 6

153rd Infantry Brigade Order No 249
                                                                24.9.18
Reference Map... A NW 1/20000

1. In the event of the operation on Y/day 1 night against
BARTLETT FARM being successful the line now held by the
Brigade will be advanced and readjusted as follows:
(a) 1st Bn. East Lancashire Regt will advance the posts
now on the line H.20.b.75.00 - H.19.d.70.20
approximate line BARTLETT FARM (inclusive) - junction
Road and Light Railway at H.20.c.00.40.
(b) North'd Fusiliers will advance the posts now
on the line H.19.d.00.50 - YORK POST to the
H.20.c.60.90 - H.13.d. ...
The enclosures at H.20.c.55.35 will be ...
(c) 1st ... Lancashire Regt.

2. If the operation against BARTLETT FARM is not
successful the following advance and readjustment
will take place:-
1st Bn North'd Fusiliers will advance the ... line
to the following points:
H.19.d.05.05 along track running N.E. to reach at
H.19.d.70.70 and thence back to our present line
through the P in YORK POST.

3. The readjustment either under paras 1 or 2 above will
take place on Y/day 2 night.

4. Ample preparation must be made by all units
immediate consolidation.

5. Commanding Officers of Battalions concerned will
arrange all details for the advance by personal
... .

6. ... will be ... as ... as possible on Y/day 2 night.

ACKNOWLEDGE   M.G...
                                                     Brigade Major 153 Inf. Bde.
Issued at 8 pm

Copy 1 - War Diary   Copy 12 - 1/1 M.G.C
     2 - file   13 - 470 Field Coy RE
     3 - GOC   14 - Gen Div ...
     4 - Bde Major   15 - CRA
     5 - S.C.   16 - 306 Bde RFA
     6 - ... ...   17 - Liaison Officer ... RFA
     7 - R. Inf Bde   18 - 152 Inf Bde
     8 - 1st ...   19 - 154 ...
     9 - 153 LTMB   20 - 173 Inf Bde
    10 - B ... RE   21 - ...
    11 - ...   22 - 51st Division

APPENDIX "B"

ORDERS 9th (NH) Battn
Northumberland Fusiliers

SECRET.   Copy No 1
          9th (NH) Bath Northumberland Fusiliers
Ref Map Sheet   Order No 11.
36 A N.W. 1/20000   27.9.18
              Not to be taken beyond Coy HQ

1.   In the event of operation ~~11~~ being
successful against BARTLETTE FARM the
Battalion line will be readjusted as follows:-
The posts now on line H.19 b.00.58 – YORK
POST to the line H.20 a.60.40 – H.13 d.70.00
The line now held by 1st E Lancs REGT
will move to conform with above.
Enclave at H.20 c.55.35 will be inclusive
to 1st E Lancs REGT.

2.   If the operation against BARTLETTE
FARM is unsuccessful the following
readjustment will take place.
     9th (or 4) Bn Nths Fus. will advance the
outpost line to following points –
H.19 d.05.05 along track running
NE to road at H.19 d.70.70, and
thence back to present line through
the P in YORK POST.

3. The readjustment, either under para 1 or 2 will take place on night 27/28th inst.

4. ACKNOWLEDGE

Issued by runner from 2-10 am

M. [signature]
Capt [illegible]
O.C. (NH) Bath. Works [illegible]

Copy No 1 Retained
       2 Covering Officer
       3 O.C. A Coy
       4 " B "
       5 " C "
       6 " D "

SECRET   Copy No.

9" (N.F.) Batt. Northumberland Fusiliers
Ref Map 36A.   Order No 70.
NW 1/20,000   27.9.18

Not to be taken beyond Coy H.Q.

1. In the event of an enemy withdrawal the Advance Guard Brigade will make the following objectives:-
Road Junction H.33.d.40.10 — CROIX BLANCHE — FLEURBAIX — ERQUINGHEM at H.4.d.9.7.

2. The advance will be made in three bounds as follows:-

(A) An intermediate bound from H.4.c.45.45 — H.9.d.6.4 (Strong point inclusive), thence along railway line to H.9.d.1.0 — H.15.a.5.7, S.W. to road at H.14.d.70.25 and S. to H.20 Central.

(B) Road H.32.d.7.0 — JUNCTION POST — Cross Road H.26.d.0.1 — H.20.c.9.0, thence N.E. to H.21.a.5.4, Strong Point in H.9.b. (inclusive) to Canal at H.4.c.45.45.

(2) (c) To the objective given in para 1. Orders for first bound will be given by the Commanding Officer and The Battalion will be disposed as follows:-

'B' Coy   LEFT FRONT
'D' Coy   RIGHT FRONT
'C' Coy   LEFT SUPPORT
'A' Coy   RIGHT SUPPORT

Boundaries as follows:-

<u>B Coy</u>   The grid line running E and W between H9 and H15 to Hospital H4d.

<u>D Coy</u>   From grid line mentioned above to grid line running E and W of H19 central to H22 central.

3/ When Companies are established on line of Bound 'B' Battalion HQ. will move forward to H8d 1.4.

4/ Move to Bound 'C' will not be made without orders.

ACKNOWLEDGE   Copy No 1 Retained
Issued at 7.0 am   2 Commd'g Officer
   3 A Coy
   4 B "
   5 C "
   6 D "

Capt
9th (N.Z.) Bn Northd Fus

SECRET   Copy No 1

                    9th (North Mimms) Bn, North'd Fus
Ref Map Sheet   Order No 62.
36 A N.E. 1/1000
SHEET
36A

1. INTENTION   The Battalion will be relieved in close
                   support of the 184th Infy Bde by the
                   2/6th Bn Warwicks Regt at about
                   3.30 pm today

2. RELIEF   On relief Companies will move out
                   by platoons at not less than 100 yard
                   interval to MEREDITH STATION where
                   they will entrain for LA LACQUE CAMP
                   Companies will close at junction of
                   light railway and LA MOTTE – MERVILLE
                   Road

3. TRENCH   All paper maps, air photos, and
   STORES etc.   Stores, excepting SOS, Very lights and
                   ground flares will be handed over
                   and receipts in duplicate obtained.
                   These receipts to be in Orderly Room
                   by 9.0 am tomorrow the 2nd inst.

4. LEWIS GUNS   D Coy L.G. limber will be packed
   COOKERS   at Battn HQ.   A B and C Coys
                   L.G. limbers will be at junction
                   of light railway and LES PURESBECQUES

Read where guns, magazines etc will be packed.

Dinners will be at 12.30 pm. O.C Coys. will then order drivers to report with cookers at Battn. H.Qrs. from whence they will proceed under Sergt. Topping to LA LACQUE CAMP.

5. GUIDES. 1 per platoon and 1 per Coy HQ to be at Battn. HQ at 1.30 pm

6. SAA O.C Coys will take steps to make up all deficiencies of S.A.A. on the man and for Lewis Guns before handing over.

7. TELEPHONE EQUIPMENT Telephone instruments will not be handed over.

8. COMPLETION OF RELIEF Will be notified to Battn. HQ. by code word on phone "PARTRIDGE" and also by runner.

ACKNOWLEDGE
Dated 1st Sept. 1918

A.W. Frankston
Capt & Adjt.
9th (N.H.) Bn Northd. Fus.

Copies To
No 1. - WAR DIARY
2. - Retained
3. - O.C A Coy
4. - " B "
5. - " C "
6. - " D "
7. - " HQ "
8. - Q.M & T.O

"A" Form
MESSAGES AND SIGNALS.

Army Form C. 2121
(In pads of 100.)
No. of Message. 2

Prefix: SM Code: 2A Words: 37
Office of Origin and Service Instructions

R.o.F.U

This message is on a/c of:
MOZI
Service
1/9/18

Recd. at 10.35 a.m.
Date 1/9/18
From R.U.T.U
By Pte Gibbs 9

TO: MOLI VIA RUTU

Sender's Number: V171
Day of Month: 1
In reply to Number: —
AAA

Train arrangement as follows aaa Train takes back VOPA leaving MEREDITH 3.30 pm for CROWE aaa Train takes back MOLI leaving MEREDITH 4.30 pm for CROWE aaa LOGI will match

From: RUFU

Appendix "C"

Orders:

Royal Warwicks Regt
Royal Berks Regt
1st Bn East Lancs Regt

SECRET   Copy No. 16

9th (Northd Hussars) Battn Northumberland Fusiliers
Order No. 68.   19-9-1918.

1. INTENTION	The Battalion will relieve the 9/th Battn Royal Warwick Regt. in the Left Battn Subsection of the advance guard tomorrow night (20/21 September 1918). On completion of relief the Battalion come under orders of G.O.C 182nd Infantry Brigade until night of 21/22 September when the Battalion reverts to Command of G.O.C 183 Infantry Brigade.
2. DISPOSITIONS.	Companies will be disposed as follows:— "B" Coy Left Front Coy. H.Q. H8.a.8.4. "C" Coy Centre Front Coy H.Q. H7.b.9.1. "D" Coy Right Front Coy H.Q. H19.c.5.8. "A" Coy Support Company H.Q. G.24.a.2.8. Battn. H.Q. G.18.a.15.15.
3. MOVE and INTERVALS	Companies and H.Qs will move off in the following order. B. C. D. A. and H.Q. Details commencing with B Coy at 5.15 pm. The remainder at intervals of 5 minutes. After passing L.9.d.1.1. Companies will move by platoons at 100 yards interval.
4. ROUTE	By light railway to L.9.d.1.1. thence across the LYS by the footbridge at 9.16.b.5.6. and thence to No 83 billet in the BAC-ST-MAUR – SAILLY Road.
5. GUIDES	One guide per platoon and Coy HQ to be at No 83 Billet at 6.45 p.m.
6. TRENCH STORES	All S.O.S. grenades, flares, tools, reserve S.A.A, maps and air photos will be taken over and detail of work in hand asked.
7. GREATCOATS & HAVERSACKS	All greatcoats, haversacks and stores to be left at Quartermasters Stores will be stacked at entrance to camp by 10.0 a.m. – L.22.A.central
8. LEWIS GUNS & COOKING UTENSILS	Lewis Gun Limbers and cooking utensils will be at No 83 Billet at 6.45 pm. Company Commanders will decide where to unload Lewis Guns and Magazines.
9. TAKING OVER PARTY	O.C. Companies, 1 Officer per Company, 1 N.C.O. per platoon, 1 Lewis Gunner per Team, 1 Signaller per Company, all Battalion observers, 2 H.Q. Signallers and 4 H.Q. runners will parade at Battn. H.Q. at 9.30 a.m. to reconnoitre dispositions in the line. The Company Commanders and H.Q. Runners will return on Completion.
10. SKETCHES	A sketch showing dispositions in detail will be forwarded to Battn H.Q. by 12 noon the 21st September 1918.
11. COMPLETION OF RELIEF.	Completion of relief will be forwarded to Battalion H.Q. by TELEPHONE and by RUNNER using the code word "LAUGH"

ACKNOWLEDGE.
Issued by runner at 8.30 pm

Copy No. 1 OC 9/th Bn Royal Warwick Regt.
          2 H.Q. 183 Infy Bde
          3 OC A Coy
          4   B "
          5   C "
          6   D "
          7 Liaison Officer
          8 Adjutant
          9 Officer i/c H.Q.
         10 Medical Officer
         11 Quartermaster
         12 Transport Officer
         13 Battn S/Bearer
         14 Orderly Book
         15 War Diary
         16 FILE

A. Freshwater
Captain & Adjutant
9th (Northd Hussars) Battn
Northumberland Fusiliers

Job

SECRET   9th (N'the Hussars) Batt. Northumberland
REF. MAP SHEETS   Fusiliers   Order No. 05   24th Oct. 1918
36A N.W. 1/40,000
36A N.E. 1/20,000

1. INTENTION	The Battalion will be relieved in the fast Sect. sector of the Advance Guard Brigade zone, on the night of 29th by the 7th Royal Berkshire Regiment.
2. DISPOSITION	D Coy will be relieved by 'A' Coy Royal Berks Regt. C " " " 'B' " B " " " 'C' " H " " " 'D' " On completion of relief the Battalion will proceed by march route via L.16.a. S.(?) (Hd Qrs) YHM I.II.M).
3. ROUTE	Any route to G.9.d.11, thence by light Railway to L.16.a. 3 where guides from details will be met. On arrival of the guides the platoons will be entrained as per at G.9.d.11.
4. GUIDES	1 Guide per platoon, and 1 per Coy H.Q. and 1 per Battn. will meet above Ties at No 3 Billet at 8.0 p.m.
5. TRENCH STORES	All S.A.A. Grenades, Flares, Tools, Reserve S.A.A., flags, His props(?), details of work in hand and food containers will be handed over and receipts obtained in duplicate. These receipts to be in Orderly Room by 12 noon 24th inst.
6. PISTOL TINS	All pistol tins are to be brought in and loaded on a limber which will be provided for them at Regimental Aid Post.
7. LEWIS GUNS & COOKING UTENSILS	B. C. and D. Companies own Gun limbers will be loaded at G.18.C.5.15. A Coy's own Gun Limber at A Coy H.Q.
8. TRANSPORT	Transport Officer will arrange for Mess Cart to be at Regt. Aid Post at 5.0 p.m. and one and a half limber to be at Battn H.Q. at 6.0 p.m.
9. ARRIVAL IN BILLETS	The Quartermaster will arrange if possible to have hot tea or soup ready for Companies on arrival.
10. COMPLETION OF RELIEF	Notification of completion of relief will be forwarded to Battn old H.Q. by telephone and by runner using code word:- "BULGARIA". ACKNOWLEDGE Issued by runner 3.0 p.m.

Copy No 1. CO A de Royal Berks Regt.
         2. I/3 Inf'y Bde
         3. OC A Coy
         4. " B "
         5. " C "
         6. " D "
         7. Signalling Officer
         8. Adjutant
         9. Intelligence Officer
         10. Medical Officer   15. RSM
         11. Lewis Gun Officer   16. Spare
         12. Transport Officer
         13. Hd Qrs Coy
         14. Files

A.E. Roberts
Captain & Adjutant
9th (NH) Battn Northd Fusiliers

War Diary

SECRET
                    9th Battn (NH) Northumberland Fusiliers
                         Orders No 67 Sept 12th 1918
                                                        Copy No 10
          Ref map Sheet
          36 NNE & NW
          1/20,000

(1) INTENTION   While the Brigade is in Reserve it will man the SOUTHERN
                 sector of the CORPS battle line — E Battn will be in Brigade
                 Reserve

(2) BOUNDARIES (a) SOUTHERN LYS CANAL EASTWARD to NOUVEAU MONDE —
                   G34 c 30.70 — G35 c 00.30 — & to G35 c 00.35
               (b) NORTHERN. Grid line between L13 and L19 EAST to
                   L17 do.o thence on a straight line to L29 Central

(3) FRONTAGE
    OF   NOUVEAU MONDE (G27c) - WEST bank of the LYS - WEST bank
    CORPS   of STILBECQUE

(4) DISPOSITIONS 4th E LAN R. FRONT LINE NOUVEAU MONDE and along W bank
                  of LYS. To be held by defended localities
                  11th SUFFOLK SUPPORT. Two Companies in area L24 and
                  L25 std. Remainder of Battalion stand by.
                  9th NORTHD FUS. RESERVE. General line from LYS BRIDGE
                  to LEAM FARM. Two Companies in front line and Two in
                  Support.

(5) BATTALION   "D" Company Right Front Company "A" Coy Right Support Coy
    DISPOSITIONS   "C"   "   Left Front Company   "B" " Left Support Coy

                  INTER COMPANY BOUNDARY. MERVILLE — ESTAIRES ROAD
                  inclusive to D and A Companies
                  "D" Company will hold the Front line with:-
                      One platoon at L28d 70.50. One platoon at L28 B 70.90.
                      Two platoons in Support at L28 b 40.85
                  "C" Company will hold the Front line with:-
                      Two platoons at L33 c 30.30. One platoon at L28a 50.75
                      Two platoons Support at L27 b 30.42
                  "A" Company in Support at L28 b 75.65
                  "B" Company in Support at WANDLE FARM L22 c 75.40
                  Company Headquarters of D & C will be their Supporting
                  Platoons. Company H.Q.'s of A & B with their Companies
                  Battalion H.Q. will be at YAPP FARM

(6) VERY LIGHTS   On receipt of orders to man VERY LIGHTS — S.O.S. Ground flares
                  &c will be issued by Coy Stores Etc

(7) TRANSPORT   On receipt of order to move Bn. Tpt Officer will send teams
                  for all vehicles at Batt H.Q. and all riding horses. Lewis
                  Gun limbers will accompany their Companies. All other
                  vehicles will await order at Bn H.Q.

(8) COMMUNICATIONS When in position Coys will immediately establish visual
                    communication with Bn H.Q. Station

(9) REPORTS   Coys will report by visual and runner when in position

(10) ACKNOWLEDGE

(11) DISTRIBUTION   Copy No 1. 103 Infty Brigade   Copy No 9. QM
                         " 2. County Officer   " 10. WAR DIARY
                         " 3. Adjutant   " 11. FILE
                         " 4. OC "A" Coy
                         " 5. " "B"
                         " 6. " "C"
                         " 7. " "D"
                         " 8. T Officer

                                              [signature]
                                              Lt Colonel & Adjutant
                                              9th (NH) Battn Northd Fusiliers

War Diary

SECRET   Copy No 9.

Reference Map.
Sheet 36A NE   9th (NF) Batt Northumberland
1/20.000   Fusiliers Order No 64.
                              5.9.1918.

1. **INTENTION.** The Battalion will move tomorrow 6th inst to RUE MONTIGNY and occupy the area vacated by the 11th Bn SUFFOLK REGT.

2. **ROUTE.** Any.

3. **STARTING POINT.** Each Company from its own area.

4. **TIME**
       A Coy   10.40 am
       B "   10.50 am
       C "   11.0 am
       D "   11.10 am
       HQ "   11.20 am

5. **COMPANY AREAS.** Each Company will take over the area of corresponding Coy of the 11th SUFFOLK REGT.

6. **TRANSPORT.** Lewis Gun Limbers and Cookers will proceed with their Coys. The Mess Cart, Mess cart & Water carts will move with Battn HQrs.

7. VALISES &) The Valise Cart and Mess
   MESS STORES.) Cart will return to NEUF
   BERQUIN for valises, these to be ready
   at each Company H.Q. at 9.30a
   Mess Stores will be taken on L.G.
   Limbers.

8. BATTN H.Q.   Will be established at
                K.7.d.25.30.

9. REPORTS.   Companys will report their
               arrival in new area giving map
               references as early as possible.

10. TRENCH   To be taken to new
    SHELTERS   area. These will go with
               valises.

11. ACKNOWLEDGE.
     By this runner.

     Issued at 10 pm

     Copy No 1-4. Companies
          5. O ½ H.Q
          6. T.O & Q.M.
          7. 183 Infy Bde
          8. FILE
          9. WAR DIARY.

     W. Grankurt
     Capt & Adjt
     9th (N.H.) Roy. North'd
     Fusiliers

SECRET   COPY N° 2

REF. MAP   9th (N.H) Bn Northumberland Fus.
SHEETS.   Order N° 65   7/9/18.
36ᴬ ᴀɴᴅ 36
1/40,000

INTENTION.   The 183rd Inf Brigade will relieve
             the 182nd Inf Bde as Adv. Guard
             on the night 6/7 and 7/8th Sept.
                  This Batt. will relieve the
             2/6th Royal Warwick Regt in support
             on the night 7/8th.

ROUTE.   L.14.C.80.60 — ESTAIRES RD —
             G.25.D.55.70 — G.24.C.55.20 —
             G.22.C.15.15.

STARTING   Road junction L.14.C.90.60
POINT

TIME   5.30 p.m.

ORDER OF   B — D — A — C — H.Q.
MARCH

AREA.   B Coy to G.24.A — G.18.C
               (Coy H.Q. G.17.D.55.45)

             D Coy to G.23.D

             A Coy to G.22.B — G.17.C (Coy HQ G.22.B.7.3)

             C Coy to G.28.B.

BATTN. H.Q. at G.26.B.1.4.

INTERVALS — 200 yards between companies

GUIDES — 1 Per Coy and 1 per platoon to be at G.22.C.15.15 at 7.15 pm

TAKING OVER — 2/Lt Y. Curson, 2 signallers for Battn H.Q. will proceed this morning to take over for Battn H.Q.

1 Officer per Coy, with 1 N.C.O per platoon + 1 signaller per coy will parade at Battn H.Q. at 1 pm to move forward & take over

All flares, S.O.S. rockets, Verey Lights, shovels, & work in hand will be taken over, receipts given

HANDING OVER — A party from 2/Bat R Warwick Regt will arrive this morning to take over Coy areas here. Our trench shelters will be handed over & receipts obtained in triplicate

VALISES, STORES, GT COATS, TENTS, HAVERSACKS etc — All will be ready for loading at Coy H.Q. at 11 am. Greatcoats to be tied up in bundles by sections. Coats & haversacks to be plainly marked.

RATIONS
AND
WATER — Cookers will return to Transport after tea. Cooking will be done at Coy H.Q. by cooks in Camp kettles. Rations to each Coy HQ and Battn HQ by limbers. Both water carts will accompany Battn. 20 petrol tins per Coy + 10 for H.Q. will be sent up nightly.

Mess Cart and half limber will be required for Battn HQ.

LEWIS
GUNS — Lewis Gun limbers will accompany their companies and will proceed as far as practicable before being unloaded.

DISPOSITIONS — Coys will forward sketch showing dispositions by 10 am 8th inst.

RELIEF — Will be notified to Bun H.Q. by wire & runner by code as follows

    'A' Coy   TWICE
    'B' "   TWO
    'C' "   ARE
    'D' "   FOUR

Issued by runner at
7.30 am.   ACKNOWLEDGE

Copy N° 1   1Bn Infy Bde
      2   C O
      3   ADJT
      4   OC A Coy
      5   " B
      6   " C
      7   " D
      8   " QM
      9   " T O
     10   " M O
     11   " O/C H.Q.
     12   " File
     13   " War diary
     14   " S + Cook
     15   " 2/6 R. Warwick Regt

A W Freshwater
Capt & /Adjt

SECRET   Copy No 15
REF MAP SHEET 9th (N.H.) Batt. Northumberland
36A NE & 36 F.   Fusiliers Order No 66
1/20000 1/40 000   11. 9. 18.

1. __INTENTION__.   The Battalion will be relieved in
Support of the Advance Guard by the 2/4
Batt. Royal Berkshire Regt on the night of
the 11/12th Sept 1918.
   On completion of relief Coys
will proceed to bivouacs at YAM FARM
L 22 a 4.8. when the Battalion will be
in Support to the Brigade which is allotted
the Northern Section of the Battle Line.

2. __TRENCH STORES__   All S.O.S. Grenades, S.A.A, Hand
grenades, flares, Shovels and air photos will
be handed over and details of work in
hand. Receipts in triplicate to be taken.

3. __ADVANCE PARTIES__ Advance parties of the 2/4 Royal
Berks will arrive at Companies at about
12 noon. 1 Officer per Coy and 1 N.C.O.
per platoon will assemble at this Batt.
H.Q. at 11.0 am and proceed to take
over accommodation at YAM FARM.

4 GUIDES 1 Guide per platoon and 1 per Coy. H.Q. of A, B & C Coys will rendezvous at the bridge at G.16.c.75.60 at 6.30 p.m. where they will report to Lieut V Curson. These guides must be taken to the bridge given above by a Coy runner. B Coy Commander will provide post guides for the platoon in posts at his Coy HQ at about 7.30 pm. Two guides from Battn H.Q. will meet the Lewis Gun Limbers of the 3 Coys 1/4 Royal Berks disposed on the SOUTH SIDE of the LYS at road junction G.22.c.10.20 at 7.0 pm and guide them as follows:-

The Limber of Coy relieving C Coy at C Coy H.Q.

The Limbers of the Coys relieving A & B Coys to No 2 Billet (Cookhouse) at SAILLY where they will be handed over to their Company Commanders.

5 ROUTE Companies of 1/4 Royal Berts moving to South Side of river will move as follows. Companies relieving A & B Coys will cross LYS at G.16.b.40.40
Company relieving C Coy will cross LYS at G.21.b.80.50.

Companies of the Battn will move by platoons at 200 yards interval to road junction at 925 d 85.70 from thence by Coys independently at at least 200 yards interval

6. **WATER TINS** Companies will ensure that all water tins supplied to them by Battalion are brought to Coy dumps to go out on transport

7. **TRANSPORT** The Transport Officer will arrange for the necessary transport to convey Lewis Guns, water tins, medical stores, signalling equipment, camp kettles, Mess Kit etc to YAN FARM. These vehicles to be at the various dumps at 7.15 pm.

8. **COMPLETION OF RELIEF** The Completion of relief will be wired to Battn HQ by following Code:-
    - A Coy — WOULD'NT
    - B " — DO
    - C " — US
    - D " — HARM.

Should wire be disconnected Completion will be forwarded to Battn HQ by runner.

ACKNOWLEDGE
Issued by runner at 7.30 am

Copy No. 1	1/4-Bn Royal Berk. Regt.
2	183 Inty Bde
3	OC A Coy
4	- B -
5	- C -
6	- D -
7	Comdg Officer
8	Adjutant
9	O. i/c H.Q.
10	M.O.
11	Q.M.
12	T.O
13	Batt. S.M.
14	War Diary
15	FILE

J Also dfray 2 Lt
for Capt & Adjt
9th (Northumberland Hussars) Batt.
Northumberland Fusiliers.

SECRET.   COPY No. 2

Reference Map:
1:36A. 1/40,000

9th (Northumberland Hussars) Battn Northumberland Fusiliers
Order No 63.   5. September 1918

1. INTENTION.	The Battalion will move to NEUF BERQUIN area by light railway and march route today 5th September 1918
2. ROUTE.	Entrain at CROWE STATION thence by train to GURNARDS CROSS. March route – Road junction K29 b 05.50 – ROBEKMETZ – NEUF BERQUIN.
3. STARTING POINT.	CROWE STATION.
4. TIME.	12-45 pm
5. DRESS.	Marching Order. Steel helmets. Care to be taken that mess tins, mugs and plates etc are packed in the packs and haversacks. No squad bags or bundles are to be carried in the hand or tied on to the equipment.
6. ORDER OF MARCH.	Hd.Qrs, D. A. B. C. This order also for entraining
7. INTERVALS.	After detraining, intervals of 100 yards will be maintained between Companies.
8. MESS KIT STORES, VALISES ETC.	All valises, stores, etc to remain behind are to be stacked at the entrance to the Camp by 12 noon. The Transport Officer will arrange for their collection. O.C. Companies are held responsible that Lewis Gun Limbers are correctly packed.
9. TRANSPORT.	The following Transport will accompany the Battalion. Lewis Gun Limbers – Cookers – Watercarts (full) – Maltese Cart – Mess Cart. These vehicles will proceed by march route to Road junction L13 b 95.05 moving by road running through J21-25-29-30 and MERVILLE.
10. TAKING OVER & HANDING OVER.	Lieut J.H. Godfrey, 1 NCO per Coy and 1 for the H.Q. for billeting, 1 man per Coy and Battn. H.Q. for rations, and all Pioneers will parade at 9.00 am at Orderly Room to move forward. The Quartermaster will hand over Camp. Billets and Company areas are to be left scrupulously clean.
11. WATCHES.	One Officer per Company will report to the Adjutant at 12 noon to synchronise watches.
12.	ACKNOWLEDGE. Issued by runner at 7.0am.

A.V. Freshwater
Captain & Adjutant
9th (NH) Battn. Northumberland Fusiliers

Copies to:-
No 1. War Diary
2. File
3. OC A Coy
4. OC B Coy
5. OC C Coy
6. OC D Coy
7. Commg. Officer
8. Quartermaster
9. Transport Officer
10. Medical Officer
11. O. i/c H.Q.
12. 183 Infy Bde
13. Spare
14. Spare

Appendix "D"

Special Order of the Day

SPECIAL ORDER OF THE DAY
By FIELD-MARSHAL SIR DOUGLAS HAIG
K.T., G.C.B., G.C.V.O., K.C.I.E
Commander-in-Chief, British Armies in France.

The following citations which appeared in the Orders of the Day, No. 371, of the 5th French Army, on August 20th, 1918, on behalf of 2nd Battalion Devonshire Regiment, and 1/4th Battalion King's Shropshire Light Infantry, are published for the information of all ranks:—

(Translation.)

2ND BATTALION DEVONSHIRE REGIMENT.

On the 27th May, 1918, at a time when the British trenches were being subjected to fierce attacks, the 2nd Battalion the Devonshire Regiment repelled successive enemy assaults with gallantry and determination, and maintained an unbroken front till a late hour. The staunchness of this Battalion permitted defences south of A——— to be organized and their occupation by reinforcements to be completed.

Inspired by the sangfroid of their gallant Commander, in the face of an intense bombardment, the few survivors of the Battalion, though isolated and without hope of assistance, held on to their trenches north of the river and fought to the last with an unhesitating obedience to orders.

Thus the whole Battalion—Colonel, 28 Officers, and 552 Non-Commissioned Officers and men—responded with one accord and offered their lives in ungrudging sacrifice to the sacred cause of the Allies.

1/4TH BATTALION KING'S SHROPSHIRE LIGHT INFANTRY.

On the 6th June, 1918, when the right flank of a British Brigade was being seriously threatened by the progress of a heavy enemy attack, the 1/4th Battalion of the King's Shropshire Light Infantry, which had been held in reserve, was called upon to counter-attack an important position from which their comrades had just been ejected.

With magnificent dash this Battalion rushed the hill on which the enemy had established themselves, inflicting heavy losses on them, and in the course of hand-to-hand fighting captured an officer and 28 other ranks.

Thanks to this gallant and spirited recapture of the key to the whole defensive position the line was completely restored.

The dash, energy, and intrepidity with which, on this memorable occasion, the 1/4th Battalion King's Shropshire Light Infantry carried all before it was largely responsible for the retrieval of a situation which had temporarily become critical.

BERTHELOT,
General Commanding Fifth Army

Commander-in-Chief,
British Armies in France.

General Headquarters,
September 26th, 1918.

PRINTED IN FRANCE BY ARMY PRINTING AND STATIONERY SERVICES.

PRESS A—9/18

SECRET.   COPY No.

2/7TH BATTALION THE ROYAL WARWICKSHIRE REGIMENT.

ORDER NO. 37.   30TH SEPTEMBER 1916.

Ref. Maps. Sheet. 36.N.W. and 36A.S.W. 1/20000.

---

1. The 9TH Batt. NORTHUMBERLAND FUSILIERS will relieve 2/7th.Batt. R.WAR.R. in the left Sub-Sector on night 30/31st inst.

2. **TABLE OF RELIEF.**

NORTH. FUS.	2/7.R.WAR.R.	DISPOSITIONS.
"B" Coy.	"W" Coy.	LEFT FRONT.
"G" "	"X" "	CENTRE FRONT.
"D" "	"Y" "	RIGHT FRONT.
"A" "	"Z" "	SUPPORT.

3. **GUIDES.**
   1 Guide per Platoon, and one for Coy H.Q. will report to Battn. Headquarters at 7 p.m.

4. **TRENCH STORES.**
   All Trench Stores including S.O.S.Grenades, Flares, Tools, Air photos, Gas Suits, and documents in connection with Sector will be handed over and receipts obtained.
   Copy of receipts will be forwarded to Battn.H.Q. by 9 p.m. 31st inst.

5. Care will be taken to hand over all information including disposition of Vickers Guns and Trench Mortars to incoming Coys. Water arrangements will also be handed over.

6. Completion of relief will be reported to Battn. Headquarters by code word "PERU".

7. On completion of relief Coys will move to area L.23. (sketch attached).

   ROUTE. Optional to G.15.a.90.15. - thence S.W. to MEEALREN - Road Junction at G.26.d.90.50. - L.30.c.b.6. - thence N.N.W. to Road Junction at L.23.c.4.0. where C.S.M.'s will meet Coys and act as Guides to Billets.

8. **TRANSPORT.** See Administrative Instructions.
   Coy Commanders chargers will be at cross roads at G.15.a.90.15.

9. Arrival in new area will be reported to Battalion Headquarters by code word "BRAHE".

   Battalion Headquarters in new area is situated at LES FARM at L.23.a.2.7.

10. **ACKNOWLEDGE.**

                                        sgd.   D.L.APPLETS. Capt. & A/Adjt.
    Issued at 11-30 A.M.   2/7th.Batt. R.War.R.

    Distribution.   Copy. No. 1. Commanding Officer.
                              2. "W" Coy.
                              3. "X" "
                              4. "Y" "
                              5. "Z" "
                              6. 9TH.Bn.North.Fus.
                              7. T/14.TRENCH.
                              8. Recs.
                              9. File.

SECRET.   COPY NO. 10

2/4th BATTALION, ROYAL BERKSHIRE REGIMENT.

OPERATION ORDER NO. 4.
By
Lieut.-Col. C.R.C. BOYLE, D.S.O., Cmdg.   10.9.1918.

Reference Map Sheet 36.A. N.E. 1/20,000.
& 36 N.W. 1/20,000.

1. The Battalion will relieve the 9th Bn. Northumberland Fusiliers in Reserve tomorrow night.

2. Companies will relieve Companies of the 9th N.F. letter for letter.

3. Coy. Commanders will arrange with Coys of the 9th N.F. they are relieving for Guides, Cooking, etc.

4. Advance Party of 1 Officer per Company and 1 N.C.O. per Platoon will be at H.Q. of 9th N.F. at G.9.d.1.1. at 11 a.m.

5. Coys. will move off from present positions in the following order :- H.Q., "B", "A", "C", "D". starting at 5.30 p.m. 200^x between Platoons. Route - LEAM FARM - PETIT BOIS BRIDGE - thence along Railway. One Limber per Coy. with Lewis Guns and Rations will meet Coys. on Road G.9.d.4.0. and go forward with Coys at at 6.30. p.m.

6. All Flares, Very Lights, S.O.S. Grenades, Tools, Reserve S.A.A. and Grenades will be taken over and receipts forwarded to Battn. H.Q. by 9.0 a.m. 12th.

7. Completion of Relief will be wired to Bn. H.Q. by Code message :- "Operation Order No. 4 Noted".

8. All Packs, Officers' Kits & Coy. Stores to be stacked on the Road by Coys by 2.0 p.m.

9. All Trench Shelters, etc., will be left standing as at present.

10. Acknowledge.

        Issued at 10.0 p.m.   (Signed) F. ASHWORTH,
                                        Captain & A/Adjutant,
                                   2/4th Bn. Royal Berkshire Regt.

        Distribution :-

            Copy Nos. 1 - 4   O.C. Coys.
                      5   Q.M.
                      6   T.O.
                      7   R.S.M.
                      8   War Diary.
                      9   File.
                      10   Spare.

Copy No. 12

1st Bn. E. Lancashire Regt. O.O. No P38

Reference Sheet 36 N.W.

War Diary.

1. On night 25/26 inst. fighting patrols of B and D Coys of 1st E. Lan. Regt. will advance and occupy BARLETTE FARM H.26.a.4.4 and JUNCTION POST H.32.a.8.3 respectively.

2. ARTILLERY SUPPORT
   (a) Divnl Artillery have co-operated in firing on selected targets during the past few days. On night 25/26 inst. Howers. will concentrate on BARLETTE FM. and JUNCTION POST from Zero to Zero plus 5 minutes, when they will lift from these two localities and concentrate on roads running North and East from them where they will remain until Zero plus 35 minutes, when fire will cease. A proportion of Howers. is being detailed for counter battery work, if required.
   (b) The Divnl. Field Artillery of 18 pdr. batteries and 4.5" How. batteries will carry out a creeping barrage and will put down a box barrage to each objective (vide attached barrage traces).
   (c) 6" Howers. will assist in the concentration of Howers. on BARLETTE FM. and JUNCTION POST from Zero plus 5 minutes to Zero plus 5 minutes. After Zero plus 5 minutes they will fire on selected targets as detailed in 306 Bde. R.F.A. O.O. No. 140.
   (d) O.C. 183rd L.T.M.B. will report to O. 1st E. Lan. Regt. for orders.

3. During the period of fire of 18 pdrs. from Zero plus 11 minutes to Zero plus 13 minutes gas (lacrymatory) and 40 incendiary gas drums will be fired on BARLETTE FM. and JUNCTION POST.

4. MACHINE GUNS will co-operate as follows:-
   (a) Guns from about H.14.c. and H.19.a. will fire on enclosures in H.20.b. and d.
   (b) Guns from H.31. will fire on H.32.c. and d.
   (c) Guns from C.36. will fire on the Cross Roads H.26.d.10.15 and Roads thence running N.E. to FLEURBAIX.
   Guns to open fire will be Zero plus 5 minutes.

5. The lines of departure for fighting patrols will be
   (a) In case of BARLETTE FM.
       1. One platoon from about H.25.d.8.8
       2. One platoon from line of light railway H.25.b.85.95.
   (b) In the case of JUNCTION POST
       1. One platoon from H.31.b.90.70
       2. One platoon from H.31.b.90.20
   Patrols will advance at Zero plus 5 minutes keeping as close under the 18 pdr. barrage as possible.

6. DRESS Fighting Order. Every man will have tied on his right arm above the elbow a strip of 4" x 6" for identification purposes.

7. SUBSIDIARY OPERATION At Zero plus 5 minutes the A. Coy. will detail a fighting patrol of strength of one platoon to advance and occupy building and orchard about H.20.c.50.40

8. CONSOLIDATION.
All consolidation will be carried out EAST of the objectives.
Advanced dumps of R.E. Stores have been formed at H.25.d.4.3
and H.31.b.6.4. for this purpose.

9. COMMUNICATION.
Relay posts will be established at A & D Coy H.Q.
Runners will stand by throughout the operation to relay messages at the double to Bn. H.Q.

10. PRECAUTIONS IN THE EVENT OF COUNTER ATTACK
(a) In the event of counter attack and reinforcements being required the Officers commanding the garrisons at BARLETTE FM. or JUNCTION POST will fire WHITE very lights in quick succession. Should this signal be given from BARLETTE FARM the O.C. A. Coy. will at once reinforce with one platoon, if from JUNCTION POST O.C. C Coy. will reinforce with one platoon.

(b) The O.C. 11th Suffolk Regt. has been ordered in the event of above signal being given to order the Coy. of 11th Suffolks now in Q.21.a & b. to occupy our now held by the left Coy. in the Outpost line of Resistance.

(c) O.C. Advanced Guard Artillery will arrange for a protective barrage to come down in the form of a box playing round BARLETTE FM. and JUNCTION POST when called for by the garrisons. This barrage will be supplemented by M.G. fire by arrangements to be made by O.C. Machine Gun Battalion.
The signal for this barrage will be a rifle grenade bursting into Red over GREEN over YELLOW. S.O.S. Signal for remainder of front remains unchanged.

11. IDENTIFICATIONS
Prisoners of War, documents, and identifications of any sort (eg. shoulder straps) will be sent to Bn H.Q. as quickly as possible.

12. Zero hour will be notified later.

13. ACKNOWLEDGE.

W Parkin
Lieut & Adjt
for Lt Col Commdg.

Distribution

Copy No 1   O.C. A Coy
       2   B
       3   C
       4   D   (without Barrage tracing)
       5   193rd Inf Bde   (without Barrage tracing)
       6   11th Suffolks   (— do —)
       7   3rd .... (— do —)
       8   B Coy. 61st M.G. Bn. (— do —)
       9   C Coy. 61st M.G. Bn. (— do —)
      10   183 L.T.M.B.   (— do —)
      11   File   (— do —)
      12   War Diary

Appendix F

Training Programmes

Sept. 1918

9th (Northd. Hussars) Batn (Northumberland Fusiliers)

Programme of Work for period 3rd – 7th September 1918.

DAY	9 – 10	10 – 11	11 – 12	12 – 1	2 – 3
Tuesday	Regtl Parade 9.58	[drawing/running drill]	Rifle Exercises	Rifle — Hours of COs Inspn — Kiev practice R.B. & L.E – Regimental	NCOs Bayonet fighting
Wednesday	All Officers and NCOs	[training notes]	Night Training Night Firing Musketry	Platoon Rifle & LG Bayonet Platoon drill	Relief of Platoons in line, working SG Lewis Gun
Thursday	Route March	A Full will be made in Types of [?] for Ranging	Bn Sports in Effort
Friday	Platoon drill	Platoon drill	2 hour P.T. & D.E. ½ hour Musketry	Battalion drill	NCOs Bombs Musketry

NOTES:
1. Private Soldier's NCOs to perfect latrines
2. Bombs to be made when not needed. Drill Order N.S.R. Steel Helmets
3. All panels "Steel in profile"

9th (Northumberland) Battn Northumberland Fusiliers.

TRAINING PROGRAMME for PERIOD 12th - 15th SEPTEMBER 1918.

DAY.	9.0 am to 10.0 am	10.0 am to 10.30 am	10.30 am to 11.0 am	11.0 am to 11.30 am	11.30 am to 12 noon	12 noon to 1.0 pm
THURSDAY/	Inspection of Arms, equipment etc.		Recreational training	Section Drill	Platoon drill	Platoon attack
FRIDAY/	All Officers & NCOs Gas Exp. Demonstration		Box Respirator drill		Platoon Attack	P.T. & B.F.
SATURDAY/	All Officers & NCOs		P.T. and B.F.		Battalion attack enemy out post line	
SUNDAY/	DIVINE SERVICES					

W Wickworth
Capt & Adjt

4th (N.H.) Battn Northumberland Fusiliers

Training Programme for Period 16-18 October 1918

	8am	1pm	3pm
MONDAY	Company training. Extended order drill by Coy Comdrs for good Coy Sergt Regt during grenade attack		Inspection of N.C.O's by Lieutenant Colonel Lectures on machine guns and bren drawing
TUESDAY	Company training. M.G's and L.T. M.B schools		Lectures & training from act. Infantry. Spl Class & Conference
WEDNESDAY	Battalion attack from 10-12. Proceed to camp for rest of day		Inspection by Brigadier Return to Canteens & General Reserve Billets

Ult. Thrichman
Lt Col u/c/4th

D. D. & L., London, E.C.
P 1487. Wt. W 9660/1669. 100,000 12/14. W 21.

COVER
FOR
BRANCH MEMORANDA.

Unregistered.

Referred to	Date	Referred to	Date
9th N. Fus: Oct 1918			

36d

Army Form C. 2118.

9th (Northumberland Hussars) Battn.
Northumberland Fusiliers

WAR DIARY
or
INTELLIGENCE SUMMARY.
(Erase heading not required.)

22/6/18

G⁹ North Hussars Battⁿ Northern Fusiliers

APPENDICES

A. 183 Inf⁽ᵞ⁾ Bde Operation Orders
B. 9 (N.H) Batt. North Fusiliers Orders
C. Reports on attempted capture of Works at H—
D. Special Order of the day.

G. Thorne, Major
O.C. 9. N.F.

WAR DIARY
INTELLIGENCE SUMMARY

9th (Northumberland Hussars) Battn. Northumberland Fusiliers

October 1918

Army Form C. 2118.

Place	Date	Hour	Summary of Events and Information	Remarks and references to Appendices
YAM FARM	Oct 1		Training am for Brigade 9.0-9.30 am Commanding Officers Inspection. Orders Received to move to STOZNISCZOWE (See order No 2.24)	AW
YAM FARM	2		Battalion moved by route march to LES CISEAUX via Pont ROSSIGNEZ NEUVILLE - BUDOIGNIES THUM STEENBECQUE Battalion arrived in billets about 5.0 pm having had dinner en route	APP B Oct 13
LES CISEAUX	3		Coys turned out their own training areas. Drill, turning into artillery formation from column of four, extended file ahead and control parties. Afternoon Payment parade and games. Bayonet fighting and games	AW
-do-	4		Companies parade am arrangements by Brigade artillery formation and attached rate Coy work out am B.F. and games	AW
-do-	5		Companies cleaning and fitting of equipment. Orders received to move by train.	AW

9th (Northumberland Hussars) Batt:
Northumberland Fusiliers

October 1918   Army Form C. 2118.

WAR DIARY
or
INTELLIGENCE SUMMARY.
(Erase heading not required.)

Place	Date	Hour	Summary of Events and Information	Remarks and references to Appendices
LES 6 ESSARTS	6		Battalion paraded at 8700 hours and marched to STEENBECQUE Station arriving about 900 hours. Large kit breakfast at Station and entrained at 1200 hours. Arrived detraining station DOULLENS about 1700 hours. Battalion formed up and marched to billets at POMMERA arriving about 2000 hours.	App A & B
POMMERA	7		Conformed shew & morning cleaning up and inspection of Coys afterwards at disposal of Company Commanders.	App
-do-	8		Battalion training. Practice in attack formation, extended order, fire discipline and Control. Also practice in the field Signal. Battalion Runners and one officer & Atkinson in conjunction with HK's Conferences goes on.	App
-do-	9		Battalion left billets at 1000 hours and marched to MONDICOURT STATION and entrained for forward area. Arrived near HAVRINCOURT about 1830 hours and marched to bivouac South of MOEUVRES (Sheet 57c E.27.67040) Arrived 2151 PM on the 9th and paraded by Coys	App 19 B

WAR DIARY
or
INTELLIGENCE SUMMARY.
(Erase heading not required.)

Northumberland Hussars
Northumberland

20/4th 1918

Army Form C. 2118.

Place	Date	Hour	Summary of Events and Information	Remarks and references to Appendices
BIVOUACS (E.7 b 70 40)	10		Battalion training in open warfare	AWF
-do-	11		Battalion training during the morning. Orders received about 1730 hours and moves off April 1730 hours 6. forward area. (ANTHING) (Sheet 5/c-L 3 @ 2. S)	AWF
BIVOUACS (L 3 a 2 S)	12		Continued training in open warfare. Salvage work and organised games during afternoon. Waving order issued to prepare for move forward.	AWF
-do-	13		SUNDAY. DIVINE SERVICES.	AWF
-do-	14		Battalion carried out operations as per Batta. Order No 71. Afternoon devoted to PT and B.F. and organised games.	APP 13. AWF

WAR DIARY
or
INTELLIGENCE SUMMARY.

(Erase heading not required.)

8th (Northumberland Hussars)
Northumberland Fusiliers

October 1918.

Army Form C. 2118.

Place	Date	Hour	Summary of Events and Information	Remarks and references to Appendices
BIVOUACS (L.9.2.5)	15th		Platoon and Company in attack. Company in Skirmishing in attacking strong points. Salvage work and organised games.	WK
-do-	16		Training as the previous day as the afternoon was devoted to Salvage work and organised games.	WK
-do-	17		Battalion training. Scheme was carried out on 1st and 2nd reception of A.T.C. by front line and B. Coys in support. A section devoted to salvage work and organised games. A feature was A Brigade Commander for all Officers (Order Issued) for next experience area forward area	WK
-do-	18		Battalion paraded at 0900 hours and marched to billets in outskirts of TO.AM.BRM South of a NOYELLES arriving about 1230 hours.	WK APPX E APPX E

WAR DIARY
INTELLIGENCE SUMMARY

9th (Northumberland Fusiliers)
Northumberland Fusiliers

October 1918

Army Form C. 2118.

Place	Date	Hour	Summary of Events and Information	Remarks and references to Appendices
Billets (H.Q. Ayette 28C.6.4)	19		Battalion training scheme Bath & attack. Received further move to forward area. Orders received and Battalion moved off about 1900 hours and arrived in Billets at AVESNES-LES-AUBERT about 23.15 hours.	M/F
AVESNES LES-AUBERT	20		Inspection of billets. Inspection of arms etc by Bde etc. R.A.A. Etc. During afternoon inspection of	M/F
-do-	21		In Billets. Battalion training in area @ 4.5.10.11 (Sheet 11 N.W.) 5 minutes Arms Drill, 15 minutes Close Order Drill and High Specialist. Exercise Battalion in attack. Was to be carried out by was cancelled.	M/F
-do-	22		Battalion training on same ground as on previous day. Where following was arrived out. 5 minutes Arms Drill 15 do Close Order Drill And exercise Company in attack. Move to forward area next day. Orders received for	M/F

WAR DIARY or INTELLIGENCE SUMMARY

Army Form C. 2118.

9th (Northumberland Hussars) Batt.
Northumberland Fusiliers

October 1918

Place	Date	Hour	Summary of Events and Information	Remarks and references to Appendices
AVESNES-LES-AUBERT	23		Battalion paraded at 0845 hours and marched to ST AUBERT preparatory to the advance and during night 23/24 Oct. Battalion left ST AUBERT about 2000 hours and relieved 5th Gloucesters Regt (19th Division) about 2345 hours in the line.	APPX A/B WD
Bath 48. (MAISON ROUGE)	24		The 153 Infy Bde (11th Bn Suffolk Regt on the LEFT and 9th N.F. Bn North Lancashire (RGH) with 4th Division on left attacked at 0400 hours. The Battalion made good progress and captured the villages of ST MARTIN and BERMERAIN and capturing 6 Officers and 150 other ranks, 4 trench mortars and M.G. machine guns. '17' and '9' Companies were in the front line with C & D Companies in support. The Battalion reached its final objective being the high ground 1500 yards NE of BERMERAIN but had to withdraw slightly owing to the Battalion on its left being held up by strong resistance of the enemy in the village of VENDEGIES. The 1/4 Bath & E.S. London Regt. took over in support and also served the two line Battns. and 184 Brigade came into supp.t	WD

WAR DIARY or INTELLIGENCE SUMMARY

Army Form C. 2118.

9th (Northumberland Hussars) Battn
Northumberland Fusiliers

Oct 7th 1918

Place	Date	Hour	Summary of Events and Information	Remarks and references to Appendices
BUSIGNY (Map ref. D.10.b)	Oct 7th		The enemy made a counter attack about 1800 hours but were repulsed. Battalion ordered to move forward about 1900 hours to a cellar in the village of ST MARTIN. Orders were received about 2230 hours to withdraw the Battalion and to be in reserve. Companies ordered to withdraw and arrive in billets during the early hours of 25. Bty being last arrived at about 1600 hours. The casualties in the Battalion were very heavy especially in the East of the NCO's whom it appears they kept charged the enemy posts and at same time encouraging and urging on the men under him. The Casualties of Officers were:— Killed Captain V.H. Hamlin (acting Adjt) 2nd Lieut H.C. Foreman (O Coy) Wounded Lieut J. Pearson (OC B Coy) 2nd Lieut Quinn 2nd Lieut Elvin 2nd Lieut W. Hamlin Lieut n/ Henson (Transport Officer wounded whilst taking up the rations)	

WAR DIARY or INTELLIGENCE SUMMARY

Army Form C. 2118.

9th [Northumberland Fusiliers] Battn.
Northumberland Fusiliers

October 1918

Instructions regarding War Diaries and Intelligence Summaries are contained in F. S. Regs., Part II. and the Staff Manual respectively. Title pages will be prepared in manuscript.

Place	Date	Hour	Summary of Events and Information	Remarks and references to Appendices
ST MARTIN	25		Battalion in cellar having moved forward in support of 184 Brigade. Orders received abt 1400 hours to move forward at 1400 hours and look up position (the front open) of the positions. Then we close and were in position Battn H.Q. at LA FOLIE at abt 1330 hours.	APP A
				APP
LA FOLIE	26		Quiet morning. Towards midday enemy shelled Batt H.Q. and continued during afternoon on to abt 1600 hours. Lieut Col W. Cpt. Bryan D.S.O. Battalion from Lieut Col W. Cpt. Bryan D.S.O. to relieve 84 but Batt in Advance Guard Batt. Battalion to be in Bois Plemont.	APP B
				APP
LA FOLIE	27		Orders received during early morn for Battalion to move forward. Battn. H.Q. moved to CHATEAU in SEPMERIES. A new B Coy moved up towards SEPMERIES and B Coy been arrived in their own position being in support. The move was complete at abt about hours.	APP A

WAR DIARY
INTELLIGENCE SUMMARY

Army Form C. 2118.

9th (Northumberland Hussars) Battn. Northumberland Fusiliers

20/9/1918

Place	Date	Hour	Summary of Events and Information	Remarks and references to Appendices
SEPMERIES	27		The Brigade attacked with 1st Bn Lent Jones and 1st Suffolks Regt. Bn was unsuccessful and the two Companies and Battn H.Q. Withdrew during afternoon and resumed their own original position by 17:15 hours. Enemy shelled very heavily during the afternoon but Battn had no casualties.	AWR
LA FOLIE	28		Orders received for the Battalion to relieve 1st Battn Suffolk Regt in the SEPMERIES - YOUI line A3 & C and D Coy in support. Relief carried out successfully and no casualties.	APRA'S AWR
LA FOLIE	29		Quiet day in line. Battn H.Q. and been received a few slight scattered shelling. Advance Battn H.Q. (just O.C.O.L.) when 2 horses near west (railway) SEPMERIES	AWR

WAR DIARY
INTELLIGENCE SUMMARY

7th (Northumberland Fusiliers) Battn.
Northumberland Fusiliers

Sept. 1918

Army Form C. 2118.

Place	Date	Hour	Summary of Events and Information	Remarks and references to Appendices
LA FOLIE	30		Quiet day with a fair amount of back gun shelling. Both Bns. moved forward to tunnel in railway near the village of SEPMERIES. Battalion attempts to capture Buzzoldun and village of MARCHES but the a unsuccessful owing to the enemy being on alert. Four fighting patrols went out. Pte C.H. Clawson in charge of No 1 patrol encountered 3 or 4 Germans from their horses near bridge over the trail RHONELLE. Harris was killed and 2 others wounded. He enemy set fire to a Natives Cottage which destroyed our men and brought down a heavy machine gun barrage.	APP 'C' (M.K.)
SEPMERIES	31		In the line. Intermittent shelling all day. An in. prisoners from the division patrol and captive the village of SEMERIES and high ground E of the village. In the following day 1 Nov 1918 ZERO HOUR to be 0515. Orders were issued to Company and preparations were made. Lieut A.T. Bowman was killed at night by a enemy shell He was acting C/O "B" Coy.	(M.K.)

Army Form C. 2118.

WAR DIARY
or
INTELLIGENCE SUMMARY.
(Erase heading not required.)

9th Northumberland Fusiliers
Manchester Regt

OCTOBER. 1918.

Instructions regarding War Diaries and Intelligence Summaries are contained in F. S. Regs., Part II. and the Staff Manual respectively. Title pages will be prepared in manuscript.

Place	Date	Hour	Summary of Events and Information	Remarks and references to Appendices

			Strength at the beginning of the month = 40 Officers 915 O.R.
			 " " " end " " = 44 " 717 O.R.
			
			 Casualties.
			     Killed Wounded Missing Evacuated Transfers Commissions Total = 284
			     H H 159 1 7/1 6 3
			
			 Drafts week ending 5th October = 15
			      " " 12 " = 40
			      " " 19 " = 10
			      " " 26 " = 9
			      " " 31 " = 12
			     Total = 86.
			
			 Officers
			 Joined Killed
			 Lieut B.C. Cocks Lieut A. Milling 10/10 Capt Webb Bowler } 2/4/18
			 Lieut J.C. Nutten Lieut J. Attayla 4/15 Lieut N.C. Foreman }
			 Lieut A.H. Beets Lieut G.A. Graham } 27/18
			 Captain & McClury Lt W. Hitter **Died of Wounds**
			 Lieut C.D.S.Hopper Tulnon Lt E. Holden H.C.M.M. 3/13 Lt W. Munson 24/18
			 Major E.P. Thompson 2 Lt G. Wood } 3/10/18 **Wounded**
			 Lieut P. Woods 2Lt S. Brown } Lieut F. Pearson
			 2Lieut N.C. Foreman 13 To England Sick Lieut C.G. Oliver } 24/18
			 Lieut C.G. Oliver Lieut F.J. Turter 25/18 2/Lt Quinn
			 Lieut E.C. Brown 10/18 Transfer Lieut J.D. Mackay
			 Lieut A.A. Quinn 15 Lieut M. Babbitt. 29/18 Lieut J. Attayla. 29/18
			      Lt C.D.S. Hopper Tulnon 28/18
			
			 AWARDS.
			 Bar to Military Cross
			 Lieut J.L. Porter.
			
			 In Stockfield in France.
			 Lieut A. Milling
			 Lieut C.P. Tulgon
			 Lieut M.J. Mealing	

SECRET.   Copy No. 8

183rd INFANTRY BRIGADE ORDER NO. 254.   1/10/18.

Reference Sheet 36A. 1/40,000.
            36.N.E.1/20,000.
            36.N.W.1/20,000.

1. The 59th Division is relieving the 61st Division.

2. 183rd Infantry Brigade will move to STEENBECQUE tomorrow 2nd inst. by March Route in accordance with March Table issued with this Order.

3. Nucleus Garrisons in the Corps Battle Line will be relieved by 8 a.m. tomorrow 2nd instant by detachments of 182nd Infantry Brigade.
   Guides for relieving detachments will be supplied as under, and will report to Headquarters 182nd Inf. Bde. (G.6.a.8.1.) at 7 a.m. tomorrow 2nd instant.

   Right Subsector.   2 Guides.   For 2 Platoons.
   Left Subsector.   3 Guides.   For 3 Platoons less 2 Sections.

   Garrisons of 11th Bn. The Suffolk Regt. and 1st Battn. The East Lancashire Regiment will, on relief, march independently to STEENBECQUE where Units will arrange to meet them.

4. Command of Corps Battle Line will pass to G.O.C. 182nd Inf. Bde. at 8 a.m.

5. Personnel at Brigade School will rejoin Units at STEENBECQUE tomorrow 2nd instant, under arrangements to be made by Commandant, Brigade School.
   Detachments of Units will not leave THIENNES before 5 p.m.

6. Half way halt for Units marching will be LA RUE LES MORTS area. Units will halt for midday meal as under:-
   9th Bn. Northumberland Fusiliers.   J.4.a.
   11th Bn. The Suffolk Regt.   J.11.b.
   H.Q. 183rd Inf. Bde.   J.12.a.
   1st Bn. East Lancashire Regt.   J.12.b.

7. Units will report arrival in billets to this H.Q.

8. Brigade H.Q. will close at present location, and reopen at STEENBECQUE at 1300 hours.

9. Administrative Instructions are issued separately.

   ACKNOWLEDGE. → Done

                                                                    Captain,
                                             Brigade Major, 183rd Infantry Brigade.

Issued at 2355 hours.

Copy 1 - War Diary.   Copy 11 - 183rd L.T.M.B.
     2 - File.   12 - 61st Division "G"
     3 - G.O.C.   13 - 182nd Inf. Bde.
     4 - S.C.   14 - 184th Inf. Bde.
     5 - B.T.O.   15 - C.R.A.
     6 - B.S.O.   16 - C.R.E.
     7 - S.I.O.   17 - A.D.M.S.
     8 - 9th Northd Fus.   18 - No. 3 Coy, Div. Train.
     9 - 11th Suffolks   19 - 61st Div. Train.
    10 - 1st E.Lancs.

MARCH TABLE ISSUED WITH 183rd INFANTRY BRIGADE ORDER NO. 254 LATED 1/10/18.

Serial No	Date.	Unit.	From	To	Starting Point.	Time (hours)	Route	Remarks
1.	2/10/18	9th Bn. Northd Fus.	YAK FARM Area.	STEENBECQUE	K.29.b.00.40	1035.	Road Junction L.13.t.90.00. ROBERMETZ - Rd. Junction K.29. b.00.40 - LES LAURIERS - Road Junction K.1.c.50.25 - J.4.b. 55.35 - Rd. Junction J.8.a. 95.70 - Rd. Junction J.2.c. 50.70 - Rd. Junction I.12.b. 90.20 - thence N.W.	Not to pass Rd. Junction L.22. c.35.75 before 0927 hours.
2.	do	11th Battn Suffolk R.	MAURIANNE FARM Area.	do	do	1102.	ditto.	
3.	do	183 Inf. Bde.H.Q. 183 T.M.B. (Capt.A.F. MORTIMER Command'g)	CHAPELLE DUVALLE Area.	do	do	1200.	L.26.d.10.65 - K.29.b.00.40 - thence as for Serial 2.	
4.	do	1st Bn. E. Lancs.Regt.	KENNET CROSS Area.	do	do	1230.	ESTAIRES - CHAPELLE DUVELLE - K.29.b.00.40.	

NOTE:
1. 1st Line Transport will accompany units.
2. Intervals to be maintained as follows:-
   Between Battalions   500 yards.
   Between Companies   200 yards.
   Between each Section of 6 Vehicles 25 yards.

SECRET. Copy No 10

183rd INFANTRY BRIGADE ORDER NO. 235.

4/10/18.

Reference Sheet 36A. 1/40,000.

1. The Division is transferred from the XI Corps to the XVII Corps.

2. 183rd Infantry Brigade Group will move from the STEENBECQUE area on the 5th and 6th instant.

   183rd Infantry Brigade Group is composed as follows:-

   183rd Infantry Brigade.
   478 Field Coy, R.E.
   No. 3 Coy, 61st Divl. Train.
   2/3rd (S.M.) Field Ambulance.

3. Units will entrain at STEENBECQUE Station (D.25.d.30.40).
   Units will march to the Station and entrain in accordance with attached Table.

4. Administrative Instructions are issued separately.

5. On arrival in the new area the Division will be in G.H.Q. Reserve at 24 hours notice.

6. Units will report arrival in billets after detraining, giving location of H.Q.

7. Brigade Headquarters will close at STEENBECQUE and reopen at destination at times which will be notified.

ACKNOWLEDGE.

Issued at 12 noon.

Captain,
Brigade Major, 183rd Infantry Bde.

```
Copy  1 - War Diary.
      2 - File
      3 - G.O.C.
      4 - B.M.
      5 - S.C.
      6 - B.T.O.
      7 - B.S.O.
      8 - B.I.O.
      9 - Major A.B.Wright M.C.
     10 - 9th North'd Fus.
     11 - 11th Suffolks.
     12 - 1st R.Lancs Regt.
     13 - 183rd L.T.M.B.
     14 - 478 Field Coy, R.E.
     15 - No. 3 Coy, 61st Divl. Train.
     16 - 2/3rd Field Ambulance.
     17 - 61st Division "G"
     18 - 182nd Inf. Bde.
     19 - 184th Inf. Bde.
     20 - C.R.A.
     21 - C.R.E.
     22 - A.D.M.S.
```

SECRET.   MARCH AND ENTRAINING TABLE ISSUED WITH 183rd INFANTRY BRIGADE ORDER NO. 255 DATED 4/10/18.

Ser. No.	Date.	Unit.	From.	To	Starting Point.	Time Transport	Time Dismtd. Prsnl.	Route.	Travel by Train No.	Leaving at	Remarks
1.	4/10/18	183 Bde) H.Q.Sig.) Sect.183) L.T.M.B.) 478 Fd.Co R.E.	STEENBECQUE	STEEN-BECQUE Statn.	I.3.a.35.	1943.	2143.	Rd. thro' I.3. a. and b.			A. Transport will be at Station 3 hours before train is due to leave. Dismounted personnel 1 hour before.
			I.4.b.10.50.	do	do	1945.	2145.	STEENBECQUE thence as above.	3	2310. 2310 2010 2230	
		1 Coy. complete with Cooker & Team of 1/E.Lancs	STEEN-BECQUE	do	do	1952.	2152.	Rd. through I.3.a. & b.			
2.	5/10/18	1/E.Lancs less 1 Coy,Cooker team 1/Suff-	do	do	do	2252	0052	do	6	2310.	B. The Company moving on train No. 21 will provide the loading party at STEENBECQUE under instructions issued by Staff Captain.
3.	do	olks,less 1 Coy, Cooker & Team.	DORBECHE	do	do	0152	0352	STEENBECQUE - Rd. thro' I.3.a. and b.	9	0510.	
4.	do	2 Rhd. Fus.less 1 Coy, Cooker tea.	CISEAUX	do	do	0452	0652	Rd. Junction I.3.b.50.80 - I.3.b.30.60 STEENBECQUE Rd. thro' I. 3.a. and b.	12.	0810. 7.10 6.10	

MARCH TABLE DETAILING UNITS COMING (U.K.)

Ser. No.	Date.	Unit.	From.	To	Starting point	Time Arrive Trans.Front	Time Leave Trans.Front	Route	Travel by train No.	Leaving at	Remarks.
1.	7/12/39	2/5 Fld.Art. 7 Cav.Div.Train. 1 Coy with Cooker & Team 11th Suffolks	ST. JACQUES do	ST. LEGER Station. do	L.a.35. 30.	1040 1047.	1250. 1247.	ST.JACQUES - Road thro' T.T.3. & h.	19	1410.	
2.	do	1 Coy. Cooker team 9th Norfolks.	CRAY do	do	do	1052. 1352.	1252. 1552.	As for Ser. No. 1.	21.	1710.	

ADDENDUM TO 183rd INFANTRY BRIGADE ADMINISTRATIVE
INSTRUCTIONS ISSUED IN CONNECTION WITH MOVE BY RAIL.

WINTER TIME.
Reference G.R.O.5185
In consequence of the revision to Winter time on the night of 5/6th., the times mentioned in Administrative Instructions after 0100 on the 6th inst. should read one hour earlier.

B.H.Q.
4.10.18.

A.R.Ball
Captain
Staff Captain, 183rd Infantry Brigade

SECRET.   Copy No. 6

183rd. INFANTRY BRIGADE
ADMINISTRATIVE INSTRUCTIONS ISSUED IN CONNECTION WITH MOVE BY RAIL.   NO. 2

4th. October 1918

1. Reference Administrative Instructions dated 3rd October.

   "A" Battalion is   1st. East Lancs.
   "B"   "   "   11th. Suffolks.
   "C"   "   "   9th. Northd. Fus.

2. **DETRAINING STATION.**
   Reference para.1 Administrative Instructions No.1, Detraining Station is DOULLENS.

3. **TIMES OF DEPARTURE OF TRAINS.**

Train No.	Date	Departs
3	5th.	2310 hours
6	6th.	0210 "
9	6th.	0510 "
12	6th.	0810 "
15	6th.	1110 "
18	6th.	1410 "
21	6th.	1710 "

4. **LORRIES.**
   3 Lorries are allotted to this Brigade Group for taking blankets and surplus stores etc to Entraining Station and are allotted to Units as follows :-

Date.	Unit.	No. of Lorries.	Remarks.
5th.	Bde.H.Q. & L.T.M.B. 478 Fld.Coy.	2 1	(Guides to be at (STEENBECQUE Church (at 1715 to meet (Lorries.
5th.	1st. East Lancs.	3	Guides to be at STEENBECQUE Stn. at 2200 to take over lorries from above Units.
6th.	11th Suffolks.	3	Guides to be at STEENBECQUE Stn at 0100 to take over Lorries from above Unit.
6th.	9th. Northd. Fus.	3	Guides to be at STEENBECQUE Stn. at 0400 to take over lorries from above Unit.
6th.	2/3rd. Field Amb.	2	Guides to be at STEENBECQUE Stn. at 0700 to take over Lorries from above Unit.

   Units will ensure that the Lorries are offloaded as quickly as possible on arrival at Entraining Station, and handed over to the next Unit.
   Lorries will meet trains at Detraining Station.

5. SURPLUS KIT.

Immediately on arrival in the new Area all Units will at once overhaul all stores and personal kit, with a view to dumping everything that is not actually required for active operations.

Units will probably only be able to rely on their baggage wagons, and it is essential that all stores and kit be reduced to a minimum. A Surplus Kit store will be established at DOULLENS. Units will be notified later exact location and arrangements for dumping.

6. SUPPLIES.

October 4th.   After second refilling (for consumption 5th) all Supply Wagons will report back to No.2 Coy. Div.Train immediately after dumping at Q.M.Stores.

October 5th.   Refilling Point will be at 1400 at STEENBECQUE Church, for consumption 7th.

Supply Wagons will report to Units and will travel loaded with Units on their Trains.

Immediately on arrival at New Q.M.Stores Supply Wagons will be offloaded, and will be sent to report to S.S.O. at Bde.Transport Lines.

Baggage wagons will remain with Units.

Grouping Table attached marked "Table A".

7. LOADING AND UNLOADING PARTIES.

Reference para.2 of Administrative Instructions No1.

The Loading and Unloading Parties detailed therein will consist of a complete Company and not 1 Officer and 50 O.R. as stated.

8. ACKNOWLEDGE.

B.H.Q.

A.R.Ball   Captain.
Staff Captain, 183rd. Infantry Brigade.

DISTRIBUTION as for Administrative Instructions No1.

RAILHEAD.   Railhead changes to ROSEL on the 7th. inst

TABLE "A".

SUPPLY GROUPING.

183rd. Brigade Group.

183rd. Brigade Headquarters.
183 L.T.M.B.
9th. Northumberland Fus.
11th Suffolks
1st East Lancs.
478 Field Coy. R.E.
2/3rd Field Amb.
523 Coy. A.S.C.
1/5th D.C.L.I. (after 2nd issue 4th & onwards.)
"A" Battery 307 Brigade R.F.A.
"B"   - do -
"C"   - do -
"D"   - do -
No. 2 Section D.A.C. (4 G.S. Wagons and 16 limbered Ammn. Wagons & Teams).
Half of S.A.A. Section, D.A.C.

REFILLING POINT.   ST.ENDECQUE Church.

TIME.   1400.

SECRET.   Copy No...6...

183rd. INFANTRY BRIGADE
ADMINISTRATIVE INSTRUCTIONS ISSUED IN CONNECTION
WITH MOVE BY RAIL. NO.3

                                                    4th. October 1918.

1. **ENTRAINMENT.**
   No personnel or stores will be allowed in the Brake Van.
   No covered trucks should be used for baggage, as it restricts the space available for personnel.

2. **ENTRAINING OFFICER.**
   Lieut. E.G.BATES.M.C. representing the Division will be at the Station throughout the hours of entrainment.

3. **STRENGTH.** Bde. Entraining Officer for transmission to
   All Units will hand in to Divisional Entraining Officer at Entraining Station, a statement shewing numbers of Vehicles, Horses, Officers and Other Ranks proceeding.

4. **TENTS, TRENCH SHELTERS ETC.**
   No Tents, Trench Shelters or Marquees surplus to authorised establishment will be taken out of the area. Any such in possession will be handed in to the nearest Area Commandant prior to departure.

B.H.Q.   Captain.
                    Staff Captain, 183rd. Infantry Brigade.

            Distribution as for Administrative Instructions Nos.1 & 2.

SECRET.   Copy No. 9

183rd INFANTRY BRIGADE ORDER NO. 253.   7/10/18.

Reference Maps: LENS 1/100,000.
            VALENCIENNES   do

1. 183rd Infantry Brigade Group will move from the POMMERA - AUTHIEULE Area to the MOEUVRES - GRAINCOURT Area (Area "D") commencing on the 8th instant as follows:-

   <u>8th instant.</u> Transport (less Transport moving by Tactical Train) by march route.

   <u>9th instant.</u> Remainder of Brigade Group by tactical trains.

   March Table for Transport and Entraining Table ("A" and "B") are attached.

2. (a) Major I.G.C.BRADY, M.C. 9th Bn. The Northumberland Fusiliers will command the Transport of the Brigade Group. Captain A.E. MORTIMER, Brigade H.Q. will act as Adjutant.

   (b) Reconnaissances of positions for halts for the night within the areas shewn in the March Table ("A") will be made daily.
   The route which Transport will take will also be previously reconnoitred. Some of the roads shewn on the maps do not exist.

3. Units will report arrival in the areas allotted to them to Brigade H.Q.

4. The following distances will be maintained on the March:

Between Battalions	500 yards.
Between Transport of Units	100 yards.
Between Groups of 3 Vehicles	25 yards.

6. Advance Parties to forward area are moving under instructions issued by Staff Captain.
   Administrative Instructions are issued separately.

7. Brigade H.Q. will close at POMMERA and reopen in Forward Area at a place and time to be notified later.

8. ACKNOWLEDGE.

                                                    Captain,
Issued at 8 p.m.   Brigade Major, 183rd Infantry Bde.

    Copy 1 - War Diary.   Copy No. 13 - Major BRADY, M.C.
         2 - File.   14 - 478 Field Coy, R.E.
         3 - G.O.C.   15 - No. 3 Coy, Div. Train.
         4 - B.M.   16 - 2/3rd Field Ambulance.
         5 - S.C.   17 - 61st Division "G"
         6 - B.T.O.   18 - 61st Division "Q"
         7 - B.S.O.   19 - 182nd Inf. Bde.
         8 - B.I.O.   20 - 184th Inf. Bde.
         9 - 9th North'd Fus.   21 - C.R.A.
        10 - 11th Suffolks   22 - C.R.E.
        11 - 1st E.Lancs.   23 - A.D.M.S.
        12 - 183 T.M.B.   24 - A.P.M.

TABLE "A" (MOVE OF TRANSPORT) ISSUED WITH 183rd INFANTRY BRIGADE ORDER NO. 256 OF 7/10/18.

Serial No	Date	Unit.	From	To	Starting Point.	Time hours	Route.	Remarks.
1.	Oct. 8	Bde.H.Q.	POMMERA.	BRETONCOURT - BAILLEULMONT Area.	X Rds above L in MONDICOURT.	1030.	MONDICOURT - LE BAC DU SUD (Main Road).	
2.	8	9th Nthd.Fus.	do	do	do	1032	ditto	
3.	8	5 Coy.Div.Trn.	BEAUREPAIRE.	do	do	1035	ditto	
4.	8	11th Suffolks.	HALLOY.	do	do	1041.	L'ESPERANCE - thence as for Serial 1.	Not to pass X Rds at L'ESPERANCE until 3 Coy.Train has passed.
5.	8	1 E.Lancs.R.	AUTHIEULE.	do	do	1044.	AMPLIER - HALLOY - L'ESPERANCE - thence as for Serial 1.	
6.	8	478 Fld.Coy.	do	do	do	1047		To follow Transport of 1 E.Lancs.from AUTHIEULE.
7.	8	2/3 Fld.Amb.	BEAUREPAIRE.	do	do	1053		Not to pass X Rds at L'ESPERANCE until 478 Fld.Co have passed.
-	9	183 Bde.Group	BRETONCOURT - BAILLEULMONT Area.	BOYELLES - BOISLEUX Area.	To be notified to Units by O.C.Column.		BRETONCOURT - BLAIR-VILLE - FICHEUX.	Not to arrive at FICHEUX before 1100 hours & to be clear by 1200 hrs.
-	10	ditto	BOYELLES - BOISLEUX area	MOEUVRES - GRAINCOURT area.	do	do	HENIN - CROISELLES LAGNICOURT - X Rds ⅓ mile N.W. of DOIGNIES	Not to arrive at HENIN before 0900 hours & to be clear by 1000 hrs

NOTE. Each Unit will detail 1 Mounted N.C.O. and 1 Bicycle Orderly to report to O.C. Column at 1030 hours on the 8th instant at the Starting Point.

TABLE "A".

ENTRAINING TABLE.

No. of Train.	Unit.	Entraining Station.	Time for loading Train.	Time of Departure of Train.	Nature of Train.	Detraining Station.	REMARKS
1.	Bde. H.Q. & 183rd Inf. Bde. Grouped Transport.	MONDICOURT.	0800	0906	Transport.	FREMICOURT.	Entraining & Detraining Officer (as far as this Bde. is concerned to be detailed by 11th Suffolks.
2.	9th Northd. Fus. 11th Suffolks.	MONDICOURT.	1100	1206	Personnel.	HERMIES.	- ditto - by 9th Northd. Fus. HERMIES Station is on the Canal Bank due South of HERMIES.
3.	1st L. Lancs. 478 Fld. Coy. 2/3 Fld. Amb.	MONDICOURT.	1400	1506	Personnel	HERMIES.	Entraining & Detraining Officer (as far as this Brigade is concerned) to be detailed by 1st Lst Lancs.

NOTE. The journey should take between 4 & 5 hours.

TABLE "E".

COMPOSITION OF TRANSPORT TRAIN.

1. Train No.1 will carry the following :-

Unit.	Personnel Offrs.	Personnel O.R.	Horses.	G.S. Limbers.	2 wheeled carts.	Remarks.
Bde.H.Q.			9	1		
Bde.Sig.Sect.	1	27	9	1	1	
Transport of Lewis Gun Detachments, 4 limbers per Bn.		8	8	4		
2 Cookers per Bn.		2	4	2		
1 Water Cart per Bn.		1	2	1		
11 Chargers & 6 Pack Animals per Bn.		17	17			
Field Coy.R.E.		3	4	1		Includes 2 chargers
Field Amb.		2	4	2		Includes 1 Water Cart.
L.T.M.B.	4	50				

2. In addition the following will be carried :-
   1 Water Cart and 1 Cooker of M.G.Bn.

3. The personnel of the M.G.Coy,n will act as loading party at the entraining Station. They will also act as unloading party on Detrainment.

4. All blankets will be carried on the Transport Train.

SECRET.   Copy No............

183rd. INFANTRY BRIGADE

ADMINISTRATIVE INSTRUCTIONS ISSUED IN CONNECTION WITH BRIGADE ORDER NO.256.

7th Oct. 1918.

1. The Brigade less portion proceeding by March Route will entrain on 9th inst. as shown in Table "A" attached.

   The composition of the Transport Train is shewn in Table "B".

   All remaining Transport will proceed by March Route.

2. LORRIES. to move blankets to the Station will be provided. Details follow later.
   Special attention is directed to paras. 1 and 2 of 61st Division No.Q57/5/1 issued under this Office S.C.7560 of to-day.
   NOTE. The allotment will probably be One Lorry per Battalion to do one journey only. This is the only additional transport available, and Units must make their arrangements accordingly.

3. SUPPLIES (a) Units have now been issued with rations for consumption up to and including the 9th. inst.
   On account of the Brigade proceeding by road and also by rail the rations will have to be split accordingly.
   (b) WAGONS. After 2nd refilling to-day one Supply wagon has remained with Units. This wagon will travel with Transport of Units and carry rations for consumption 9th. for the mounted personnel travelling by road. This wagon will report back to No.3 Coy.Train immediately on arrival at halting place on evening of 9th inst.
   Baggage wagons will remain with Units.
   (c) REFILLING.
   8th inst. There will be no refilling for all Units who had a double refil to-day.
   9th inst. (a) Troops travelling by train. There will be a refilling point on the road running due North from HAVRINCOURT to the main BAPAUME - CAMBRAI road, one mile South of its junction with the latter road.
   Time. On arrival; advance parties should get in touch with the Supply Officer at the dump early on the 9th inst. and inform him exact location of Units.
   Supplies will be delivered by lorry.
   (b) Troops marching by road. There will be a refilling for each of the Groups marching by road on arrival at the halting place on the 9th. on the ARRAS - BAPAUME road, immediately North of BOYELLES.
   Supply grouping for the 9th inst will be notified later.
   10th inst. All Refilling points will be as in (a) above, unless Units are notified to the contrary at Refilling point on the 9th.

4. ADVANCE PARTIES. One Lorry will be at Brigade Headquarters at 0700 on 8th inst to take advance parties as under to new area. They will proceed to Cross roads about 1 mile due south of M in MOEUVRES on the BAPAUME - CAMBRAI road where they will await till met by Staff Captain or D.A.A.G. 61st Division.

          Each Battalion 5
          Brigade H.Q.   1
          183 L.T.M.B.   1
          478 Field Coy 1
          2/3rd Fld Amb.............. 1
          No.3 Coy.Train 1

5. All Transport will move complete to establishment.

6. WATER. Water carts will travel full.
   All personnel will travel with Water Bottles filled.

7. BILLETS. Clean Billet and No Damage Certificates will be obtained before leaving the area, and forwarded to this Office as soon as possible.

8. ACKNOWLEDGE.

B.H.Q.

(signed)
Captain.
Staff Captain, 183rd. Infantry Brigade.

DISTRIBUTION.

```
Copy No 1 & 2  Retained.
 "   "  3      G.O.C.
 "   "  4      Brigade Major
 "   "  5      Staff Captain
 "   "  6 & 7  9th Northd Fus
 "   "  8 & 9  11th Suffolks
 "   " 10 & 11 1st East Lancs
 "   " 12      478 Field Coy. R.E.
 "   " 13      No.3 Coy. Div. Train.
 "   " 14      2/3rd Field Amb.
 "   " 15 & 16 183 L.T.M.B.
 "   " 17      Major I.G.C.BRADY.M.C.
 "   " 18      R.T.O.
 "   " 19      Bde Signal Offr.
 "   " 20       "   Supply Offr.
 "   " 21       "   Q.M.S.
 "   " 22      N.C.O. i/c M.M.P.
 "   " 23      Offr. i/c Entraining & Detraining 11th Suffs.
 "   " 24       "   "      "          "        "  9th N.F.
 "   " 25       "   "      "          "        "  1 E.Lancs.
 "   " 26      61st Div. 'Q' } for information.
 "   " 27      A.P.M.        }
```

SECRET   9th (North'd Fusiliers) Battalion Northumberland   Copy No. B
Ref maps Fust   Fusiliers Order No. 72
36A '40,000   2.10.1918
36A N.E.'20,000
36 N.W.'20,000

1. INTENTION.   The Battalion will move today to STEENBECQU by
                     march route

2. TIME.   Head of Column at starting point (A.M.
                     Stores facing N.W.) at 0900.

                     Reveille   0430
                     Breakfast   0530
                     No Sick parade. Men who are unable to march
                     will report to Regt. Aid post at 0630.

3. ORDER OF
   MARCH.   B. C. Band D. A. Bat'n H.Q.

4. ROUTE   Road Junction L13 b 9.0. – ROBERMETZ – Road junction
                     K 29 b 00.40 – LES LAURIERS – Road junction I 13 c 50.25 –
                     J 4 b 55.35 – Road junction J 8 a 95 40 – Road junction
                     J 2 c 50.70 – Road junction I 12 b 90.20 – Thence N.W.

5. INTERVALS   Between Battalion 500 yards, between Companies 200yds,
                     between each section of 6 vehicles 25 yards.

6. HALT   A halt will be made for midday meal in J4d.

7. BILLETING   Billeting party consisting of 1 N.C.O per Coy, 1 N.C.O.
   PARTY   for Bat'n H.Q., 1 N.C.O for A.M. Stores and 1 N.C.O. for Transport
                     will report to Lieut. F. Curson, at A.M. Stores at 0930.

8. OFFICERS
   VALISES, MESS   Will be ready for Collection at corner of field
   KIT, SIG. EQUIP. SOUTH of A Company lines at 0730
   ORDERLY Room
   BOXES & CANTEEN
   STORES S.

9. TENTS, TRENCH   Will be handed over to Relieving Units (of 182 Inf
   SHELTERS, AREA   Bde). Lieut. H. Godfrey will stay behind to see that
   STORES ETC   this is done and obtain usual receipt.

10. BILLETS   Company Commanders are held responsible that the
                    billets are left in clean and sanitary condition.

                    ACKNOWLEDGE
                    Issued by runner at 0500

Copies 15.   No. 1   183 Inf. Bde
                    2   OC A Coy
                    3   OC B "
                    4   OC C "   A. V. Trustwater
                    5   OC D "   Captain & Adjutant
                    6   OC HQ.   9th (NF) Bat'n North'd Fusiliers
                    7   Comm'g Officer
                    8   Adjutant
                    9   Medical Officer
                    10   Quartermaster
                    11   Transport Officer
                    12   RSM
                    13   War Diary ✓
                    14   File
                    15   Spare.

SECRET   Copy No 17

4th (North'd Hussars) Battalion Northumberland Fusiliers Order 73.

Ref Map Sheet 36A 1/40000   4.10.1918

1. INTENTION
The Division is transferred from XI Corps to XVII Corps and will be in G.H.Q. Reserve under 24 hours notice.

2. MOVE
The Battalion will entrain at STEENBECQUE D.15.d.30.40 and will debus at DOULLENS.

3. TIME
The Battalion (less "A" Coy, complete with cooker and team) will parade with head of column at road junction T.3.A.50.60 at 0500 hours on 6th October 1918.

4. ORDER OF MARCH
D, C, B Coys, Headquarters.

5. ROUTE
Road junction 30 & 50.30 – D.9.b.80.60 – STEENBECQUE – Road length A.6 & 10.

6. LOADING PARTY
"A" Coy will report to Major A.B. Wright I.P.C. at STEENBECQUE Station at 2040 hours on 5th inst. They will travel by train No.2 leaving STEENBECQUE at 1610 hours on 6th October 1918. All personnel to be at the station 1 hour before time of departure of train.

7. ADVANCE PARTY
An advance party consisting of Lieut. J. Bowden and 1 N.C.O. each from A, B, C & D Coys to collect at STEENBECQUE Church at 0700 hours on 5th inst. A lorry will take this party to Town Major's Office, DOULLENS where it will be met by Staff Captain. Bicycles will not be taken.

8. WATER
Water carts will travel full. All ranks will travel with water bottles full.

9. DISCIPLINE
The Senior Officer on each train will detail two guards of 1 N.C.O. and 3 men each who will be posted and travel at the head and tail of each train.
Their duties will be to prevent troops straggling from train and out of stations when train is at rest. Also to prevent troops travelling on steps, footboards etc and particularly to prevent men from attempting to relieve nature at various and unauthorised places.

10. CERTIFICATES
O.C "A" Coy will detail an Officer whose duty it will be to obtain "Clean billets and no damage" certificates from the Mayor.

11. TRANSPORT
Transport will be at the station at 0430 hours on the 6 October 1918.

12. NOTE
For the purpose of the move the Battalion will be referred to as "C" Battalion.

ACKNOWLEDGE.

Issued by runner at 2410 hours.

T.J. Leonards
Captain & Adjutant
4/(North'd Hussars) Batt. Northd Fus.

Copies to. No 1 1st Supply Batt
2 O.C. A Coy
3 O.C. B Coy
4 O.C. C Coy
5 O.C. D Coy
6 O.C. H.Q. Coy
7 Loading Officer in Command
8 Adjutant
9 Intelligence Office
10 Medical Officer
11 Transport Officer
12 Quartermaster
13 R.S.M.
14 Sgt Cook
15 M.G. Office
16 File

Administrative Instructions
to
Battalion North'd Fusiliers Order No 73

Copy 17

5.10.18

___

(1) All officers Valises will be ready for collection at 1700 hrs

(2) Mess Kit will be carried on Company Cookers. Teams will be sent for these at 2200 hrs to-day

(3) 'A' Coy Cooker will travel with Company. Team will be sent for this at 1800 hrs to-day

(4) All Camp Kettles and Consolidated Stores will be ready to pack on returning ration limbers

(5) Horse will be sent for Maltese Cart 1800 hrs

(6) Transport officer will send a limber to Orderly Room for Signallers Equipment Orderly Room Boxes etc, at 1800 hrs

(7) ~~Advance~~ all officers chargers will ~~be issued~~ ~~late~~ go forward by Transport

ACKNOWLEDGE

Issued by runner at 1230

Copies No 1
2 OC 'A' Coy
3 " B "
4 " C "
5 " D "
6 Officer i/c H.Q. Coy
7 Commanding Officer
8 2nd in Command
9 Adjutant
10 Intelligence Officer
11 Medical Officer
12 Transport Officer
13 Quartermaster
14 a/ R.S.M
15 Sgt Cook
16 War diary
17 FILE

J.V. Brackworth
Capt & a/Adj
9 (N.F.) Batt'n North'd Fusiliers

SECRET.   Copy No. 12

9th (North'd Hussars) Batt'n Northumberland Fusiliers Order No. 74   8.10.1918

1. INTENTION	The Battalion will entrain tomorrow 9th inst at MONDICOURT.
2. TIME	The Battalion will parade at 1000 hours and march to MONDICOURT STATION
3. STARTING POINT	Head of Column on road junction South of T in LE GROS TINSON at 1040 hours.
4. ORDER OF MARCH	Band H.Q. C. A. B. D. Coys.
5. TRANSPORT	All Officers valises, Mess Kit, transport (other than portion moving by road) will travel on train No 1, loading at 0600 hours.
6. PERSONNEL	All personnel will travel on train No 4, loading at 1100 hours. This train is for personnel only.
7. MESS KIT VALISES &c	All officers valises, mess kit, band back and rifles, Company boxes and all bicycles, stores which cannot be carried on the train will be sent to Q.M. Stores before 0445 hours on 9th inst.
8. BREAKFAST	Bacon and Meat for consumption on 9th inst will be cooked tonight 8th inst and distributed to the men. Breakfast only at 0630. B and D Coys will use the boilers from their field kitchens. A and C Coys will use Camp Kettles. All these cooking utensils will be taken immediately breakfasts are finished and carried to MONDICOURT STATION in time to be loaded on train No 1 which leaves at 0830 hours.
9. ENTRAINING OFFICER	Captain H.B. Parkinson is detailed as entraining Officer at MONDICOURT STATION at 1030 hours 9th inst. Loading and unloading parties will be found by M.G. Battalion.
10. WATER BOTTLES	Company Commanders will see that all water bottles are filled before starting.
11. BILLETS	Company Commanders are responsible that billets are left in a clean and sanitary condition. OC D Coy will detail an Officer to stay behind after the Battalion has moved off to obtain clean billet and No damage certificates. He must be at the station by 1145 hours.

ACKNOWLEDGE
Issued by runners at   hours.

Copies to. No 1. 183 Inf'y Bde
         2. OC A Coy
         3.   " B "
         4.   " C "
         5.   " D "
         6. Comm'g Officer
         7. Adjutant
         8. 2nd in Command
         9. Quartermaster
         10. A/RSM
         11. War Diary
         12. File.

A.V. Freshests
Captain & Adjutant
9th (NH) Batt'n North'd Fusiliers

SECRET 9th (N.H.) Batn Northd Fusiliers   Copy No 13
Ref Map Sheet   Order No. F.1.   CANTAING
Sh. N.E. 1/20,000   14 October 1918

1. INFORMATION
The enemy's main position is purposed to be along line NOYELLES - NINE WOOD - FLESQUIERES.

2. INTENTION
The advance guard (183 Brigade) will continue the advance and occupy this position in conjunction with Brigades on Right and Left.
The 9th (N.H.) Bn Northd Fusiliers will be on the Right of the Brigade front keeping in touch with K Bath on its LEFT and Y Bath of X Brigade on the Right.
The Batn will pass through the present outpost line which is along road from L.3.c.y.5. - L.7.d.8.0. at 1030 hours.
The objective is the high ground from edge of NINE WOOD L.16.a.5.6. to L.20.6.7.6.

3. STARTING POINT
The Battalion will parade on road running EAST - WEST, just NORTH of bivouacs ready to march off at 0900.

4. ORDER OF MARCH
C. A. B. D.   Batn HQ.   Dress: Fighting Order with pack.

5. ROUTE
Along road due WEST to Sunken Road at L.2.a. 05. 08.

6. RECONNOITRING PARTY
The line of advance will be reconnoitered by all officers from L.2.a. 05. 05.

7. PLACE OF DEPLOYMENT
L.2.a. 05. 05.

8. ADVANCE FORMATION
Frontage one mile along present outpost position running from L.3.c.1.5. - L.7.d.8.0.
A Coy on "L" from L.3.c.1.5. to L.8.a.9.5. (250x S.W. of Cross Roads)
C Coy on R from this point to L.7.d.8.0.
B and D Coys in Support at distance of 500x.
The Directing Officer will march on "L" of A Coy on a compass bearing of 134° True from Trench Meeting Road at L.3.c.1.7.
The dividing line between Coys will be a point at L.8.b.9.5. (250x S.W. of Cross Roads) thence to LAINE TRENCH at L.9.d.8.6. and along that trench to objective.

9. MACHINE GUNS
1 Section will be allotted to the Battalion. Two guns will be in rear of B Coy and two in rear of D Coy.

10. L.M.B.
1 Section allotted to no Battalion and will be on Left flank of B Coy.

11. ARTILLERY
1 Section allotted to the Battalion and will be about 500x in rear of Battalion.

12. REPORTS
Situation reports will be submitted every quarter of an hour to Batn HQ. which will move forward at a distance of 500x in rear of B Coy.

13. NOTES
Strong points will be marked by BLUE flags.
Occupied trenches by BLUE and WHITE flags.
Green Verey lights denote Artillery fire.
Red Verey lights denote Heavy artillery and machine gun fire.
All Companies to carry smoke bombs for use against strong points.

14. ACKNOWLEDGE. Issued at 2100 hours.

                                                A. S. _____
                                                Lieut & Adjutant
                                                9th (N.H.) Batn Northd Fusiliers

Copies
No 1   183 Infy Bde
   2   O.C. C Coy 61st M.G. Batn
   3   O.C. 183 T.M. Battery
   4   Gunner Officer
   5   2ic in Command
   6   Adjutant
   7-11 Companies
   12 R.S.M.
   13-15 File.

SECRET.   Copy No.

Ref Map Sheet   9th (North'd Hussars) Batn North'd Fusiliers
S/c 1/40,000
S/c 1/10,000   Order No 75.   17.10.18

1. INTENTION.	The 61st Division will become the supporting group of the XVII Corps from 0600 hours tomorrow the 18th inst.
2. MOVE.	The Battalion will move tomorrow 18th inst. to new area in H.22.b
3. TIME.	Battalion will parade 0830 hours with head of column at road junction by Q.M. Stores ready to move off.
4. ORDER OF MARCH.	D. H. Band B C A D
5. ROUTE.	NOYELLES – Bridge L.6.c.2.3 – Cross roads R.15.a.1.3 – Road junction A.22.a.5.
6. INTERVALS	An interval of 100 yards between Companies, Units, and their transport, 300 yards between Battalions and 25 yards between each group of six vehicles will be maintained.
7. ADVANCE PARTY	An advance party consisting of Lieut R. Wade, 1 N.C.O per Coy and 1 N.C.O for Batn HQ will report to Staff Captain at road junction A.22.6.1.5 at 0900 hours tomorrow when areas will be allotted.
8. HANDING OVER.	A Guard of 1 N.C.O and 6 men will be detailed by O.C. C Coy to hand over this camp to a Unit of the 184th Infy Brigade. Lieut C. Wilkinson will be in charge of this party who will obtain usual clean billet certificates. These certificates to be in Orderly room by 1600 hours tomorrow. Tents and trench shelters to be handed over will not be struck.
9. VALISES ETC.	Officers Valises, Mess kit, specialist equipment Orderly room boxes etc will be dumped at Q.M. Stores by 0700 hours. No unauthorised articles will be carried on limbers, cookers, etc.
10. MALTESE CART & MESS CART.	Transport Officer will arrange for Maltese Cart and Mess Cart to be on road near Batn HQ by 0745 hours.
11. Discipline	Company Commanders are held responsible that their Company lines are left in a clean and sanitary condition.
12.	ACKNOWLEDGE.

Copies to   No 1. 83 Infy Bde
             2. County Officer
             3. 2nd in Command
             4. Adjutant
             5/8. O.C. Companies
             9. Quartermaster
             10. Transport Officer
             11. Medical Officer
             12. O.C. HQ Coy
             13. R.S.M.
             14. War Diary
             15. File

                                   D. Winchester.
                                   Captain & Adjutant
                                   9th (North'd Hussars) Batn North'd Fus.

SECRET   9th (North'd Hussars) Batt'n North'd Fusiliers   COPY No. 11
Ref. Map Sheet   Order No. T.2.
57B. N.W. 1/20.000   AVESNES-LES-AUBERT 21.10.18

INFORMATION   The enemy holds an outpost line extending along ridge C.11. central to C.11.b central.

INTENTION   The G.O.C. has decided to take this position tonight.

PARADE   The Battalion will parade at 1700 hours with head of column facing SOUTH at "B" Coy Mess.
  ORDER OF MARCH   "A" "B" "C" "D" and Batt'n H.Q.
  DRESS   Battle Order.
    Batt'n H.Q. will carry a very light pistol and 6 each Red, Green and White very lights.

RENDEZVOUS   C.9.b.30.70. thence on a compass bearing of 139°.M.10.

PLACE OF DEPLOYMENT   C.10.a.80.50 (Captain V.H. Thornton will act as guide)

ATTACK FORMATION   The Battalion will attack on a frontage of 500x —
250x on either side of place of deployment (along a track) "A" Coy on Right, "B" Coy on Left, "C" Coy Right Support "D" Coy Left Support. Batt'n H.Q. immediately in rear of "D" Coy. Companies will advance in two lines in extended order. Captain V.H. Thornton will direct the advance and will march on left of "A" Coy. Intervals between Coy. lines 50 yards. This to be maintained by connecting files. Distance between front line and Support 100x.

OUTPOSTS   On reaching objective outposts will be immediately put out.

SIGNALS   The following Light Signals will be used:—
  GREEN   GAS.
  WHITE   Stand fast for 5 minutes then continue advance.
  RED   Close and march home independently.

REPORTS   All reports to be sent to Batt'n H.Q. and to be rendered every 15 minutes from ZERO onwards.

ACKNOWLEDGE.
Copies to   No.1. B Duty Bks
            3   Commd Officer
            3   O. in Command
         5- 4   Adjutant
            9   O.C. Coys
            10 R.S.M.
            11 War Diary

                                    A.W. Freshwater
                                    Captain & Adjutant
                                    9th (N.H.) Batt'n North'd Fusiliers

War Diary

SECRET   COPY No.

9th (NORTHUMBERLAND HUSSARS) BATTN. NORTHUMBERLAND FUSILIERS

REF MAP SHEETS   ORDER No. 76.   22-10-1918
51a. 1/40,000
51a. SE. 1/20,000.

1.	Intention	The Battalion will move to St AUBERT tomorrow morning 23rd inst.
2.	Move	The Battalion will parade with head of column at "D" Corps Mess ready to move off at 0900 hours
3.	Order of March	D. A. B. C. Battn HQ. Transport.
4.	Route	Direct road through U.23.
5.	Surplus Kit etc.	All surplus stores including kits of officers going into the line, mens greatcoats, haversacks and entrenching tools of men carrying shovels and picks, all blankets (neatly rolled in bundles of 10 and marked plainly) will be dumped at No 2 GRAND PLACE AVESNES-LES-AUBERT at 0800 hours. O.C. "B" Coy will detail a guard of 1 N.C.O. and 2 men to stay in charge. Valises of Officers not going forward will be sent to Q.M. Stores by 0800 hours.
6.	Yukon Packs	Two pack mules and Yukon pack carriers (Drummers) with yukon packs and equipment with haversack at side, rifles and 50 rounds S.A.A. to be at Battn H.Q. ready to move off with guide from T.M. Battery at 0845 hours.
7.	Tools.	These will be drawn at the rate of 3 shovels and 1 pick per section from the transport lines at 0700 hours under the supervision of Sergt. Mitchelmore J.
8.	Grenades.	Grenades Nos 27 and 36 will be drawn on arrival at St AUBERT. Lieut C.W. Hardwick will arrange to detonate them there.
9.	Billeting Party.	A Billeting party consisting of Lieut F.A. Jung, 1 N.C.O. per Coy and 1 N.C.O. Battn. H.Q. will report to 56 Bde H.Q. U.24b.5.1. at 0830 hours tomorrow to take over billets from 9th Battn CHESHIRE REGT. Advance party for Q.M. Stores and Transport will report at Bde Q.M. Sergt. 75th Brigade U.24.b.4.6. Billet No 6 at 0830 hours to take over from 8th Battn GLOUCESTER REGT.
10.	Handing Over.	Lieut J. Burman will report to Brigade H.Qrs. to hand over present billets to the incoming Unit. Usual certificates will be obtained.
11.	Synchronization	Lieut R. Woods will report to Bde HQ. at 0830 hours to synchronize watches.
12.	Water Bottles	Company Commanders will see that all Water Bottles are filled.
13.	Transport.	Mess Cart and limbers for Orderly Room boxes and Signalling equipment will be at Battn H.Q. at 0800 hours prompt.

ACKNOWLEDGE.
Issued by runner at 2320 hours.   Reveille 0530 hours
                                              Breakfast 0600 "

Copies to   No 1 - 188 Infy Bde.
            2 - Commanding Officer
            3 - 2nd in Command
            4 - Adjutant
            5-9 - O.C. Company's
            10 - Quartermaster
            11 - Transport Officer
            12 - R.S.M
            13 - War Diary
            14 - File.

A.W. Freshwater
Captain and Adjutant
9th (N.H.) Battn Northumberland Fus.

SECRET   COPY No. 15

9th (North'd Hussars) Batt'n Northumberland Fusiliers

REF. MAP SHEET   **ORDER No. 77**   23.10.1918
51 & S.E. 1/20.000

1. INFORMATION
The enemy is holding lightly line running CAPELLE – ST MARTIN – SOMMAINE.

2. INTENTION
It is intended to attack this position at dawn tomorrow 24th inst to push through these villages and establish an outpost line 1500 yards N.E. of these positions.
Second objective the high ground N.E. of BERMERAIN from G.23 central to G.6 central.

3. DISPOSITIONS FOR ATTACK
The Brigade will attack with two Battalions in front line and 1 in support. The boundaries are shown on supplied to O.C. Companies.
The 9th (N.H.) Batt'n North'd Fus'rs will be on the Right 11th Batt'n Suffolk Regt on the Left and 1st East Lancashire Regt in Support. On our right will be the 1st Bn Berkshire Regt of 2nd Division. 102nd Infy Bde will be on the left of 103rd Infy Bde.

4. MOVE TO FORWARD AREA
The Battalion will parade in following order at ~~1715~~ 1915 hours:–
D, A, B, C, Bn. HQ, Transport (L.G. Limbers in rear of Coys)
Head of Column at turning near Batt'n H.Q.
There will be no lights shown and no smoking on the march.
An interval of 100 yards will be maintained between Companies.

5. TRANSPORT DETAILS
Will remain at ST AYBERT when Battalion moves forward. Usual S.O.S. grenades, very lights (white) ground flares (red) will be taken forward.

6. WATER BOTTLES
To be carried full and not to be used unless absolutely necessary as water will be scarce.

7. CONTACT
Red Flares will be called for by aeroplane at ZERO plus 3½ hours, 5 hours, and 7 hours. They will only be lit by most forward bodies of men.

8. TRANSPORT
The following transport will proceed with the Battalion
4 Lewis Gun Limbers (each in rear of its Company)
2 S.A.A. & Grenade "
1 Limber for Signals "
Water Cart and Mess Cart
4 pack animals.

9. GUIDES
Guides will meet the Battalion at V.16.a.5.6.

10. DEPLOY
The Battalion will deploy N.E. of HARPIES RIVER along which tapes will be laid out.

11. ATTACK POSITIONS
Battalion front 400 yards. Order of attack
    D   A
    B   C
Companies will deploy in artillery formation (square) 2 platoons in front line, 2 in support. 100 yard distance will be maintained between sections in section formations and 20 yards distance between front and second wave platoons. 50 yards distance between leading and immediate support platoons. Support Companies in same formation at a distance of 200 yards.

12. BARRAGE
Barrage table as already notified

9th (NH) Batt. Northumberland Fusiliers Order No 77

13. ZERO.   Zero hour will be 0400 hours.

14. COMPASS   Compass bearing for advance approximate 48° True
    BEARING

15. PRISONERS   P.O.W. Cage is at VH.645. Not more than
                  1 guard will be sent with each 25 prisoners.

16. AID POST   R.A.P. will be found of all established at MAISON
                  DIJON.

17. CIVILIANS   Civilians should be treated as walking wounded
                  and sent down to HAYCOX and ST AUBERT where
                  they will be dealt with under arrangements made
                  by 2/1st Field Ambulance.

18. SYNCHRONIZAT- Lieut C. Moody will report to Brigade HQ with his
    ION   watches at 1815 hours today.

19. R.E.'s   A detachment of R.E.'s have been detailed to
                  the Battalion for bridging etc. They will follow
                  up the attack closely in the rear of "D" and "A" Coys.

20. T.M.'s   183rd T.M. Battery will send 1 gun each to
                  "D" and "A" Companies.

ACKNOWLEDGE
Issued by runner at   hours

                                          A.V. Freshwater.
                                          Captain & Adjutant
                                  9 (NH) Batt. Northumberland Fusiliers

Copies to:-
No. 1   183 Infy Bde
    2   General Officer
    3   O in Command
    4   Adjutant
    5-9 H.Q. Companies
    10   Transport Officer
    11   Quartermaster
    12   M.O.
    13   I.O.
    14   S.M.
    15   War Diary
    16   File.

War Diary

SPECIAL ORDER OF THE DAY
By FIELD-MARSHAL SIR DOUGLAS HAIG
K.T., G.C.B., G.C.V.O., K.C.I.E
Commander-in-Chief, British Armies in France.

The following messages are published for the information of all ranks:—

To FIELD MARSHAL SIR DOUGLAS HAIG from THE LORD MAYOR, LONDON.
10-10-18.
    In the name of the citizens of London I warmly congratulate you and the gallant and indomitable forces under your command on the signal and successive victories which time after time have crowned the brilliant efforts of the troops. The capture of Cambrai is a great historic event which will stand out prominently in the annals of the war, and ever redound to the credit and renown of the British and Imperial forces. Again I offer you our heartiest congratulations on your magnificent leadership which has been an all important feature and factor in the series of successes, and fills us with complete confidence in the final victory of our great cause.

FROM FIELD MARSHAL SIR DOUGLAS HAIG to THE LORD MAYOR, LONDON.
11-10-18.
    On behalf of all ranks of the British Army in France and of myself I beg that you will accept and convey to the citizens of London our gratitude for the inspiring message you have been good enough to send us. We always gratefully remember the encouragement and whole-hearted support given to us by you and your stout-hearted citizens during the critical days of last Spring. It is a great source of strength to us in the Field to know how absolutely we may always rely, in bad as well as good days, on the support of our great capital. I can assure you that your message will strike deep into the hearts of all the troops of the Empire in their great fight for what we believe is right. Your very generous reference to myself has greatly touched me. I thank you very heartily for it, but none of us must ever forget how dependent my leadership is upon the skill of my Army Commanders and the many subordinate commanders of all ranks.

To FIELD MARSHAL SIR DOUGLAS HAIG from THE MAYOR, CAPE TOWN, SOUTH AFRICA.
11-10-18.
    Citizens Capetown send congratulations magnificent advance heroic forces under your command. We pray God sustain all and give victory.

FROM FIELD MARSHAL SIR DOUGLAS HAIG to THE MAYOR, CAPE TOWN, SOUTH AFRICA.
11-10-18.
    All ranks under my command are grateful for the congratulations you have so kindly sent us from the citizens of Cape Town, and join with me in sending our heartiest thanks.

To FIELD MARSHAL SIR DOUGLAS HAIG from THE CHAIRMAN, FOLESHILL BRANCH, NATIONAL FEDERATION OF DISCHARGED AND DEMOBILISED SAILORS AND SOLDIERS, ANGEL HOTEL, COVENTRY.
10-10-18.
    Heartiest congratulations to all ranks on brilliant successes.

From FIELD MARSHAL SIR DOUGLAS HAIG to THE CHAIRMAN, FOLESHILL BRANCH, NATIONAL FEDERATION OF DISCHARGED AND DEMOBILISED SAILORS AND SOLDIERS, ANGEL HOTEL, COVENTRY.
11-10-18.

    Heartiest thanks from myself and the Army under my command for the kind congratulations which you have been good enough to send us from yourself and from the Discharged and Demobilised Sailors and Soldiers of the Foleshill Branch.

To FIELD MARSHAL SIR DOUGLAS HAIG from THE CHAIRMAN, EFFRA CONSERVATIVE CLUB, BRIXTON, LONDON.
10-10-18.

    At a meeting of members and friends held last night at the Effra Conservative Club, Brixton, London, and addressed by Sir Harry Samuel, a very hearty message of congratulation was passed to you, your officers and men, on the splendid results of your united efforts during the past week. May God prosper you and bring you all back very soon to our dear homeland.

From FIELD MARSHAL SIR DOUGLAS HAIG to THE CHAIRMAN, EFFRA CONSERVATIVE CLUB, BRIXTON, LONDON.
11-10-18.

    All ranks join with me in sending our heartiest thanks to you and to the Effra Conservative Club for your message of generous appreciation which we all greatly value.

To FIELD MARSHAL SIR DOUGLAS HAIG from THE TOWN CLERK, TOWN HALL, CAMBERWELL, S.E.5
4-10-18.

    The Camberwell Local Tribunal at their meeting on Thursday last, passed the following resolution:—
" Moved by the Chairman (Alderman G. J. Molony),
Seconded by Sir Evan Spicer, J.P., L.C.C. and
RESOLVED (Unanimously):—That this, Camberwell Tribunal representing a population of 280,000, an area from which so many thousands have joined H.M. Forces, send their most sincere and hearty congratulations to the Commander-in-Chief for the glorious achievements of our Armies in conjunction with our Allies on all Fronts, together with an assurance of our unceasing gratitude, sympathy, and support."

From FIELD MARSHAL SIR DOUGLAS HAIG to THE TOWN CLERK, TOWN HALL, CAMBERWELL, S.E.5.
10-10-18.

    The moving resolution which you have sent me on behalf of the Camberwell Tribunal, representing so great a population, has gratified the whole British Army in France. On behalf of myself and the Army, to whose ranks so many citizens of Camberwell belong, I beg you to accept and convey to your Tribunal our very warmest thanks.

D. Haig. F.M.

Commander-in-Chief,
British Armies in France.

General Headquarters,
13th October, 1918.

SPECIAL ORDER OF THE DAY
By FIELD-MARSHAL SIR DOUGLAS HAIG
K.T., G.C.B., G.C.V.O., K.C.I.E
Commander-in-Chief, British Armies in France.

The following messages are published for the information of all ranks:—

To FIELD-MARSHAL SIR DOUGLAS HAIG FROM THE PRIME MINISTER, 10, DOWNING STREET, LONDON.

9-10-18.

I have just heard from Marshal Foch of the brilliant victory won by the First, Third and Fourth Armies, and I wish to express to yourself, Generals Horne, Byng and Rawlinson, and all the officers and men under your command, my sincerest congratulations on the great and significant success which the British Armies, with their American brothers-in-Arms, have gained during the past two days. The courage and tenacity with which the troops of the Empire, after withstanding the terrific enemy onslaught of the Spring of this year, have again resumed the offensive with such decisive results is the greatest chapter in our military history. The smashing of the great defensive system erected by the enemy in the West, and claimed by him to be impregnable, is a feat of which we are justly proud and for which the Empire will be ever grateful.

FROM FIELD-MARSHAL SIR DOUGLAS HAIG TO THE PRIME MINISTER, 10, DOWNING STREET, LONDON.

10-10-18.

On behalf of the General Officers commanding the First, Third and Fourth Armies, and all officers and men of those Armies under my command, as well as myself, I beg to send you our best thanks for your kind message of congratulation on the results gained during the past two days. We are all determined to continue to do our utmost to justify the confidence that is placed in us by the Empire. I have communicated your message to the American troops operating with the British Forces.

D. Haig. F.M.
Commander-in-Chief,
British Armies in France.

General Headquarters,
11th October, 1918.

SPECIAL ORDER OF THE DAY
By FIELD-MARSHAL SIR DOUGLAS HAIG
K.T., G.C.B., G.C.V.O., K.C.I.E
Commander-in-Chief, British Armies in France.

The following telegrams are published for the information of all ranks:—

To FIELD-MARSHAL SIR DOUGLAS HAIG from THE MAYOR OF BOURNEMOUTH.

2-10-18.

    The Mayor, Aldermen and Councillors of Bournemouth, in council assembled, on behalf of themselves and the borough at large, desire to convey to you sincerest congratulations on recent events in the West, and heartfelt admiration of bravery of the splendid troops under your command, and devoutly trust that success may be maintained and speedily result in assured final victory for Allies and a dictated peace.

From FIELD-MARSHAL SIR DOUGLAS HAIG to THE MAYOR OF BOURNEMOUTH.

3-10-18.

    All ranks join with me in sending you and the Aldermen and Councillors of Bournemouth our heartiest thanks for the message of congratulation and generous appreciation you have been good enough to send us. We share your trust in final victory for the Allies.

To FIELD-MARSHAL SIR DOUGLAS HAIG from THE SECRETARY, HULL BRANCH OF THE COMRADES OF THE GREAT WAR, 41 GEORGE STREET, HULL.

2-10-18.

    Hull branch, Comrades of the Great War, representing 450 discharged sailors and soldiers of Hull, send their congratulations to comrades in the field on recent splendid successes.

From FIELD-MARSHAL SIR DOUGLAS HAIG to THE SECRETARY, HULL BRANCH OF THE COMRADES OF THE GREAT WAR, 41, GEORGE STREET, HULL.

3-10-18.

    Warmest thanks from myself and all ranks of the British Army in France to the Hull Branch, Comrades of the Great War, for their friendly message of congratulation.

To FIELD-MARSHAL SIR DOUGLAS HAIG from THE SUPERINTENDENT, ROLLING MILLS, SOUTHAMPTON.

1-10-18.

Employees at this factory, responsible for producing large quantities of cartridge metal, wish me to express their intense admiration of the heroic achievements of all your troops, and to congratulate you on magnificent victories recently achieved. They assure you of their fixed determination to increase output to meet all future requirements.

From FIELD-MARSHAL SIR DOUGLAS HAIG to THE SUPERINTENDENT, ROLLING MILLS, SOUTHAMPTON.

3-10-18.

The kindly congratulations which you have sent us from the employees of your factory are very welcome to us all. Please convey to them the best thanks of myself and of the Army in France, and assure them of our grateful appreciation of their assurance to support us in the future in even greater measure than they have done in the past.

D. Haig. F.M.

Commander-in-Chief,
British Armies in France.

General Headquarters,
5th October, 1918.

SPECIAL ORDER OF THE DAY
By FIELD-MARSHAL SIR DOUGLAS HAIG
K.T., G.C.B., G.C.V.O., K.C.I.E
Commander-in-Chief, British Armies in France.

The following messages are published for the information of all ranks:—

To FIELD-MARSHAL SIR DOUGLAS HAIG FROM THE CONSEIL GENERAL DES ALPES-MARITIMES, PARIS.

1-10-18.

A motion proposed by the President, the Deputy M. Raiberti, and carried unanimously:—

"The Conseil General des Alpes-Maritimes desire to express to His Excellency Field-Marshal Sir Douglas Haig their admiration of the splendid valour of the British Armies, of the incomparable feats of arms which they have accomplished, and of the magnificent victories which they have gained under his command."

FROM FIELD-MARSHAL SIR DOUGLAS HAIG TO THE CONSEIL GENERAL DES ALPES-MARITIMES, PARIS.

10-10-18.

I have been greatly touched by the message of generous appreciation you have been good enough to send to me and to the Army under my command on behalf of the Conseil General des Alpes-Maritimes. I beg you to accept for yourself and convey to your Council our very warmest thanks. We are all very confident that the triumph of Justice and Right is in sight.

D. Haig. F.M.

General Headquarters,
14th October, 1918.

Commander-in-Chief,
British Armies in France.

PRINTED IN FRANCE BY ARMY PRINTING AND STATIONERY SERVICES.   PRESS A—10/18.

SPECIAL ORDER OF THE DAY
By FIELD-MARSHAL SIR DOUGLAS HAIG
K.T., G.C.B., G.C.V.O., K.C.I.E
Commander-in-Chief, British Armies in France.

The following telegrams are published for the information of all ranks:—

From FIELD-MARSHAL SIR DOUGLAS HAIG to GENERAL MILNE, COMMANDING-IN-CHIEF, SALONICA.

5-10-18.

The achievements of our comrades under your command in Salonica have filled us with intense pride and admiration. Will you please accept, on behalf of myself and of the British Armies in France, and convey to your Army, our heartiest congratulations on the magnificent victory which has crowned your perseverance and patience so admirably displayed during many weary months of waiting.

To FIELD-MARSHAL SIR DOUGLAS HAIG from GENERAL MILNE, COMMANDING-IN-CHIEF, SALONICA.

6-10-18.

Many thanks for your telegram. Nothing can give the British Army in Macedonia more satisfaction than the approbation of their comrades in France, and they are glad to have been able to take a small part in the general success.

General Headquarters,
14th October, 1918.

Commander-in-Chief,
British Armies in France.

PRINTED IN FRANCE BY ARMY PRINTING AND STATIONERY SERVICES.

PRESS A—10/18.

SPECIAL ORDER OF THE DAY
By FIELD-MARSHAL SIR DOUGLAS HAIG
K.T., G.C.B., G.C.V.O., K.C.I.E
Commander-in-Chief, British Armies in France.

The following messages are published for the information of all ranks:—

To FIELD-MARSHAL SIR DOUGLAS HAIG from LORD METHUEN, MALTA.
11-10-18.
May Malta congratulate you for your splendid work from beginning to end.

From FIELD-MARSHAL SIR DOUGLAS HAIG to LORD METHUEN, MALTA.
12-10-18.
Grateful thanks to you and your command for your kind telegram. We all greatly appreciate your thinking of us in this friendly way.

To FIELD-MARSHAL SIR DOUGLAS HAIG from THE LAMPETER PATRIOTIC COMMITTEE.
11-10-18.
Your success greatly admired by the Lampeter Patriotic Committee, who send you heartiest congratulations and best wishes for complete victory.

From FIELD-MARSHAL SIR DOUGLAS HAIG to THE LAMPETER PATRIOTIC COMMITTEE.
12-10-18.
Many thanks to you and the Lampeter Patriotic Committee for the kindly congratulations and good wishes which we all greatly appreciate.

To FIELD-MARSHAL SIR DOUGLAS HAIG from MRS. OGILVIE GORDON, HARROGATE.
11-10-18.
The National Council of Women of Great Britain and Ireland offer their heartfelt congratulations on the brilliant achievements of the troops under your command on the Western front.

From FIELD-MARSHAL SIR DOUGLAS HAIG to MRS. OGILVIE GORDON, HARROGATE.
12-10-18.
All ranks join with me in sending heartiest thanks to the National Council of Women of Great Britain and Ireland, and take this opportunity of expressing their appreciation of their splendid services during the war.

To FIELD-MARSHAL SIR DOUGLAS HAIG from THE SECRETARY, NATIONAL FEDERATION OF DISCHARGED AND DEMOBILIZED SAILORS AND SOLDIERS, DUNFERMLINE.
11-10-18.
Congratulations to yourself and our serving comrades capture Cambrai. We are with you all in spirit.

From FIELD-MARSHAL SIR DOUGLAS HAIG to THE SECRETARY, NATIONAL FEDERATION OF DISCHARGED AND DEMOBILIZED SAILORS AND SOLDIERS, DUNFERMLINE.

11-10-18.

Please convey to the members of your Branch heartiest thanks, on behalf of myself and all ranks under my command, for the welcome message you have sent us.

To FIELD-MARSHAL SIR DOUGLAS HAIG from THE HON. SECRETARY, EXECUTIVE COMMITTEE OF THE UNITED COUNCIL OF THE EVANGELICAL CHURCHES, TORQUAY.

7-10-18.

I am requested by the Executive Committee of the United Council of the Evangelical Free Churches in Torquay and neighbourhood to write and assure you, of our sincere gratitude for the long and strenuous service that you have rendered to our King and Country.

We rejoice in the great successes which have attended the efforts of the noble men under your command, and we are especially proud of the victories which have been won by the British Army and the Colonial troops.

We feel confident that, with the blessing of God, the future is safe in your hands and those associated with you, and we earnestly pray that He will so sustain and strengthen you, that you will be enabled to bring this Great War to an early and satisfactory conclusion.

Trusting that you will be pleased to accept this expression of our gratitude.

From FIELD-MARSHAL SIR DOUGLAS HAIG to THE HON. SECRETARY, EXECUTIVE COMMITTEE OF THE UNITED COUNCIL OF THE EVANGELICAL CHURCHES, TORQUAY.

11-10-18.

We are all greatly touched by the kind message which you have sent us from the Executive Committee of the United Council of the Evangelical Churches of Torquay and neighbourhood. All ranks join with me in sending our grateful thanks for your congratulations, and for the support which your prayers will mean for us in the carrying out of our endeavours.

To FIELD-MARSHAL SIR DOUGLAS HAIG from THE GENERAL SECRETARY, ABERCARN AND CROSSKEYS BRANCH, NATIONAL FEDERATION OF DISCHARGED AND DEMOBILISED SAILORS AND SOLDIERS, CROSSKEYS, MON.

8-10-18.

The members of the above Branch wish me to convey to you, and all ranks under your command, their sincere congratulations upon your recent successes. We having left the field of activity feel secure in the knowledge that the safeguarding of our beloved Country could not have been placed in more capable hands. We are proud of you, and our late comrades-in-arms, and shall pray for the continued success of your glorious offensive.

From FIELD-MARSHAL SIR DOUGLAS HAIG to THE GENERAL SECRETARY, ABERCARN AND CROSSKEYS BRANCH, NATIONAL FEDERATION OF DISCHARGED AND DEMOBILISED SAILORS AND SOLDIERS, CROSSKEYS, MON.

11-10-18.

Please convey to the members of your Branch the heartfelt thanks of myself and their late comrades-in-arms now serving in France for their welcome message of congratulation.

I should like to add how much I personally appreciate your kind words about myself.

To FIELD-MARSHAL SIR DOUGLAS HAIG from THE ORGANIZING SECRETARY, BRITISH WORKERS' LEAGUE, NORTHWICH.

3-10-18.

I have the honour to ask your acceptance of the accompanying resolution passed at an Open Air Meeting of the British Workers' League, and submitted by Councillor Millar, of Widnes, on Thursday evening, the 3rd October:—

RESOLUTION.

"That this Public Meeting here assembled beg to send their hearty congratulations to Field-Marshal Sir Douglas Haig on the great victories he has achieved over the German Army, and desire to assure him that the people of Northwich will continue to watch with interest the future march of his glorious and unconquerable troops to the complete destruction of Prussian Militarism and restoration of a full measure of freedom to all Nations."

From FIELD-MARSHAL SIR DOUGLAS HAIG to THE ORGANIZING SECRETARY, BRITISH WORKERS' LEAGUE, NORTHWICH.

11-10-18.

I beg that you will convey to the members of the Northwich Branch of the British Workers' League, on behalf of myself and all ranks of the Army in France, our grateful thanks for the inspiring message of congratulation which you have been good enough to send us on their behalf. We are all gratified to hear of the interest the people of Northwich take in our doings, and of their confidence in our ability to achieve a victorious peace.

D. Haig. F.M.
Commander-in-Chief,
British Armies in France.

General Headquarters,
14th October, 1918.

SPECIAL ORDER OF THE DAY
By FIELD-MARSHAL SIR DOUGLAS HAIG
K.T., G.C.B., G.C.V.O., K.C.I.E
Commander-in-Chief, British Armies in France.

The following messages are published for the information of all ranks:—

To FIELD-MARSHAL SIR DOUGLAS HAIG FROM THE SECRETARY, NATIONAL FEDERATION OF DISCHARGED AND DEMOBILIZED SAILORS AND SOLDIERS, CLAPHAM, BRIXTON AND STOCKWELL BRANCH, LONDON.

9-10-18.

On behalf of the members of the Clapham, Brixton and Stockwell Branch of the National Federation of Discharged and Demobilized Sailors and Soldiers, I have been requested to convey to you our heartiest congratulations on the brilliant victories recently achieved by all sections of the British Army serving under your command.

Although rendered incapable of taking any further part in the actual fighting, our thoughts are always with our gallant comrades we have left behind on the various fronts with our sincerest wishes for a continued success.

FROM FIELD-MARSHAL SIR DOUGLAS HAIG TO THE SECRETARY, NATIONAL FEDERATION OF DISCHARGED AND DEMOBILIZED SAILORS AND SOLDIERS, CLAPHAM, BRIXTON AND STOCKWELL BRANCH, LONDON.

20-10-18.

Please convey on behalf of myself and all ranks under my command to the members of your Branch our heartiest thanks for their kind message and the best greetings from their old comrades.

To FIELD-MARSHAL SIR DOUGLAS HAIG FROM THE HON. SECRETARY, 8TH WIGAN TROOP BOY SCOUTS, 30, DICCONSON STREET, WIGAN.

9-10-18.

The officers of the above Troop at the meeting of the "Court of Honour" held on the 7th inst. expressed their admiration of the splendid successes which have attended the Armies under your command, and I am asked to convey to you their warmest congratulations.

They remember with pride that some of their comrades of the Court of Honour have taken part and borne their share in the heat of the battle.

They are filled with sorrow, too, for some will never return.

FROM FIELD-MARSHAL SIR DOUGLAS HAIG TO INSTITUTE FRANCAIS DE LONDRES, INCORPORATED UNIVERSITE DE LILLE.

23-10-18.

All ranks of the British Army in France send warmest thanks for your friendly message, and are proud of the share they have taken in regaining the great town with whose University you are incorporated

To FIELD-MARSHAL SIR DOUGLAS HAIG FROM THE PRESIDENT, INSTITUTE OF GAS ENGINEERS, GREAT GEORGE STREET, WESTMINSTER, LONDON.

17-10-18.

Institution, Gas Engineers, in special meeting assembled, desire to express their pride in, and gratitude for, the magnificent victories achieved by you and the forces under your command, and give assurance they will maintain supply raw materials for production high explosives essential to complete victory.

FROM FIELD-MARSHAL SIR DOUGLAS HAIG TO THE PRESIDENT, INSTITUTE OF GAS ENGINEERS, GREAT GEORGE STREET, WESTMINSTER, LONDON.

23-10-18.

All best thanks to you and the members of the Institution for their welcome message of congratulation and their promise to maintain supplies of raw materials for producing high explosives which all ranks greatly appreciate.

To FIELD-MARSHAL SIR DOUGLAS HAIG FROM SIR THOMAS DUNLOP, GLASGOW.

19-10-18.

On behalf of meeting organized by the Merchant Seamen's League, and addressed by Havelock Wilson, I convey to you and to the gallant British Armies under your command our heartfelt gratitude and profound admiration for your unparalleled victories over the barbarians. We are irrevocably determined that after you have smashed the Prussian military machine beyond hope of restoration or repair we shall for our part equally render for all time impossible the commercial domination of Prussia. Our sailors and firemen will carry no German passengers or goods until full atonement and reparation have been made by the huns for their unspeakable crimes against humanity, including the murder of 15,000 non-combatant seafaring men and the torture inflicted upon prisoners of war. In this policy we feel assured that we can rely upon the support of His Majesty's fighting services. I am to tell you that Scotland is triumphantly proud of her son whose calm courage never quailed in the darkest days of disaster and ill-fortune, and whose brilliant leadership in the hour of victory is the admiration of the civilised world.

FROM FIELD-MARSHAL, SIR DOUGLAS HAIG TO THE TRADES AND LABOUR COUNCIL, OLDHAM AND DISTRICT.

23-10-18.

All ranks join with me in sending heartiest thanks for your kind congratulations on results of recent fighting.

To FIELD-MARSHAL SIR DOUGLAS HAIG FROM THE SECRETARY, BATTERSEA AND WANDSWORTH BRANCH, NATIONAL FEDERATION OF DISCHARGED AND DEMOBILISED SAILORS AND SOLDIERS, 38a, BATTERSEA RISE, LONDON.

19-10-18.

The Battersea and Wandsworth Branch, National Federation Discharged and Demobilised Sailors and Soldiers offer their hearty congratulations to Sir Douglas Haig and all ranks under his command on their heroic achievements and the success attending their courageous fighting.

FROM FIELD-MARSHAL SIR DOUGLAS HAIG TO THE SECRETARY, BATTERSEA AND WANDSWORTH BRANCH, NATIONAL FEDERATION OF DISCHARGED AND DEMOBILISED SAILORS AND SOLDIERS, 38a, BATTERSEA RISE, LONDON.

23-10-18.

On behalf of myself and all ranks under my command please convey to the Battersea and Wandsworth Branch, National Federation of Discharged and Demobilised Sailors and Soldiers, our grateful thanks for their kind message.

To FIELD-MARSHAL SIR DOUGLAS HAIG FROM THE SECRETARY, GROCERS' FEDERATION, LONDON.

20-10-18.

Grocers' Federation meeting at Brighton tenders its most respectful and heartiest congratulations to Sir Douglas Haig upon the unexampled victories achieved by the heroism and bravery of the officers, non-commissioned officers, and men under his command, with those of our great Allies.

FROM FIELD-MARSHAL SIR DOUGLAS HAIG TO THE SECRETARY, GROCERS' FEDERATION, LONDON.

23-10-18.

The congratulations of the Grocers' Federation are very welcome to all ranks, who join with me in sending grateful thanks.

To FIELD-MARSHAL SIR DOUGLAS HAIG FROM INSTITUTE FRANCAIS DE LONDRES, INCORPORATED UNIVERSITE DE LILLE.

20-10-18.

Beg to convey to yourself and splendid Armies boundless admiration and gratitude.

It seems only a short time since they were young knights errant with their bare knees.

May you and your gallant Armies soon achieve complete victory and a speedy return to the homes that have been so nobly defended by the valour of your arms.

From FIELD-MARSHAL SIR DOUGLAS HAIG to THE HON. SECRETARY, 8TH WIGAN TROOP BOY SCOUTS, 30, DICCONSON STREET, WIGAN.
20-10-18.

Please convey to the 8th Wigan Troop Boy Scouts on behalf of myself and all ranks under my command our heartiest thanks for the message of congratulation and good wishes to which they have given such kindly expression.

To FIELD-MARSHAL SIR DOUGLAS HAIG from THE PROVOST OF LEITH.
5-10-18.

Excerpt from minute of meeting of the Town Council of the Burgh of Leith of date 3rd October, 1918:—

On the motion of Bailie Finlayson, seconded by Bailie Coull, the Members of Council unanimously adopted the following resolution:—

"The Provost, Magistrates and Councillors of the Burgh of Leith on behalf of the Citizens of the Burgh, in view of the contemplated visit of the Provost and Town Clerk to the Western Front, welcome this opportunity to express to Field-Marshal Sir Douglas Haig their deep appreciation of his personal services and the utmost admiration and pride in the great achievements, endurance and fighting qualities of the Troops under his command.

Further instruct the Provost to convey this resolution to the Field-Marshal."

From FIELD-MARSHAL SIR DOUGLAS HAIG to THE PROVOST OF LEITH.
10-10-18.

All ranks join with me in heartiest thanks to you, the Magistrates and Councillors of Leith, for the message of generous appreciation you have been so good as to convey to me on behalf of the citizens of your ancient Burgh.

I am personally very much touched by the kind reference to myself, which I greatly value.

To FIELD-MARSHAL SIR DOUGLAS HAIG from R. W. ELLETT, ESQ., CLERK TO THE URBAN DISTRICT COUNCIL, CIRENCESTER.
11-10-18.

I am directed by the Cirencester Urban District Council, on behalf of the inhabitants of Cirencester and District, to tender to you and to the gallant troops under your command, their hearty congratulations and grateful thanks for the brilliant victories which the British Army has recently achieved in conjunction with the forces of our Allies, and also for the splendid courage and steady perseverance which they have displayed throughout this great struggle on behalf of our beloved country, and in the cause of Justice and Freedom.

From FIELD-MARSHAL SIR DOUGLAS HAIG to R. W. ELLETT, ESQ., CLERK TO THE URBAN DISTRICT COUNCIL, CIRENCESTER.

20-10-18.

All ranks join with me in conveying to the inhabitants of Cirencester and district our heartiest thanks for their very kind message of congratulation which they have been good enough to send us from your District Council, and which we all appreciate.

To FIELD-MARSHAL SIR DOUGLAS HAIG FROM HOWARD CHAPMAN, ESQ., TOWN HALL, BANBURY.

15-10-18.

At a full meeting of the Special Constables of this Borough held last night the enclosed Congratulatory Message to you, Sir, was assented to with acclamation.

I pray that you will believe it to convey the sincere admiration and good wishes of us all.

Congratulatory Message.

The Special Constables of the Borough of Banbury beg to tender to Field-Marshal Sir Douglas Haig their hearty congratulations on the glorious achievements of the British Forces under his command.

They recall with pride that the one, who with undaunted courage and marvellous success is directing the British Arms to victory, was once a familiar figure in this neighbourhood, and they hope it will not be long before the gallant Field-Marshal will again be seen in the Hunting Field here.

From FIELD-MARSHAL SIR DOUGLAS HAIG to HOWARD CHAPMAN, ESQ., TOWN HALL, BANBURY.

20-10-18.

The extremely kind message which you have been good enough to send me on behalf of the Special Constables of the Borough has given me the very greatest pleasure. I am delighted to feel with what interest and encouragement all my old friends in your neighbourhood are following the doings of the British Armies in France. Please convey to them all my very best thanks and all good wishes.

To FIELD-MARSHAL SIR DOUGLAS HAIG FROM THE TRADES AND LABOUR COUNCIL, OLDHAM AND DISTRICT (through War Office).

19-10-18.

Following resolution received from Oldham and District Trades and Labour Council:—

"This representative meeting of the Trades' Unionists of Oldham, covering all sections of industry, congratulate the British and Allied Naval and Military Forces on their magnificent achievements on sea and land, believing that the gratitude of the whole civilized world is due to officers and men of all ranks for their gallant and heroic services and self-sacrifices in the fight for the world-wide freedom and for the crushing of militarism."

From FIELD-MARSHAL SIR DOUGLAS HAIG to SIR THOMAS DUNLOP, GLASGOW.

23-10-18.

The inspiring message of congratulation and generous praise which you have sent us on behalf of meeting organized by the Merchant Seamen's League has caused the liveliest satisfaction to all ranks of the British Armies in France. We are filled with admiration at the splendid spirit of the Merchant Seamen which has enabled them to triumph over all danger and difficulties during the war and render inestimable service to the Empire and the cause of Liberty. I cannot adequately thank you and them for the kind words about myself which have touched and pleased me beyond expression.

D. Haig, F.M.

General Headquarters,
25th October, 1918.

Commander-in-Chief,
British Armies in France.

SPECIAL ORDER OF THE DAY
By FIELD-MARSHAL SIR DOUGLAS HAIG
K.T., G.C.B., G.C.V.O., K.C.I.E
Commander-in-Chief, British Armies in France.

The following messages are published for the information of all ranks:—

FROM FIELD-MARSHAL SIR DOUGLAS HAIG TO GENERAL READ, II AMERICAN CORPS.

20th October, 1918.

I wish to express to you personally and to all the Officers and men serving under you my warm appreciation of the very valuable and gallant services rendered by you throughout the recent operations with the Fourth British Army. Called upon to attack positions of great strength held by a determined enemy, all ranks of the 27th and 30th American Divisions under your command displayed an energy, courage and determination in attack which proved irresistible. It does not need me to tell you that in the heavy fighting of the past three weeks you have earned the lasting esteem and admiration of your British comrades in arms whose successes you have so nobly shared.

TO FIELD-MARSHAL SIR DOUGLAS HAIG FROM GENERAL READ, II AMERICAN CORPS.

20th October, 1918.

In acknowledging receipt of your telegram of this date permit me to say that every officer and other soldier of the II American Corps will always remember with great pride your generous commendation of the services rendered in the important operations of the past three weeks, during which time we have had the honour to be in action as a part of your superb Fourth Army. We are under the greatest obligation to all British units attached to us. Their splendid co-operation, especially that of the VII Corps Royal Artillery, insured at all times the success of our operations.

D. Haig, F.M.
Commander-in-Chief,
British Armies in France.

General Headquarters,
26th October, 1918.

PRINTED IN FRANCE BY ARMY PRINTING AND STATIONERY SERVICES.   PRESS A—10/18.

War Diary.

SPECIAL ORDER OF THE DAY
By FIELD-MARSHAL SIR DOUGLAS HAIG
K.T., G.C.B., G.C.V.O., K.C.I.E
Commander-in-Chief, British Armies in France.

The following messages are published for the information of all ranks:—

To FIELD-MARSHAL SIR DOUGLAS HAIG from THE CLERK, THE GUILD OF FREEMEN OF THE CITY OF LONDON (INCORPORATED), CANNON STREET HOTEL, CANNON STREET, E.C. 4.

16-10-18.

I am directed to inform you that at a meeting of this Guild, which includes nearly a thousand Freemen of the City of London, a resolution was passed conveying to you and the officers and men under your able command, our sincere congratulations upon your recent brilliant successes and our heartfelt thanks for all the gallant and skilful work which you and they have so devotedly accomplished throughout four years of fighting. It is our fervent hope and belief that your tremendous task is now approaching a glorious and triumphant termination which will secure the accomplishment of all your aims.

From FIELD-MARSHAL SIR DOUGLAS HAIG to THE CLERK, THE GUILD OF FREEMEN OF THE CITY OF LONDON.

24-10-18.

All ranks greatly appreciate the friendly message you have been good enough to send us from the Freemen of the City of London, and join with me in begging you to convey to your Guild our hearty appreciation and thanks.

To FIELD-MARSHAL SIR DOUGLAS HAIG from THE GENERAL SECRETARY, HARNESS AND SADDLERY, FURNITURE TRADES ASSOCIATION, WALSALL, STAFFS.

19-10-18.

I am directed by the members of the above Society at a general meeting of the Trade held last Tuesday, October 15th, to forward you the following copy of a resolution that was unanimously adopted at the meeting:—

"That this mass meeting congratulates the Allied Armies on the splendid success which they have achieved on the Battle Fields. Pledging ourselves to give all the support possible to help the Commanders to bring the War to a successful issue. Believing that in the interest of the Allied Nations it is necessary to carry on the War until there is a complete surrender of the Enemies of Mankind."

To FIELD-MARSHAL SIR DOUGLAS HAIG FROM H. LEE, ESQ., WESLEYAN CHURCH, ASHFORD, KENT.
22-10-18.

Brotherhood mass meeting supporting the League Nations, at Wesleyan Church, Ashford, Kent, with Urban District Council present, heartily congratulates you and all ranks, rejoices thankfully at the glorious news of continued successes and earnestly prays for early decisive victory, leading to lasting peace for Glory of God and good of humanity.

From FIELD-MARSHAL SIR DOUGLAS HAIG To H. LEE, ESQ., WESLEYAN CHURCH, ASHFORD, KENT.
24-10-18.

I beg you to convey to the Brotherhood mass meeting the warmest thanks of all ranks of the British Armies in France and of myself for their welcome message which we all greatly value.

To FIELD-MARSHAL SIR DOUGLAS HAIG FROM THE CHAIRMAN, DISTRICT COUNCIL, CHURCH, LANCS.
18-10-18.

Sincere congratulations from the Chairman and members of the District Council and residents of Church on your splendid achievements.

From FIELD-MARSHAL SIR DOUGLAS HAIG To THE CHAIRMAN, DISTRICT COUNCIL, CHURCH, LANCS.
24-10-18.

Warmest thanks to you and the members of the District Council from myself and all ranks under my command for your friendly wire.

To FIELD-MARSHAL SIR DOUGLAS HAIG FROM THE PRINCIPAL, UNIVERSITY, ST. ANDREWS.
21-10-18.

The Court and the Senate congratulate Sir Douglas Haig on the great victories won by the British Armies under his command, and are proud to think that the illustrious Field-Marshal is the Rector of the University.

From FIELD-MARSHAL SIR DOUGLAS HAIG To THE PRINCIPAL, UNIVERSITY. ST. ANDREWS.
24-10-18.

Please accept for yourself and convey to the Court and Senate of your ancient University, of which I have the honour to be Rector, my most grateful thanks and appreciation of the kind message which you have been good enough to send to me. My best greetings to you all.

From FIELD-MARSHAL SIR DOUGLAS HAIG To THE HON. SECRETARY, NORTHERN COUNTIES UNION OF SPIRITUALISTS AND SPIRITUALIST SOCIETIES, NEWCASTLE-ON-TYNE.
24-10-18.

The very kind message which you have sent to me personally on behalf of the Conference of Northumberland and Durham Spiritualists has given me the very greatest pleasure. The generous appreciation which we have all received from our fellow-countrymen at home is a source of continual encouragement to us in our work out here. Please accept and convey to the members of your Societies our very warmest thanks.

To FIELD-MARSHAL SIR DOUGLAS HAIG FROM THE SECRETARY, THE SCOTTISH FEDERATION OF DISCHARGED AND DEMOBILISED SAILORS AND SOLDIERS, DUNDEE BRANCH.
22-10-18.

The Scottish Federation of Discharged and Demobilised Sailors and Soldiers, Dundee Branch congratulate you and the Armies under your command on recent great victories gained and hope that similar success will attend your efforts in the future. The discharged men of Dundee will follow your efforts for a speedy victory with the same feelings of confidence that they held when they had the honour to fight under you.

From FIELD-MARSHAL SIR DOUGLAS HAIG To THE SECRETARY, THE SCOTTISH FEDERATION OF DISCHARGED AND DEMOBILISED SAILORS AND SOLDIERS, DUNDEE BRANCH.
24-10-18.

Please convey to our discharged and demobilised comrades of the Dundee Branch the cordial thanks of myself and all ranks of the Army in France for the message of congratulation to which they have given such kind expression.

To FIELD-MARSHAL SIR DOUGLAS HAIG FROM THE CONVENER, COUNTY COUNCIL OF FIFE, CUPAR.
18-10-18.

The County Council of Fife in statutory meeting assembled desire me to express their warmest congratulations to yourself and the troops under your command on the success of the Armies in the field, and their profound admiration of, and gratitude for, the valour and devotion displayed by all ranks in overcoming the resistance of the enemy.

From FIELD-MARSHAL SIR DOUGLAS HAIG To THE CONVENER, COUNTY COUNCIL OF FIFE, CUPAR.
24-10-18.

The generous message of congratulation and appreciation which you have sent us from the County Council of Fife has given us all great pleasure. The Army joins with me in sending best thanks.

From FIELD-MARSHAL SIR DOUGLAS HAIG to THE GENERAL SECRETARY, HARNESS AND SADDLERY, FURNITURE TRADES ASSOCIATION, WALSALL, STAFFS

24-10-18.

All best thanks to the members of your Society on behalf of myself and the Army under my command for the welcome message of congratulation you have been good enough to send us. Please tell them how much we value their splendid spirit at this time.

To FIELD-MARSHAL SIR DOUGLAS HAIG from THE HON. SECRETARY, NATIONAL FEDERATION OF DISCHARGED AND DEMOBILISED SAILORS AND SOLDIERS, SOUTH WEST HAM AND DISTRICT BRANCH.

16-10-18.

I am directed to forward to yourself the following resolution, adopted unanimously by the above Branch at their Quarterly Meeting, and to request you to kindly bring same to the notice of Marshal Foch:—

"That this meeting of 700 men broken in the war do express our great admiration for our old comrades who are now doing such splendid work, and tender to all ranks our very hearty congratulations.

"With our old comrades who are still in the field we demand the reward of our sufferings:—

"An unconditional surrender from Germany and No Peace by Negotiation."

From FIELD-MARSHAL SIR DOUGLAS HAIG to THE HON. SECRETARY, NATIONAL FEDERATION OF DISCHARGED AND DEMOBILISED SAILORS AND SOLDIERS SOUTH WEST HAM AND DISTRICT BRANCH.

24-10-18.

All ranks join with me in sending our warmest thanks to the meeting of seven hundred of our discharged and demobilised comrades for their heartening message of congratulation. They can rely on us to see that full results are reaped from their past sacrifices and endurance.

To FIELD-MARSHAL SIR DOUGLAS HAIG from THE SECRETARY, OLDHAM AND DISTRICT TRADES AND LABOUR COUNCIL, 151 UNION STREET, OLDHAM.

17-10-18.

At our quarterly meeting of Delegates held on Tuesday night, the 15th October, in the Weavers Institute, Oldham, representing over 25,000 Trades Unionists of all sections of Trade, passed the following resolution unanimously, and they instructed me to send same on to you and hope you will convey these congratulations to all your men of all ranks:—

Congratulations to our fighting men.

"That this representative meeting of the Trades Unionists of Oldham covering all sections of industry, congratulate the British and Allied Naval and

To FIELD-MARSHAL SIR DOUGLAS HAIG from THE WORKERS, LILLE SHELL FACTORY, HAILEY'S INDUSTRIAL MOTORS, LTD., YOKER, GLASGOW.

18-10-18.

The workers of Lille Shell Factory at Yoker, Glasgow, desire us to convey to you and your troops their hearty congratulations on the re-capture of Lille.

From FIELD-MARSHAL SIR DOUGLAS HAIG to THE WORKERS, LILLE SHELL FACTORY, HAILEY'S INDUSTRIAL MOTORS, LTD., YOKER, GLASGOW.

24-10-18.

On behalf of myself and all ranks under my command please accept our warmest thanks for your congratulations on the re-capture of Lille.

To FIELD-MARSHAL SIR DOUGLAS HAIG from THE PRESIDENT, DISTRICT COUNCIL, REGIMENTAL ASSOCIATIONS, EDINBURGH.

20-10-18.

The Edinburgh, Leith, and District Council of Regimental Associations, respectfully offer heartiest congratulations to you and the soldiers of the Empire on the magnificent and far reaching victories achieved under your splendid leadership, which bring us within view of peace.

From FIELD-MARSHAL SIR DOUGLAS HAIG to THE PRESIDENT, DISTRICT COUNCIL, REGIMENTAL ASSOCIATIONS, EDINBURGH.

24-10-18.

Very many thanks for your friendly message of congratulation. All ranks greatly appreciate your confidence in the final results of our efforts.

General Headquarters,
28th October, 1918.

D. Haig. F.M.
Commander-in-Chief,
British Armies in France.

PRINTED IN FRANCE BY ARMY PRINTING AND STATIONERY SERVICES.

Military forces on their magnificent achievements on sea and land, believing that the gratitude of the whole civilised world is due to officers and men of all ranks for their gallant and heroic services and self sacrifices in the fight for the world wide freedom and for the crushing of Militarism.

From FIELD-MARSHAL SIR DOUGLAS HAIG to THE SECRETARY, OLDHAM AND DISTRICT TRADES AND LABOUR COUNCIL, 151 UNION STREET, OLDHAM.

24-10-18.

Please convey to the Trades Unionists of Oldham the best thanks of myself and all ranks under my command for their message of congratulation which we all were delighted to receive.

To FIELD-MARSHAL SIR DOUGLAS HAIG from THE HON. SECRETARY, MAIDSTONE LOCAL CENTRAL COMMITTEE, NATIONAL WAR SAVINGS COMMITTEE, MAIDSTONE.

15-10-18.

I have much pleasure in transmitting to you the following resolution, passed at a meeting of the Maidstone War Savings Associations:—

"That the Maidstone War Savings Associations tender their hearty congratulations to you, and the British Generals and troops under your Command, on their Great Victory, and pledge themselves to increase their endeavours to find funds for the completion of the grand work of the British Forces".

From FIELD-MARSHAL SIR DOUGLAS HAIG to THE HON. SECRETARY, MAIDSTONE LOCAL CENTRAL COMMITTEE, NATIONAL WAR SAVINGS COMMITTEE, MAIDSTONE.

24-10-18.

Warmest thanks to the members of the Maidstone War Savings Association from all ranks of the British Army in France for their friendly message and for their promise to increase their present endeavours, which the Army greatly appreciates.

To FIELD-MARSHAL SIR DOUGLAS HAIG from THE HON. SECRETARY, NORTHERN COUNTIES UNION OF SPIRITUALISTS AND SPIRITUALIST SOCIETIES, NEWCASTLE-ON-TYNE.

15-10-18.

At conference to-day of Spiritualists representing Northumberland and Durham it was resolved to send you our felicitations re turn of events, and at the same time express our confidence and thanks for your personal work. We fully realize, during the terrible days through which our country has passed, what a tremendous responsibility has been yours, and we rejoice with you, the way things stand to-day as a result of your work. We pray that health, strength and happiness may be yours for many years to come, and that the supreme pleasure born from a consciousness of duty well and nobly done, may fill your cup overflowing.

PRESS A—10/13

War Diary

SPECIAL ORDER OF THE DAY
By FIELD-MARSHAL SIR DOUGLAS HAIG
K.T., G.C.B., G.C.V.O., K.C.I.E
Commander-in-Chief, British Armies in France.

The following messages are published for the information of all ranks:—

FROM HER MAJESTY QUEEN ALEXANDRA, SANDRINGHAM, TO FIELD-MARSHAL SIR DOUGLAS HAIG.

18-10-18.
Please accept my renewed congratulations on the victorious progress of your wonderful Army. The re-occupation of Cambrai, Douai, Lille and Ostend is the result and reward of their fine spirit, their untiring energy and their splendid courage under leadership that they trust and believe in.

TO HER MAJESTY QUEEN ALEXANDRA, SANDRINGHAM, FROM FIELD-MARSHAL SIR DOUGLAS HAIG.

24-10-18.
Your Majesty's gracious message of congratulation has given universal pleasure to the whole Army. I beg that you accept on behalf of all ranks and of myself our most grateful thanks for this fresh proof of your Majesty's unfailing interest and encouragement.

TO FIELD-MARSHAL SIR DOUGLAS HAIG FROM GENERAL SMUTS.

21-10-18.
I have received a telegram from General Botha, dated 17th October, in which he says.
"Please convey my warmest congratulations to Haig on the magnificent success obtained by his Army, and on the admirable manner in which the operations have been carried out."
I am sure it will give you great pleasure to have this direct message from General Botha, whose greatest pleasure is to hear of the success of the British Army.

FROM FIELD-MARSHAL SIR DOUGLAS HAIG TO GENERAL SMUTS.

24-10-18.
Will you be kind enough to convey to General Botha the grateful thanks of myself and of the British Army in France for his kindly message. All ranks greatly value his appreciation and join with me in sending him very cordial greetings.

General Headquarters,
28th October, 1918.

Commander-in-Chief,
British Armies in France.

PRINTED IN FRANCE BY ARMY PRINTING AND STATIONERY SERVICES   PRESS A—10/18.

SECRET.   Copy No. 4

183rd. INFANTRY BRIGADE.

ADMINISTRATIVE INSTRUCTIONS ISSUED IN CONNECTION WITH BRIGADE ORDER NO.258 of to-day.

17th. October 1918

1. **ADVANCE BILLETING PARTIES.**
    The Area now allotted to this Brigade Group (subject to mutual arrangement with 182nd Infantry Bde) is Map Squares A.22 & A.17 south of Railway.
    This Area is clear of troops of the 24th. Division.
    Advance Billeting parties will report to Staff Captain at road junction A.16.c.6.4. at 0900 to-morrow 18th inst. when areas will be allotted.

2. **SUPPLIES.**
    Refilling Point will be at 0730 to-morrow at the same place as for to-day.
    After refilling Supply Wagons will report direct to Q.M.Stores and proceed to new area with Units.
    IMMEDIATELY on arrival in new area Supply Wagons will be off-loaded and return to No.3 Coy.Div.Train. (It is most important that they should be offloaded as soon as possible as they are required for drawing from CAMBRAI Railhead the same morning). If Supply Wagons cannot be loaded in time to march with Units they will travel in rear of the last column and deliver on arrival in new area.

3. **TRANSPORT.**
    LORRIES.   5 Lorries are allotted to the Brigade for the carriage of blankets, stores, etc., and are allotted as under :-

    Brigade H.Q.   1
    Each Battalion   1
    2/1st.Field Amb.   One third
    478 Field Coy.   "   "
    183 L.T.M.B.   "   "

    These Lorries will report at Brigade H.Q. at 0830, and Units concerned will have guides at Brigade H.Q. at 0820 to take over the Lorries as allotted by Staff Captain.
        They will do <u>one</u> journey only, as they are required at CAMBRAI Railhead the same morning.
    NOTE.   Blankets will <u>not</u> be dumped in this area.
    BAGGAGE WAGONS will remain with Units.

4. **TENTS AND TRENCH SHELTERS.**
    184 Infantry Bde. are taking over Camps at present occupied by this Brigade Group.   Camps will therefore not be struck, but guards will be left in charge to hand over to 184 Bde.   Receipts for all Tents and Trench Shelters handed over will be obtained and copies sent to the Staff Captain as soon as possible.

5. **TRANSPORT** will move complete to establishment.

6. Clean billet certificates will be obtained before leaving the area and forwarded to this Office as soon as possible.

7. **ACKNOWLEDGE.**

B.H.Q.

A. Ball.
Captain.
Staff Captain, 183rd. Infantry Brigade.

DISTRIBUTION.

No.1	G.O.C.	No. 8 & 9	1st E.Lancs	No. 18	Bde.Sig.Off
" 2	B.M.	" 10 & 11	183 T.M.B.	" 19	S.T.O.
" 3	S.C.	" 12 & 13	478 Fld.Coy.	" 20	Bde.Supply O.
" 4 & 5	9th Northd. Fus.	" 14 & 15	2/1st Fld.Amb.	" 21	Bde.Q.M.S.
" 6 & 7	11th Suffolks.	" 16 & 17	3 Coy.Div.Train	" 22	S.C.182 Bde.
				" 23	" 184 Bde.

No.24 61st.Div."Q"   No.25 A.P.M.   No.26 & 27 Retain.

SECRET.   Copy No. 4

ADMINISTRATIVE INSTRUCTIONS ISSUED IN CONNECTION WITH MOVE.

1st October 1918.

1. ADVANCE BILLETING PARTIES.

Billeting parties will proceed on lorries allotted for Q.M.Stores (see para 2).

Advance billeting parties will proceed to STEENBECQUE where they will report to Staff Captain at Church at 1300. Staff Captain will allot billeting areas.

Each Billeting party will include at least One N.C.O. from Q.M. Stores personnel, who will, immediately on arrival in new area, select new Q.M.Stores, and then proceed to Church STEENBECQUE to meet Supply Wagons and guide them to new Q.M.Stores. Supply Wagons will be at STEENBECQUE Church about 1500.

Refilling point on 3rd inst will be at STEENBECQUE Church at 0930.

2. TRANSPORT.

(a) Baggage wagons will report to Units at 0900 to-morrow.

(b) Lorries will report at Q.M.Stores 11th Suffolks L.21.b.5.3 at 0930 to-morrow to assist Units to move Q.M.Stores, Kits, blankets etc, and are allotted as follows :-

9th Northd. Fus.	2
11th Suffolks	2
1st East Lancs.	2
Bde. H.Q.	2
183 L.T.M.B.	1
	9

The 3 Battalions will have guides at L.21.b.5.3 at 0925 to meet lorries and to guide them to Q.M.Stores.

Lorries to do one journey only, and drivers will be instructed to report back to their park on completion of duty.

3. SUPPLIES.

Supplies for consumption 3rd inst will be delivered to-morrow to Q.M.Stores in new area.

Units will ensure that guides meet Supply wagons at STEENBECQUE Church at 1500. (see para 1) and guide wagons to new Q.M.Stores.

NOTE. Personnel at Brigade School are rejoining Units to-morrow.

4. FIRST LINE TRANSPORT
will move complete with tools, S.A.A., Grenades etc. and certificates will be rendered to this Office to that effect. Any deficiencies will be distinctly stated.

5. TENTS, TRENCH SHELTERS AND AREA STORES ETC.
will be handed over to relieving Brigade (182 Bde). If necessary an Officer will be left behind to hand over. Receipts will be obtained and copies will be submitted to this Office as soon as possible after relief.

6. ACKNOWLEDGE. Done

B.H.Q.

A.E. Bull
Captain
Staff Captain, 183rd. Infantry Brigade.

DISTRIBUTION.

Copy Nos. 1 & 2	Retained	Copy No. 14	Bde. Signal Officer
" No. 3	G.O.C.	" " 15	" Supply Officer
" Nos 4 & 5	9th Northd.Fus.	" " 16	" Q.M.S.
" " 6 & 7	11th Suffolks	" " 17	No 3 Coy Train.
" " 8 & 9	1st East Lancs	" " 18	A.P.M.
" " 10 & 11	183 L.T.M.B.	" " 19	61 Div "Q"
" " 12	Brigade Major	" " 20	182 Bde.
" " 13	R.T.O.		

To all recipients 183rd. Infantry Brigade Order
    No.23 dated 4.10.18.

    In consequence of the reversion to winter time on the night 5/6th.inst. the hours of all trains timed to run after 01.00 hours on the 6th.inst should read one hour earlier.
    Similarly all timings in 183rd.Infantry Brigade Order No.253 of 4.10.18 after 01.00 hours will read one hour earlier.

                                            [signature]
                                              Captain,
                                    Brigade Major, 183 Inf. Bde.
HQ.
4.10.18.

SECRET.   Copy No. 6

183rd. INFANTRY BRIGADE
ADMINISTRATIVE INSTRUCTIONS ISSUED IN CONNECTION WITH MOVE BY RAIL.

3rd. October 1918.

1. **MOVE.**

    The Brigade Group complete with Transport will move by Rail from STEENBECQUE Station on the 5th inst, in accordance with attached Table. The actual times of departure and Detraining Station will be notified later.

    The journey will take approximately 5 hours.

    Transport will arrive at Station 3 hours, and personnel 1 hour before schedule time of departure of train.

2. **LOADING AND UNLOADING PARTIES.**

    (a) ENTRAINING. Major A.F.WRIGHT.M.C. 11th Suffolk Regt. will be in charge of Entrainment and will travel on last train (Train No.21).

    "C" Battalion will detail a party of 1 Officer and 50 O.R. to be at Entraining Station 3 hours before the time of departure of the first train (Train No.3). This party will report to Major A.D.WRIGHT.M.C. and will load all trains down to train No.21, on which train they will travel.

    (b) DETRAINING. The Staff Captain or Brigade representative will be in charge Detraining Station.

    "A" Battalion will detail a party of 1 Officer and 50 O.R. to travel on the first train (Train No.3) to report to Staff Captain or representative and remain at Detraining Station until train No 21 has been unloaded.

    (c) Care will be taken to ensure that loading and unloading parties are provided with sufficient rations for consumption until they rejoin their Units.

    NOTE. The Officers detailed should have had experience in Entraining and Detraining.

3. **ADVANCE PARTIES.**

    Advance billeting parties of all Units will proceed by Train No.3, and will report to Staff Captain immediately on arrival at Detraining Station. These parties should include two or three Regimental Police to act as guides to Units on arrival.

4. **SUPPLIES.**

    (a) Arrangements for supplies will be notified later.
    (In all probability there will be two refillings to-morrow 4th. inst. and supply wagons will travel loaded with Units).
    (b) Railhead changes to AIRE on 4th inst.

5. **LORRIES.**

    Lorries to take Stores and Blankets to Entraining Station and from Detraining Station will be provided. Arrangements will be notified later.

6. **TRANSPORT.**

    Transport will travel loaded with complete establishment.

    Horses will be watered and fed before entraining. (There is a Water Point at D.25.d.8.8. where horses can be watered from buckets). Petrol tins at the rate of 1 per animal will be carried filled on all vehicles. Canvas buckets must be kept handy.

    All horses will travel harnessed. O.C.Units will ensure that head collars and head ropes are provided for every horse.

    No detonated grenades will be carried on Transport.

7. **WATER.**

    Water carts will travel full.

    All personnel will travel with water bottles filled.

    NOTE. There is a pump at Station but this is not in working order at present. 478 Field Coy.R.E. have been asked to put this in order, but this cannot be relied on as the exact nature of the necessary repairs are not known.

8. **DISCIPLINE**

The Senior Officer proceeding on each train will detail two guards of 1 N.C.O. & 3 men each, who will be posted and travel at the Head and Tail of each train. Their duties will be to prevent troops from straggling away from the train and out of the Station when the train is at rest, and when train is in motion to prevent troops from travelling on steps, footboards, and roofs or otherwise breaking the general rules laid down for "transport by rail" - particularly to prevent men from attempting to relieve nature at various and unauthorised places.

The N.C.O. i/c M.M.P. attached to Brigade Headquarters will detail two M.M.P. to report to Major A.E.WRIGHT.M.C. at Entraining Station to assist him to organise the traffic at Station. They will travel on the last train (Train No.21). The remainder of M.M.P. personnel will travel on the first train (Train No.3) and will report to Staff Captain or representative immediately on arrival at Detraining Station.

9. **MEDICAL**.

There will be a Medical Officer and an Ambulance in attendance at Entraining and Detraining Stations.

10. **DIVISIONAL BULK CANTEEN**.

The Divisional Bulk Canteen will be open from 7 am to 6 pm on the 4th inst. at AIRE H.29.a.2.4. on the Canal Bank on the HAZEBROUCK side of the Cathedral. All Units may draw their allotment on that day.

Statements shewing the amounts Units are entitled to draw will be given to representatives at time of drawing.

Stores which Units are unable or unwilling to draw will be conveyed to the new Area under Divisional arrangements, but no guarantee can be given as to when they will be available for issue.

11. **BILLETS**.

Clean Billet and No Damage Certificates will be obtained before leaving the area, and forwarded to this Office as soon as possible.

12. **ACKNOWLEDGE**.

B.H.Q.

A E Ball Captain.
Staff Captain, 183rd. Infantry Brigade.

DISTRIBUTION.

```
Copy No. 1 & 2   Retained
 "    "  3       G.O.C.
 "    "  4       Brigade Major
 "    "  5       Staff Captain
 "    "  6 & 7   9th Northd Fus.
 "    "  8 & 9   11th Suffolks
 "    "  10 & 11 1st East Lancs.
 "    "  12      478 Field Coy.R.E.
 "    "  13      No.3 Coy. Div.Train.
 "    "  14      2/3rd Field Amb.
 "    "  15 & 16 183 L.T.M.B.
 "    "  17      1/5 D.C.L.I.
 "    "  18      S.A.A.Sect.D.A.C.
 "    "  19      Major A.E.WRIGHT.M.C.
 "    "  20      R.T.O.
 "    "  21      Bde.Sig.Offr.
 "    "  22      Bde.Supply Officer.
 "    "  23      Bde.Q.M.S.
 "    "  24      N.C.O.i/c M.M.P.
 "    "  25      61st Division "Q" ) for information.
                 A.P.M.            )
```

Train No.	Entraining STEENBECQUE.
3	183 Inf.Bde.H.Q.& Signal Section. 183 L.T.M.B. 478 Field Coy.R.E. 1 Coy. complete with Cooker & Team of "A" Bn.
6	"A" Battalion, less 1 Coy. Cooker and Team.
9	"B" Battalion, less 1 Coy. Cooker and Team.
12	"C" Battalion, less 1 Coy. Cooker and Team.
15	1/5th D.C.L.I.
18	2/3rd Field Ambulance. No 3 Coy. Div.Train. 1 Coy. Complete with Cooker & Team "B" Battalion.
21	½ S.A.A.Section D.A.C. 1 Coy. complete with Cooker & Team "C" Battalion.

TABLE "B" ISSUED WITH 183rd INFANTRY BRIGADE ORDER NO. 249 DATED 7/10/18.

Serial No	Date Oct	Unit	From	To	Starting Point	Time hrs	Route	Leaving by train No	Time for loading train	Time of departure	Detraining Station	Remarks
1.	9	Bde. H.Q., L.T.M.B. & all remaining Transport of 183 Bde. Group.	Present locations.	MONDICOURT Station.	Rd.Junction on Main Rd. Sth of T in LE GROS TISON	0545.	Any.	1.	0600	0905	FREMICOURT.	
2.	9	9 Rthd. Fus.	BO... ERA.	do	do	1040	Direct.	4	1100	1206	HELLIES.	
3.	9	11 Suffolks	HALLOY.	do	do	1045	thro' POMMERA	4	do	do	do	Not to enter POMMERA before 1035
4.	9	2/3 Fld. Ambulance.	BEAUR- PAIRE.	do	do	1335	Direct.	7	1400	1508	do	
5.	9	1st East Lancs.R.	AUTHIEULE	do	do	1340	AUTHIER - HALLOY - POMMERA.	7	do	do	do	Not to enter POMMERA before 1320.
6.	9	478 Field Coy, R.E.	do	do	do	1345	do	7	do	do	do	To follow 1st East Lancs.R.

SECRET.   Copy No 6

183rd INFANTRY BRIGADE ORDER NO. 257.   10/10/18.

Reference Map Sheet 57c, 1/40,000.
VALENCIENNES, 1/100,000.

1. From all information to hand the enemy is carrying out a retirement on a large scale.
   At 0900 this morning, 10th instant, Troops of 17th Corps had reached the general line INCHY - BETHENCOURT - BEVILLERS - BOUSSIERES - RIEUX, and were still advancing.

2. The pursuit of the enemy has been ordered to be carried out with the utmost determination. The one aim and object of troops of the 17th Corps is to get at the enemy's main forces, and bring them to battle.

3. The attached map shows the boundaries of the Corps for the advance:

4. The organisation of the advance will be, for the present, as follows:

   (a) <u>Leading Group.</u>   24th Division.
                                      Corps Mounted Troops.
                                      5 Brigades Field Artillery.
                                      1 Brigade Heavy Artillery.

   (b) <u>Support Group.</u>   19th Division.
                                      4 Brigades Field Artillery.

   (c) <u>Reserve Group.</u>   61st Division.
                                      61st Division Artillery.

5. In the event of the Division being ordered to advance through the leading and support Groups (as in paras. 4 (a) and (b)) the following will form the Advanced Guard of the Division:-

          Commander: Brigadier-General B.D.L.G.ANLEY, CMG, DSO.
             183rd Infantry Brigade.
             306 Brigade R.F.A.
             1 Company 61st Bn. M.G.C.
             478 Field Coy, R.E.

6. In accordance with the above, and as a preparatory measure, 183rd Infantry Brigade Group, will move forward today, 10th instant, to areas as follows:

              H.Q. 183 Inf.Bde. & L.T.M.B.   to Westpil L.2.c
              11th Suffolk Regt.   to L.4.b. and d.
              9th North'd Fusiliers.   to L.4.a. and c.& L.3.b.
              1st E.Lancs. Regt.   to L.3.a. and c.
              306 Bde. R.F.A.   to L.2.a.b.and c.
              M.G.Coy.   to L.2.d.
              478 Field Coy, R.E.   to L.3.d.

   Battalions and Field Coy will move in the order given above, following each other, on receipt of this order.
   Usual distances will be maintained.
   306 Bde. and M.G.Coy. are moving under separate instructions.

7. Route: SUGAR FACTORY - Cross Roads F.19.c.10.90 - ANNEUX.

8.   Communication by visual will be established with this H.Q. immediately on arrival in the new area.

9.   Completion of move, and location of Headquarters will be reported by all Units.

10.   Brigade H.Q. will close at E.21.a.05.20, and reopen at new Headquarters at a time to be notified.

11.   ACKNOWLEDGE.

Roland Le Mesurier
Captain,
Brigade Major, 133rd Infantry Bde.

Issued at 5.20 p.m.

```
Copy  1 - War Diary
      2 - File
      3 - S.C.
      4 - B.S.O.
      5 - B.T.O.
      6 - 9th North'd Fus.
      7 - 11th Suffolks.
      8 - 1st E.Lancs.
      9 - 133 T.M.B.
     10 - 306 Bde. R.F.A.
     11 - M.G.Coy, 61st M.G.C.
     12 - 478 Field Coy, R.E.
     13 - 61st Division "G"
     14 - 182nd Inf.Bde.
     15 - 184th Inf.Bde.
     16 - C.R.A.
     17 - C.R.E.
     18 - 61st Bn. M.G.C.
     19 - 2/1st Field.Ambulance.
     20 - No. 3 Coy, Divl. Train.
```

=====

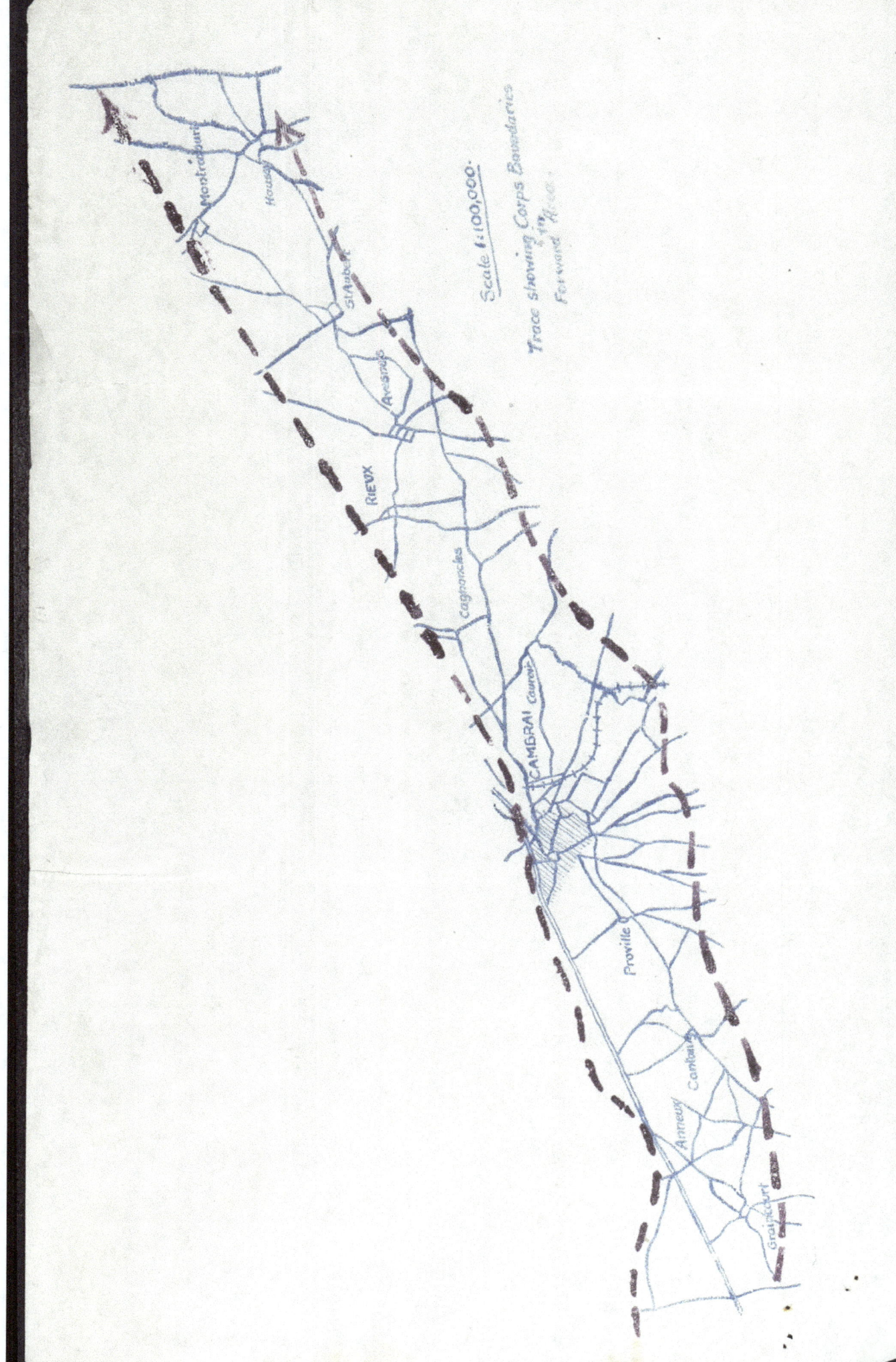

SECRET.   Copy No 9

193rd INFANTRY BRIGADE ORDER NO. 253.

Reference Map, Sheet 57c, 1/40,000.
                57b,   do

1. The 61st Division will become the Supporting Group of XVII Corps from 0600 hours on 18th instant. Order of Groups will then be:

   Leading Group   = 19th Division.
   Supporting Group = 61st Division.
   Reserve Group   = 24th Division.

2. The leading Brigade Group of the 61st Division (less "C" Coy, 61st Battalion, M.G.C.) will march to the area A.16, A.22 on the 18th instant in accordance with attached movement Table.

3. First and Second Line Transport will march with Units.

4. Steel Helmets will be worn on the Line of March.

5. The following distances will be maintained by Units on the Line of march.

   (a) Between Companies, Units & their transport = 100 yards.
   (b) Between Battalion.   = 500 yards.
   (c) Between Groups of 3 Vehicles   = 25 yards.

6. Brigade H.Q. will close at CANTAING at 0800 hours and reopen on arrival at a location to be notified later.

7. Completion of move and location of new H.Q. to be reported to this office.

8. Acknowledge.

                                                           Captain,
Issued at 8.15 p.m. 17/10/18   Brigade Major, 193rd Infantry Brigade.

           Copy 1 - War Diary.
                2 - File.
                3 - G.O.C.
                4 - Brigade Major.
                5 - S.C.
                6 - B.T.O.
                7 - D.S.O.
                8 - B.I.O.
                9 - 9th North'd Fus:
               10 - 11th Suffolks.
               11 - 1st D.Lancs.
               12 - 193 L.T.M.B.
               13 - 476 Field Coy, R.E.
               14 - 2/1 Field Ambulance.
               15 - 61st Divl. Train.
               16 - No. 3 Coy, Div. Train.
               17 - 61st Division "G"
               18 - C.R.E.
               19 - A.D.M.S.
               20 - 182nd Inf.Bde.
               21 - 184th Inf.Bde.
               22 - A.P.M.

MOVE SEE TABLE ISSUED WITH 123rd INFANTRY BRIGADE ORDER NO. 258.

Serial No	Unit.	From	To	Route.	Starting Point	Starting time hours.	Remarks
1.	Bde.H.Q. and L.T.M.Bty.	CANTAING.	Area A.16 & A.22.	NOYELLES - Bridge A.8.a.2.5 - X Rds G.15.a.1.3 - Road Junction A.22.c.3.3.	Road Junction L.T.c.0.5.	0830.	
2.	11 Suffolks.	L.4.	do	do	do	0840.	
3.	9 North'd Fus.	L.5.	do	do	do	0932.	
4.	10 K.Lancs.	L.6.d.	do	do	do	0954.	
5.	473 Fld.Coy.	L.2.d.	do	do	do	1006.	
6.	2/1 S.M.F.A.	CANTAING.	do	do	do	1021.	
7.	8 Coy. Divl. Train.	do	do	do	do	1035.	To clear Bridge L.8.a. 2.3. by 1100 hours.

SECRET.   Copy No 11

183rd INFANTRY BRIGADE ORDER NO. 259.   19/10/18.

Reference Map: Sheet 57b.(N.E.1a) 1/40,000.
                   51a.   do   do

1. The Leading Brigade Group will move by march route to AVESNES LEZ AUBERT tonight 19th October in accordance with March Table "A" attached.

2. Leading Brigade Group consists of:

    H.Q. 183rd Infantry Brigade.
    183rd Infantry Brigade.
    473 Field Coy, R.E.
    2/1st (S.M.) Field Ambulance.
    No. 3 Coy, Div. Train.

3. 1st and 2nd Line Transport will NOT accompany Units but will march separately under a Field Officer to be detailed by 9th North'd Fusiliers in accordance with March Table "B" attached.

4. Dismounted Personnel of 478 Field Coy, R.E. 2/1st (S.M.) Field Ambulance will march with Transport in accordance with March Table "B" attached.

5. Major G. WEST, 11th Suffolk Regt. will be at the starting point as in Table "A" attached with an Electric Torch and will guide the dismounted personnel column to its destination.

6. Guides will meet the dismounted personnel of Units and also their transport at Cross Roads C.3.a.7.5.

7. Distances to be maintained on line of march are:

    (a) Between Companies   = 50 yards.
    (b) Between Units, and between transport of Units = 100 yds
    (c) Between each Section of 4 Vehicles, horse or,
        mechanical.   = 25 yds.

8. Connecting files will be put out by Units as required.

9. Dress. Steel Helmets and Packs will be worn.
           Greatcoats in the pack.
           Waterproof sheet on the pack.

10. Should the transport column find the dismounted personnel column crossing its line of march the transport column will halt until the dismounted personnel column is clear.

11. 9th North'd Fusiliers, 11th Suffolks and 1st E.Lancs. Regt will synchronise watches by telephone at 1800 hours.
    183rd L.T.M.B. 478 Field Coy, R.E., 2/1st Field Ambulance and No. 3 Coy, Div. Train will each send a representative with a watch to synchronise at Brigade H.Q. at the same hour (1800 hrs)

12. All Commanders are warned that the enemy have been shelling AVESNES LEZ AUBERT with Gas Shell and will be ready to order Gas Masks to be put on if occasion arises.

13. Brigade H.Q. will close at A.16.c.60.35 at 1830 hours and reopen at AVESNES-LEZ-AUBERT on arrival.

1.

12.   Completion of moves and location of new H.Q. will be forwarded to this office as soon as possible.

13.   ACKNOWLEDGE.

                                                                Captain,
Issued at 6 p.m.   A/Brigade Major, 183rd Infantry Brigade.

              Copy 1 - War Diary.
                   2 - File.
                   3 - G.O.C.
                   4 - B.M.
                   5 - S.C.
                   6 - D.T.O.
                   7 - E.S.O.
                   8 - D.I.O.
                   9 - Major WEST, 11th Suffolks.
                  10 - Field Officer, 9th North'd Fus.
                  11 - 9th North'd Fus.
                  12 - 11th Suffolks.
                  13 - 1st E.Lancs.
                  14 - 183 T.M.B.
                  15 - 2/1st Field Ambulance.
                  16 - 472 Field Coy. R.E.
                  17 - No. 3 Coy. Div. Train.
                  18 - 31st Division "G"
                  19 - 182nd Inf.Bde.
                  20 - 184th Inf.Bde.
                  21 - C.R.E.
                  22 - A.D.M.S.
                  23 - 31st Div. Train.

MARCH TABLE "A"

DISMOUNTED PERSONNEL.

Serial No	Unit.	From.	To	Route	Starting Point.	Starting time. hours.
1.	Bde.H.Q. L.T.M.B.	A.16.c.	AVESNES-LEZ-AUBERT.	Rd.Junction A.18.b.2.3 - Junction of Rd. and Track B.13.c.7.5 - B.13.b.1.7 thence S of Track leading S.E.S.E. through B.13.b., B.14.a. and b, B.15. a. and c., B.16.c. & d. to B.13.d.9.3 thence by track Northwards to B.16.d. 9.9. - thence by Road to CARNIÈRES - through Village past Church to the CARNIÈRES - AVESNES-LEZ-AUBERT Road at C.13.d.9.5.	Cross Roads A.23.b.9.0.	1910.
2.	11 Suffolks	do	do	do	do	1913.
3.	9 North d Fusiliers	A.22.	do	do	do	1920.
4.	1 E.Lancs	do	do	do	do	1927.

MARCH TABLE "B" (1st and 2nd LINE TRANSPORT PLUS 478 FIELD COY. R.E. & 3/1 FIELD AMBULANCE COMPLETE).

Serial No	Unit.	From	To	Route.	Starting Point.	Starting time. hours.	Remarks.
1.	Bde.Signal Sect. Bde.H.Q.1.T.M.B.	A.16.c.	AVESNES LEZ AUBERT.	Rd Junction A.21.d.9.2 - Rd.Junction A.18.b.2.3 - X Rds A.20.b.8.4 - thence thro' GAUROIR to X Rds B.2.d.1.1.- X Rds.C.3.a. 7.3.- AVESNES LEZ AUBERT.	X Roads A.17.c. Central.	2000.	
2.	11th Suffolks.	A.16.	do	do	do	2004.	
3.	9th Northd Fus.	A.22.	do	do	do	2011.	
4.	1st E.Lancs.	do	do	do	do	2018.	
5.	3 Coy.Div.Train.	A.16.c.	do	do	do	2024.	
6.	478 Fld.Coy. R.E.	A.22.	do	do	do	2028.	(Complete Unit)
7.	3/1 Field Amb.	do	do	do	do	2032.	ditto

SECRET.   Copy No...5...

183rd. INFANTRY BRIGADE.

ADMINISTRATIVE INSTRUCTIONS ISSUED IN CONNECTION WITH BRIGADE ORDER No. 259

18th. October 1918.

1. **ADVANCE BILLETING PARTIES.**

   Advance billeting parties will proceed to-morrow and report to Staff Captain at Cross roads 400 yards South West of A in AVESNES LEZ AUBERT at 1100 hours. (VALENCIENNES 12 1/100,000).

   Advance billeting party will provide guides for lorries, and also guides for Battalion marching in.

2. **SUPPLIES.**

   Refilling Point will be as arranged with the Supply Officer to-day (at 0900 hours on road just South of No.3 Coy.Train H.Q. A.14.a.8.1.)

   Supply Wagons will march loaded with Units. They will remain with Units for night 19/20th and report to O.C. No.3 Coy.Div.Train on the morning of the 20th.

   Refilling Point for 20th. will be notified later.

   Coal can be drawn from the Lines of No.1 Coy.of the Train at CAGNONCLES.

3. **TRANSPORT.**

   5 Lorries will report at Bde.H.Q. about 0900 hours to-morrow to assist Units in the carriage of blankets, etc., and are allotted as under :-

Bde.H.Q.	1.
Each Battalion	1.
9th.Northd.Fus.	One third.
No.3 Coy.Train.	" " "
183 L.T.M.B.	" " "
478 R.E.	" " "

   Units concerned will send guides for each lorry to report at Bde.H.Q. at 0900 hours to guide lorries to Q.M.Stores.

   Lorries will do one journey only.

   A competent guide should be sent with each lorry to new area, and Units should arrange for guide from advance billeting party to meet lorry at a prearranged rendezvous in new area.

   As lorries must be back at CAMBRAI ANNEXE Railhead by 1800 hours to draw supplies they will be offloaded immediately on arrival in new area, and if necessary stores dumped until Q.M.Stores are fixed. BAGGAGE WAGONS will remain with Units.

4. **AMMUNITION.**

   The Subsection of S.A.A.Section D.A.C. allotted to the Advance Guard Brigade will be prepared to join this Bde. immediately on receipt of orders.

   There are dumps of S.A.A. and Grenades at B.6.c.central, and Cross Roads in C.8.b.

5. **LOCATIONS.**

   As soon as possible after arrival in new area Units will report to this Office location of Q.M.Stores and Transport Lines.

6. **TRANSPORT** will move complete to establishment.

7. **ACKNOWLEDGE.**

B.H.Q.

A.E.Pugh Captain.
Staff Captain, 183rd. Infantry Brigade

DISTRIBUTION.

No.1	G.O.C.	No.10 & 11	183 T.M.B.	No.19	Bde.Sig.Off.
" 2	B.M.	" 12 & 13	478 Fld.Coy.	" 20	B.T.O.
" 3	S.C.	" 14 & 15	2/1 Fld.Amb.	" 21	Bde.Supply Off.
" 4 & 5	9th Northd.F.	" 16 & 17	3 Coy.Train.	" 22	Bde.Q.M.S.
" 6 & 7	11th Suffolks	" 18	S.A.A.Sec.	" 24	61stDiv."Q"
" 8 & 9	1st E.Lancs.		D.A.C.	" 25	A.P.M.
				" 26 & 27	Retain.

To:-
 9th. Northd Fus.
 11th. Suffolks.
 1st. E.Lancs.
 183 L.T.M.B.
 478 Field Coy.
 2/1 Field Amb.
 No.3 Coy.Div.Train.
Copy to Staff Captain.
 "   E.T.O.
 "   E.S.O.

B.M.27.

                Reference move of Brigade Group today.
1. Probable time for 1st. Unit to pass Starting Point is 7.0pm.
2. Transport will be Brigaded.
3. Routes across country are being reconnoitred for dismounted personnel and great care must be taken to keep touch between units.
4. Detailed Orders follow.

                                                Captain,
                                      A/Brigade Major,183 Inf.Bde.

BHQ.
19.10.18.

Army Form C. 2123.
(In books of 100.)

"C" FORM.

MESSAGES AND SIGNALS.

No. of Message..............

Prefix.......Code......Words.........	Received.	Sent, or sent out.	Office Stamp.
£ s. d. Charges to Collect	From............ By............	At..........m	34
Service Instructions		To..........	
		By..........	

Handed in at. ....Office..........m. Received..........m.

TO Duyé

* Sender's Number.	Day of Month.	In reply to Number.	AAA
Bde x 32	25	—	

Refce Bde x 32 & P.A. order No. 6
para 6 of today [illegible]
will proceed [illegible]
to [illegible]
[illegible] Q17 and deploy
in artillery formation
as ordered in para 3
aaa KANA will remain
in Bde Reserve in
BERMERAIN for present aaa
addsd all concerned

FROM
PLACE & TIME [illegible] 18 05

* This line should be erased if not required.

(11201.) W528/M1970. 25,000 Pads. 10/5/17. P. & C. Ltd., B. (E 1213).

SECRET 35 Copy No
183 Inf. Bde. Order No 262   25/10/18

Ref: Map 1/20000 51A SE
       1/40000 51A

1. 184 Inf Bde (front line) is at present established from Q.12.d - thorough Q.11 Central - LA JUSTICE - Q.3. Central.

   184 Inf Bde is about to advance N.E. from that line as Corps Advance Guard in touch with 2nd Division on Right & 4th Division on Left. 2/4th Oxfords on Right, 2/4th Bucks on Left, 2/5 Gloucesters in Support.

2. 182nd & 183rd Inf Bdes are to be prepared to follow in support of 184 Inf Bde on original Brigade Boundaries.

3. On receipt of further orders 183rd Inf Bde will deploy on line of Stream through Q.10.Central - Q.17.a & b in readiness to advance further by bounds.

   4th North'd Fus on right, 1st E.Lancs on left, dividing line junction of Stream & Road in Q.17.a to Road junction Q.6.d.5.9 - PARQUIAUX inclusive to 1st East Lancs Regt.

   11th Suffolks will follow in Bde Reserve in rear of 4th North'd Fus.

4. Units will advance in artillery

1

formation on two Company front.
General direction of advance magnetic bearing of 58°.

5. Two Stokes Guns & one section of MGs will be attached & cooperate with Each leading Battalion. Section Commanders will get into touch at once with Commanders concerned.

6. Preparatory to above advance 1st East Lancs & 11th Suffolks will withdraw from their present positions & assemble and reorganize in Billets as quickly as possible in BERMERIAN and ST MARTIN.
  1st E Lancs about Q 22 a N of Road.
  11th Suffolks in ST MARTIN in Q 27 b - between Road & Rly, &
  9th North'd Fus in present billets about Q 22 c
  "C" Coy 6 MG Bn less 2 Sections now in position on LA FOLIE SPUR will withdraw to Area about Q.22 c 3 3.

7. Completion of assembly & location of Hdqrs will be reported priority to Bde Hdqrs at MAISON BLEUE Q 31 b. 9.9

8. All 1st Line Transport & Q M Stores of Units are being moved to HAUSSY today

9. Units will complete SAA Lewis Gun Magazines Flares &c as soon as possible

10. Acknowledge
Issued at 0900.   A/Bde Major 183 Inf Bde

Distribution

Copy to —
9th North'd Fus
11th Suffolks
1st E/ancs
183 F MB
C Coy 61 MGC
Mortar Group
478 Field Coy RE
61 Div G
182 Inf Bde
184 " "
AC
War Diary
File.
BSO.
A.D.M.S.

(6392) Wt. W6192/P575 1,500,000 4/18 McA & W Ltd (E 2815) Forms W3091/4.   Army Form W.3091.

Cover for Documents.

Nature of Enclosures.

Nov.r 1918.

9th (North.d Hussars) B.n Northumberland Fusiliers

War Diary.

Notes, or Letters written.

Army Form C. 2118.

WAR DIARY
or
INTELLIGENCE SUMMARY.
(Erase heading not required.)

9th (N.M.d Hussars) Bn. Northumberland Fus:ro

November 1918

Summary of Events and Information

APPENDICES.

A 163rd Infantry Brigade Operation Orders.
B 9th (N.H.) Bn. North'd Fus:rs Orders.
C Special Orders of the day.

In the Field
30.11.1918

WAR DIARY or INTELLIGENCE SUMMARY

Army Form C. 2118.

November 1918.

Place	Date	Hour	Summary of Events and Information	Remarks and references to Appendices
SEPMERIES	1		Enemy shelled back areas and around Bolton H.Q. Orders were received in the B[n] to get to carry out an attack to effect a crossing of the river RHONNELLE. The object of the attack was the high ground East of the village. Arty attacked with C of D in support. About 1115 the enemy made a counter attack on our left (Worcesters) and forced them back a little but on C Coy moved up and closed the gap. The enemy infantry came down in number. Our Lewis gun put out of action, inflicted 6 prisoners prior to our entry. The enemy put up a fair resistance to the entry to MARESCHES and at 2 p.m. the village was in our hands. B[n] consolidated and about 30 prs wounded. Our captures were 3 offrs & 170 O.Rs. 2 M.Gs. The B[n] was relieved at night by the 11th Batt[n] Duke Regt. (1st-5th Div) and returned to LA FOLIE while the Bren stayed overnight.	A.H.
LA FOLIE	2		B[n] as in bivouac and marched to SOMAING and slept in billets overnight.	A.H.
SOMAING	3		Bolton paraded at 1100 hrs and marched to AVESNES-LES-AUBERT via MONTRECOURT — ST AUBERT) arriving in billets about 1630 hrs.	A.H.
AVESNES- LES AUBERT	4		Battalion in billets, day spent in cleaning up and inspection of arms & equipment.	A.H.
do	6		Coy parade & parade at 0900 hrs for Battn. Training. General parade postponed for enquiry Roll of effects of men in action. Germany. Major E.L. Thomson took over command of the Battn. sent Col W 2nd/Lt Burns Adams proceeded to England.	A.H.

WAR DIARY / INTELLIGENCE SUMMARY

Army Form C. 2118.

November 1916

Place	Date	Hour	Summary of Events and Information	Remarks and references to Appendices
AVESNES-LES-AUBERT	6th		Prophylaxis carried out. A rail hunt on the Cavaria Road near the village. Afternoon devoted to lectures by Company Commanders & Platoon Commanders.	
do.	7th		Battalion in Training (Ground). 900 – 1100 hrs. Demonstration 1000 – 1100 hrs. Battalion in attack. Afternoon – Lectures. Orders received for move next day but were cancelled about midnight.	
do.	8		Orders received at about 10 a.m. that Brown Div. to move to Ghissignies. Move to take place three hours later than originally ordered. Battalion marched off about 1200 hrs and arrived to billets at BERMERAIN around about 1500 hrs.	
BERMERAIN	9.		S. I. Drills. Training in area S. of BERMERAIN – RUESANES Road.	
do.	10.		Church Service. Night Operations as per Order No. T.O.	
do.	11.		Battalion training. 0900 – 1100 Rifle Exercise, L.G. Drill & Bayonet fighting. 1030 – 1200 Platoon Schemes as per train. T.S. 1430 – 1600 Kicquet games. Fire received at 0915 hrs that Hostilities had to cease at 1100 hrs on 11th November as per wire in Appendix A.	
do.	12.		Battalion Training. 0900 – 1000 Drill & P.T. Drill & sports. 1030 – 1130 Battalion Drill. 1145 – 1245 Coy training.	
do.	13		Battalion Training as per programme. Warning orders received to move.	
do.	14		Bn. moved at 0845 hrs for move to St. AUBERT. Battalion of 1000 hrs and marched to St. AUBERT arriving about 1400 hrs. Warning order received for moving next day.	
ST. AUBERT	15		Bn. less 1st Echelon & Battle Bn. moved by march route to CAMBRAI at 1115 hrs arriving at 1430 hrs.	

WAR DIARY or INTELLIGENCE SUMMARY

Army Form C. 2118.

November 1918

Place	Date	Hour	Summary of Events and Information	Remarks and references to Appendices
CAMBRAI	16th		General cleaning up of billets & fort picket. Drill would be arranged by company. B.H.Q. at Cross Killet.	W.D.
do.	17th		Church Parades. C of E (Revd People) Football match between Officers & 1st Foot Lance & Officers of this Battalion. Won it 1st Foot Lance 3 goals nothing.	W.D.
do.	18th		Battalion Training. 0715 – 1015 hrs PT 1045 hrs PT 1015-3. 1030 – 1130 hrs Brigade Saluting Drill, Squad & Company Drill. 1145 – 1245 hrs Battalion Drill. 1430 – 1600 hrs Organized Games etc.	W.D.
do.	19th		Battalion training at P.H. 1st. Inspection of Billets & Kit of open men.	W.D.
do.	20th		Battalion training as per programme	W.D.
do.	21st		Battalion training as per programme	W.D.
do.	22nd		Battalion Schemes took during morning (Attack and F. Bayonet) Games in afternoon as usual. Orders Received to move on 24th/25th by train to BERNAVILLE (sta CONTEVILLE Stn)	W.D.
	23rd		Companies made ordinary Company arrangements. Orders during morning that Bn will Entrain. Battalion on Saturday 23rd during afternoon. By Football today concert on evening in Style hired Ste. Kr. Ors. Transport would eventually road to BERNAVILLE area.	W.D.
do	24th		Church Parade & Sermile & football. Orders were to move in the evening. H Officers & men battalion. Order received to stand fast and await orders before filling in.	W.D.

Army Form C. 2118.

WAR DIARY
or
INTELLIGENCE SUMMARY.   November 1918.
(Erase heading not required.)

Instructions regarding War Diaries and Intelligence Summaries are contained in F. S. Regs., Part II. and the Staff Manual respectively. Title pages will be prepared in manuscript.

Place	Date	Hour	Summary of Events and Information	Remarks and references to Appendices
CAMBRAI	25th		Still shunting by trains running some late. At 1200 hrs Orders received "Stand to, ready to fall in at 10 mins notice." Orders received & Battalion fell in at 1400 hrs & marched to CAMBRAI VILLE STN. Entrained at about 1530 hrs & moved out at about 2000 hrs. (Retour train from RSV for 170 miles — 1 day).	WP?
LONGUEVILLERS	26.		Arrived CONTEVILLE STN at about 1100 hrs. Battn HQrs & D Coy billeted at LONGUEVILLERS. B & A Coys at DOMLEGER. C Coy Transport & MT Store at EGENVILLE.	WP?
do.	27.		Companies at the disposal of Company Commanders for cleaning up & billet repairing.	WP?
do.	28.		Companies at the disposal of Company Comdrs to be cleaning up & repair of billets. Scout & Signallers Pltns to inspire into a/c and cos of Platoons & MSS M? to take the B Coy.	WP?
do.	29.		Prov. Pioneers Coys training according to programme. Co?.	WP?
do.	30.		under Coy Commdrs for interior economy &c. Training as per programme on Company & under Company arrangements.	WP?

A10260 W.W.5300/P713 750,000 7/16 Sch. 82 Forms/C2118/16
D. D. & L., London, E.C.

Army Form C. 2118.

WAR DIARY
or
INTELLIGENCE SUMMARY.
(Erase heading not required.)

NOVEMBER 1918.

Instructions regarding War Diaries and Intelligence Summaries are contained in F. S. Regs., Part II. and the Staff Manual respectively. Title pages will be prepared in manuscript.

Place	Date	Hour	Summary of Events and Information	Remarks and references to Appendices

Strength at the beginning of month — 47 Officers. 914 O.Rs.
Strength at the end of month — 53 Officers. 981 O.Rs.

Casualties.
Killed — 6
Wounded — 39
Evacuations — 57
Deaths — 1
Taken on Enemy — 1
Total — 104.

Drafts for week ending Nov 9 = 282
" " " " " 16 = 18
" " " " " 23 = 16
" " " " " 30 = 52
Total = 368

Killed
Lieut. E.O. Bowman 30th

Wounded
Lieut. J.O. Jury 16th
Lieut. C. Wilkinson 30th

To England
Lieut Colonel H. Cock Brown

Officers Joined
Lieut. G. Belford 5th
Lieut. A.J. Fraser 17th
Lieut. J. Starling 18th
Major J.R. Walker 21st
Lieut. C. Wilkinson 19th
Lieut. A. Cairns 24th
Lieut. A.J. Bigott 24th
Lieut. B.G. Rikard 24th
Lieut. B.J. Aggott 24th
Lieut. B.J. Bjoran 27th

Decorations.
Military Medal
41172 C.S.M. R. Jordan
35508 Pte. R. Bell
09858 " J.G. Wilson
23571 " J.R. Kerr
38964 " G. Garbough
36642 " G. Starry
73567 " Hall
60770 Sgt. E. Greenwood
24049 Pte. Hunter
46307 Major E. Marshall
39026 Pte. R. Moss
22744 " " Way
60938 " Bewick-Suman
203126 " Thornton
38217 " T. Beaumont
20454 " T. Clayton
557445 Cpl. W. Cottle
201482 " Yeatby
14738

Bar to Military Medal
41070 Pte. Wilson
20468 Sgt. Peverson

In Hospital in France
Lieut C.W. Hardwicke
Lieut C.W. Tupper

J. Newmarch Lt. Col.

War Diary
November
1918

Appendix
B

9th (S) Bn North'n Lancs   Copy No. 11
Order No 81
                              2.11.18

The Batt. will proceed by march
route tomorrow 3rd inst to AVESNES-LES-
AUBERT.

        Reveille   0700 hours
        Breakfast   0800   "
        Sick Parade   0700   "
        Parade ready to march off 1000 hours
at Q.13.A.4.2 Bn. Starting point 1015 hrs (P 24 C 9 L)

        First line transport will march
in rear of column under command
of Ounm Transport Officer.

        The usual intervals will be
maintained.
        Order of March.

        HQ Coy   9th North'n Lancs
        B   "   "
        C   "   "
        D   "   "
        A   "   "
        Batt. Details
        No 1 Coy 7th Batt Own Lancs.
        No 2 "   1st Batt East Lancs.

ROUTE STARTING POINT (P.24 C 9 L) - MONTRECOURT
       - ST HUBERT - AVESNES - LES AUBERT.

       Tea will be served on arrival at
AVESNES-LES-AUBERT.
       Dinner at 1600 hours

2.

All baggage, including Officers
Mess Kit will be ready for collection
at 0900 hours.

Mess Cart to be at HQ Offrs
Mess at 0930 hours.

Head of Transport will be
at fork-road at ?24 B 22 at 0945 hrs.

Detail   All personnel of detail from
BERMERAIN to be at cross roads at
Q13 a 4 2 at 1000 hours facing S.W.

Transport Transport from BERMERAIN
to be at cross roads Q13 a 4 2 at 1000
hours facing S.W.

Clean billets certificates will
be obtained in duplicate and rendered
to Orderly Room by 2000 hours on 3rd inst.

ACKNOWLEDGE

Copies to
No 1 RDE
   2 Coying Offrs
  3/6 OC Coys
   7 O/C HQ
   8 QM + T.O
   9 O/C Details
  10 RSM
  11 War Diary
  12 O/C Pnr 2nd Lines

W.S. Roberts
Capt Asst
Q^m (WA) 1st N.S. Bn

SECRET.   Copy No.

Ref. Map Sheet   9th (North'd Hussars) Batt'n North'd Fusiliers
51A /40.000   Order No. 82.   7.11.1918.

1. INTENTION	The Battalion will move tomorrow to BERMERAIN by march route
2. MOVE	1200 Battalion will parade ready to march off at ~~0800~~ hours. Head of column outside Orderly Room
3. ORDER OF MARCH	H.Q. Band. A. B. C. D. Coys. Rearguard. Transport will march in rear of Battalion
4. STARTING POINT	Solitary House at U.22.d.9.6.
5. ROUTE	St AUBERT – HAUSSY – Cross Roads W1d. – Cross Roads Q.21.b.9.9.
6. INTERVALS	Usual intervals will be maintained
7. OFFICERS VALISES, MESS KIT ETC.	Officers Valises and Mess Kit to be at Q.M. Stores at ~~0800~~ 1100 hours.
8. BLANKETS	To be lightly rolled in bundles of 10 and plainly marked to be in Q.M. Stores by ~~0800~~ 1150 hours.
9. MESS CART, MALTESE CART & R.Sig.LIMBER	Will report at their respective places at ~~0800~~ 1100 hours
10. SYNCHRONIZATION	Lieut B. C. Cocks will report at Bde H.Q. at ~~0730~~ 1030 hours to synchronize watches.
11. CLEAN BILLET CERTIFICATES	Will be obtained and sent in to Orderly Room by 1800 hours tomorrow 8th inst.

ACKNOWLEDGE.

Copies to
No 1. 83 Inf Bde
    2. Commanding Officer
    3. 2. in Command.
    4. Adjutant
    5/9. O.C. Coys
    10. Quartermaster
    11. Transport Officer
    12. R.S.M.
    13. War Diary
    14. File.

R.F. Hauss......
Captain & Adjutant
9th (NH) Bn North'd Fusiliers

SECRET.   Copy No.

Nº MAP SHEET.   9th (North'd Hussars) Batn (Northumberland
S.A.S.E. 1/40000.   Fusiliers) Order No. T.2.   10. 11. 18

INFORMATION	Saint The enemy is holding an outpost line CAPELLE to RUESNES – along road through Pont à Bois to cross roads in R.30 WEST of RUESNES
INTENTION	The G.O.C. 83 Infy. Bde. intends making a surprise attack on this position tonight.
DISPOSITION OF TROOPS	The 9th & 11th Battns North'd Fusiliers will be the centre Battalion with 8 Battn on right and 8 Battn on the left. One Battalion is in Reserve.
OBJECTIVE	The objective of the Battalion will be road running through Q.24.d.4.4. - Q.24.c.
PARADE	The Battalion will parade at 1710 hours. Head of column at Q.22.d. . Order of march. D.C.B.A. and Bn H.Q. and will march on a compass bearing of 90° true to Q.23.c.4 and thence to Q.23.a.4.5. on a bearing of 50° true. Drill Fighting Order will pack.
PLACE OF DEPLOYMENT	Along track from Q.23.d.1.5. to Q.23.b.5.2.
DISPOSITIONS	O.C. C Coy. – Front line. A Coy. – In reserve. Battn H.Q. in front of Reserve Company. Company frontage 200 yards to be taken up in two lines of Sections at 25 yards interval and 100 yards distance.
DIRECTION	B Coy will direct. Each Company will attach one Officer to march on a compass bearing of 90° true with the front line to the left of their Company.
MACHINE GUNS	One section of M.G. Company will be with the Reserve Coy.
CONSOLIDATION	On objective being taken no fences will be captured by front line troops and outpost line to be formed 100 yards EAST of the objective. Battn H.Q. and Reserve Coy will dig in 200 yards WEST of the objective.
DRUMMERS	12 Drummers will report to Major S.F.C. Brady M.C. at 1700 hours at Battn H.Q. each carrying 1 very light pistol and 5 white cartridges. Drum Major will arrange to draw same from Company.
Issues to	No 1 83 Infy Bde 2 Liaison Officer 3 2nd in Command 4/5 O.C. Coys 9 O.C. A Coy 11th Bn N.F. 10 R.S.M. 11 Drum Major 12 War Diary copy

R. F. Ha————
Lt Captain and Adjutant
9th (N.H.) Battn North'd Fusiliers

Copy No. 11

9th (Northd Hussars) Battn (Northumberland Fusiliers
Order No. T 3.   10·11·1918

TO 1" SHEET.
5 A.S.E.

1. **INFORMATION**   The enemy is holding an Outpost line CREVE to RUESNES along road through PONT de BUAT to cross roads in R.13.c WEST of RUESNES

2. **INTENTION**   The G.O.C. 183 Infantry Brigade intends to attack this position tomorrow 11" inst.

3. **OBJECTIVE**   Road running from Q 24 d 4.0 to Q 24 b 9.2.

4. **DISPOSITIONS FOR ATTACK**   The 9th (NH) Battn Northd Fusiliers will be the centre Battalion, with X Battalion on right and Y Battalion on the left.

5. **DISPOSITIONS**   The Battalion will form up for attack on line running from Q.22.c. 4.8. to Q 22 b. 4.0. East of BERMERI O.
      "A" Coy   "B" Coy
      "C" Coy   "D" Coy

    Battn H.Qrs. will be at house Q 22 a. 2.1.
    Company frontage 400 yards to be taken up in two lines of sections at 50 yards interval and 100 yards distance.

6. **DIRECTION**   "A" Company will direct.

7. **ZERO.**   1100 hours.

8. **MACHINE GUNS.**   One gun will be attached to Coy.Hd.Qrs. of each of the two front Companies and 2 guns will be in reserve at Battn H.Qrs.

9. **CONSOLIDATION**   An outpost line will be formed on objective being taken.

10. **SMOKE BOMBS.**   Will be carried by all Companies.

R. F. Harrison.
Captain & Adjutant
9th (NH) Battn Northumberland Fusiliers

Copies to
No 1 183 Infy Bde
   2 Comdg Officer
   3 2nd in Command
  4/8 O.C. Coys.
   9 O.C. 3 Coy 61 M.G. Bn
   6 C.O. M
  11 Spare
   2

Spare

SECRET.   Copy No 16

9th (Cyclist Hussars) Battn. North Somerset.

Ref Map Sheet.   Order No 83.
51A 1/50.000.   14.11.1918

INTENTION	The Battalion will move today to ~~Avesnes Les~~ St AUBERT.
MOVE	The Battalion will parade ready to march off at 1015 hours. Head of column outside B. Coy H.Q.
ORDER OF MARCH.	Signallers, Band, H.Q. B. A. C. D. Coys. Rear Guard. Transport will march in rear of the Battalion.
STARTING POINT.	LES FORRIÈRES
ROUTE	Cross Roads Q.21 & G.9. — Cross Roads W.1.d. — HAUSSY - ST. AUBERT.
INTERVALS	Usual intervals will be maintained
OFFICERS VALISES & MESS KIT.	Officers Valises and Mess kit will be at Q.M. Stores at 0845 hours.
BLANKETS.	To be tightly rolled in bundles of 10 and plainly marked to be in Q.M. Stores by 0830 hours
MESS CART.	Will report at Battn. H.Q. Mess at 0930 hours.
ORD. ROOM & SIGNALS LIMBER	Will report at B.H.Q. at 0900 hours.
SCOUT OFFICER	Lieut B. C. Cook will report at Bde H.Q. at 0845 hours to Synchronize watches.
ARMY BILLET CERTIFICATES	Will be obtained by Lieut W. Godfrey and sent in to Orderly Room by 1015 hours today 14 inst.
DINNERS	Will be served on arrival.
REAR GUARD	2nd-Lt. L. Fletcher M.C. will be in charge of Rear Guard.
ACKNOWLEDGE	Sent by runner 0830 hrs.

                                                                R. F. Harrison
                                                                Captain & Adjutant
                                                        9th (N.H) Battn. North Somerset

Copies to:-
No 1   1st Army Bde
    2   Carrying Officer
    3   2nd in Command
    4   Adjutant
    5/10 O.C. Coys.
    11 R.M.O.
    3   T.O.
    13 R.S.M.
    14 Sig Sergt
    15 Sigs. Sect
    16 War Diary
    17 Spare.

SECRET   Copy No 13
9th (NH) Battn North'd Fus
         ORDER No 84

Ref Maps Sheet   14·11·1918
51A ¹/₄₀₀₀₀ 57B ¹/₄₀₀₀₀

1. INTENTION	The Battalion will move tomorrow by march Route to CAMBRAI
2. MOVE	The Battn will parade ready to march off at 1105 hrs. Head of Column at U17 d.7.0
3. ORDER OF MARCH	Sigs, Bomd, HQ, C, B, A, D, Rear Guard. Transport will march in rear of Battn
4. STARTING POINT	Road Junction U 24 a 3.6
5. ROUTE	AVESNES – Cross Roads C 3. 68. 4 – SOLESMES – CAMBRAI RD
6. INTERVALS	Usual intervals will be maintained
7. BILLETING PARTY	A Billeting Party consisting of 2/Lt V. Carson & 1 NCO per Coy, 1 from QM Stores & 1 Transport will Rendezvous at BHQ at 0730 hours. Tomorrow 15th to proceed by Cycles to meet Staff Captain at Town Commandant's Office CAMBRAI at 0915 hours. Guides from above Billeting will meet Battalion on main SOLESMES RD at Railway Crossing A 11 & 8.3.
8. OFFICERS VALISES & MESS KIT	Officers Valises & Mess Kit will be at QM Stores at 0915 hours.
9. BLANKETS	To be tightly rolled in bundles of 10 & plainly marked, to be in QM Stores by 0900 hours.
10. MESS CART	Will report at Batt HQrs mess at 1030 hours.
11. SYNCHRONIZATION	2/Lt Woody will report at Bde HQrs at 0930 hrs to Synchronize watch.
12. CLEAN BILLET CERTIFICATES	Will be obtained by O/C's Units, Sent in to Orderly Room by 1100 hours
13. MEALS	Tea will be served on arrival. Dinners 1 hour after arrival.
14. REAR GUARD	2/Lieut W Doon will be in charge of the Rear Guard.

ACKNOWLEDGE
Issued by Runner 2359 hrs.
Copies to   10 T.O
1 183 Inf Bde   11 R.S.M
2 CO   12 Sgt Cook
3 Adjutant   13 War Diary
4/5 OC Coys   14 Spare   (Sd) R.J. Hanson
9 QM   Capt a/Adj
                                  9 (NH) Bn North'd Fus.

SECRET
COPY No 13

9th (North'd Hussars) Bn. Northumberland Fus'rs.
ORDER No 85.
23.11.1918

The Battalion will entrain at CAMBRAI VILLE Stn.
& will detrain at CAUDRY(?) Stn.
The Battalion less transport will parade, facing
on the west side of column at D Coy. H'qrs. at 0255 hrs
ORDER OF MARCH — B, C, D, A & B'n H.Q. Coys.
A B.(?) Guard of 1 N.C.O. & 3 men, detailed by us.
D Coy will report to the Quartermaster at 1830 hrs on
[illegible]

Water bottles will be carried full.
Blankets will be carried by all ranks.

Officers' valises & men's kit will be handed in to
Quartermaster Stores by 16.00 hrs on 24th inst.

The Senior Officer on each train will detail two
parties of 1 N.C.O. and 3 men each, who will be posted
and travel at the first and last of each train.
Their duties will be to prevent troops straggling from
train in event of stations when train is at rest. Also
any particularly to prevent men from attempting to
obtain rations at various and unauthorised places.

[illegible] Kindle(?) or us will obtain clean billets & no
damage certificates from the Town Commandant and
hand same in to Orderly Room by 20:15 hrs 24th inst.

Supper at 2000 hrs on 24th inst. Hot tea & Rum
will be issued at [illegible] before departure. Dinners
will be issued on detraining on the 25th inst. Tea
on arrival at destination.

Transport & H.Q. staff will arrive at CAMBRAI
Stn. at 2130 hours on 24th inst.

ACKNOWLEDGE.

Issued by Runner at 19:05 hrs.

Captain &
Adjutant
9th N'd Hr Bn. N'd Fus'rs.

SECRET. AMENDMENT TO   COPY No. 13
9th (Northd Hussars) Bn. Northumberland Fus.
ORDER   No. 85.   24:11:1918

1. MOVE	Read 2300 hrs. 24th inst., instead of 0255 hrs. 25th inst.
8. MEALS.	Breakfasts will be cooked on the train by men with Tommies Cookers. Dinners at destination
9. TRANSPORT & Q.M. STORES	Read 0130 hrs. 25th inst., instead of 2130 hrs. 24th inst.

ACKNOWLEDGE.
Issued by runner at 2000 hrs.

R. F. Harrison,
Capt. & Adjt.
9th (N.H.) Bn. North Fus.

Copies to.
No. 1 183 Infy Bde.
  2   Senior Officer
  3   Adjutant
4/8   O.C. Coys.
  9   Q'Master
 10   T.O.
 11   R.S.M.
 12   Sergt. Cook
 13   War Diary
 14   Spare.

Army Form C. 2118.

WAR DIARY
or
INTELLIGENCE SUMMARY
(Erase heading not required.)

DECEMBER 1918.

Instructions regarding War Diaries and Intelligence Summaries are contained in F. S. Regs., Part II. and the Staff Manual respectively. Title pages will be prepared in manuscript.

Place	Date	Hour	Summary of Events and Information	Remarks and references to Appendices
			9th. (Northumberland Hussars) Battalion Northumberland Fusiliers.	
			APPENDICES	
			A. 182rd Infantry Brigade ⎫ Operation 9th (N.H.)Bn. Northd. Fus. ⎭ Orders.	
			B. Training Programmes.	
			C. Special orders of the Day.	

Army Form C. 2118.

WAR DIARY

9th (Northd. Hussars) Battalion Northumberland Fusiliers.
DECEMBER 1918.

INTELLIGENCE SUMMARY.

(Erase heading not required.)

Instructions regarding War Diaries and Intelligence Summaries are contained in F. S. Regs., Part II. and the Staff Manual respectively. Title pages will be prepared in manuscript.

Place	Date	Hour	Summary of Events and Information	Remarks and references to Appendices
LONGVILLERS.	1st.	Sunday.	Non-Conformist Service at 0915 hours. Other Services cancelled on account of Lecture delivered by Revd. Studdart Kennedy (Woodbine Willy) on Demobilization at the Hangar at CONTEVILLE Station. Battalion present.	out
LONGVILLERS.	2nd.	Monday.	Battalion training as far as bathing arrangements permit. Football during the afternoon.	with APP B out
LONGVILLERS.	3rd.	Tuesday.	Brigade Ceremonial Parade. This was postponed owing to bad weather.	out
LONGVILLERS.	4th.	Wednesday.	Battalion Training. Notice of move received. R.S.M. A. Richardson proceeded to England. C.S.M. Naisby J. took over the duties of acting R.S.M.	out
LONGVILLERS.	5th.	Thursday.	Battalion Tactical Scheme carried out. Rear Guard and Advance Guard exercises.	out
LONGVILLERS.	6th.	Friday.	Battalion Training as per programme. C.S.M. Hornby T. rejoined the Battalion from Hospital and took over the duties of R.S.M.	out
LONGVILLERS.	7th.	Saturday.	Companies devoted the morning to Interior Economy. The Move ordered for today postponed 24 hours.	out
LONGVILLERS.	8th.	Sunday.	Battalion paraded on Main St, Riquier–Abbeville Road at 1000 hours and proceeded by march route to Billets in new area. Battn. H. Q., B. and D. Companies in the village of VAUCHELLES-LES-QUESNOY, C. Coy, in billets on the outskirts of ST. RIQUIER, A. Coy and Transport at NEUF MOULIN.	APP A. out

Army Form C. 2118.

WAR DIARY
INTELLIGENCE SUMMARY.
(Erase heading not required.)

DECEMBER 1918.

Instructions regarding War Diaries and Intelligence Summaries are contained in F. S. Regs. Part II. and the Staff Manual respectively. Title pages will be prepared in manuscript.

Place	Date	Hour	Summary of Events and Information	Remarks and references to Appendices
VAUCHELLES-LES-QUESNOY.	9th. Monday.		Day devoted to cleaning up and settling in new billet.	out APP.B
VAUCHELLES-LES-QUESNOY.	10th. Tuesday.		Battalion Training as per programme.	out —
VAUCHELLES-LES-QUESNOY.	11th. Wednesday.		Battalion Training as per programme.	out —
VAUCHELLES-LES-QUESNOY.	12th. Thursday.		Route march as per programme. A and C Companies. Bn. H.Q., B and D Companies. Lieut-Colonel R. J. Morris, D.S.O. joined the Battalion and assumed Command.	out —
VAUCHELLES-LES-QUESNOY.	13th. Friday.		Battalion Training as per programme.	out —
VAUCHELLES-LES-QUESNOY.	14th. Saturday.		Companies devoted the morning to interior economy.	out —
VAUCHELLES-LES-QUESNOY.	15th. Sunday.		Divine Services.	out —
VAUCHELLES-LES-QUESNOY.	16th. Monday.		Battalion Training as per programme. C Company firing on the range.	out APP.B

Army Form C. 2118.

WAR DIARY DECEMBER 1918.
INTELLIGENCE SUMMARY.
(Erase heading not required.)

Instructions regarding War Diaries and Intelligence Summaries are contained in F. S. Regs., Part II. and the Staff Manual respectively. Title pages will be prepared in manuscript.

Place	Date	Hour	Summary of Events and Information	Remarks and references to Appendices
VAUCHELLES-LES-QUESNOY	17th	Tuesday.	Training as per programme. C. Company on the range.	APP.B
- do -	18th	Wednesday.	Training as per programme. The route march was cancelled owing to bad weather.	
- do -	19th	Thursday.	Training as per programme. B. Company on the range. Forms for the demobilisation of 125 miners (4 forms and 1 postcard per man) received and orders for them to embus next day for Cambrai.	
- do -	20th	Friday.	Training as per programme. The 125 miners (mostly original battalion men) paraded at Battalion H. Q. and embussed for Cambrai.	
- do -	21st	Saturday.	Morning devoted by Companies to Interior Economy.	
- do -	22nd	Sunday.	Divine Services.	
- do -	23rd	Monday.	Training as per programme. Lieut-Colonel R. J. Morris D.S.O. took over the Command of the 183rd Infantry Brigade on Brigadier General B. L. Anley, C.M.G. D.S.O. proceeding to United Kingdom on leave. Major E. L. Thomson assumed command of the Battalion.	APP.B

Army Form C. 2118.

WAR DIARY DECEMBER 1918.
INTELLIGENCE SUMMARY.
(Erase heading not required.)

Instructions regarding War Diaries and Intelligence Summaries are contained in F. S. Regs., Part II. and the Staff Manual respectively. Title pages will be prepared in manuscript.

Place	Date	Hour	Summary of Events and Information	Remarks and references to Appendices
VAUCHELLES-LES-QUESNOY.	24th	Tuesday.	HOLIDAY. XMAS FESTIVITIES.	AWT
	25th	Wednesday.	do. do.	AWT APP. B.
	26th	Thursday.	do do.	AWT
- do. -	27th	Friday.	Battalion training as per programme. Squad drill and Company drill substituted in place of Battalion drill, Ceremonial.	AWT
- do. -	28th	Saturday.	Companies devoted the morning to Interior economy. A further batch of miners (57 in all) left the Battalion for Cambrai.	AWT APP B
- do -	29th	Sunday.	Divine Services.	AWT
- do -	30th	Monday.	Training as per programme. Companies at the disposal of Company Commanders for the first hour in place of Battalion Drill Ceremonial. Another batch of miners 26 left the Battalion for Cambrai.	
- do -	31st	Tuesday.	Training as per programme. Companies at the disposal of Company Commanders for the first hour in place of Battalion Drill Ceremonial.	

E. Thomson, Major
Comdg. 9th (Northumberland Hussars) Battn. Northumberland Fusiliers.

Army Form C. 2118.

WAR DIARY

~~INTELLIGENCE~~ SUMMARY

(Erase heading not required.)

DECEMBER 1918.

Instructions regarding War Diaries and Intelligence Summaries are contained in F.S. Regs. Part II. and the Staff Manual respectively. Title pages will be prepared in manuscript.

Place	Date	Hour	Summary of Events and Information	Remarks and references to Appendices
			Strength at beginning of month. 53 Officers 981 O.R.	
			Strength at end of month. 56 " 860 " 200 total.	
			CASUALTIES.	
			TRANS. Home Depot. Evacs. To England for Demobilisation Taken on in error.	
			6. 67. 126 1 79 total.	
			DRAFTS.	
			For week ending 7/12/18. -- 23	
			" " 14/12/18. -- 17	
			" " 21/12/18. -- 18	
			" " 31/12/18. -- 21	
			Officers Joined.	
			Lieut. E.J.Barker. 1/12/18.	
			Lieut. G.P.LeFebvre, MC. 9/12/18.	
			Lieut-Colonel R.J.Morris,D.S.O. 12/12/18.	
			Officers in Hospital.	
			Lieut. C.W. Hardwicke.	
			Lieut. C.H.V. Turpin.	
			2nd.Lieut. A.H. Becke.	
			Decorations.	
			D.S.O.	
			Major I.G.C. Brady, M.C.	
			Military Cross.	
			Captain E.M.Parkinson	
			Lieut. H. Robinson.	
			2nd.Lieut. F. C. Melvin.	
			2nd.Lieut. M. Babbitt.	
			2nd.Lieut. A. H. Becke.	
			2nd.Lieut. C. Wilkinson.	
			D.C.M.	
			No.25/227 Pte. W. Granville.	
			Mentioned in Despatches.	
			Lieut-Col. W.A.Vignoles DSO,	
			No.12885 Cpl. Morse W.	
			15620 Pte. Stobbart G.S.	

APPENDIX "B"

Training Programme
Of (NH) Bn. North'd Fus.

SPECIAL ORDER OF THE DAY
By FIELD-MARSHAL SIR DOUGLAS HAIG
K.T., G.C.B., G.C.V.O., K.C.I.E
Commander-in-Chief, British Armies in France.

The following telegram addressed to Field-Marshal Sir Douglas Haig has been received :—

FROM THE MAYOR OF CAPETOWN.

16-11-18.

Citizens, Capetown, desire to tender hearty congratulations on magnificent achievement of arms of Allies resulting in an armistice equivalent to decisive victory. We ask you kindly to communicate felicitations to Springboks who have been privileged under your command to bring imperishable renown to the young South African Nation.

REPLY :—

Please accept for yourself and convey to all your fellow citizens the hearty thanks of myself and all ranks of the British Armies in France for your telegram of congratulation which has been communicated to all Springboks serving here. The gallant achievements of South African troops have won the admiration of all ranks.

Suitable replies have been sent to the following :—

FROM THE FOURTH PORTUGUESE INFANTRY REGIMENT, FARO, PORTUGAL.

14-11-18.

The Commanding Officer and Officers of the 4th Portuguese Infantry Regiment, stationed at Faro, salute, in your person, the valorous British Army, whose wondrous help has gained so brilliant a victory for Right and Liberty.

FROM THE SECRETARY, TERRITORIAL FORCE ASSOCIATION, COUNTY OF ESSEX, CHELMSFORD.

21-11-18.

I have the honour by direction of my Association to append hereto a resolution passed by them at a special meeting held 20th November, 1918 :—

"Resolved that the Territorial Force Association of the County of Essex at a special meeting this day assembled, desire to convey to the Commanders-in-Chief of His Majesty's Naval, Military and Air Forces engaged in the war their grateful thanks for the great sacrifices made by them and all ranks under their command, and heartiest congratulations upon the magnificent victory attained."

FROM THE TOWN CLERK, BATH.

20-11-18.

I have the honour to inform you that the resolution, a copy of which is set out below, was carried with acclamation at a meeting of the Council of this City held yesterday.

Resolution.

"That the Bath City Council do place upon record their profound appreciation of the valour and fortitude of His Majesty's Forces and of their splendid achievements which have gained for the Empire victory over our enemies and full promise of a satisfactory and lasting peace, and do express on behalf of the City their unbounded gratitude to all members of the Forces for the heroic tasks accomplished by them on behalf of their countrymen and in maintaining the cause of Freedom and Justice."

FROM THE CLERK OF THE URBAN DISTRICT COUNCIL, TIPTON.

19-11-18.

I am directed by the above Council to forward you, which I do herewith, copy of a resolution which was unanimously adopted at an Extraordinary Meeting of the Council held last night, thanking the British Army for their great services rendered during the past four years, and congratulating them upon the success which has attended their efforts.

"To Admiral Sir David Beatty, Commander-in-Chief of the British Navy; to Sir Douglas Haig, Commander of the British Forces; and to Lord Weir, Commanding the Royal Air Force :—

Resolved—That the Members of the Tipton Urban District Council, realizing the important part which has been played by the Navy during the period of the war, beg to tender to Admiral Sir David Beatty and those under his command their most sincere appreciation of the courage and fortitude displayed under most trying and difficult circumstances, which have to such a large extent brought about the collapse of the enemy and proved the British Tars to be "Masters of the Ocean and Rulers of the Waves."

The Council also desire to express to Sir Douglas Haig and those under his command hearty congratulations on, and grateful thanks for, the results which have been achieved as the result of four years' strenuous warfare. The indomitable pluck and courage displayed by our brave boys has added further lustre and glory to the British Army, of whose achievements the British public will ever be justly proud.

To Lord Weir and those under his command the Council also desire to extend their grateful thanks appreciating, as they do, that the security of this country against attacks by the enemy has resulted only from the constant vigilance of this section of His Majesty's Forces."

FROM THE DISTRICT SECRETARY, UNITED KINGDOM SOCIETY OF AMALGAMATED SMITHS AND STRIKERS, GATESHEAD-ON-TYNE.
20-11-18.

I am requested by the members of the above Society, employed in the Engineering and Shipbuilding Yards on the Tyne and Wear, to tender to you, and the officers and men under your command, their heartfelt thanks for the glorious victory achieved on behalf of liberty and civilization.

They desire you to accept this as a token of their appreciation for the noble services which you have rendered for the Mother Country.

FROM THE CLERK TO THE URBAN DISTRICT COUNCIL OF BEDWELLTY, CLERK'S OFFICE, BARGOED, GLAMORGANSHIRE.
19-11-18.

I am directed by the Bedwellty Urban District Council on their behalf, and on behalf of the residents of the Bedwellty Urban Area, to send you their sincere congratulations on the great victory of right against might achieved under your command.

FROM THE MINISTER, NEW GRAVEL PIT CHURCH, HACKNEY, E.9.
20-11-18.

I am desired by the members of my congregation to forward to you a copy of the following resolution passed unanimously at the close of a special Service of Gratitude held on November 11th :—

"The congregation of the New Gravel Pit Church, Hackney, offer to Sir Douglas Haig and all ranks serving under him their sincere congratulations on the great victory that has crowned their work of the past four years, and their appreciation of their achievements, and in gratitude pledge themselves to do all that lies in their power to work for the betterment of this country."

FROM THE CLERK TO THE PARISH COUNCIL, CHUDLEIGH, S. DEVON.
19-11-18.

At the first meeting of the Parish Council of Chudleigh, held after the signing of the armistice, the members of the Council unanimously desired to express to you and those under your command the admiration of the glorious victories in France, and their thankfulness to those who for more than four years have protected us from our powerful foes.

Our traditions of the past have been more than upheld by you in the present in a contest of such magnitude as our forefathers never dreamed of, and fresh and undying glory has been added to the flag that for so many centuries has waved the battle and the breeze.

That every blessing may rest upon you in the future is our earnest prayer for those who have deserved well of their country.

FROM THE CHAIRMAN, URBAN DISTRICT COUNCIL, KIRBY-IN-SHEFFIELD, NOTTS.
22-11-18.

Urban District Council congratulate you and officers and men on your great success.

D. Haig, F.M.

Commander-in-Chief,
British Armies in France.

General Headquarters,
26th November, 1918.

PRINTED IN FRANCE BY ARMY PRINTING AND STATIONERY SERVICES.

PRESS A—11/18.

SPECIAL ORDER OF THE DAY
By FIELD-MARSHAL SIR DOUGLAS HAIG
K.T., G.C.B., G.C.V.O., K.C.I.E
Commander-in-Chief, British Armies in France.

The following message addressed to Field-Marshal Sir Douglas Haig has been received:—

FROM THE PRESIDENT, THE CHARTERED INSTITUTE OF SECRETARIES, LONDON.

19-11-18.

I have the honour to transmit to you the following resolution passed at its meeting on the 13th November by the Council of this Institute:—

"Resolved—That the Council of the Chartered Institute of Secretaries takes the occasion of the conclusion of the Armistice to offer its thanks and congratulations to the Armed Forces of the Crown under the command of Field-Marshal Sir Douglas Haig. The sacrifices which the soldiers of all ranks have made can never be repaid by those whom they have saved from the destruction with which they were threatened by the crime of the German High Command in precipitating the great war. But as far as lies in the power of the Council and the Members of the Institute no effort will be spared by them to assist the transfer back to civil life of those who may so desire it and who have gained such glory and suffered so much in the course of their military duty."

REPLY :—

Please convey to the Council of the Chartered Institute of Secretaries the sincere thanks of all ranks of the British Armies under my command for their kind message of congratulation. The results achieved more than repay the sacrifices demanded of us, but we trust that the nation will not forget the disabled, and the widows and children of those whose sacrifice has been supreme.

Suitable replies have been sent to the following:—

FROM THE TOWN CLERK, GREENWICH.

21-11-18.

I have the greatest honour to transmit to you the following copy of a resolution passed at a meeting of the Council of this Borough held last evening, being the first meeting after the signing of the armistice:—

"In view of the great victories granted by Almighty God to our arms and those of our Allies, which have led to the signing of the armistice on 11th November, and the prospect of a victorious peace, the Council desires to offer to Marshal Foch, the Commander-in-Chief of the Allied Forces, and to Admiral Sir David Beatty, Field-Marshal Sir Douglas Haig and to all the officers and men of the Royal Navy, the Army and the Royal Air Force and the Mercantile Marine its hearty congratulations on the successful result of their great sacrifice and arduous labour, and to express its profound admiration and gratitude for their splendid service in defence of the Country and Empire and the homes of our people, always remembering with affectionate regard those heroic men who have given their lives for the cause of justice, right and freedom."

FROM THE DISTRICT CLERK AND TREASURER, COUNTY OF LANARK.

20-11-18.

As instructed at a meeting of the District Committee held here on Monday last, I send you herewith an Excerpt from the minutes of that meeting:—

"The Chairman said he was sure that it would be the unanimous wish of the members that he should give expression to their heartfelt satisfaction at the cessation of hostilities, and for the splendid terms of the armistice and the prospects of enduring peace won by the glorious arms of the British Empire and her Allies. They would also desire at this time to express for themselves and the people of the District their continued and unswerving devotion and loyalty to the Throne and Person of His Most Gracious Majesty the King, and he moved accordingly. The motion was received with unanimous acclamation, the members rising and singing the National Anthem."

General Headquarters,
27th November, 1918.

Commander-in-Chief,
British Armies in France.

PRINTED IN FRANCE BY ARMY PRINTING AND STATIONERY SERVICES.   PRESS A—11/18.

SPECIAL ORDER OF THE DAY
By FIELD-MARSHAL SIR DOUGLAS HAIG
K.T., G.C.B., G.C.V.O., K.C.I.E
Commander-in-Chief, British Armies in France.

The following messages addressed to Field-Marshal Sir Douglas Haig have been received and suitable replies have been sent :—

FROM THE PRESIDENT, LONDON COMMITTEE OF DEPUTIES OF THE BRITISH JEWS, FINSBURY SQUARE, LONDON.
21-11-18.

At a meeting held on the 17th inst. of this Board, which is the Representative Body of the Jews of the British Empire, it was unanimously resolved that the Board desired to convey its heartfelt thanks to you and to the Officers, Non-commissioned Officers and Men of His Majesty's Army, through whose skill, gallantry, self-sacrifice and courage, combined with that of the rest of His Majesty's Forces, this country has been freed from the peril which menaced its existence, its enemies vanquished and their plans of world domination thwarted.

FROM THE PRESIDENT, THE CAVERSHAM AND READING VETERANS' ASSOCIATION, CAVERSHAM, READING.
21-11-18.

We, the Executive Committee of the Caversham and Reading Veterans' Association, beg leave to tender our cordial and hearty congratulations on the successful and glorious termination of the greatest war in history.

We recognize that this gratifying result has been achieved by the high motives, great abilities and energetic actions of the directing authorities; the splendid strategy of our Admirals and Generals; the self-sacrifice and strenuous exertions of our populace both on land and sea; and last, but not least, the valour, endurance and tenacity of all the rank and file of our sailors and soldiers, and our magnificent merchantmen.

We respectfully submit that the memories of the gallant heroes who have fallen in the fight may be best perpetuated by the establishment of Governmental Working Homes for the disabled.

FROM THE SECRETARY, SCOTTISH UNIONIST ASSOCIATION, EDINBURGH.
22-11-18.

I have the honour to transmit to you the following resolution which was unanimously passed at a meeting of the Eastern Divisional Council of the Scottish Unionist Association held yesterday, on the motion of Sir Henry Dundas, Bart., His Grace the Duke of Buccleuch being in the chair :—

"The Eastern Divisional Council of the Scottish Unionist Association at their first meeting after the armistice tender to Sir Douglas Haig and all the officers, non-commissioned officers and men of His Majesty's Land and Air Forces their heartfelt admiration of the magnificent courage, indomitable will and supreme individual efforts with which they have sustained, during more than four years, a fight for liberty unexampled in the history of the world; they record with pride the heroism of the original Expeditionary Force, the memory of whose devotion and supreme sacrifice will never die; they tender their grateful thanks and rejoice that the splendid efforts of all ranks have been crowned with splendid victory."

FROM THE PRESIDENT, NATIONAL POLITICAL LEAGUE, WESTMINSTER.
23-11-18.

I have the greatest pleasure in forwarding you the following resolution passed unanimously at a Public Meeting held in the Central Hall (large), Westminster, on Nov. 21st.

It is especially gratifying to me to be able to express to you the thanks of the women of the Country at the first large public meeting convened after the signing of the armistice :—

"At this meeting held in the Central Hall, Westminster, by the National Political League, women unanimously voice their gratitude to the men of the Army and the Air Service, who have defended their country and their homes with unbounded heroism, noble sacrifices and indomitable pluck, and whose deeds for ever immortal in the history of the Empire have achieved through a gigantic and terrible struggle the most glorious victory of all times.

Women, on their part, pledge themselves to do all in their power to build up a Country and Empire worthy of the freedom won at so great a cost."

From The Hon. Secretary, Southern Counties Cross-Country Association, Sutton, Surrey.
21-11-18.
I am instructed to forward to you a copy of the resolution passed at our meeting last night.

* * *

Resolution.

"The Southern Counties Cross-Country Association desires to tender its sincere congratulations to Field-Marshal Sir Douglas Haig on the magnificent achievements of the Empire Armies under his command. It feels that the success of the British Arms is a vindication of the sporting spirit, the spirit of playing for your side, and not for yourself, which it is the prime object of cross-country associations to foster."

From The Prefect of the Pas-de-Calais, Arras.
19-11-18.

Translation.

I have the honour to send you the text of a motion voted unanimously by the Municipal Council of Arras in session on the 15th November at which I was present.

"The Municipal Council of Arras in session at Arras on the 15th November, 1918, under the presidency of the Mayor, sends its congratulations and expresses its gratitude to Monsieur Georges Clemenceau, President of the Council and Minster of War, whose glowing patriotism and far-seeing energy stimulated the gallantry of all the Allied troops, to the illustrious Marshal Foch, to General Petain, to Field-Marshal Sir Douglas Haig, to General Pershing, commanding the French, British and American Armies, who with their heroic troops and their able assistants, broke the enemy's front; to the tenacious and intrepid Armies, and to the valiant dead who brought victory again to the Allied flag in this fight for Right and Justice."

D. Haig. F.M.

Commander-in-Chief,
British Armies in France.

General Headquarters,
29th November, 1918.

SPECIAL ORDER OF THE DAY
By FIELD-MARSHAL SIR DOUGLAS HAIG
K.T., G.C.B., G.C.V.O., K.C.I.E
Commander-in-Chief, British Armies in France.

The following telegrams addressed to Field-Marshal Sir Douglas Haig have been received:—

FROM THE MAYOR OF HUDDERSFIELD.

23-11-18.

The inhabitants of Huddersfield at a Town Meeting held this evening, Friday, November 22nd, 1918, in support of the Huddersfield thanksgiving week, desire to offer to Sir Douglas Haig their most sincere and hearty congratulations on the signing of the armistice with the enemy Powers, and on the prospect of an early and victorious peace. The meeting begs that Sir Douglas Haig will kindly accept its most sincere congratulations on the conclusion of hostilities, to which Sir Douglas Haig's masterly abilities have so largely contributed, and for which the Armies under his command, and following his most notable example, have striven so splendidly. Out-generalled and out-fought the enemies of freedom have been defeated and the world made safe.

REPLY :—

The forces under my command join with me in asking you to convey to the inhabitants of Huddersfield our warmest thanks for the message of congratulation to which you have given such very kind expression. Though the way has been long and steep, each one of us has ever been sustained in our difficulties by the confidence, encouragement, and loyal support of the people at home, and now in the hour of victory we find our greatest reward in the wholehearted appreciation of our countrymen and women of which your telegram is a moving example.

TO GENERAL DE GOUTTE, COMMANDING SIXTH FRENCH ARMY.

24-11-18.

On your return to the command of the French Sixth Army, may I be permitted to express my deep appreciation of the great services rendered by you to the Allied cause throughout the brilliant operations of the Flanders Group of Armies. All ranks of the British forces who took part in the successful attacks delivered by the Allied Armies under the command of His Majesty the King of the Belgians will esteem it an honour that in those operations they had the advantage of the ability and experience of so distinguished a French General.

REPLY :—

The Sixth French Army is very proud of the congratulations sent to it by the Field-Marshal, Commanding-in-Chief of the British Armies in the Field. It feels that it has been fortunate in having fought alongside the Second British Army, whose good comradeship in action, shewn by the valour of the troops and the gallantry of their leaders, has again been demonstrated. The General Officer Commanding the Sixth French Army considers it a great honour to have been associated with so distinguished an Army Commander as General Plumer in carrying out to a successful issue their common task, which end has been happily realized owing to the efforts made by all ranks. He retains for the troops of Great Britain as great a feeling of sympathy as he does of admiration.

Suitable replies have been sent to the following:—

FROM THE SECRETARY, CALEDONIAN SOCIETY, MELBOURNE.

26-11-18.

Members wholeheartedly unite in congratulating you on your glorious achievements in the great cause for which the Allies have been fighting. We feel proud that as a Scot you have proved your worth and have fought hard and brilliantly in the cause of humanity.

From The Secretary, The Our Boy's Lodge, No. 149, R.A.O.B., Plymouth.
 24-11-18.

   The members desire to express to you their feelings of relief and spirit of thankfulness on the cessation of hostilities.

   They recognize with feelings of gratitude the debt they and our country owe to you, and they admire the singleness of purpose which has actuated your every effort and appreciate to the full the loyal way in which you have brought this war to a successful climax.

   They feel it an honour to have been associated in this great war and to have contributed to it in no small degree.

From The Sailors and Soldiers Widow, Wives and Dependents Scottish Federation, West End Branch, Edinburgh.
 26-11-18.

   We thank you for the noble and valuable services you have rendered us and mankind, and through you, all officers and men under your command who through devotion to duty have rendered our homes secure. For this grand victory and prospects of a glorious peace we thank you.

From The Order Sons of Empire, Montreal.
 25-11-18.

   Sends warmest congratulations to self and brave Armies on great victories.

From The English and Allied Colonies, Linares.
 -11-18.

   The English and Allied Colonies and Spanish sympathies in Linares send greetings to the holder of the rights of the little nations, the weak and the oppressed against tyranny, which has always been the desire of England in the war.

D. Haig. F.M.

General Headquarters,
 1st December, 1918.

Commander-in-Chief,
British Armies in France.

SPECIAL ORDER OF THE DAY
By FIELD-MARSHAL SIR DOUGLAS HAIG
K.T., G.C.B., G.C.V.O., K.C.I.E
Commander-in-Chief, British Armies in France.

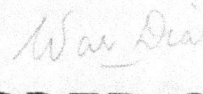

The following telegrams addressed to Field-Marshal Sir Douglas Haig have been received:—

FROM THE MUNICIPAL CHAIRMAN, COIMBATORE, INDIA.
26-11-18.
  Please accept hearty congratulations of Coimbatore Public, India, on success of Allied arms, to which the British Empire and your generalship so largely contributed.

REPLY:—
  Warmest thanks on behalf of all ranks of the Army under my command and of myself to you and the inhabitants of Coimbatore for your kind message which we greatly value.

FROM THE PRESIDENT, ST. ANDREW'S SOCIETY, TORONTO.
25-11-18.
  Recognising the heroic part played by troops under your splendid command, the Saint Andrew's Society, Toronto, on near approach of Scotland's National Day, desire to express unbounded admiration for steadfast spirit displayed under most trying circumstances, and assure you that your fellow countrymen are proud and grateful for the brilliant part your forces had in bringing the war to such a glorious end.

REPLY:—
  Warmest thanks from all ranks of the Armies in France and from myself for your very friendly message. St. Andrew's Day will never have dawned brighter than it will this year—for the sons of Scotland throughout the world have indeed played a glorious part in the triumphant vindication of those ideals for which all free nations stand.

Suitable replies have been sent to the following:—

FROM THE CLERK TO THE COMMITTEE, NATIONAL HEALTH INSURANCE, GATESHEAD.
25-11-18.
  I am instructed to forward to you a copy of a resolution unanimously passed by the Gateshead Insurance Committee at a meeting held on the 12th instant.
  1. "That this Gateshead Insurance Committee expresses its grateful thanks to the Allied Commanders and all ranks of the Navy, Army, and Air Forces and Mercantile Marine for their magnificent services rendered during the war, and to congratulate them on the splendid victories achieved and final triumph in their fight for Freedom's Cause which they hope has laid a foundation of a just and lasting peace.
  2. That copies be sent to Field-Marshal Haig and Sir David Beatty."

FROM THE CLERK OF THE URBAN DISTRICT COUNCIL, BLAENAU-FESTINIOG. N.W.
26-11-18.
  At the last meeting of the above Council, the following resolution was unanimously passed:—
  "That the warmest congratulations of the Council be tendered to Sir Douglas Haig upon the complete victory of the Allied arms, and in particular upon his excellent leadership of the British Army."

From The Clerks of the Urban District Council, Blyth, Northumberland.
23-11-18.
At the last ordinary Monthly meeting of the above Council held on the 14th instant, we were directed to convey to you the following resolution which was unanimously agreed to :—

"That this Council expresses its grateful thanks to Marshal Foch, the Allied Commanders, and all ranks of the Navy, Army and Air Forces for their magnificent services rendered during the great war, and for the splendid victories and final triumph of the Allies, in their effort for Freedom's Cause, which we hope has laid the foundation of a just and righteous peace."

From The Chairman, Mountayliff Board.
15-11-18.
Bravo. Inhabitants congratulate you and your victorious troops.

From The Overseas Club, Benonis.
14-11-18.
Benonis Overseas Club profoundly thankful for glorious triumph, and offer you sincere congratulations.

D. Haig, F.M.

General Headquarters,
2nd December, 1918.

Commander-in-Chief,
British Armies in France.

SPECIAL ORDER OF THE DAY
By FIELD-MARSHAL SIR DOUGLAS HAIG
K.T., G.C.B., G.C.V.O., K.C.I.E
Commander-in-Chief, British Armies in France.

A large number of men are now being withdrawn from Tunnelling Companies for urgent work at home.

Before they leave the Country I wish to convey to the Controllers of Mines and to all ranks of Tunnelling Companies, both Imperial and Overseas my very keen appreciation of the fine work that has been done by the Tunnelling Companies throughout the last four years.

At their own special work, Mine Warfare, they have demonstrated their complete superiority over the Germans, and whether in the patient defensive mining, in the magnificent success at Messines, or in the preparation for the offensives of the Somme, Arras and Ypres, they have shown the highest qualities both as Military Engineers and as fighting troops.

Their work in the very dangerous task of removing Enemy Traps and Delay action charges, on subways, dug-outs, bridging, roads, and the variety of other services on which they have been engaged has been on a level with their work in the mines.

They have earned the thanks of the whole Army for their contribution to the defeat of the enemy. Their fighting spirit and technical efficiency has enhanced the reputation of the whole Corps of Royal Engineers, and of the Engineers of the Overseas Forces.

I should like to include in the appreciation the work done by the Army Mine Schools and by the Australian Electrical and Mechanical, Mining and Boring Company.

D. Haig, F.M.

General Headquarters,
4th December, 1918.

*Commander-in-Chief,
British Armies in France.*

SPECIAL ORDER OF THE DAY
By FIELD-MARSHAL SIR DOUGLAS HAIG
K.T., G.C.B., G.C.V.O., K.C.I.E
Commander-in-Chief, British Armies in France.

The following messages addressed to Field-Marshal Sir Douglas Haig have been received :—

FROM THE REGISTRAR, THE UNIVERSITY OF LIVERPOOL.
27-11-18.

I am instructed by the Council and Senate of the University to forward to you the following resolution :—

"The Council and Senate of the University of Liverpool would express to Field-Marshal Sir Douglas Haig their grateful admiration for the services that he with the Forces under his command has rendered to the nation. They are proud of the bravery that has won so great a victory for the cause of the Allies, but still more proud of the spirit that days of disaster could not break, of the endurance that withstood suffering, hardship and the unimaginable horrors of war, and of that kindliness of heart which our troops have carried with them among the folk of many lands. To the men whom we hope soon to welcome to their homes, and to the heroic dead, by whom we have been shielded and saved, we owe it that the new world of peace and safety which they have won for us shall be a better world than the old."

REPLY :—

Please convey to the Council and Senate of the University of Liverpool, on behalf both of myself and of the officers, non-commissioned officers and men under my command, our deep appreciation of the sentiments of gratitude and pride so generously expressed in the resolution you have sent to me. We ourselves are both proud and grateful that it has been given us to uphold victoriously the honour of our country through the long years of war. With you we look forward to the day when the seeds of unselfishness and disinterested devotion to duty which the war has planted in the hearts of the nation shall bear fruit in peace.

Suitable replies have been sent to the following :—

FROM THE SECRETARY, LEITH CHAMBER OF COMMERCE.
22-11-18.

On behalf of the Leith Chamber of Commerce, I have the honour to send you the following resolution passed by its members on the occasion of the signing of the armistice, of which they respectfully beg your acceptance.

They instruct me also to express to you and the Forces under your command, their highest appreciation of your unwearied services to the Nation, and their cordial congratulations on the successful termination of the war.

Resolution of General Meeting—18th November, 1918.

"We, the members of the Leith Chamber of Commerce, now assembled, desire to record our satisfaction at the virtual conclusion of the war by terms of armistice imposed by the Allies and accepted unconditionally by Germany; and our deep thankfulness that the cause of Justice and Right should thus have been triumphantly vindicated.

At this happy termination of the ordeal through which the nation has had to pass, our thoughts turn first to our King, who, by his personal example, has given so inspiring a lead to his whole people in facing and surmounting the difficulties and anxieties, and in accepting the privations, inseparable from such a time; and we respectfully offer to him the tribute of our admiration and of our enduring loyalty.

Conscious as we are of the tremendous burden of duty and responsibility which has fallen on the Government, on the Navy, and on the Army, we desire to express our sense of the unfaltering courage and devotion with which these duties and responsibilities have been carried through to a victorious issue. To Mr. Lloyd George, to Sir David Beatty, and to Sir Douglas Haig we tender our grateful thanks for the brilliant services which they have been able to render, and our congratulations that success should now have crowned their labours."

But even such distinguished services must have failed had they not been supported by the resolute and united will of the British people, and reinforced by the loyalty of the Dominions beyond the Seas. Nothing, perhaps, has been more memorable in the four years that have passed than the oneness of spirit which has bound the whole Empire together in the performance of its great task. Whether in the actual fighting by land or sea or in the air, whether in munition factories, in hospitals, or wherever the organization or the executive detail of War Work had to be done, there, loyal and untiring workers were to be found for whom no labour was too irksome and no sacrifice too heavy. Women claimed their part with men in discharging the great responsibility laid on our generation, and the story of that united effort is one of which the country will long be proud.

Least of all in the hour of victory can we forget the dead, who have laid down their fair and gallant lives that not ruthless Force, but Truth, Justice and Mercy should rule the affairs of men. They sleep well, and their great sacrifice has not been made in vain. To them no honour can be added. But their names and their deeds are unforgotten, and their memories live and endure in the hearts of those who mourn for them.

FROM THE HON. SECRETARY, BENEVOLENT SOCIETY OF ST. ANDREW, BELFAST.

30-11-18.

Belfast Benevolent Society of St. Andrew, assembled at anniversary dinner, send you cordial greetings and congratulations on the magnificent victory won by the Forces under your command, especially do we appreciate the services of our gallant Scottish lads.

FROM THE CALEDONIAN SOCIETY, BLOEMFONTEIN.

16-11-18.

Gratitude and admiration for you and your gallant Armies on glorious issue, won through grim endurance, noble fortitude, and fine fighting.

FROM THE CONSULTATIVE COMMITTEE OF WOMEN'S SOCIETIES WORKING FOR EQUAL CITIZENSHIP, LONDON.

27-11-18.

We, the undersigned representatives of constituent societies of the Consultative Committee of Women's Societies Working for Equal Citizenship, wish to convey, through you, our thanks to the men and women of the British Army for their services rendered during the war.

(*Signed*)

BLANCHE STANLEY,
  Actresses' Franchise League.

H. C. NEWCOMB,
  British Dominions Women Citizens' Union.

FFLORENS ROCH,
  Catholic Women's Suffrage Society.

LOUISE CORBEN,
  Church League for Women's Suffrage.

E. L. KELSALL,
  Fabian Society (Women's Group).

ETHEL MACNAGHTEN,
  Irishwomen's Civic Federation.

ETHEL E. FROUD,
  National Federation of Women Teachers.

MILLICENT GARRETT FAWCETT,
  National Union of Women's Suffrage Societies.

ANNIE G. FERRIER,
  Scottish Churches League for Women's Suffrage.

General Headquarters,
4th December, 1918.

Commander-in-Chief,
British Armies in France.

SPECIAL ORDER OF THE DAY
By FIELD-MARSHAL SIR DOUGLAS HAIG
K.T., G.C.B., G.C.V.O., K.C.I.E
Commander-in-Chief, British Armies in France.

The following telegrams are published for the information of all ranks:—

To HER MAJESTY QUEEN ALEXANDRA, BUCKINGHAM PALACE, LONDON.

1-12-18.

All ranks of the British Armies in France offer Your Majesty their most respectful congratulations and good wishes on the anniversary of your birthday.

FIELD-MARSHAL SIR DOUGLAS HAIG.

REPLY:—

With a deeply grateful heart I thank you and all our splendid and brave Army in France for kind wishes on my old birthday. Accept all my heartfelt congratulations for your splendid and glorious achievements and peace.

ALEXANDRA.

D. Haig. F.M.

Commander-in-Chief,
British Armies in France.

General Headquarters,
4th December, 1918.

SPECIAL ORDER OF THE DAY
By FIELD-MARSHAL SIR DOUGLAS HAIG
K.T., G.C.B., G.C.V.O., K.C.I.E
Commander-in-Chief, British Armies in France.

The following telegram addressed to Field-Marshal Sir Douglas Haig has been received :—

FROM THE G.O.C., 5TH CAVALRY DIVISION, ALEPPO.
30-11-18.
    Fifth Cavalry Division sends heartiest congratulations on glorious victory. Their only regret is that they were not with you.

REPLY :—
    Very sincere thanks for your telegram of congratulation from myself and from all ranks of the Armies under my command. We in our turn heartily congratulate you and the 5th Cavalry Division on your brilliant work in Palestine. We have never ceased to regret the departure of yourself and your splendid squadrons from my command in France during the critical battles of this year.

Suitable replies have been sent to the following :—

FROM THE CLERK TO THE URBAN DISTRICT COUNCIL, SHIPLEY.
28-11-18.
    At the Monthly Meeting of this Council held on the 26th instant—the first meeting since the signing of the armistice—the Chairman referred to the great victory which has been achieved by our Military, Naval and Air Forces, and I am instructed to forward, on behalf of the people of Shipley, heartfelt congratulations and thanks to you and to all Officers, Non-commissioned Officers and Men in all Forces of the British Empire under your command on the splendid victory which has been achieved.
    In doing this I have to say that this district, with a population of less than 30,000 has sent into the Army and Navy 3,500 men, and the people of this district are proud to know that their sons have had a share in the overthrow of the enemy, and that they have exhibited courage, devotion, endurance and heroism, which have helped to secure the freedom of the world.

FROM THE TOWN CLERK, NEWPORT, MON.
28-11-18.
    I am desired to forward to you the following copy of a resolution passed at Massed Thanksgiving Service held here last Sunday, the 24th instant :—
    Resolved : "That at this Massed Thanksgiving Service, convened by the Salvation Army, representative of the people and Local War Organizations of the Borough of Newport, it is desired to place on record heartfelt gratitude to Almighty God who has graciously allowed the light of victory to shine upon our banners with the cessation of hostilities, also a deep appreciation of the magnificent services rendered by the gallant men of our Navy and Army, also our Doctors, Nurses and Mercantile Marine, together with our Allies and the United States Forces, in defeating the sinister designs of the enemy, and so vindicating the cause of righteousness, the right of small Nations, and the freedom of all peoples.
    An expression of deepest sympathy is also offered to the relatives of those brave men who have made the supreme sacrifice with the prayer that the consoling ministrations of the Holy Spirit may be vouchsafed to them.
    Further, that a message of congratulation and expression of loyalty be sent to His most gracious Majesty the King, The Prime Minister, The Right Hon. David Lloyd George; The Naval Commander-in-Chief, Admiral Sir David Beatty; and Field-Marshal Sir Douglas Haig."

FROM MR. W. T. HESLOP, HATTINGSPRUIT, NATAL.
27-11-18.
    Residents, Natal Navigation Collieries, Glencoe Colliery, and St. Georges Colliery, Hattingspruit, in public meeting assembled, desire to express to you and all Forces under your command their heartfelt gratitude for the long years of brave and strenuous efforts which have culminated in such brilliant success, which we trust, after the sacrifice of so many lives, have secured to humanity peace and liberty for all time.

D. Haig, F.M.

General Headquarters,
5th December, 1918.

Commander-in-Chief,
British Armies in France.

Ivor Dean

War Diary

SPECIAL ORDER OF THE DAY
By FIELD-MARSHAL SIR DOUGLAS HAIG
K.T., G.C.B., G.C.V.O., K.C.I.E
Commander-in-Chief, British Armies in France.

The following messages addressed to Field-Marshal Sir Douglas Haig have been received and suitable replies have been sent :—

FROM THE GRAND REGISTRAR, GRAND ROYAL ARCH PURPLE CHAPTER OF IRELAND, BELFAST.

27-11-18.

I am directed by Grand Royal Arch Purple Chapter of Ireland to convey to you the following resolution of congratulation :—

"That we, the Grand Royal Arch Purple Chapter of Ireland, composed of loyal and devoted subjects of our Sovereign, (many of whom freely enlisted to serve their King and Country), at Annual Meeting assembled, desire to offer our most sincere and hearty congratulations to the officers and men of the Navy, Army, and Royal Air Force for their great valour, devotion, and sacrifice which have secured us victory over all our foes, and led to a successful armistice with the near prospect of a lasting peace.

We desire also to place on record our heartfelt appreciation of the bravery and devotion of those who have fallen in the fight for freedom, justice, and right; and our deep gratitude for the sacrifice made by them in laying down their lives to secure for us and our children, and for the world at large those inestimable blessings—Peace and Liberty."

FROM THE TOWN CLERK, LUTON.

Mayor and Councillors of Borough of Luton express their great appreciation of the magnificent and heroic services you and the officers and men under your command have so persistently rendered in the great war, culminating in the complete defeat and collapse of the Central Powers and cessation of hostilities. The Empire will be ever grateful to and proud of you and all under your command, not forgetting our Indian and Colonial troops whose heroism and efforts to maintain the cause of freedom have been crowned with victory.

FROM THE CLERK, YELL SCHOOL BOARD, MID YELL, SHETLAND.

27-11-18.

I am directed by my Board to convey to you their sincere and heartiest congratulations on the great success which has at last crowned your labours, their appreciation of the services you have rendered to your country, and to civilization; their admiration and gratitude to your Army for their valour in the field, and the heroic manner in which officers and men have endured unexampled hardships.

FROM THE SECRETARY, CHAMBER OF COMMERCE, SWANSEA.

2-12-18.

At the first meeting of the Swansea Chamber of Commerce held subsequent to the signing of the armistice, it was unanimously resolved that the heartiest congratulations and grateful thanks of the members be extended to you for the magnificent results that have been attained by you and the men under your command. We appreciate fully the great valour and sacrifices that have been necessary to bring about the complete overthrow of our enemies, as clearly shown in the terms of the armistice which they have been compelled to accept.

FROM THE SECRETARY, MINISTRY OF LABOUR, EMPLOYMENT EXCHANGE, LOWESTOFT.

30-11-18.

I am instructed by my Committee to convey to you their congratulations upon the successful termination of hostilities, contributed to so largely by the British Army under your command. I am to add that they wish to express their great admiration and gratitude for the wonderful bravery and self-sacrifice displayed.

From the National Master Farriers' Association, Swindon Branch, Banbury.

8-12-18.

I am desired by the Chairman and Members of the Swindon and District Branch of the National Master Farriers' Association to convey to you and all ranks of the British Armies in France our hearty congratulations on the successful issue of the signing of the armistice and the end of fighting in the terrible war now brought to a close.

We all honour and admire the ungrudging way in which you and the troops of all ranks have done your duty.

D. Haig. F.M.

General Headquarters,
9th December, 1918.

Commander-in-Chief,
British Armies in France.

SPECIAL ORDER OF THE DAY
By FIELD-MARSHAL SIR DOUGLAS HAIG
K.T., G.C.B., G.C.V.O., K.C.I.E
Commander-in-Chief, British Armies in France.

The following telegrams addressed to Field-Marshal Sir Douglas Haig have been received :—

FROM THE PRESIDENT, ASSOCIATION OF HIGHLAND SOCIETIES OF EDINBURGH.
7-12-18.

At the Annual General Meeting of the Association of Highland Societies of Edinburgh, representing many thousands of Highland men and women, just held, it was resolved to ask you to accept our heartiest congratulations on the magnificent results achieved by all ranks of the British Army during the past four and a half years. May we also respectfully tender to you our appreciation of your inestimable services. We remember with pride that under your command our Highland Regiments in whose interests we have steadfastly laboured in the provision of comforts, have more than maintained their traditional honours.

REPLY :—

Please accept for yourself and convey to the members of the Association of Highland Societies of Edinburgh my warmest thanks, together with those of all ranks of the Armies under my command, for their kind telegram of congratulation. Throughout the war Highland Regiments have not only upheld the glorious traditions handed down to them by their forebears, but have greatly added to them, and your unwearied labours at home on their behalf have materially helped them in their task.

Suitable replies have been sent to the following :

FROM THE SECRETARY, THE GRIMSBY FISHING VESSEL OWNERS' EXCHANGE CO. LTD., FISH DOCKS, GRIMSBY.
3-12-18.

At a meeting of the Committee of this Company (which comprises the whole of the Owners of Fishing Vessels of this Port) held on the 28th ult., the following resolution was unanimously carried :—

"Grimsby Fishing Vessel Owners tender to you and the officers and men serving under you their grateful thanks and sincere appreciation of the magnificent services rendered by you and them and for the gallant and strenuous efforts and sacrifices made during the Great War, and which have so materially contributed towards the preservation and maintenance of our homes and liberties and the complete and final defeat of our enemies."

I have pleasure in forwarding you this resolution.

FROM THE SECRETARY, R.A.O.B., MIDDLETON, MANCHESTER.
3-12-18.

At a meeting of the above held at the Ackrington Lodge of the Oldham Province, I was instructed to convey the congratulations of the brethren to you and the excellent troops under your command for the excellent victory you have achieved in the cause of freedom. We cannot express too highly the admiration we feel for all those who are deserving of our thanks. Assuring you of our sincerity.

FROM THE PRESIDENT, BRITISH AND CONSTITUTIONAL LABOUR PARTY, LONDON, N.5.
3-12-18.

At the first meeting of the National Executive of the British and Constitutional Labour Party since the declaration of the armistice, held to-day, I am instructed to write you their best wishes and congratulations on the splendid consummation of the great struggle which has attended the gallant and noble conduct of yourself, staff and officers, and men of the British Army in France; and to assure you on their behalf of their full appreciation of the great sacrifices which have been made by all ranks on behalf of Freedom, Liberty and Democracy.

With every personal good wish.

D. Haig, F.M.

General Headquarters,
10th December, 1918.

Commander-in-Chief,
British Armies in France.

PRINTED IN FRANCE BY ARMY PRINTING AND STATIONERY SERVICES.   PRESS A—12/18

SPECIAL ORDER OF THE DAY
By FIELD-MARSHAL SIR DOUGLAS HAIG
K.T., G.C.B., G.C.V.O., K.C.I.E
Commander-in-Chief, British Armies in France.

The following messages addressed to Field-Marshal Sir Douglas Haig have been received, and suitable replies have been sent :—

FROM THE CLERK TO THE URBAN DISTRICT COUNCIL, ISLE OF AXHOLME, EPWORTH, NR. DONCASTER.
6-12-18.

At the first meeting of this Council following the signing of the Armistice and the cessation of hostilities, the Chairman (Mr. Arthur Knapton) voiced the feeling of the Council in giving expression to words of congratulation to, and appreciation of the services of, those who have been responsible for the splendid world victory which has been achieved.

The Council resolved to place upon record this expression of appreciation and congratulation.

Furthermore, I am desired to convey to yourself these sentiments and at the same time to express to you the Council's full appreciation of the splendid and unselfish services which you have rendered to the cause of the Empire, and which, through the incomparable deeds of the British Army have brought victory to the Allied Forces.

FROM THE SECRETARY, EXECUTIVE COMMITTEE, FARMERS' UNION, LEICESTER.
7-12-18.

At a meeting of the Leicestershire Farmers' Union held at Leicester on Saturday, Nov. 30, a resolution was unanimously passed of thanks and congratulations to you and the whole of your Forces on the splendid Victory achieved after so many years of strenuous efforts.

FROM THE SECRETARY, HARTLEPOOL NO. 2 BRANCH, BOILER MAKERS, IRON AND STEEL SHIP BUILDERS SOCIETY, HARTLEPOOL.
-12-18.

I have very great pleasure in forwarding to you the following resolution, passed at our meeting last night :—

"That we, the members of the above Branch, desire to record our satisfaction with the brilliant victory attained by the Allied Fleets and Armies, as represented in the terms of the armistice. Also to express our appreciation of those who have led us to this glorious termination of the world conflict, and of those who have fallen in the effort. This meeting further emphasizes the continuous loyalty of our members to the Crown and Empire."

FROM THE SECRETARY, THE PADDINGTON AND BAYSWATER CHAMBER OF COMMERCE, WESTBOURNE GROVE, W.2.
3-12-18.

I am instructed and have the honour to forward you herewith the following resolution which was unanimously passed at the meeting of my Executive Committee on the 2nd inst. :—

"That the Members of the Paddington and Bayswater Chamber of Commerce desire respectfully to convey to yourself and our gallant and victorious troops upon land and in air under your command their congratulations upon the signing on the 11th November last the armistice, and upon the terms accompanying the same which have been justly exacted from the defeated German Army and Navy."

We earnestly trust that the united efforts of our Allies and ourselves may soon establish peace and justice and order in the World, and that we and the friendly Nations may be enabled to form a League against war and enjoy the fruits of victory and truth and peace for all time.

From the President, the Bolton and District Chamber of Commerce, Bolton.
25-11-18.

I have the honour to submit to you the following resolution unanimously adopted by this Chamber :—

"The Council of the Bolton Chamber of Commerce assembled in special meeting hereby record their deep satisfaction and thankfulness for the brilliant termination of the war by the victory of the Forces representing right and justice, the respect of solemn treaties, and the protection of weaker Nations, and offer their sincere thanks to His Majesty's Navy, Army and other combatants and non-combatants actively engaged in the War, for their gallantry and endurance through four and a quarter years of intense warfare, and to the members of His Majesty's Government for their successful carrying through of the greatest effort any country has ever made for the defence of Freedom and Justice."

From the Clerk to the Parish Council, Brislington, Nr. Bristol.
30-11-18.

At a meeting of the Brislington Parish Council held on Thursday last it was unanimously resolved :—

"That the best thanks of this Council, on behalf of the Parishioners of Brislington, be tendered to Sir Douglas Haig and the men of the fighting Forces for the splendid part they had played in attaining such a glorious victory over our enemies."

I was requested to forward a copy of such resolution to you.

D. Haig. F.M.

Commander-in-Chief,
British Armies in France.

General Headquarters,
14th December, 1918.

Printed in France by Army Printing and Stationery Services.

Press A—12/18.

SPECIAL ORDER OF THE DAY
By FIELD-MARSHAL SIR DOUGLAS HAIG
K.T., G.C.B., G.C.V.O., K.C.I.E
Commander-in-Chief, British Armies in France.

War Diary

The following messages addressed to Field-Marshal Sir Douglas Haig have been received and suitable replies have been sent:—

FROM THE GENERAL SECRETARY, POSTAL AND TELEGRAPH CLERKS' ASSOCIATION, WESTMINSTER, S.W.1.
9-12-18.

I have much pleasure in forwarding to you the following resolution which was unanimously adopted at a recent Special Conference of this Association:—
"This Special Conference of the Postal and Telegraph Clerks' Association sends its congratulations to our Naval and Military Forces everywhere on their great achievements towards the furtherance of the ideals and aims that inspire British Democracy."

FROM THE TOWN CLERK, MUNICIPAL OFFICES, WEYMOUTH.
11-12-18.

I am directed by the Council of the Borough of Weymouth and Melcombe Regis as representing the inhabitants of this Borough to convey to you and the Forces under your command their heartfelt congratulations on the conclusion of the armistice and the prospect of a victorious peace.

FROM THE SECRETARY AND TREASURER, THORNCLIFFE AND ROCKINGHAM PERMANENT RELIEF SOCIETY, THORNCLIFFE IRON WORKS, NR. SHEFFIELD.
2-12-18.

At a meeting of the Board of Management of this Society, held on the 28th November, 1918, and representing about 4,500 miners and surface workers at the Collieries of Newton Chambers and Co. Ltd., I was instructed to convey to you their high admiration at the brilliant military victory achieved by the British Army under your wise and distinguished leadership, and also their high appreciation of the determination and devotion to duty under very many trying ordeals and difficulties.

The highest traditions of the British Army have been upheld, and but for the bravery, tenacity, endurance and self-sacrifice of our Army, it is admitted that our country must have shared the fate of France, Belgium, Serbia and other countries where homes and country have been devastated by the actions of the most relentless and vicious enemy recorded in history.

This Society wishes to place on record their gratitude to, and high appreciation of, the noble deeds of our Armies, and their distinguished leaders in the protection of the homes of Old England, and in vindication of the noble traditions of our Country in supporting the weak against the strong, right as against might, and in the maintenance of those Christian principles which form the basis of all our highest traditions and noble Institutions.

Many of our members have fought and died for their Country, and those of us whose duty has been at home feel we cannot do less than pay the highest possible tribute to all who have helped in the titanic struggle, and also to congratulate you on the high distinction which has been conferred upon you, and which was never more nobly deserved; we also hope that your life will long be spared to enjoy the repose and rest you have so richly merited.

I feel sure you may rely upon the best wishes of a grateful Country for your future welfare and a long life of happy reflections on such a brilliant achievement in the interest of Humanity and Civilization.

D. Haig, F.M.

General Headquarters,
16th December, 1918.

Commander-in-Chief,
British Armies in France.

PRINTED IN FRANCE BY ARMY PRINTING AND STATIONERY SERVICES.   PRESS A—12/18.

SPECIAL ORDER OF THE DAY
By FIELD-MARSHAL SIR DOUGLAS HAIG
K.T., G.C.B., G.C.V.O., K.C.I.E
Commander-in-Chief, British Armies in France.

The following message addressed to Field-Marshal Sir Douglas Haig has been received and a suitable reply has been sent :—

FROM THE TOWN CLERK, HASTINGS.

12/12/18.

I have the honour of forwarding you herewith copy of a resolution which was unanimously passed at a meeting of the Council of this Borough held on the 6th instant :—

"On the motion of the Right Worshipful the Mayor seconded by the Deputy Mayor (Councillor Mannington) it is Unanimously Resolved :—

'That this Council representing the inhabitants of the County Borough of Hastings, the Premier Cinque Port, at this its first meeting after the signing of the armistice congratulates His Most Gracious Majesty The King upon the success attained by His Majesty's Forces and those of His Allies and places on record the very high appreciation of the Borough of the magnificent and exceptional courage, skill and endurance exhibited by all ranks and sections of His Majesty's Forces during the whole period of the greatest War the world has ever known.'"

General Headquarters,
20th December, 1918.

Commander-in-Chief,
British Armies in France.

SPECIAL ORDER OF THE DAY
By FIELD-MARSHAL SIR DOUGLAS HAIG
K.T., G.C.B., G.C.V.O., K.C.I.E
Commander-in-Chief, British Armies in France.

This Christmas Day sees our united efforts crowned with a glorious victory.

I desire to wish all ranks of the Armies under my command a very happy Christmas and a brighter and happier New Year.

The self-sacrifice, endurance, and devotion to duty of our troops have gained the admiration of the whole world, and at this time, when everything is being done to accelerate demobilization, I feel sure that the same splendid qualities, which have carried us through these past years of war, will help us and strengthen us in reconstructing our Empire.

My thoughts are with you all on this memorable Christmas Day, and I wish you God Speed.

D. Haig. F.M.

Commander-in-Chief,
British Armies in France.

General Headquarters,
23rd December, 1918.

PRINTED IN FRANCE BY ARMY PRINTING AND STATIONERY SERVICES.   PRESS A—12/18.

SPECIAL ORDER OF THE DAY
By FIELD-MARSHAL SIR DOUGLAS HAIG
K.T., G.C.B., G.C.V.O., K.C.I.E
Commander-in-Chief, British Armies in France.

CHRISTMAS MESSAGE FROM THEIR MAJESTIES THE KING AND QUEEN.

Another Christmas has come round and we are no longer fighting. God has blessed your efforts. The Queen and I offer you our heartfelt good wishes for a happy Christmas and many brighter years to come. To the disabled, sick, and wounded, we send a special greeting, praying that with returning health you may be comforted and cheered by the vision of those good days of peace for which you have sacrificed so much.

GEORGE, R.I.

To HIS MAJESTY THE KING FROM FIELD MARSHAL SIR DOUGLAS HAIG.

Your Majesty's gracious message has given universal pleasure to all ranks of the Armies in France. They join with me in sending most respectful thanks, and beg to be allowed to send to their King and Queen earnest hope that the years to come may bring your Majesties all happiness. The never failing confidence and encouragement which we have received from you, Sir, throughout all the fluctuating fortunes of four and a half years of war have ever been a source of strength to us, and the gracious message which your Majesty has sent to the disabled, sick, and wounded will bring them comfort and reward.

D. Haig. F.M.

General Headquarters,
23rd December, 1918.

Commander-in-Chief,
British Armies in France.

PRINTED IN FRANCE BY ARMY PRINTING AND STATIONERY SERVICES.   PRESS A—12/18.

SPECIAL ORDER OF THE DAY
By FIELD-MARSHAL SIR DOUGLAS HAIG
K.T., G.C.B., G.C.V.O., K.C.I.E
Commander-in-Chief, British Armies in France.

The following telegram addressed to Field-Marshal Sir Douglas Haig has been received :—

FROM THE GENERAL OFFICER COMMANDING-IN-CHIEF, GREAT BRITAIN.

24/12/18

On behalf of the troops in Great Britain I wish a Happy Christmas to all troops under your command.

Reply :—

All ranks under my command send heartiest good wishes for Christmas and the coming year to you and their comrades in Great Britain.

D. Haig. F.M.

Commander-in-Chief,
British Armies in France.

General Headquarters,
26th December, 1918.

SPECIAL ORDER OF THE DAY
By FIELD-MARSHAL SIR DOUGLAS HAIG
K.T., G.C.B., G.C.V.O., K.C.I.E
Commander-in-Chief, British Armies in France.

The following message is published for the information of all ranks:—

FROM GENERAL PERSHING, COMMANDER-IN-CHIEF, AMERICAN EXPEDITIONARY FORCE, TO JUDGE ALTON B. PARKER, CHAIRMAN NATIONAL COMMITTEE ON ARRANGEMENT FOR BRITISH DAY, 233 BROADWAY, NEW YORK CITY.

7/12/18.

The achievements of the British Empire for humanity are too manifold to enumerate in a short message. Entering the war to defend the rights of nations she has unhesitatingly given her sons and her wealth. Gathered from her loyal Dominions, the men of the British Empire have carried their victorious eagles over many a bloody field. Steadfast in adversity, wounded with a thousand wounds, Britain's hammer blows have never weakened nor faltered. But for the tenacity of her people the war would have been lost. To those of us who have been associated with them and who fought beside their gallant troops words of praise seem inadequate to express our admiration. These things our kinsmen have done and these things have brought an inseparable union between them and ourselves. To the British people we extend our thanks for the powerful aid her Navy has given, and offer our great respect for the resolute Anglo-Saxon determination with which she has held on, and we offer our right hand of friendship that our two nations may be more firmly linked together to insure the future peace of the world.

The following telegram addressed to Field-Marshal Sir Douglas Haig has been received:—

FROM GENERAL PERSHING, COMMANDER-IN-CHIEF, AMERICAN EXPEDITIONARY FORCE.

26/12/18.

Please accept for our gallant British comrades the heartiest Christmas greetings of all members of this command. May the New Year bring to all of you a full measure of happiness which you so well deserve.

Reply:—

All ranks under my command heartily reciprocate the Christmas greetings you have sent us from our American comrades. May the years to come strengthen still further the ties of friendship we have formed in our common and triumphant progress.

D. Haig. F.M.

General Headquarters,
31st December, 1918.

*Commander-in-Chief,
British Armies in France.*

War Diary

SPECIAL ORDER OF THE DAY
By FIELD-MARSHAL SIR DOUGLAS HAIG
K.T., G.C.B., G.C.V.O., K.C.I.E
Commander-in-Chief, British Armies in France.

The following telegram addressed to Field-Marshal Sir Douglas Haig has been received:—

From The G.O.C. Portuguese Corps.

31/12/18.

Portuguese troops under my command greet their Commander-in-Chief, and express their best wishes that the New Year be prosperous to him and to all our British comrades in arms.

Reply:—

Very many thanks for your message which I heartily reciprocate on behalf of all ranks under my command.

D. Haig. F.M.

Commander-in-Chief,
British Armies in France.

General Headquarters,
3rd January, 1919.

SPECIAL ORDER OF THE DAY
By FIELD-MARSHAL SIR DOUGLAS HAIG
K.T., G.C.B., G.C.V.O., K.C.I.E
Commander-in-Chief, British Armies in France.

The following telegram addressed to Field-Marshal Sir Douglas Haig has been received:—

From THE LORD PROVOST, EDINBURGH.

24/12/18.

The citizens of Edinburgh send you and the Forces of all ranks under your command warmest greetings and best wishes for Christmas and the New Year, with special remembrance of the various Scottish Regiments. We deeply appreciate the Armies' great achievements and the glorious result of their heroic services for the Country, and our thoughts and heartiest feelings go forth to all ranks at this time.

Reply:—

All ranks under my command, and especially the Scottish Regiments, associate themselves with me in sending our heartiest thanks to you and the citizens of Edinburgh for your welcome greetings. We are grateful for the interest and appreciation we have always received from the capital of Scotland throughout the war and are glad to receive this message from you at the commencement of what we trust will be a happy New Year for all of us.

D. Haig. F.M.

General Headquarters,
4th January, 1919.

Commander-in-Chief,
British Armies in France.

PRINTED IN FRANCE BY ARMY PRINTING AND STATIONERY SERVICES.   PRESS A—1/19.

SPECIAL ORDER OF THE DAY
By FIELD-MARSHAL SIR DOUGLAS HAIG
K.T., G.C.B., G.C.V.O., K.C.I.E
Commander-in-Chief, British Armies in France.

The following telegram addressed to Field-Marshal Sir Douglas Haig has been received :—

From HIS MAJESTY THE KING OF THE BELGIANS.
1-1-19.

In my name, and in the name of the Belgian Army, I send you and all ranks of your splendid troops my most sincere wishes for a Happy New Year.

Reply :—

All ranks of the British Armies under my command beg your Majesty will accept our warmest thanks for the kind message of good wishes which you have been gracious enough to send us. We hope that the years which lie ahead of us may bring peace and prosperity to your Majesty, and the whole Belgian nation.

D. Haig. F.M.

General Headquarters,
9th January, 1919.

Commander-in-Chief,
British Armies in France.

PRINTED IN FRANCE BY ARMY PRINTING AND STATIONERY SERVICES.   Press A—1/19.

TRAINING PROGRAMME

FOR

WEEK COMMENCING 2nd DECEMBER 1945

DAY	0400-1000 hrs	1015 - 1115 hrs	1130 - 1230 hrs	REMARKS
MONDAY	P.T.	SALUTING. COY DRILL.	Bn CEREMONIAL	Organised games in afternoon. Lectures in evening.
TUESDAY	ROUTE MARCH combined with TACTICAL SCHEME — Own Guard			
WEDNESDAY	P.T.	SALUTING. COY DRILL	Bn CEREMONIAL	Organised games in afternoon. Lectures in evening.
THURSDAY	FIELD DAY .... TACTICAL SCHEME			
FRIDAY	P.T.	SALUTING COY DRILL	Bn DRILL	Organised games in afternoon. Lectures in evening.
SATURDAY	Interior Economy — Kit inspection etc.			

9th (Northumberland Fusaars) Battalion
Northumberland Fusiliers.

TRAINING PROGRAMME for the period :-   23/12/18   28/12/18

DECR.23.   0900-1200   EDUCATIONAL TRAINING (each day excepting
                            Wednesday and holidays) Shorthand,
                            Bookkeeping, Arithmatic, French classes, English.

                0900-0945   Platoon Drill.
                1000-1045   Squad Drill. Handling of Arms, etc.
                1100-1200   Guards and Sentries Drill.
                                                                MAP SHEET.
                                                                ABBEVILLE 14.
DECR. 24   HOLIDAY. Xmas Festivities.   5.K.63.12.
      25   do.   Xmas Festivities.   5.K.73.18.
      26   do.   Xmas Festivities.   5.K.98.64.
                                                                5.K.75.24.
                                                                5.L.13.57.

DECR. 27   0900-0945   Platoon Drill.
                1000-1100   Saluting Drill.
                1100-1200   Battalion Drill (Ceremonial) weather
                            permitting.

                            INTERIOR ECONOMY.

                            AFTERNOONS   EVENINGS.

                            Organised Games.   Lectures, Debates, Smokers,
                                                    as per Amusement programme.

DECR.28.

183rd INFANTRY BRIGADE.

TRAINING PROGRAMME FOR PERIOD 30/12/18 to 4/1/1919.

Unit.	Date	Time.	Nature of Training	Training Area	Remarks (To show Routes of Route Marches).
	1918. Decr. 30.	1500 hrs.	Conference of Officers and Specialist N.C.O's.		In Theatre Hut. All N.C.O's who are specialists whether employed as such or not.
		1000-1230	Educational Training (Each day excepting Wednesday) and Shorthand, Bookkeeping, Arithmetic, French classes, English.		
	Decr. 31.	0900-0945 1000-1045 1100-1200	Battalion Drill. Ceremonial. Squad Drill, Handling of Arms. Guards and Sentries Drill.	MAP SHEET. ABBEVILLE 14	
	1919. Jan. 1.	0900-0945 1000-1045 1100-1200	Battalion Drill. Ceremonial. Saluting Drill. Platoon Drill. HOLIDAY.	5.K.63.13. 5.K.75.18. 6.K.95.64. 5.K.75.24. 5.L.13.57.	AFTERNOONS Organised Games. EVENINGS. Lectures,Debates,Smokers as per amusement programme. In Theatre Hut.
	Jan. 2.	0900-0945 1000-1045 1100-1200 1700	Battalion Drill. Ceremonial. Handling of Arms. Saluting Drill. Guards & Sentries Drill. Brigade Commander's Conference.		
	Jan. 3.	0900-0945 1000-1045 1100-1200	Battalion Drill. Ceremonial. Saluting Drill. Guards & Sentries Drill. Squad Drill.		
	Jan. 4.		INTERIOR ECONOMY.		

Appendix 'C'

Special Orders of the Day

Army Form C. 2118.

WAR DIARY

~~INTELLIGENCE SUMMARY.~~ JANUARY 1919.

(Erase heading not required.)

9th (Northumberland Hussar) Battalion. Northumberland Fusiliers.

APPENDICES

A. Training Programme.

B. Special Orders of the Day.

Army Form C. 2118.

WAR DIARY
or
INTELLIGENCE SUMMARY.
(Erase heading not required.)

Instructions regarding War Diaries and Intelligence Summaries are contained in F. S. Regs., Part II. and the Staff Manual respectively. Title pages will be prepared in manuscript.

Place	Date	Hour	Summary of Events and Information	Remarks and references to Appendices
VAUCHELLES-LES-QUESNOY.	1st	Wednesday.	Holiday. The Drums sounded the Last Post at 2355 hours on the 31st December 1918, and Reveille at 0005 hours on the 1st January 1919 and then played the Regimental March Past.	Out
VAUCHELLES-LES-QUESNOY.	2nd	Thursday.	Training as per programme.	Out
VAUCHELLES-LES-QUESNOY.	3rd	Friday.	Training as per programme.	Out
VAUCHELLES-LES-QUESNOY.	4th	Saturday.	Training as per Programme. Companies devoted the morning to Interior Economy.	Out
VAUCHELLES-LES-QUESNOY.	5th	Sunday.	Divine Services.	Out
VAUCHELLES-LES-QUESNOY.	6th	Monday.	Training as per programme. The Commanding Officer gave a lecture on "Leadership" to the Officers in the Theatre Hut at 1200 hours.	Out
VAUCHELLES-LES-QUESNOY.	7th	Tuesday.	Training as per programme.	Out
VAUCHELLES-LES-QUESNOY.	8th	Wednesday.	Battalion Route March, route as per training programme.	Out
VAUCHELLES-LES-QUESNOY.	9th	Thursday.	Training as per programme. A lecture was given by the Brigade Commander to all the Officers, in the Theatre Hut at 1430 hours. Subject "Interior Economy".	Out

Army Form C. 2118.

WAR DIARY
of
INTELLIGENCE=SUMMARY.
(Erase heading not required.)

Instructions regarding War Diaries and Intelligence Summaries are contained in F. S. Regs., Part II. and the Staff Manual respectively. Title pages will be prepared in manuscript.

Place	Date	Hour	Summary of Events and Information	Remarks and references to Appendices
VAUCHELLES-LES-QUESNOY.	10th	FRIDAY.	The COLOURS were presented to the Battalion by Major General F.J.Duncan,C.B., C.M.G.,D.S.O.Commanding 61st Division. Lieut H.Robinson.M.C. received the Colours, which were Consecrated on the parade ground with the Battalion on parade.	
VAUCHELLES-LES-QUESNOY.	11th	Saturday.	The morning was devoted to interior economy.	
VAUCHELLES-LES-QUESNOY.	12th	Sunday.	Divine Services were held at Vauchelles-les-Quesnoy, St Riquier and Neuf Moulin.	
VAUCHELLES-LES-QUESNOY.	13th	Monday.	Training as per programme as far as bathing arrangements will permit.	
VAUCHELLES-LES-QUESNOY.	14th	Tuesday.	Training as per programme as far as bathing arrangements will permit. "C" Coy moved from St Riquier to Vauchelles-les-Quesnoy, and occupied billets in latter village.	
VAUCHELLES-LES-QUESNOY.	15th	Wednesday.	Route March, route as per programme.	
VAUCHELLES-LES-QUESNOY.	16th	Thursday.	Training as per programme. Lecture by the Brigade Commander at 1450hours in the Theatre Hut for Officers, Subject "Organization for Home Defence" (Part I.)	
VAUCHELLES-LES-QUESNOY.	17th	Friday.	Training as per programme. Battalion Drill on Football Ground. "B.C & D"Coys only.	

Army Form C. 2118.

WAR DIARY
or
INTELLIGENCE SUMMARY.
(Erase heading not required.)

Instructions regarding War Diaries and Intelligence Summaries are contained in F.S. Regs., Part II. and the Staff Manual respectively. Title pages will be prepared in manuscript.

Place	Date	Hour	Summary of Events and Information	Remarks and references to Appendices
VAUCHELLES-LES-QUESNOY.	18th	Saturday.	The morning was devoted to interior economy.	Ant
VAUCHELLES-LES-QUESNOY.	19th	Sunday.	Devine Services were held at Vauchelles-les-Quesnoy, St Riquier and Neuf Moulin.	Ant
VAUCHELLES-LES-QUESNOY.	20th	Monday.	Training as per programme as far as bathing arrangements permit. Concert in the evening by "The Travelling Tinkers" Concert Party.	Ant
VAUCHELLES-LES-QUESNOY.	21st	Tuesday.	Training as per programme as far as bathing arrangements permit. Concert in the evening by "The Travelling Tinkers" Concert Party.	Ant
VAUCHELLES-LES-QUESNOY.	22nd	Wednesday.	Route March; route as per programme. Concert in the evening by the 2/5 Glosters Concert Party.	Ant
VAUCHELLES-LES-QUESNOY.	23rd	Thursday.	Training as per programme. Lecture by the Brigade Commander at 1450 hours in the Theatre Hut, Subject "Organization for Home Defence" (Part 2.).	Ant
VAUCHELLES-LES-QUESNOY.	24th	Friday.	Training as per programme. Brigade Inter-Platoon Competition Final. The Brigade Cup was won by No 9 Platoon ("C" Coy) of this battalion.	Ant
VAUCHELLES-LES-QUESNOY.	25th	Saturday.	Companies at the disposal of Company Commanders for interior economy. Brigade Compritition - Platoon best turn out & drill - Cup won by platoon of "A" Company of this battalion under 2nd Lieut G.Bestford.	Ant
VAUCHELLES-LES-QUESNOY.	26th	Sunday.	Devine Services were held at Vauchelles-les-Quesnoy, St Riquier and Neuf Moulin.	Ant

Army Form C. 2118.

WAR DIARY
INTELLIGENCE SUMMARY.
(Erase heading not required.)

Instructions regarding War Diaries and Intelligence Summaries are contained in F. S. Regs., Part II. and the Staff Manual respectively. Title pages will be prepared in manuscript.

Place	Date	Hour	Summary of Events and Information	Remarks and references to Appendices
VAUCHELLES-LES-QUESNOY.	27th Monday.		Training as per programme as far as bathing arrangements permit. Concert in the evening by the "Nightlights" (2/6 Warwicks) Concert Party in the Theatre Hut.	AW7
VAUCHELLES-LES-QUESNOY.	28th Tuesday.		Training as per programme as far as bathing arrangements will permit. Concert in the evening by the "Nightlights" Concert Party in the Theatre Hut.	AW7
VAUCHELLES-LES-QUESNOY.	29th Wednesday.		Route March as per programme cancelled. Companies carried out a series of schemes in "Tracking" from 0900 - 1200 hours.	AW7
VAUCHELLES-LES-QUESNOY.	30th Thursday.		Training as per programme.	AW7
VAUCHELLES-LES-QUESNOY.	31st Friday.		Training as per programme. Lecture by the Brigade Commander at 1400 hours in the Theatre Hut, Subject "Organization for Home Defence"(Part 3.)	AW7

* *

Demobilization developed very quickly during the month, the Battalion strength now being 51 Officers & 712 Other Ranks, included in these figures are 7 Officers & 298 Other Ranks who have left the Battalion for demobilization but no authority has yet been received to strike them off the strength.

Army Form C. 2118.

WAR DIARY
of
INTELLIGENCE SUMMARY. JANUARY 1919.

(Erase heading not required.)

Instructions regarding War Diaries and Intelligence Summaries are contained in F. S. Regs., Part II. and the Staff Manual respectively. Title pages will be prepared in manuscript.

Place	Date	Hour	Summary of Events and Information	Remarks and references to Appendices
			Strength at the beginning of month = 55 Officers 860 O.Rs.	
			Strength at the end of the month = 51 Officers 712 O.Rs.	
			240 O.Rs	
			CASUALTIES. Demobilized. Evacuations. Posted to Depot.	
			216. 21. 3.	
			92 O.Rs	
			DRAFTS. For week ending January 4th = 10	
			11th= 13	
			18th= 8	
			25th= 60	
			31st= 1	
			OFFICERS. Demobilized. Transferred.	
			2nd Lieut A. Darwent. Lt-Col R.J.Morris D.S.O.	
			(21/1/19.) (1/1/19)	
			2nd Lieut W.Cain.	
			(18/1/19)	
			2nd Lieut H.Stewart.	
			(11/1/19)	
			DECORATIONS.	
			Distinguished Conduct Medal.	
			37708 Sgt. L.R.Nainby.	
			Officers in Hospital.	
			Lieut C.H.V.Turpin.	
			Lieut C.W.Hardwicke.	

9th (NORTH. NURSING) BATTALION NORTH BRIGADE NURSING.

TRAINING PROGRAMME for the period 30/12/19 to 4/1/1920.

DATE.	TIME.	NATURE OF TRAINING.	TRAINING AREA.	REMARKS. (to shew routine of route marches).
1919. DECR. 29.	Two hours.	Conference of Officers and Specialist N.C.O's.		In theatre hut. All N.C.O's who are specialists whether employed as such or not.
	1000-1230	Educational Training (Each day excepting Wednesday) Shortened, Bookkeeping, Arithmetic, French, Classes, English.		
	0900-0945 0945-1045 1045-1200	Battalion Drill. Ceremonial. Squad Drill, Handling of Arms. Guards and Sentries Drill.	Company Parade Grounds.	
	0900-0945 0945-1045 1045-1200	Battalion Drill. Ceremonial. Saluting Drill. Platoon Drill.	Battalion Drill Ceremonial on Parade found at 5.1.20.42.	
DECR. 31.		HOLIDAY.		
1920. JANY. 1.				
JANY. 2.	0900-0945 0945-1045 1045-1200	Battalion Drill. Ceremonial. Handling of Arms. Saluting Drill, Guards & Sentries Drill.		
JANY. 3.	0900-0945 0945-1045 1045-1200	Battalion Drill. Ceremonial. Saluting Drill, Guards & Sentries Drill. Squad Drill.		Two hours Brigade Commander's Conference in the Theatre Hut.
JANY. 4.		INSPECTION REPORT		
		AFTERNOONS. Organised Games.		EVENINGS. Lectures, Debates, Smokers as per amusement programme.

9th (... [illegible]) BATTALION NORTHUMBERLAND FUSILIERS.

TRAINING PROGRAMME for the period 6-1-18 to 11-1-18.

DATE.	TIME.	NATURE OF TRAINING.	TRAINING AREA.	REMARKS (to show Routes of Route Marches.
	1800-1900	Educational Training (daily excepting Wednesday) Shorthand, Bookkeeping, Arithmetic, French Classes, English.		
Jan. 6.	0900-0945	Company Drill.		
	1000-1045	Squad Drill, Handling of Arms.		
	1100-1200	Guards and Sentries Drill.		
	1800	Lecture by the Commanding Officer for Officers on Leadership.		Theatre Hut.
Jan. 7.	0900-0945	~~Battalion~~ Company Drill, Ceremonial.	Company parade Grounds	
	1000-1045	Musketry.		
	1100-1200	Platoon Drill.		
Jan. 8.	0900-1200	Route March and Tactical Scheme.	Battalion parade ground S.E.70.42. Map Sheet ARMENTIERES 1A.	Starting point-Cross Roads at S.E.65.60. thence [illegible] S.W. to Cross Roads S.E.15.35., thence East striking main ARMENTIERES-ST.[illegible] Road at S.F.[illegible], thence to Cross Roads S.E.[illegible] where Companies will separate and march independently to their billets.
Jan. 9.	0900-0945	Company Drill.		
	1000-1045	Guards Drill and Saluting Drill.		
	1100-1200	Musketry.		
Jan. 10.	0900-0945	Battalion Drill, Ceremonial.		
	1000-1045	Squad Drill.		
	1100-1200	Guards and Sentries Drill.		
	1800	Lecture by the Commanding Officer for Officers on Esprit de Corps. in Theatre Hut.		
Jan. 11.		INTERIOR ECONOMY.		

AFTERNOONS.
Organised Games.

EVENINGS.
Lectures, Debates, Smokers,
as per educational programme.

6th (North'd Hussars) Battalion NORTHUMBERLAND FUSILIERS.

TRAINING PROGRAMME for the period 13/1/1919 to 19/1/1919.

Date	Time	NATURE of TRAINING	TRAINING AREA	Remarks to shew routes of route marches.
	10.30 – 12.30.	Educational training (daily excepting Wednesday) Shorthand, Bookkeeping, Arithmetic, French Classes, English.		
Jan 13th	0900 – 0945	Company Drill		
	1000 – 1030	Guards & Sentries Drill } "B" Coy.Musketry.		
	1045 – 1200	Squad Drill, Handling of Arms, Signals etc Lewis Gun Instruction and Practice on Range.		
Jan 14th	0900 – 0945	Platoon Drill		
	1000 – 1030	Saluting Drill } "A" Coy Musketry & L.G. Instruction and firing on range.		
	1045 – 1200	Extensions etc Field Signals.		
	1200	Lecture by Commanding Officer to Officers on INTERIOR ECONOMY in Theatre Hut at Vauchelles.	Company Parade	
Jan 15th	0900 – 1200	ROUTE MARCH.	Grounds.	Starting point 5.6.70.40. thence to X roads S.W. 5.10. thence to X roads, 5..53. 12. and home.
Jan 16th	0900 – 0945	Company Drill	"B" Coy Musketry	
	1000 – 1030	Squad drill and Saluting Drill }		
	1045 – 1400	Guards and Sentries Drill, Lewis Gun Drill and Practice on Range.		
	1430	Lecture by Brigade Commander to Officers.		
Jan 17th	0900 – 0945	Battalion Drill.		
	1000 – 1030	Squad Drill		
	1045 – 1200	Semaphore Instructions, Lewis gun Drill.		
	1200	Lecture by Commanding Officer to Officers on "Work in the Field" in Theatre Hut Vauchelles.		
Jan 18th	0900 – 1200	INTERIOR ECONOMY		

EVENINGS

Lectures, Debates, Speakers, Training games. as per amusement programme.

9th (Northd Hussars) BATTALION NORTHUMBERLAND FUSILIERS.

TRAINING PROGRAMME for the period 20/1/1919 to 25/1/1919   Ref Map Abbeville 14

Date	Time	NATURE OF TRAINING	TRAINING AREA	Remarks (To show Routes of route Marches
Jan 20	1030 - 1230	Educational training (daily excepting Wednesday) Shorthand, Bookkeeping, Arithmetic, French, English.		
	0900 1000 1045 1200	Company Drill Guards and Sentries Drill } /, Coy Musketry. Squad Drill, Handling of Arms, Signals etc Lewis Gun Instruction and Practice on range-		
Jan 21	0900 1000 1045 1200	Platoon Drill } Saluting Drill } @, Coy Musketry and L.G. instruction. Extensions etc Field Signals, (and firing on range) Lecture by Commanding Officer to Officers on "Interior Economy in Theatre Hut at Vauchelles.		Starting point Vauchelles thence N. to X roads 5 K 68.40 thence N.E. to X roads 5 L 20.52. thence to X roads 5 L 34.51. thence S to X roads 5 L 25.20 thence W to home.
Jan 22	0900 1200	ROUTE MARCH		
Jan 23	0900 1000 1045 1200 1450	Company Drill Squad Drill and Saluting Drill } B,Coy Musketry. Guards and Sentries Drill, Lewis Gun & Practice on Range Lecture by Brigade Commander to Officers,		
Jan 24	0900 1000 1045 1200	Battalion Drill Squad Drill Semaphore instruction, Lewis Gun Drill Lecture by Commanding officer to Officers on "Work in the Field" in Theatre Hut, Vauchelles,		
Jan 25	0900 1200	INTERIOR ECONOMY		

AFTERNOONS
Organized Games

EVENINGS
Lectures, Debates, Smokers,
as per Amusement Programme,

9th (Northd Hussars) BATTALION NORTHUMBERLAND FUSILIERS.

TRAINING PROGRAMME for the period 20/1/1919 to 25/1/1919

Date	Time	NATURE OF TRAINING	TRAINING AREA	Remarks (To show Routes of route marches &c Map Abbeville 1
	1030 - 1230	Educational training (daily excepting Wednesday) Shorthand, Bookkeeping, Arithmetic, French, English.		
Jan 20	0900	Company Drill)		
	1000	Guards and Sentries Drill) /, Coy Musketry.		
	1045	Squad Drill, Handling of Arms, Signals etc Lewis Gun Instruction and Practice of range-		
Jan 21	0900	Platoon Drill)		
	1000	Saluting Drill) B, Coy Musketry and L.G. Instruction.		
	1045	Extensions etc Field Signals, (and firing or range)		
	1200	Lecture by Commanding Officer to Officers on "Interior Economy" in Lecture Hut, at Vauchelles.		
Jan 22	0900	ROUTE MARCH		Starting point Vauchelles, thence N. to X roads S 4. 68.40 thence N.W. to X roads S L 20.58. thence to X roads S L 24.51. thence S to X roads S L 25.20 thence E to home.
Jan 23	0900	Company Drill)		
	1030	Squad Drill and Saluting Drill) B, Coy Musketry.		
	1045	Guards and Sentries Drill, Lewis Gun & Practice on Range		
	1430	Lecture by Brigade Commander to Officers.		
Jan 24	0900	Battalion Drill		
	1000	Squad Drill		
	1045	Semaphore Instruction, Lewis Gun Drill		
	1200	Lecture by Commanding Officer to Officers on "Work in the Field" in The Brewer Hut, Vauchelles.		
Jan 25	0900 1200	INTERIOR ECONOMY		

AFTERNOONS
Organized Games

EVENINGS
Lectures, Debates, Smokers, as per Amusement Programme.

2nd (Res) BN SASKATOON LIGHT INFANTRY (M.G.).

TRAINING PROGRAM for the period 27/1/42 to 1/2/42.

Time	Nature of Training	Training Area	Remarks (To be miles of route marches)
TUES — 1-30	REGIMENTAL PARADE (Drill Shooting Shining). Vertical, Bookkeeping, Arithmetic, French, English.		
WED — 6:00 – 8:45 7:00 – 9:30 8:45 – 9:00	Scouting Drill. Guards and Sentries Drill.) & hr ancestry Fuel Drill, Handling of Arms, Light & etc. Lewis Guns Instruction and Practise on Range.		
THUR — 8:00 – 9:00 9:15 – 10:15 10:30 – 12:00	Platoon Drill. Saluting Drill. } & hr Infantry / L.G. Instruction Stretchers etc. Foot Drill. (3 MFII, on Ranges.	Compass	Starting Point, Main Road, Baroo 1 to 2 Roods Easter, Value 8 X 30.19, thence to Route 01 N 26.05, thence S to 6 Route 6 N 28.19, thence back to Vancouver.
FRI — 8:00 – 9:00	MUSKETRY.	Parados	
SAT — 6:00 – 9:00 9:15 – 10:15 10:30 – 12:00 1:00	Compass Drill. Guards and Sentries Drill. } & hr Musketry Nursing Sentries Drill. Lewis Gun & Practise on Range. Lecture by Brigade Commander to Officers.	Lavender	
MON — 8:00 – 9:00 9:15 – 10:30 10:45 – 12:00 1:00	Battalion Drill. Squad Drill. Demonstration Instruction Lewis Gun Drill.		
TUES — 1:00 – 1:30	MUSKETRY Parades.		

ALL RANKS:
Lectures, Debates, Conferences, Discussions, etc.,
as per, or according to Regiment Program etc.

Operation: Order

J C Cox

Army Form C. 2118.

WAR DIARY
or
INTELLIGENCE=SUMMARY.

(Erase heading not required.)

FEBRUARY 1919.

Summary of Events and Information

9th. (NORTHUMBERLAND HUSSARS) BATTALION NORTHUMBERLAND FUSILIERS.

APPENDICES.

A. 133rd. Infantry Brigade. } OPERATION ORDERS.
   9th. (N.H). Bn. Northumberland }
                Fusiliers. }

B. Training Programme.

Place	Date	Hour		Remarks and references to Appendices

Army Form C. 2118.

WAR DIARY
or
INTELLIGENCE SUMMARY.

(Erase heading not required.) (1). February 1919.

Place	Date	Hour	Summary of Events and Information	Remarks and references to Appendices
VAUCHELLES LES-QUESNOY.	1st.		Training as per Programme.	7.C
	2nd.		Voluntary Divine Services at VAUCHELLES Church.	7.C
	3rd.		Baths as per Programme. Battalion re-organised on a two Company basis and called Nos. 1 and 2 Companies. (A and C = No. 1. B and D = No. 2 Company.)	7.C
	4th.		Training as per Programme. Street Football Match. Lecture at 1400 hours on "Australia" by Capt. Finigan.	7.C
	5th.		Route March as per Programme.	7.C
	6th.		50 men left at 6.00 hours in lorries to ABBEVILLE to act as Guard to German Prisoners. Returned again at 1000 hours.	7.C
	7th.		Training as per Programme.	7.C
	8th.		Companies at disposal of Company Commanders for Interior Economy.	7.C
	9th.		Divine Services for Non-Conformists and Church of England in Theatre Hut.	7.C
	10th.		Parades as far as Bathing arrangements permit. No water available owing to frost. Wire received for Battalion to be ready to move to DIEPPE on the 12th. inst. Concert in Theatre Hut at 1200 hours by "Prismatics".	7.C
	11th.		100 men to report to P.O.W. Main Cage, ABBEVILLE. Party despatched at 1520 Hours, but only 30 men were available.	7.C
	13th.		Men still at P.O.W. Abbeville.	7.C
	13th.		Orders received to move to DIEPPE on Friday, 14th. inst. at 1400 hours.	7.C

Army Form C. 2118.

WAR DIARY
or
INTELLIGENCE SUMMARY.

(Erase heading not required.) (2). February 1919.

Place	Date	Hour	Summary of Events and Information	Remarks and references to Appendices
VAUCHELLES LES-QUESNOY.	14th.		Battalion marched to ST. RIQUIER and entrained at 1350 hours. Train should have departed 1400 hours but did not leave until 1530 hours.	
	15th.		Arrived at ARQUES-LA-BATAILLE Station about 0400 hours and marched off at 0700 hours. Breakfast at station. Marched to Camp at ST. MARTIN EGLISE. Arrived at 0830 hours.	
ST. MARTIN EGLISE.	16th.		Battalion to assist 15th. Essex Regt. in demobilisation in 5 Groups from tomorrow until strong enough to take over.	
	17th.		Battalion assisting 15th. Essex Regt. in demobilisation duties in B. Block containing Groups 4, 5, and 6.	
	18th.		Same duties as above.	
	19th.		Same duties as above.	
	20th.		Same duties as above.	
	21st.		Same duties as above.	
	22nd.		Draft of 4 Officers and 194 O.Rs. from 22. Battalion Northumberland Fusiliers arrived about 1900 hours.	
	23rd.		Demobilisation duties as usual, in conjunction with 15th. Essex Regt.	
	24th.		Battalion re-organised into 4 Companies, A. B. C and D Companies.	
	25th.		Demobilisation work as usual. Battalion takes over from the 15th. Essex Regt.	
	26th.		Demobilisation work as usual.	

Army Form C. 2118.

WAR DIARY
or
INTELLIGENCE SUMMARY.
(Erase heading not required.) (5). FEBRUARY 1919.

Instructions regarding War Diaries and Intelligence Summaries are contained in F. S. Regs., Part II. and the Staff Manual respectively. Title pages will be prepared in manuscript.

Place	Date	Hour	Summary of Events and Information	Remarks and references to Appendices
ST. MARTIN RIVIER.	27th.		Demobilisation work as usual.	7".
	28th.		Demobilisation work as usual.	7".
			* *	

B. Dawson Lt Col.
5th (Northumberland Hussars) Batn.
Northumberland Fusiliers.

2nd March 1919.

SECRET.   Copy No. 1

163rd INFANTRY BRIGADE ORDER NO.274.   13/2/19.

Reference Sheet.
~~ABBEVILLE.~~   1/100000
~~DIEPPE.~~   do.

1.   9th Bn, The Northumberland Fusiliers, will entrain at ST. RIQUIER
     for DIEPPE on the 14th inst.
        On arrival at DIEPPE the Battalion will come under the command
     of G.O.C., L. of C.

2.   Entrainment will commence at 10.00 hours - Personnel will entrain
     at 12.00 hours - The train will depart at 14.00 hours.

3.   Rations for the 15th, 16th, & 17th, will be delivered at ST. RIQUIER
     STATION. on the 14th inst.

4.   4 Lorries are reporting to H.Q. the Battalion to-night 13th February
     and will convey Stores to ST. RIQUIER.

5.   O.C. 9th Bn, the Northumberland Fusiliers will detail 2 men to remain
     at VAUCHELLES to act as guard over Area Stores which will be collected
     and stored under arrangements to be made by Town Major, VAUCHELLES.
        These men will be provided with rations up to the 18th February
     inclusive, after which date they will be rationed by 2/1st Field
     Ambulance.

6.   Northumberland Fusiliers to acknowledge.

                                              Roland L. Sammy
                                                   Captain,
                                         Brigade Major, 163rd, Inf. Bde.

Issued at 12.00 hours.

              Copy. 1.- 9th Northd. Fus.
                     2.- 163.L.T.M.B.
                     3.- Brigade Major,
                     4.- Staff Captain,
                     5.- No.3 Coy, Div. Train.
                     6.- 478 Field Coy, R.E.
                     7.- 2/1 Field Amb'ce.
                     8.- 61st, Division "G"
                     9.- 61st, Division "Q"
                    10.- Spare.
                    11.- File.
                    12.- War Diary.
                    13.- Town Major, VAUCHELLES.
                    14.- R.T.O. ST. RIQUIER.

                                                              A

OPERATION ORDERS.

Secret.
9th (N.H.) Bn Northumberland Fusiliers.

1. **MOVE.** The Battalion will entrain at ST RIQUIER at 1400 hours to-morrow 14th inst and will proceed to DIEPPE where it will come under the Command of G.O.C. L. of C.

2. **TRANSPORT.** Transport will arrive at St Riquier Station at 1000 hours

3. **PARADES.** Battalion will parade close column Companies in Camp field ready to move off at 1045 hours in following order Hd Qrs, "1" & "2" Coys.

4. **DRESS** Marching order less Box Respirator and Steel Hats.

5. **LORRIES.** 2 lorries will report to Camp at 0800 hours. These will carry Canteen Stores, Blankets and all stores, Officers Valises and mess kits etc of Nos "1" & "2" Coys 2 lorries will report to Q.M.Stores at 0700 hours for Regimental Stores, Hd Qrs Officers valises etc. All lorries will move off at 0930 hours.

6. **LOADING PARTY.** Loading party of 5 men "1" Coy, 5 men "2" Coy and 40 men Hd Qrs Coy will parade at Q.M.Stores ready to move off at 0900 hours. Lieut A.H.Beckwill be in charge of this party.

7. **COLOUR PARTY.** Lieut G.P.Lefebvre M.C. C.Q.M.S.Crapper, C.Q.M.Bails and Sergt McIntyre will compose the Colour Party.

8. **Billets.** Company Commanders are responsible that the billets are left clean and in sanitary condition. Certificate to this effect will be handed into Orderly Room on arrival at destination.

9. **DINNERS** Dinners will be served at St Riquier Station. Tea on arrival at destination.

10. **BLANKETS.** Blankets will be rolled in bundles of 10 and clearly marked.

Distribution.   ACKNOWLEDGE.

1. C.O.
2. Adjutant.
3.)
4.) O.C. "1" Coy.
5.)   (Signed) R.P. Harrison.
6.) O.C. "2" Coy.   Captain & A/Adjutant.
7. O.C. Hd Qrs Coy.   9th (N.H.) Bn Northumberland Fusiliers.
8. O.C. Transport.
9. R.S.M.
10. R.Q.M.
11. Master Cook.
12. War Diary.
13. 102nd Brig Hd Qrs.

Dated 13/8/19.

9th (NORTHD HUSSARS) BATTALION NORTHUMB'RLAND FUSILIERS.

TRAINING PROGRAMME for the period of 3/2/1919 to 8/2/1919.

Training Area. Ref Map Abbeville 14

Remarks to show Routes of Route marches.

Date.	Time.	Nature of Training.	
Feb 3rd.	1030 - 1230	Educational Training (Daily excepting Wednesday) Shorthand, Bookkeeping, Arithmetic, French, English.	
	0900 - 0945	Company Drill.	
	1000 - 1030	Guards and Sentries Drill.	
	1045 - 1200	Squad Drill, Handling of Arms, Signals etc, Lewis Guns instruction and Practice on Range.	
	Afternoon.	Paper Chase.	
Feb 4th	0900 - 0945	Platoon Drill.	Company Parades Ground, Starting Point 5.K 72.27. thence to 5.L. 25.17. thence to 5.L, 16.02. thence to 5.K, 81.05. to Vauchellas.
	1000 - 1200	Scouting and Tracking.	
	1400	Lecture on AUSTRALIA by Capt Flinigen.	
Feb 5th	0900 - 1200	ROUTE MARCH.	
Feb 6th	0900 - 0945	Company Drill.	
	1000 - 1030	Guards and Sentries Drill.	
	1045 - 1200	Lewis Gun Instruction, Field Signals, Semaphore.	
Feb 7th	0900 - 0945	Battalion Drill.	
	1000 - 1200	Scouting and Tracking.	
Feb 8th	0900 - 1200	INTERIOR ECONOMY.	

AFTERNOONS
Organised Games.

EVENINGS
Lectures, Debates, Smokers, & Whist Drives etc,

Army Form C. 2118.

WAR DIARY
or
INTELLIGENCE SUMMARY.
(Erase heading not required.)

MARCH. 1919.

9th. (NORTHUMBERLAND HUSSARS) BATTN. NORTHUMBERLAND FUSILIERS.

Army Form C. 2118.

WAR DIARY

~~INTELLIGENCE SUMMARY~~

(Erase heading not required.)

Instructions regarding War Diaries and Intelligence Summaries are contained in F.S. Regs., Part II. and the Staff Manual respectively. Title pages will be prepared in manuscript.

MARCH 1919.

Place	Date	Hour	Summary of Events and Information	Remarks and references to Appendices
ST. MARTIN EGLISE.	1st.		Demobilization work at Dieppe Embarkation Camp.	
	2nd.		Demobilization work, and Voluntary Church Services.	
	3rd.		Demobilization work.	
	4th.		Demobilization work. Drafts received from 9th. Battn. Yorkshire Regiment of 10 officers and 260 O.R.s. 10th. battn. East Yorkshire Regiment 2 officers and 43 O.R.s, 11th. Battn. East Yorkshire Regiment 3 officers and 111 O.R.s and 1/7th. Battn. Northumberland Fusiliers 2 officers and 64 O.R.s.	
	5th.		Demobilization work. Drafts divided amongst Companies.	
	6th.		Demobilization work. Detachment of 3 officers and 85 O.R.s proceeded to Dieppe on P.O.W. duties.	
	7th.		Demobilization work.	
	8th.		Demobilization work Detachment of 1 officer and 83 O.R.s on P.O.W. duties at Abbeville returned.	
	9th.		Demobilization work, and Voluntary Church Services.	
	10th.		Demobilization work. Committees formed for Battalion sports (football, hockey, boxing and concerts sub-Committees)	
	11th.		Demobilization Work.	
	12th.		Demobilization Work.	
	13th.		Demobilization Work.	

Army Form C. 2118.

WAR DIARY
INTELLIGENCE SUMMARY.
(Erase heading not required.) (2)

MARCH 1919.

Instructions regarding War Diaries and Intelligence Summaries are contained in F. S. Regs., Part II. and the Staff Manual respectively. Title pages will be prepared in manuscript.

Place	Date	Hour	Summary of Events and Information	Remarks and references to Appendices
ST. MARTIN EGLISE.	14th.		Demobilization work.	
	15th.		Demobilization work. Clearing up the Camp.	
	16th.		Demobilization work. Voluntary Divine Services	
	17th.		Demobilization work. Draft of 3 Officers and 150 O.R.s arrived from 2nd. Battalion Yorkshire Regiment.	
	18th.		Demobilization work.	
	19th.		Demobilization work. Conference held re "Organization of the battalion. Working Parties as far as Bathing arrangements would permit.	
	20th.		Demobilization work. Parade ground allotted to Companies. Alterations and additions to Sports Sub-Committees. Return of 3 Officers & 85 O.R.s on P.O.W. Duties on detachment from DIEPPE.	
	21st.		Demobilization work. Working parties as as Bathing arrangements would permit. 2nd. Lieut. R. M. Heasha. took over the Stores of the New Delouser from 2/6th. Royal Warwickshire Regt.	
	22nd.		Men ceased to pass through the Camp for demobilisation. Working Parties and N.C.O's classes under the R.S.M. Lewis Gun Class under 2nd. Lieut. E. Lovell.	
	23rd.		Voluntary Divine Services.	
	24th.		Company Parades and Working Parties. N.C.O's and Lewis Gun Classes.	
	25th.		Company Parades and Working Parties. N.C.O's and Lewis Gun Classes. Allotment of Battalion Parade Ground by 152nd. Infantry Brigade.	
	26th.		Company Parades and Working Parties as far as Bathing arrangements would permit. N.C.O's and Lewis Gun Classes.	

Army Form C. 2118.

WAR DIARY
OF
INTELLIGENCE SUMMARY

(Erase heading not required.) (3)   M A R C H   1919.

Instructions regarding War Diaries and Intelligence Summaries are contained in F. S. Regs., Part II. and the Staff Manual respectively. Title pages will be prepared in manuscript.

Place	Date	Hour	Summary of Events and Information	Remarks and references to Appendices
ST. MARTIN EGLISE.	27th.		Company Parades and Working parties as far as bathing arrangements would permit. N.C.O's and Lewis Gun Classes. Inspection of No 4 Group by the Commanding Officer.	
	28th.		Battalion Parade, and Drill as far as bathing arrangements would permit. Working Parties. N.C.O's and Lewis Gun Classes.	
	29th.		Battalion Parade. Drill and Working parties, N.C.O's and Lewis Gun Classes. Inspection of No 6 Group Lines and Battalion Lines by the Commanding Officer.	
	30th.		Voluntary Divine Services.	
	31st.		Battalion Parade. Drill and Working Parties, N.C.O's and Lewis Gun Classes. Inspect of Drafts from the 10th. and 11th. Battalions East Yorkshire Regiment.	

* * * * * * * * * * * * * * * * * * * *

B. Chambers
Lieut-Colonel,
Comdg. 9th. (N.H.) Battn. Northumberland Fusiliers.

Army Form C. 2118

WAR DIARY
&
INTELLIGENCE SUMMARY

(Erase heading not required.)

APRIL 1919

Instructions regarding War Diaries and Intelligence Summaries are contained in F.S. Regs., Part II. and the Staff Manual respectively. Title Pages will be prepared in manuscript.

Place	Date	Hour	Summary of Events and Information	Remarks and references to Appendices
			9th. (NORTHUMBERLAND HUSSARS) BATTN. NORTHUMBERLAND FUSILIERS.	
			Appendix "A" Education Programmes	
			Appendix "B" Training Programmes.	

1875 Wt. W593/826 1,000,000 4/15 J.B.C. & A. A.D.S.S./Forms/C. 2118.

Army Form C. 2118

WAR DIARY
INTELLIGENCE SUMMARY
(Erase heading not required.)

APRIL 1919

Instructions regarding War Diaries and Intelligence Summaries are contained in F.S. Regs., Part II. and the Staff Manual respectively. Title Pages will be prepared in manuscript.

Place	Date	Hour	Summary of Events and Information	Remarks and references to Appendices
ST. MARTIN. EGLISE.	1st.		Battalion Parade and Drill, N.C.O's and Lewis Gun Classes.	
	2nd.		Inspection of the Battalion by the G.O.C. 61st. Division.	
	3rd.		Battalion Parade and Drill, N.C.O's and Lewis Gun Classes.	
	4th.		Battalion Parade and Drill, N.C.O's and Lewis Gun Classes.	
	5th.		Company Parades and Drill. N.C.O's and Lewis Gun Classes.	
	6th.		Divine Services.	
	7th.		Battalion Parade and Drill, N.C.O's and Lewis Gun Classes. Inspection of the Battalion by the Commanding Officer.	
	8th.		Parades as per Training Programme and N.C.T's Classes.	
	9th.		Battalion Route March.	
	10th.		Parades as per Training Programme and N.C.O's Classes.	
	11th.		Parades as per Training Programme and N.C.O's Classes.	
	12th.		Parades as per Training Programme and N.C.O's Classes.	
	13th.		Divine Services.	
	14th.		Inspection of the Battalion by the Commanding Officer, Drill. N.C.O's and Educational Classes, etc.	

Army Form C. 2118

WAR DIARY

INTELLIGENCE SUMMARY

(Erase heading not required.)

APRIL 1919

Instructions regarding War Diaries and Intelligence Summaries are contained in F.S. Regs., Part II. and the Staff Manual respectively. Title Pages will be prepared in manuscript.

Place	Date	Hour	Summary of Events and Information	Remarks and references to Appendices
ST. MARTIN EGLISE.	15th		Parades as per Training Programme, N.C.O's and Educational Classes, etc.	
	16th		Battalion Route March.	
	17th		Parades as per Training Programme, N.C.O's and Educational Classes, etc.	
	18th		Divine Service.	
	19th		Parades as per Training Programme, N.C.O's and Educational Classes, etc.	
	20th		Divine Services.	
	21st		Easter Monday. Day devoted to Sports.	
	22nd		Parades as per Training Programme, N.C.O's and Educational Classes, etc.	
	23rd		St. George's Day. Ceremonial Parade. Battalion inspected by the Brigadier General. Special Dinner. Sports in the afternoon and Concert in the Evening	
	24th		Parades as per Training Programme, N.C.O's and Educational Classes, etc.	
	25th		Parades as per Training Programme, N.C.O's and Educational Classes, etc.	
	26th		Parades as per Training Programme, N.C.O's and Educational Classes, etc.	
	27th		Divine Services.	
	28th		Parades as per Training Programme, N.C.O's and Educational Classes, etc.	

Army Form C. 2118.

WAR DIARY
~~INTELLIGENCE SUMMARY~~

(Erase heading not required.)

APRIL 1919

Instructions regarding War Diaries and Intelligence Summaries are contained in F. S. Regs., Part II. and the Staff Manual respectively. Title pages will be prepared in manuscript.

Place	Date	Hour	Summary of Events and Information	Remarks and references to Appendices
ST. MARTIN EGLISE	29th.		All available men for Musketry on Arques Range under the supervision of the Musketry Officer.	
	30th.		All available men for Musketry on Arques Range under the supervision of the Musketry Officer.	

Lieut-Colonel.
Commg. 9th. (N.H.) Battn. Northumberland Fusiliers.

9th.(Northumberland Hussars) Batn NORTHUMBERLAND FUSILIERS

EDUCATIONAL SCHEMES for week ending 19th April 1919.

Date	Class Room	1000hrs to 1030hrs.	1030hrs to 1140hrs.	1140hrs to 1230hrs.
Monday	No.1. No.2. No.3.	English Adv. Mathematics	Arithmetic Shorthand	Elementary French Elementary French Book-keeping
Tuesday	No.1. No.2. No.3.	English Adv. French	Arithmetic Shorthand Adv. Mathematics	Elementary French Elementary French Adv. Maths.
Wednesday	No.1. No.2. No.3.	History Book-keeping	Arithmetic Shorthand	Elementary French Elementary French Adv. Maths.
Thursday	No.1. No.2. No.3.	Geography Book-keeping	Arithmetic Shorthand	Elementary French Elementary French Adv. Maths.
Friday	No.1. No.2. No.3.	English Book-keeping	Arithmetic Shorthand	Elementary French Elementary French Adv. Maths.
Saturday	No.1. No.2. No.3.	Letter Writing Adv. French	Arithmetic Shorthand	Elementary French Elementary French Book-keeping

9th.(Northumberland Hussars) Battn.Northumberland Fusliers.

EDUCATIONAL PROGRAMME for week ending 26th.April 1919.

Date.	Class Room.	1.000 - 1050 hours	1050 - 1140 hours	1140 - 1250 hours.
Monday.	No 1. No 2. No 3.	English. Advanced Mathematics.	Arithmetic. Shorthand.	Elementary French. Elementary French. Book-keeping.
Tuesday.	No 1. No 2. No 3.	English. Advanced French.	Arithmetic Shorthand Advanced Mathematics.	Elementary French. Elementary French. Advanced Mathematics.
Wednesday.	No 1. No 2. No 3.	History. Book-keeping.	Arithmetic. Shorthand.	Elementary French. Elementary French. Advanced Mathematics.
Thursday.	No 1. No 2. No 3.	Geography. Book-keeping.	Arithmetic. Shorthand.	Elementary French. Elementary French. Advanced Mathematics.
Friday.	No 1. No 2. No 3.	English. Book-keeping.	Arithmetic. Shorthand.	Elementary French. Elementary French. Advanced Mathematics.
Saturday	No 1. No 2. No 3.	Letter Writing. Advanced French.	Arithmetic. Shorthand.	Elementary French. Elementary French. Book-keeping.

Lieut.-Colonel,

9th.(Northumberland Hussars) Batn. NORTHUMBERLAND FUSILIERS.

EDUCATIONAL PROGRAMME for week ending 3rd. May 1919.

Date	Class Room.	1000-1050 hours.	1050-1140 hours.	1140-1230 hours.
Monday.	No 1.	English.	Arithmetic.	Elementary French.
	No 2.	Advanced Mathematics.	Shorthand.	Elementary French.
	No 3.			Book-keeping.
Tuesday.	No 1.	English.	Arithmetic.	Elementary French.
	No 2.	Advanced French.	Shorthand.	Elementary French.
	No 3.		Advanced Mathematics.	Advanced Mathematics.
Wednesday.	No 1.	History.	Arithmetic.	Elementary French.
	No 2.	Book-keeping.	Shorthand.	Elementary French.
	No 3.			Advanced Mathematics.
Thursday.	No 1.	Geography.	Arithmetic.	Elementary French.
	No 2.	Book-keeping.	Shorthand.	Elementary French.
	No 3.			Advanced Mathematics.
Friday.	No 1.	English.	Arithmetic.	Elementary French.
	No 2.	Book-keeping.	Shorthand.	Elementary French.
	No 3.			Advanced Mathematics.
Saturday.	No 1.	Letter Writing.	Arithmetic.	Elementary French.
	No 2.	Advanced French.	Shorthand.	Elementary French.
	No 3.			Book-keeping.

Lieut-Colonel,
Comg.9th.(N.H.) Batn.Northumberland Fusiliers.

9th. (Northumberland Hussars) Battn. Northumberland Fusiliers.

TRAINING PROGRAMME for week ending 12th. April 1919.

Day	Training	Place	Remarks.
Monday	0900-1130 hours Marching Order Parade (Strong as possible) 1130-1230 hours Platoon Drill	Football Field Forest 2B80.76	"C" Coy to find all Guards and duties for the week.
Tuesday	0900-1230 hours No 5 Platoon Musketry 0900-1200 hours Remainder of "B" coy Platoon Drill 0900-1200 hours "D" coy Drill 1200-1230 hours Lecture by Medical Officer	Rifle Range Forest 2B80.76 Football Field No 5 Dining Hall	All specialists will parade with Btn. on first parade for one hours drill etc. They will then "Fall Out" and be marched away for special instructions by their instructors.
Wednesday	Route March (Drill Order)	From 2B77.79-2018. 76-2016.61-2B71.61 -2B77.79.	The following are the classes under instruction:- Scouts, Lewis Gunners, Signallers and Band.
	No 6 Platoon Musketry.	Rifle Range	The Platoon for Musketry will be as strong as possible and it will not be taken for any other duties on the day allotted to it for Range Practice and all men employed will be relieved as fast as possible. Miniature Range Practices under Lt. Fisher for all bad shots put back for further training by Lt. Knight. These will parade daily at 1-45 hours.
Thursday	Same as Tuesday ex. No 7 Platoon for Musketry Lecture by Medical Officer.	Same as for Tuesday.	
Friday	Same as Thursdayex. No 8 Platoon for Musketry and Platoons for Extension Movements and Field Signals	Same as for Thursday.	
Saturday	Kit Inspection by Coy. Commdrs, Interior Economy.		

5/4/19.

Lieut-Colonel.
Commg. 9th. (N.H.) Battn. Northumberland Fusiliers.

9th. (N.H.) Battn. Northumberland Fusiliers.

TRAINING PROGRAMME for the week ending 19th. April 1919.

Day	Training	Place	Remarks.
Monday	0900-1100 hours Marching Order Parade 1100-1230 hours Platoon Drill	Football Field Forest 2B80.76.	"D" Coy to find all Guards and Duties for the week.
Tuesday	0900-1230 hours Musketry No 5 Platoon 0900-0930 hours "B" & "C" Coy Physical Training 0930-1230 hours "B" Coy Platoon Drill, Extd. Order Drill 0930-1250 hours "C" Coy Company Drill (& Field Signals 1200-1230 hours "C" Coy Lecture on Regts. History	Rifle Range Football Field Forest 2B80.76 Football Field No 5 Dining Hall.	All specialists will parade with Btn. on first parade for one hour's drill etc. They will then "Fall Out" and be marched away for special instruction by their instructors. The following at the Classes under instruction:- Scouts, Signallers, Lewis Gunners, and Band.
Wednesday	Route March (Skeleton Marching Order) No 6 Platoon Musketry	From 2B77.99-2B71. 61-2B57.58-1A86.11 -1B6.13-2B77.79½ Rifle Range	The Platoon for Musketry will be as strong as possible. It will not be taken for any duties on the day allotted
Thursday	As for Tuesday No 7 Platoon Musketry 1200-1230 hours "B" Coy Lecture on Regt. History	Same as for Tuesday Rifle Range No 5 Dining Hall.	to it for Range Practices and all employed men will be relieved as far as possible. Miniature Range Practice under Lt. Fisher for all bad shots put back for further training
Friday	As for Thrusday with simple skirmishing exercises No 8 Platoon Musketry.	Same as for Thursday	by Lr. Knight. Those will parade daily at 1.45 hours.
Saturday	Kit Inspection by Coy. Commanders		Mon. Tues. Thurs. Fri. afternoons from 1430-1600 hours are devoted to organized Recreational Training.

12/4/19.

Comng. 9th. (N.H.) Battn. Northumberland Fusiliers.

Lieut-Colonel.

9th. (Northumberland Hussars) Battn: Northumberland Fusiliers.

TRAINING PROGRAMME for week ending 26th. April 1919.

DAY.	TRAINING.	PLACE.	REMARKS.
MONDAY.	Easter Monday --- Holiday.		"B" Coy. to find all guards and duties for the week.
TUESDAY.	0900-0930 hrs. Physical Training 0945-1030 hrs. Platoon Drill. 1045-1130 hrs. Company Drill. 1145-1230 hrs. Saluting & Guards Drill	Football Field. Football Field. Football Field. Football Field.	All Specialists will parade with Bn. on first parade for one hours drill etc. They will then "fall out" & be marched away for special instruction by their instructors. The following are the classes under instruction:- Signallers, Scouts, Lewis Gunners and Band.
WEDNESDAY.	St. George's Day.-Holiday-Ceremonial Parade.	Football Field.	Regimental Sports.
THURSDAY.	0900-0930 hrs. Physical Training. 0945-1030 hrs. Platoon Drill. 1045-1130 hrs. Company Drill. 1145-1230 hrs. Saluting and Guards Drill.	Football Field. Football Field. Football Field. Football Field.	All men for Educational Classes will be marched away in time for the various classes i.e. ¼ of an hour before time scheduled to begin. Mon, Tues, Thurs. and Frid. afternoons from 1430-1600 hrs. are devoted to organised Recreational Training. Dancing and Singing Classes in the Evenings.
FRIDAY.	Route March (Skeleton Marching Order) with 1 st. Line Transport.	Dieppe 1=100000. From 2B77.79-2B71.61- 2C16.61-2C66.55- 2C61.57- 2C19.70 2B77.79.	
SATURDAY.	Kit Inspection by the Commanding Officer. 1130-1230 hrs. Lecture in First Aid by M.O.	Football Field. Dining Hall.	If wet, in huts.

Lieut-Colonel,
Commg. 9th. (N.H.) Battn. Northumberland Fusiliers.

9th (N.F.) Batt.Northumberland Fusiliers.

TRAINING PROGRAMME for week ending 3 rd May 1919.

DAY.	TRAINING.	PLACE.	REMARKS.
MONDAY.	"B" Company Musketry. 0800-0845 hours Physical Training. 0845-1130 hours Platoon Drill. 1045-1130 hours Company Drill. 1145-1230 hours Saluting and Guards Drill.	Aspen Range. Football Field. Football Field. Football Field. Football Field.	"B" Company will fire off all the amm\n and Duties for the week.
TUESDAY.	"B" Company Musketry. 0800-0900 Hours Physical Training. 0945-1030 hours Extended Order Drill, Games, Field Signals, Attack Schemes, Wood-Clearing.	Aspen Range. Football Field. Front GR 83.78.	All Specialists will parade with the Bn. on first parade for the hours drill. They will then fall off & be marched away for special instruction by their instructors. The Classes under instruction are:- Signallers, Scouts, Lewis Gunners and Bomb. All men for Educational Classes will be marched away in time for that classes to commence, i.e. 1/2 of an hour before the time scheduled to begin. Mon. Tues. Thurs. and Frid afternoons from 1630-1800 hours are devoted to organised Recreational Training. Tactics and similar Classes in the Evenings.
WEDNESDAY.	"B" & "C" Coys. Musketry (and shots etc.) 0800-0845 hours Physical Training. 0845-1130 hours Platoon Drill. 1045-1130 hours Extended Order Drill. 1145-1230 hours Saluting and Guards Drill. 1430 hours Lectures by Col.-Inhabited Economy	Aspen Range. Football Field. Football Field. Football Field. Football Field. Red Pinkus Tall.	
THURSDAY.	Route March (Skeleton Marching Order) with 1 st. Line Transport.	Dieppe 1-200000. From 5377.79-1R 83.1.— 183.12.—CR7.93.	
FRIDAY.	0800-0845 Physical Training. 0845-1030 Sudging Distance. 1045-1130 Company Drill. 1145-1230 C.O's Parade for Field Movements	Football Field. Football Field. Football Field. Football Field.	
SATURDAY.	Kit Inspection by Commanding Officer. 1130-1230 hours Lecture by Medical Officer.	Football Field. Med Dining Hall.	If wet in the huts.

Lieut-Colonel,
Comdg. 9th (N.F.) Battn.Northumberland Fusiliers.

WAR DIARY
INTELLIGENCE SUMMARY

Army Form C. 2118.

MAY 1919.

9TH. (NORTHUMBERLAND HUSSARS) BATTN. NORTHUMBERLAND FUSILIERS

Appendix "A"   Education Programme.

Appendix "B"   Training Programme.

Army Form C. 2118.

WAR DIARY
INTELLIGENCE SUMMARY.
(Erase heading not required.)

MAY 1919.

Instructions regarding War Diaries and Intelligence Summaries are contained in F. S. Regs., Part II. and the Staff Manual respectively. Title pages will be prepared in manuscript.

Place	Date	Hour	Summary of Events and Information	Remarks and references to Appendices
MARTIN EGLISE	1st.		Day very wet. Lecture to men by Platoon Commanders. Interior Economy. Special Kit Inspections.	
	2nd.		Training as per Programme. Six Officers (1 Captain, 3 Lieuts. and 2 2/Lieuts.) joined the Battn. from the Rhine Army.	
	3rd.		Kit and Hut Inspection by the Commanding Officer.	
	4th.		Church Parade cancelled owing to wet weather.	
	5th.		One Officer joined the Battalion from the Rhine Army. Training as per Programme.	
	6th.		Training as per Programme.	
	7th.		Training as per Programme.	
	8th.		Training as per Programme.	
	9th.		Training as per Programme.	
	10th.		Training as per Programme.	
	11th.		Church Parade.	
	12th.		Training as per Programme.	
	13th.		Training as per Programme. Lecture (Educational) by Capt. ~~Harvey~~ HAWKEN 61st. Divisional Headquarters entitled "Shakesperean Recitations" This lecture was well attended and all ranks showed very keen interest in it.	
	14th.		Training as per Programme.	
	15th.		Training as per Programme.	
	16th.		Training as per Programme.	

Army Form C. 2118.

WAR DIARY
or
INTELLIGENCE SUMMARY.
(Erase heading not required.)

MAY 1919.

Instructions regarding War Diaries and Intelligence Summaries are contained in F. S. Regs., Part II. and the Staff Manual respectively. Title pages will be prepared in manuscript.

Place	Date	Hour	Summary of Events and Information	Remarks and references to Appendices
MARTIN EGLISE.	17th.		Training as per Programme.	
	18th.		Church Parade. A party of 8 Officers & 200 men were warned to stand by owing to a disturbance at a Camp occupied by Allies coloured troops and Chinese Labour Corps.	
	19th.		Training as per Programme.	
	20th.		Training as per Programme.	
	21st.		Training as per Programme.	
	22nd.		Training as per Programme. First Bathing Parade of the season.	
	23rd.		Training as per Programme.	
	24th.		Training as per Programme.	
	25th.		Church Parade.	
	26th.		Training as per Programme.	
	27th.		Training as per Programme. Lecture by Mr.Johnson on Local Government in the Y.M.C.A. HUT. This lecture was well attended and all Ranks showed very keen interest in it. 3 Officers joined the Battalion from 2/4th. Battn Royal Berkshire Regiment.	
	28th.		Training as per Programme.	
	29th.		Training as per Programme.	
	30th.		Training as per Programme.	
	31st.		Training as per Programme.	
			43 O.Rs. Reinforcements joined during the month, 22 from 11th East Yorkshire Regiment. 9 from 10th East Yorkshire Regiment. 11 from 8th Northumberland Fusiliers. 1 from 2nd Yorkshire Regiment.	
	2/6/19.			

Commdg. 9th (N.F.) Battn Northumberland Fusiliers.
Lieut-Colonel.

Appendix A.

9th (Northumberland Fusrs) Battn.Northumberland Fusiliers.

EDUCATIONAL PROGRAMME for the week ending 3 rd May 1919.

Date.	Class Room.	1030-1050 hours.	1050-1140 hours.	1140-1230 hours.
Monday	No 1.	English.	Arithmetic.	Elementary French.
	No 2.	Advanced Mathematics	Shorthand.	Elementary French.
	No 3.			Book-keeping.
Tuesday.	No 1.	English.	Arithmetic.	Elementary French.
	No 2.	Advanced French.	Shorthand.	Elementary French.
	No 3.		Advanced Mathematics.	Advanced Mathematics.
Wednesday	No 1.	History.	Arithmetic.	Elementary French.
	No 2.	Book-keeping.	Shorthand.	Elementary French.
	No 3.			Advanced French.
Thursday.	No 1.	Geography.	Arithmetic.	Elementary French.
	No 2.	Book-keeping.	Shorthand.	Elementary French.
	No 3.			Advanced Mathematics.
Friday.	No 1.	English.	Arithmetic.	Elementary French.
	No 2.	Book-keeping.	Shorthand.	Elementary French.
	No 3.			Advanced Mathematics.
Saturday.	No 1.	Letter Writing.	Arithmetic.	Elementary French.
	No 2.	Advanced French.	Shorthand.	Elementary French.
	No 3.			Book-keeping.

Lieut-Colonel,
Comdg. 9 th.(N.F.) Batn.Northumberland Fusiliers.

9th. (Northumberland Hussars) Batt. Northumberland Fusiliers.   Appendix B.

EDUCATIONAL PROGRAMME for the week ending 10th. May 1919.

Date	Class Room	1000-1050 hours	1050-1140 hours	1140-1250 hours
Monday	No 1.	English	Arithmetic.	Elementary French.
	No 2.	Advanced Mathematics.	Shorthand	Elementary French.
	No 3.			Book-keeping.
Tuesday	No 1.	English	Arithmetic	Elementary French.
	No 2.	Advanced French	Shorthand	Elementary French.
	No 3.		Advanced Mathematics.	Advanced Mathematics.
Wednesday	No 1.	History.	Arithmetic	Elementary French.
	No 2.	Book-keeping.	Shorthand	Elementary French.
	No 3.			Advanced French.
Thursday	No 1.	Geography.	Arithmetic.	Elementary French.
	No 2.	Book-keeping.	Shorthand.	Elementary French.
	No 3.			Advanced French. Advanced Mathematics.
Friday	No 1.	English.	Arithmetic.	Elementary French.
	No 2.	Book-keeping.	Shorthand.	Elementary French.
	No 3.			Advanced Mathematics.
Saturday	No 1.	Letter Writing.	Arithmetic.	Elementary French.
	No 2.	Advanced French.	Shorthand.	Elementary French.
	No 3.			Book-keeping.

T. Leopkhrapady
for Lieut-Colonel,
Comdg. 9th (N.H.) Batt. Northumberland Fusiliers.

9th. (Northumberland Fusiliers) BATTN. NORTHUMBERLAND FUSILIERS

EDUCATIONAL PROGRAMME for the week ending 27th. May 1922.

DAY	9.00–10.00 a.m.	10.00–11.00 a.m.	11.00–12.00 noon
MONDAY	English	Arithmetic	Arithmetic
	Advanced Mathematics	Geography	History
			Bookkeeping
TUESDAY	English	Arithmetic	Arithmetic
	Advanced French	Geology	French
		Special Mathematics	Advanced Mathematics
WEDNESDAY	History	Arithmetic	History
	Bookkeeping	Shorthand	History
			Chemistry
THURSDAY	Hygiene	Arithmetic	Hygiene
	Bookkeeping	Shorthand	Chemistry
			Advanced Mathematics
FRIDAY	English	Arithmetic	Elementary French
	Typewriting	Shorthand	Geology
			Advanced Mathematics
SATURDAY	Letter writing	Elementary	Elementary French
	Essays etc.	Shorthand	Chemistry
			Bookkeeping

Approved. H.P.Page
Lt. Col.
Comdg. 9th. (N.F.) Battn. Northumberland Fusiliers.

Appendix B

Approved
H.Henderson

Appendix B.

9th. (Northumberland Hussars) Battn. Northumberland Fusiliers.

EDUCATIONAL PROGRAMME for the week ending 24th. May 1919.

Day	Class Room	1000-1050 hours.	1050-1140 hours.	1140-1230 hours.
Monday	No 1.	English	Arithmetic	Elementary French.
	No 2.	Advanced Mathematics	Shorthand	Elementary French.
	No 3.			Book-keeping.
Tuesday	No 1.	English	Arithmetic	Elementary French.
	No 2.	Advanced French	Shorthand	Elementary French.
	No 3.		Advanced Mathematics	Advanced Mathematics.
Wednesday	No 1.	History	Arithmetic	Elementary French.
	No 2.	Book-keeping	Shorthand	Elementary French.
	No 3.			Advanced French.
Thursday	No 1.	Geography	Arithmetic	Elementary French.
	No 2.	Book-keeping	Shorthand	Elementary French.
	No 3.			Advanced Mathematics.
Friday	No 1.	English	Arithmetic	Elementary French.
	No 2.	Book-keeping	Shorthand	Elementary French.
	No 3.			Advanced Mathematics.
Saturday	No 1.	Letter Writing	Arithmetic Elementary	Elementary French.
	No 2.	Advanced French	Shorthand.	Elementary French.
				Book-keeping.

Comdg. 9th. (N.H.) Battn. Northumberland Fusiliers.

Lieut-Colonel.

Appendix A.

9th.(Northumberland Fusurs.) Battn. No NORTHERN AREA Rt.

EDUCATIONAL PROGRAMME for week ending 31st.May 1919.

Day.	Class Room.	1000 — 1050 hours.	1050 — 1140 hours.	1140 — 1230 hours.
Monday	No 1.	English.	Arithmetic.	Elementary French.
	No 2.	Advanced Mathematics.	Shorthand.	Elementary French.
	No 3.			Book-keeping.
Tuesday	No 1.	English.	Arithmetic.	Elementary French.
	No 2.	Advanced French.	Shorthand.	Elementary French.
	No 3.		Advanced Mathematics.	Advanced Mathematics.
Wednesday	No 1.	History	Arithmetic.	Elementary French.
	No 2.	Book-keeping	Shorthand.	Elementary French.
	No 3.			Advanced French.
Thursday	No 1.	Geography.	Arithmetic.	Elementary French.
	No 2.	Book-keeping.	Shorthand.	Elementary French.
	No 3.			Advanced Mathematics.
Friday	No 1.	English.	Arithmetic.	Elementary French.
	No 2.	Book-keeping.	Shorthand.	Elementary French.
	No 3.			Advanced Mathematics.
Saturday	No 1.	Letter Writing.	Arithmetic.	Elementary French.
	No 2.	Advanced French.	The Chnnl.	Elementary French.
	No 3.			Book-keeping.

Lieut-Colonel,

Comdg. 9th.(Northumberland Fusurs.) Battn.Northumberland Fusiliers.

Appendix B

9th.(N.S.) Battn.NORTHUMBERLAND FUSILIERS.

TRAINING PROGRAMME for week ending 3rd May 1919.

DAY	TRAINING.	PLACE	REMARKS.
SUNDAY.	"C"Company Musketry 0800-0930 hours Physical Training. 0945-1030 hours Platoon Drill. 1045-1150 hours Company Drill. 1145-1230 hours Saluting and Guards Drill.	Arqued Range. Football Field. Football Field. Football Field. Football Field.	"C" Company will find all guards and duties for the week. All Specialists will parade with the Bn. On the first parade for one hour drill. They will then "fall out" and be marched away for instruction by their instructors. The following are the classes under instruction:- Signallers, Scouts, Lewis Gunners and Bnd. Allmen for Educational Classes will be marched away in time for their classes i.e. of an hour before the time scheduled to begin. Mon,Tues,Thurs,and Frid afternoons from 1430-1600 hours are devoted to organised Recreational Training. Dancing and Singing Classes in the Evenings.
TUESDAY.	"D" Company Musketry 0800-0930 hours. Physical Training. 0945-1030 hours Extended Order Drill,Games, Field Signals,Attack Scheme,Wood-fighting.	/rques Range. Football Field. Forest SW 80./6.	
WEDNESDAY.	"B" & "D" Companies(half shots etc.) 0830-0930 hours Physical Training 0945-1030 hours Platoon Drill. 1045-1130 hours Extended Order Drill. 1145-1230 hours.Saluting and Guards Drill 1400 hours Lecture by C.O.-Interior Economy.	Arques Range. Football Field. Football Field. Football Field. No 5 Lister Hall.	
THURSDAY.	Route March (Skeleton Marching Order) with 1 st.Line Transport.	Mappe 1.17000. /Nye (2377.75-1506.1- -198.10-2077.75.	
FRIDAY.	0800-0830 hours Physical Training. 0945-1030 hours.Marching Distance 1045-1130 hours.Company Drill. 1145-1230 C.O's parade for Field movements.	Football Field. Football Field. Football Field. Football Field.	
SATURDAY.	Kit Inspection by Commanding Officer 1130-1230 hours Lecture by MedicalOfficer.	Football Field. No 5 Lister Hall.	If wet in the hut.

26.4.1919

9th (Northumberland Hussars) Batt. NORTHUMBERLAND FUSILIERS.

TRAINING PROGRAMME for week ending 10th. May 1919

DAY	TRAINING	PLACE	REMARKS
MONDAY.	0900-0945 hours Physical Training 0945-1030 hours Platoon Drill 1045-1130 hours Company Drill 1145-1230 hours Saluting and Guards Drill	Football Field Football Field Football Field Football Field	"B" Squadron will find all the Guards and Duties for the week.
TUESDAY.	0900-0945 hours Physical Training 0945-1230 hours Extended Order Drill, Games Field Signals, Attack before Wood-fighting	Football Field Forest 25.B.76	All Specialists will parade with the Sqn. on Gist Parade for one hours drill. They will then "Fall Out" & be marched away for special Instruction by their Instructors. The Classes under Instruction are:- Signallers, Scouts, Lewis Gunners and M.G. All men for Educational Classes will be marched away in time for their classes i.e. 1/4 of an hour before the time is scheduled to begin. Mon. Tues. Thurs. and Frid. afternoons from 1430-1600 hours are devoted to Organised Recreational Training. Theatre and Singing Classes in the Evening.
WEDNESDAY.	0900-0945 hours Physical Training 0945-1030 hours Platoon Drill 1045-1130 hours Extended Order Drill 1145-1230 hours Saluting and Guards Drill 1400 hours Lecture by O.C. (Interior Economy)	Football Field Football Field Football Field Football Field No 5 Mining Hall	
THURSDAY	Route March (Skeleton Marching Order) with 1st. Line Transport.	Mappa 1.Le000 From 2370.53-2370.61- 2087.50-2089.58-2010.70- 2370.58	
FRIDAY	0900-0945 hours Physical Training 0945-1030 hours Pointing Distance 1045-1130 hours Company Drill 1145-1230 hours Parade for Field Movements	Football Field Football Field Football Field Football Field	
SATURDAY	Kit Inspection by Commanding Officer 1100-1230 hours Lecture by Medical Officer	Football Field No 5 Mining Hall	If not in the huts.

3.5.1919

9th (Northumberland Hussars) Batt. Northumberland Fusiliers.

TRAINING PROGRAMME for week ending 17th May 1919.

Day	Hours	Work
MONDAY	0830-Reveille Morning Inspection Drill. 1 Hour. Games Physical Drill. 1145-1215 Hours SALUTING LECTURE. 1215-1315 LECTURES. 1315-1330 Issue Of SMOKES and Reading Matter.	Football Match. Football Field. Cricket Nets. Cricket Nets. Football Field.	All Groups will find all the Reports and Prizes for the Week. All Specialists will parade for the Run, on their parade for the usual Drill. They will then fall in & be Graded by the Musical Instructors to their Instructors. The Classes note information and signatures Sports Gear (Players and Ref) All men for Educational Classes will be exempt of duty to give for these classes 2hr 4hr as long before the time scheduled by Master. The Times and Places of the actual Lectures and Practical Training will be posted on Notice Board.
TUESDAY	As above but no Morning Letter drawn	Marching Also B. Fore Classes	
WEDNESDAY	As above Board Officer -Stores	Marching Drill B. Lect classes	
THURSDAY	THIS SAME Unit School Board Inspection Until 12 Noon when Sport	No Training Movements To Posts — Lectures.	
FRIDAY	ORDERLY ROOM Meetings 1000 1000-1145 Route March Field Drill. 1045-1100 Hours Master Invitation. 1145-1215 Hour Master Visit 115	Football Match. Football Field. Cricket Nets. St Luke Hall.	
SATURDAY	Marching Shoe Heads for NH Inspection by the Commanding Officer. 1115-1200 Hour Lecture First Aid.	Medical Work. No 6 Training Hall.	

Comdg. Offr. (N.T.) Batt. Northumberland Fusiliers.

Lieut-Colonel.

9th. (NORTHUMBERLAND HUSSARS) BATTN. NORTHUMBERLAND FUSILIERS.

TRAINING PROGRAMME for week ending 24th.May 1919.

DAY	TRAINING	PLACE	REMARKS
MONDAY	Musketry. All day.	Arques Range	"C" Company will find all Guards and Duties for the week.
TUESDAY	0900-0945 hours Battalion Drill. 1000-1230 hours Education as per Programme Night Operations	Football Field. Forest d'Arques.	All Specialists will parade with the Battn.on first parade for one hours drill. They will then "Fall Out" & be marched away for special instruction by their instructors. The Classes under instruction are:- Signallers, Scouts, Lewis Gunners and Band.
WEDNESDAY	0930-1000 hours Physical Training. 1015-1230 hours Education as per Programme.	Football Field.	All men for Educational Classes will be marched away in time for their classes i.e. 2 of an hour before the time scheduled to begin.
THURSDAY.	Route March (Drill Order) 1 Coy.Advanced Guard & 1 Coy. Rear Guard.	to Bellengrieville	Mon.Tues.Thurs.and Friday afternoons from 1430-1600 hours are devoted to Organized Recreational Training.
FRIDAY.	0900-1030 hours Battalion Drill Extended Order,Artillery formations movements. 1030-1230 hours. Education as per programme	Football Field.	Dancing and Singing Classes in the Evenings.
SATURDAY.	Marching Order Parade for Kit Inspection by the Commanding Officer 1145-1230 hours Lecture—First Aid.	Football Field. No 5 Dining Hall	

Lieut-Colonel.

Commg. 9th. (N.H.) Battn. Northumberland Fusiliers.

Appendix B.

9th. (Northumberland Hussars) Battn. NORTHUMBERLAND FUSILIERS.

TRAINING PROGRAMME for the week ending 31st. May 1919.

DAY	TIME	SUBJECT	PLACE	REMARKS
MONDAY.	0900-1030 hours.	Physical Training.	Football Field.	Normal Officers' and Guards' parade for the week.
	0830-1030 hours.	Extended Order Drill, Platoon and etc.	Football Field.	
	1030-1230 hours.	Musketry as per Programme "B" Course, which see.	Lecture Room.	Lecture 3½ hrs. for instruction in rifle - ½ hour. All others to fill out at Field Service Regulations Part 1, Chap 5, Pages 67 -75.
TUESDAY.	0900-0930 hours.	Rifle Training.	Football Field.	
	0945-1130 hours.	Coy. Officers Parade. Battalion Drill.	Football Field. Football Field.	
	1030-1130 hours.	Education as per Programme C.		All Specialists will parade with their Coys. on first parade for one hour drill. They will then fall out & be marched away for specialist instruction by their instructors. The Classes under instruction are:- Signallers, Scouts, Lewis Gunners and M.M.G.
	1130-1230 hours.	Lecture by M.O. or Protestant Chaplain.	Main Hall.	
WEDNESDAY	0900-1030 hours.	Physical Training.	Football Field.	
	0930-1030 hours.	Firing Drill.	Football Field.	
	1030-1130 hours.	Question As per Programme.		
		Company Sports.	Lecture Room.	All men for Equestional Classes will be prepared away from the Coy. for their classes i.e. ½ or an hour before the time schedule begin. Non, Coms, Coys. and Trips afternoons are devoted to Organised Recreational Training from 1430 - 1800 hours. Chaplain for Lecture Classes in the Evening.
THURSDAY.		Conversation (Examination of Lectures) Fort & Platoon.		
FRIDAY.	0900-1000 hours.	Musketry Training. (Rifle.)	Football Field.	
	1000-1130 hours.	Labour Drill, Platoon & Guards Football Field.		
		(Drill)		
	1100-1230 hours.	Question As per Programme.		
		To Company Orders.		Members Ranks.
SATURDAY		Commanding Officer's Inspection of Company lines, Equipment etc, all articles in shares to be laid out.		

signature Lieut-Colonel.
Comm. 9th.(N.H.) Battn.Northumberland Fusiliers.

To:
    Brigade Major.
        182nd, Infantry Brigade.

Herewith War Diary for the month of JUNE

                                    Lieut, Colonel,
                        9th.(NH) Bn. Northumberland Fusiliers.

3/7/19.

Army Form C. 2118.

WAR DIARY

~~INTELLIGENCE SUMMARY~~

(Erase heading not required.)

JUNE 1919

9th: (NORTHUMBERLAND HUSSARS) BATTN. NORTHUMBERLAND FUSILIERS.

Appendix "A"   Education Programme.

Appendix "B"   Training Programme.

Army Form C. 2118.

WAR DIARY
INTELLIGENCE SUMMARY.
(Erase heading not required.)

Instructions regarding War Diaries and Intelligence Summaries are contained in F. S. Regs., Part II. and the Staff Manual respectively. Title pages will be prepared in manuscript.

JUNE 1919.

Place	Date	Hour	Summary of Events and Information	Remarks and references to Appendices
MARTIN EGLISE	1st.		Divine Service.	
	2nd.		As per Training Programme.	
	3rd.		As per Training Programme.	
	4th.		As per Training Programme.	
	5th.		As per Training Programme, Lecture of "Literature" by the Divisional Educational Officer. The lecture was well attended and all ranks showed a keen interest in it.	
	6th.		Training as per Programme, Lecture by the Staff Captain 182nd. Infantry Brigade on "English" This lecure was well attended and all showed a very keen interest in the subject.	
	7th.		As per Training Programme.	
	8th.		Church Parade.	
	9th.		As per Training Programme.	
	10th.		As per Training Programme.	
	11th.		As per Training Programme, 4 Other Ranks proceeded to England for demobilization.	
	12th.		As per Training Programme.	
	13th.		As per Training Programme.	
	14th.		As per Training Programme, Four Lance Corporals (under 20 years of age) proceeded to the Chinese Depot, Noyelles.	
	15th.		Church Parade.	
	16th.		As per Training Programme.	

Army Form C. 2118.

WAR DIARY
INTELLIGENCE SUMMARY

(Erase heading not required.)

Instructions regarding War Diaries and Intelligence Summaries are contained in F.S. Regs., Part II. and the Staff Manual respectively. Title pages will be prepared in manuscript.

JUNE 1919.

Place	Date	Hour	Summary of Events and Information	Remarks and references to Appendices
MARTIN EGLISE	17th.		As per Training Programme.	
	18th.		As per Training Programme. 5 Other Ranks proceeded to England for demobilization.	
	19th.		As per Training Programme. 8 Lance Corporals proceeded to Harfleur to attend a Course at 61st. Divisional School. 14 Lance Corporals (under 20 years of age) proceeded to Chinese Depot. Noyelles.	
	20th.		As per Training Programme.	
	21st.		As per Training Programme. 4 Men under 20 years of age proceeded to School of Cookery, Wimereux for training as cooks.	
	22nd.		Church Parade.	
	23rd.		As per Training Programme. Battalion Tug-of-War Team proceeded to Olympia, London, to represent British Troops in France in contest.	
	24th.		As per Training Programme. Congratulatory messages received from Divisional and Brigade Commanders on success of the Tug-of-War contesting in France.	
	25th.		As per Training Programme.	
	26th.		As per Training Programme. 5 Other Ranks proceeded to England for demobilization.	
	27th.		As per Training Programme.	
	28th.		As per Training Programme.	
	29th.		Voluntary Church Services owing to Base Sports taking place.	
	30th.		As per Training Programme.	

Lieut-Colonel,
Commg. 9th. (N.H.) Battn. Northumberland Fusiliers.

A

9th. (Northumberland Hussars) Battn. NORTHUMBERLAND FUSILIERS.

EDUCATIONAL PROGRAMME for week ending June 28th. 1919.

DAY.	1045-1145	1145-1245	Special Subjects	Special Subjects	

MONDAY	Shorthand A & B
	History
	English
	French
	C.O's Art Class
		Book-keeping
		Arithmetic A & B
		French B.
		Engineering
			Carpentry)1045
			Cobbling) to
			Tailoring)1245
			Piano (1045-1130
			     (1130-1215
			     (1330-1415
				Reading Class 1800-1900
				Officers French Class
				  1600-1800 hours
				Dancing Class 1800-1900
					Officers classes may be arranged more frequently in the course of the week.

TUESDAY	Shorthand A & B History French English	Book-keeping Arithmetic A & B French B. Engineering	ditto	Officer Book-keeping Class Dancing Class	
THURSDAY	Shorthand A & B History French English	Book-keeping Arithmetic A & B French Engineering	ditto	Reading Class 1800-1900 Dancing Class 1800-1900	It is not yet certain upon which day the Base Education Officer will give his lecture at 1130 hours.
FRIDAY	Shorthand A & B History French A. English	Book-keeping Arithmetic A & B French B.	ditto.	Dancing Class 1800-1900	
SATURDAY	Shorthand A & B History French English	Book-keeping Arithmetic A & B French B.	ditto		

21.6 1919.

(signature)
for Lieut-Colonel,
9th (N.H.) Battn. Northumberland Fusiliers.

A

9th.(Northumberland Hussars)Battn. Northumberland Fusiliers.

EDUCATIONAL PROGRAMME for week ending June 21st: 1919.

Day	1045-1145	1145-1245	Special Subjects	Special Subjects	Remarks:
MONDAY	M.O's Lecture to Battalion.	Shorthand A & B Civil Economics History French A. C.O's Art Class Piano	Carpentry) 1045 Cobbling) to Tailoring)1245 (1045-1130 (1130-1215 (1330-1415	Reading Class 1800-1900hrs. Officers French Class 1600-1800hrs. Dancing Class 18001900hrs.	Officers Classes may be arranged more frequently in the course of the week.
TUESDAY	Shorthand A & B History French	Book-keeping Arithmetic A & B. French B.	Ditto.	Officers Book-keeping Class Dancing Class	
THURSDAY	ShorthandA & B Arithmetic A & B French A. C.O's Art Class	Lecture by Capt. Taylor (see remarks)	Ditto.	Reading Class 1800-1900 hrs. Dancing Class 1800-1900 hrs.	It is not yet certain upon which day Capt. Taylor will give this lecture.
FRIDAY	Shorthand A & B History French A English	Book-keeping Arithmetic A & B French B.	Ditto.	Dancing Class 1800-1900 hrs.	
SATURDAY	Shorthand A & B History French A English	Book-keeping Arithmetic A & B French B	Ditto		

15.6.1919.

[signature]
for Lieut-Colonel,
Commg. 9th. (N.H.) Battn. Northumberland Fusiliers.

A

9th.(Northumberland Hussars)Battn. Northumberland Fusiliers.

EDUCATIONAL PROGRAMME for week ending June 14th. 1919.

Day.	1030 to 1130	1130 to 1230	Special Subjects.
MONDAY.	Shorthand A&B Civil Economics Geography French A.	Book-keeping Arithmetic A & B French	Carpentry) 1030 Bootmaking) to Tailoring) 1230 (1045-1130 Piano (1130-1215 (1330-1415	Art Classes (C.O.) 1400-1600 hours. Dancing Class 1800-1900 hours. Reading Class 1800-1900 hours.
TUESDAY.	Shorthand A & B Arithmetic History French (A)	Book-keeping Arithmetic French English	Carpentry) 1030 Bootmaking) to Tailoring) 1230 (1045-1130 Piano (1130-1215 (1330-1415	Officers Book-keeping 1400-1500hours. Dancing Class 1800-1900hrs.
WEDNESDAY THURSDAY.	Geography Arithmetic (B) English Shorthand A & B to be taken in letter writing by Educ 'Off.	French A. Shorthand A&B.	Piano Carpentry)1030 Bootmaking)to Tailoring)1230 (1045-1130 (1130-1215 (1330-1415	Dancing Class 1800-1900hrs. Reading Class 1800-1900hrs.
Friday	Shorthand A & B Arithmetic B. History French A. English	Book-keeping Arithmetic A. English French	Carpentry) 1030 Bootmaking) to Tailoring)1230 (1045-1130 Piano (1130-1215 (1330-1415	Art Classes 1400-1600hrs. Dancing Class 1800-1900hrs.
SATURDAY.	Shorthand A & B Geography French A. English	Lecture to Battn. on Literature by C.O.	Carpentry) 1030 Bootmaking) to Tailoring)1230 (1045-1130 Piano(1130-1215 (1330-1415	

Commg. 9th.(Northumberland Hussars)gt.Battn.Northumberland Fusiliers.

9th. (Northumberland Hussars) Battn. Northumberland Fusiliers.

EDUCATIONAL PROGRAMME for week ending 7th. June 1919.

Day.	Class Room.	1000-1050 hours.	1050-1140 hours.	1140-1230 hours.	1400-1500 hours.
MONDAY.	No.1.	English	Arithmetic	Elementary French	
	No.2.	Advanced Mathematics.	Shorthand.	Elementary French	
	No.3.			Book-keeping.	
	Officers Mess.				Art Class:
TUESDAY.	No.1.	English	Arithmetic	Elementary French	
	No.2.	Advanced French	Shorthand	Elementary French	
	No.3.		Advanced Mathematics	Advanced Mathematics	
WEDNESDAY.	No.1.	History	Arithmetic	Elementary French	
	No.2.	Book-keeping	Shorthand	Elementary French	
	No.3.			Advanced French	
Thursday	No.1.		Arithmetic	Elementary French	
	No.2.	Lecture by Div. Educ. Officer "Literature".	Shorthand	Elementary French	
	No.3.			Advanced Mathematics.	
FRIDAY	No.1.		Arithmetic	Elementary French	
	No.2.	Lecture by Staff Capt. "English"	Shorthand	Elementary French	
	No.3.			Advanced Mathematics.	
	Officers Mess				Art Class.
SATURDAY	No.1.	Letter Writing	Arithmetic	Elementary French	
	No.2.	Advanced French	Shorthand	Elementary French	
	No.3.			Book-keeping.	

31.5.1919

[signature]
for Lieut. Colonel,
Comng. 9th. (Northumberland Hussars) Bn. Northumberland Fusiliers.

B

9th (Northumberland Hussars) Battn. NORTHUMBERLAND FUSILIERS.

TRAINING PROGRAMME for week ending June 28th. 1919.

Day	Training	Place	Remarks.
MONDAY.	0900-0945 hours Physical Training 1 Platoon Boxing 1000-1030 hours Guards Drill. 1030-1230 Hours Education as per programme, remainder of Battn. Miniature Range.	Football Field. " "	"B" Coy. will find all Guard & Duties for the week.
TUESDAY.	0900-0945 hours Rifle Training 1 platoon Boxing 1000-1030 hours Platoon and Company Drill. 1030-1230 Hours Education as per programme, remainder of Battn. Musketry. Examination of all Sub. Officers in chapter 5 F.S.R. paras, 75-89	Football Field " " Officers Mess.	All Officers will make themselves thoroughly acquainted with chap 6 paras 90-93 F.S.R. All specialists will parade with the Battn. till 1030 hours they will "Fall Out" and be marched away for special instruction by their instructors. The classes
WEDNESDAY	0900-1230 hours Route March	Arques, St. Aubin, Tourville.	under instruction are:- Signallers Lewis Gunners, Band and N.C.O.s
THURSDAY.	0900-0945 hours Physical Training 1 platoon Boxing. 1000-1045 hours Battalion Drill, ceremonial. 1100-1230 hours Education as per programme, remainder of Battn. Miniature Range.	Football Field. Football Field.	All Men for Educational Classes will be march away in time for their various classes i.e. ½ of an hour before the time scheduled to begin. Mon. Tues. &
FRIDAY.	0900-0945 hours Physical Training 1 platoon Boxing 100-1030 hours Company in attack. 1030-1230 hours Education as per programme, remainder of Battn. Musketry.	Football Field.	Friday afternoons are devoted to Organized recreational training. Dancing and Singing classes in the evenings.
SATURDAY.	0930 hours. Commanding Officer's Marching Order and Kit Inspection(as strong as possible) Education as per programme.	Football Field	

21.6.1919.

Womersall.
Capt. & A/Adj.
for Lt.Col. Comdg. 9th(N.H.)Bn. North. Fusiliers

B

9th (Northumberland Hussars) Battn NORTHUMBERLAND FUSILIERS.

TRAINING PROGRAMME for week ending 21st June 1919.

Day.	Training.	Place.	Remarks.
MONDAY.	0900-0930 hours Physical Training 1 Platoon Boxing 0945-1020 " Guards & Saluting Drill 1030 hours Lecture by M.O. to whole Battalion 1130-1230 hours Education as per Programme, remainder of Battn. platoon Drill	Football Field Football Field Dining Hall	"D" Company will find all Guards and Duties for the week.
TUESDAY.	0900-0930 hours Rifle Training 1 Platoon Boxing 0945-1030 " Company Drill 1030-1230 " Education as per Programme, remainder of Battalion Minature Range. 1100 hours Examination of Sub.Officers on Chap.IX F.S.R.	Football Field Football Field Officers'Mess	All Officers will make themselves thoroughly acquainted with Chap.V paras 75-89 F.S.R. Part I (Outposts). All specialists will parade with the Battn till 1030 hours. They will "Fall Out" & be marched away for special instruction by their instructors. The
WEDNESDAY.	Outpost Scheme or Night Operations Education as per programme	St.Nicolas.	classes under instruction are:-Signallers Lewis Gunners. Scouts. Band & N.C.Os.
THURSDAY.	0900-0930 hours Physical Training 1 Platoon Boxing 0945-1030 " Battn.Drill.Artillery Formation etc. 1030-1230 " Education as per Programme, remainder of Battalion Musketry.	Football Field Football Field	All men for Educational Classes will be marched away in time for their various classes i.e. ½ of an hour before the time scheduled to begin.
FRIDAY.	0900-0930 Hours Rifle Training 1 Platoon Boxing 0945-1030 " Battalion Drill(Ceremonial) 1030-1230 " Education as per Programme, remainder of Battalion Musketry	Football Field Football Field	Mon. Tues. and Friday afternoons from 1430-1600 hours are devoted to Organised Recreational Training. Dancing and Singing Classes in the evenings.
SATURDAY.	0930 hours C.O's Marching Order Parade & Kit Inspection 1030-1230 hours Education as per Training Programme.	Football Field	

13/6/19.

Commdg. 9th (N.H.) Battn Northumberland Fusiliers.

B

9th (Northumberland Hussars) Battn NORTHUMBERLAND FUSILIERS.

TRAINING PROGRAMME for week ending 14th June 1919.

Day.	Training.	Place.	Remarks.
MONDAY.	0900-0945 hours Physical Training 1 Platoon Boxing	Football Field.	"C" Company will find all Guards and Duties for the week.
	1000-1030 " Guards & Saluting Drill	Football Field	
	1030-1230 " Education as per Programme		
TUESDAY.	0900-0945 Hours Rifle Training 1 Platoon Boxing	Football Field	All Officers will make themselves thoroughly acquainted with Chap IX F.S.R. Part I (Night Operations).
	1000-1020 " Company Drill	Football Field	
	1030-1230 " Education as per Programme		
	1100 hours Examination of Sub.Officers in Chap V F.S.R.	Officers Mess	
WEDNESDAY.	0900-1230 hours Route March or Night Operations. (Attack Scheme)	Archelles St.Aubin Foret d'Arques.	All specialists will parade with the Battn. on first parade for one hours drill. They will then "Fall Out" and be marched away for special instruction by their instructors. The Classes under instruction are:- Signallers.Scouts. Lewis Gunners & Band.
THURSDAY.	0900-0945 hours Physical Training 1 Platoon Boxing	Football Field	
	1000-1045 " Battalion Drill (Ceremonial	Football Field	
	1100-1230 " Education as per Programme		All men for Educational Classes will be marched away in time for their various classes i.e. ¾ of an hour before the time scheduled to begin.
FRIDAY.	0900-0945 hours Rifle Training 1 Platoon Boxing	Football Field	
	1000-1030 " Judging Distance	Football Field	
	1030-1230 " Education as per Programme		Mon.Tues.& Friday afternoons from 1430-1600 hours are devoted to Organised Recreational Training.
SATURDAY.	0930 hours Commanding Officer's Marching Order Parade (Strong as possible)	Football Field	
	1030-1230 hours Education as per Programme.		Dancing and Singing Classes in the evenings.

NOTE:- The P.T. & Rifle Training will be carried out in the Forest after the Battn. has been taken over by the Senior Officer on Parade. Rifles and Equipment will be left on the field in charge of 1 man per Company.

Lieut-Colonel.
Commdg. 9th (N.H.) Battn Northumberland Fusiliers.

6/6/19

B

9th (Northumberland Hussars) Battn NORTHUMBERLAND FUSILIERS.

TRAINING PROGRAMME for week ending 7th June 1919.

Day.	Training.	Place.	Remarks.
	0700 hours Adjutant's Roll Call Parade all Subaltern Officers to attend	Coy Parade Ground.	"B" Company will find all Guards and Duties for the week.
MONDAY. 0945	0900-0930 hours Physical Training 1 Platoon Boxing 1030-1030 " Platoon Drill 1030-1230 " Education as per Programme 1100 hours Examination of officers in Chap.V paras.64-74.	Football Field Football Field Officers Mess	Bad shots on Minature Range in the afternoons. All Officers will make themselves to read up remainder of Chap.5 F.S.R. Part 1.
TUESDAY.	0700 hours Adjt.Roll Call Parade.Sub.Officers to attend 0900-0930 hours Rifle Training 1 Platoon Boxing 0945-1030 " C.O's Parade Battalion Drill 1030-1230 " Education as per Programme 1030 hours Reconnoitering of River by all available Officers.	Coy Parade Grounds Football Field Football Field Martin Eglise to Ancourt.	1 Platoon daily for instructions in First Aid at 1400 hours. All specialists will parade with the Battn on first parade for one hours drill.They will then "Fall Out" & be marched away for special instruction by their instructors. The Classes under instruction are:-Signallers,Scouts, Lewis Gunners, and Band.
WEDNESDAY.	0700 hours Adjt.Roll Call Parade.Sub.Officers to attend 0900-1230 hours Route March (Bathing if fine)	Coy Parade Grounds Ancourt-Bellengreville-St.Nicolas.	
THURSDAY.	0700 hours Adjt.Roll Call Parade.Sub.Officers to attend 0900-0930 hours Physical Training 1 Platoon Boxing 0945-1030 " Company Drill 1030-1230 " Education as per Programme 1030 hours Further Reconn;of River by all available officers.	Coy Parade Grounds Football Field Football Field (to Ancourt. Martin Eglise	All men for Educational Classes will be marched away in time for their various classes i.e.½ hour before the time scheduled to begin.
FRIDAY.	0700 hours Adjt.Roll Call Parade.Sub.Officers to attend 0900-0930 hours Rifle Training 1 Platoon Boxing 0945-1030 hours Saluting and Guards Drill 1030-1230 " Education as per Programme.	Coy Parade Grounds Football Field Football Field	Mon.Tues.& Friday afternoons from 1430-1600 hours are devoted to Organised Recreational Training. Dancing and Singing Classes in the evenings.
SATURDAY.	0700 hours Adjt.Roll Call Parade.Sub.Officers to attend 1000 hours C.O's Kit Inspection Bn.in Marching Order	Coy Parade Grounds Football Field	

31/5/19.

Hammond Lt.Col.
Lieut-Colonel.
Commdg. 9th (N.H.) Battn Northumberland Fusiliers.

Army Form C. 2118.

WAR DIARY
INTELLIGENCE SUMMARY

(Erase heading not required.)

Vol 50

JULY 1919

Place	Date	Hour	Summary of Events and Information	Remarks and references to Appendices
			9th (NORTHUMBERLAND HUSSARS) BATTN NORTHUMBERLAND FUSILIERS.	
			Appendix "A" Education Programme	
			Appendix "B" Training Programme	

Army Form C. 2118.

WAR DIARY

INTELLIGENCE SUMMARY.

(Erase heading not required.)

JULY 1919.

Instructions regarding War Diaries and Intelligence Summaries are contained in F.S. Regs., Part II. and the Staff Manual respectively. Title pages will be prepared in manuscript.

Place	Date	Hour	Summary of Events and Information	Remarks and references to Appendices
MARTIN EGLISE	1st.		Training as per programme.	
	2nd.		Training as per programme. 6 men proceeded to England for Demobilization.	
	3rd.		Training as per programme.	
	4th.		Training as per programme.	
	5th.		Training as per programme. Lieut-Colonel S. Boyle,M.C. 10th. King's Own Scottish Borderers joined the Battalion as 2nd in Command.	
	6th.		Church Parades	
	7th.		Training as per programme. Educational Lecture by Base Education Officer.	
	8th.		Training as per programme. draft of 85 men under 20 years of age sent to 20th. General Hospital Audricq for training as R.A.M.C.	
	9th.		Training as per programme. 2 men proceeded to England for demobilization.	
	10th.		Training as per programme.	
	11th.		"B" & "C" Companies proceeded to Abancourt to relieve the 1/5th. D.C.L.I.	
	12th.		Training as per programme.	
	13th.		Church Parades.	
	14th.		Holiday owing to the Peace Celebrations of the French.	
	15th.		Training as per programme	
	16th.		Training as per programme. 3 O.R.s proceeded to England for Demobilization.	

A8834 Wt.W4973 M687 750,000 8/16 D.D.&L.Ltd Forms/C.2118/13.

Army Form C. 2118.

WAR DIARY
INTELLIGENCE SUMMARY.

(Erase heading not required.)

JULY 1919.

Instructions regarding War Diaries and Intelligence Summaries are contained in F. S. Regs., Part II. and the Staff Manual respectively. Title pages will be prepared in manuscript.

Place	Date	Hour	Summary of Events and Information	Remarks and references to Appendices
MARTIN EGLISE	17th.		Training as per programme	
	18th.		Training as per programme	
	19th.		Holiday owing to Peace Celebrations in England.	
	20th.		Church Parades.	
	21st.		Training as per programme, 3 O.R.s proceeded to Boulogne for duty under the A.D.P.S. Boulogne, 2 N.C.O.s proceeded to Etaples to sit for examination for 1st. Class Army Certificate.	
	22nd.		Training as per programme. Lecture by Major Heywood on "Anti-Bolshevism."	
	23rd.		Training as per programme.	
	24th.		Training as per programme. Lecture by the Rev. F.E. Brown on "Nature Study."	
	25th.		Training as per programme.	
	26th.		Training as per programme.	
	27th.		Church Parades	
	28th.		Training as per programme, 6 O.R.s proceeded to 21st. Vehicle Reception Park, Rouen, for training as M.T. R.A.S.C. Drivers.	
	29th.		Training as per programme, 20 O.R.s proceeded to 8th Auxiliary Steam Company, Havre, for training as R.A.S.C. Drivers.	

Army Form C. 2118.

WAR DIARY
INTELLIGENCE SUMMARY.
(Erase heading not required.)

Place	Date	Hour	Summary of Events and Information	Remarks and references to Appendices
MARTIN EGLISE	30th.		Training as per programme.	
	31st.		Training as per programme. Battalion Transport moved from Remount Camp Hautot to Remount Camp, Janval.	

E. Plowler
Lieut-Colonel,
Commg. 9th. (N.H.) Batᵗⁿ. Northumberland Fusiliers.

25th (Northumberland Hussars) Batt., NORTHUMBERLAND FUSILIERS.

TRAINING PROGRAMME for week ending August 2nd, 1919.

DAY	MONDAY	TUESDAY	WEDNESDAY	THURSDAY	FRIDAY	SATURDAY
Main under Company	3 Platoons	3 Platoons	3 Platoons	3 Platoons	3 Platoons	3 Platoons
0830–0915 hours	Physical Trng.	Rifle Exer.	Rifle Exer.	Physical Trng.	Rifle Exer.	Commander Officers
0915–1045	Range Rules & Targets	Musketry Instruction	Musketry	Extended Order Drill	Musketry Theory	Inspection of Arms
1045–1115	Latrine Drill	Guards Drill	La Drill	Marson Drill	Company Drill	Gas–M
1115–1130	Inspection				Inspection	

Course of c/s.M.2 Commences 22nd hours Aug.5
Course of Lance Commanders under to busy Templeton 1400 hours Aug.5

	Small Numbers		Small Numbers		W.O's	
STRENGTH	Total Under Trng.	N.C.Os.	O.R.	Recruits	under training	Star Traces under training
Absent without leave	12	4	58	17	17	Transport 10
Parade States	18	12	28	7	6	Shoemakers 5
						Tailors 0
Unfit to						Carpenters 4
take duties	1 Sr. 1 C.S.M.	0	0 Sr. 12 C.S.M.	1 C.		Painters 24

24.7.1919.

Capt. & A/Adjt. (signed) T. W. Prismall,

(signed) T. W. Prismall,
Lieut-Colonel,
Comdg. 25th (N.H.) Batt. Northumberland Fusiliers.

9th. (Northumberland Hussars) Batn. NORTHUMBERLAND FUSILIERS.

TRAINING PROGRAMME for week ending July 26th. 1919.

DAY	MONDAY	TUESDAY	WEDNESDAY	THURSDAY	FRIDAY	SATURDAY
Units under training.	3 Platoons.	3 Platoons.	3 Platoons.	3 Platoons.	3 Platoons.	3 Platoons.
PERIOD: 0900-0930 hrs.	Physical Trng.	Rifle Trng.	Physical Trng.	Rifle Trng.	Physical Trng.	Company Commdrs.
0945-1050 "	Guards & Sentries Drill	Platoon Drill	Extended Order Drill	Guard and Sentries Drill	Company Drill	Kit
1045-1130 "	Fire Positions, etc.	Rapid Loading	Recognition of Targets	Judging Distance.	Fire positions.	Inspection.
1145-1245 "	----------- Education -----------					

Remarks (Conference of Platoon Commanders under Company Commanders 1400 hours daily.
        (Conference of Company Commanders 1200 hours daily.

SPECIALISTS:-	Signallers Trained Under Tng.		Lewis Gunners T. U.T.		Scouts T. U.T.		Runners T. U.T.		N.C.O.s Under training		Other Classes under training	
Abancourt Martin Prize	13	15	104	53 26	7	7 5			17 6		Transport 10 Shoemakers 5 Tailors 2 Carpenters 4 Musicians 20	
Qualified to instruct	1 Off. 2 O.R.		2 Off. 12 O.R.		1 Off.							

(signed) T. W. Prismall
Capt. & A/Adjt. for Lieut-Colonel,
Comdg. 9th. (N.H.) Batn. Northumberland Fusiliers.

17.7.1919.

9th. (Northumberland Hussars) Battn. NORTHUMBERLAND FUSILIERS

TRAINING PROGRAMME for week ending July 19th. 1919.

DAY	MONDAY	TUESDAY	WEDNESDAY	THURSDAY	FRIDAY	SATURDAY
Units under training	9	2 Platoons	2 Platoons	2 Platoons	2 Platoons	
PERIOD 0900-0930 hours	HOLIDAY	Physical Trng.	ROUTE MARCH	Rifle Training	Physical Trng.	HOLIDAY
0945-1030	"	Platoon Drill	Arques & St. Nicholas	Rapid Loading, etc	Platoon Drill.	
1045-1130	"	Guards & Sentries Drill		Fire Positions	Recognition of Targets	
1145-1245	"	Education		Education		

Remarks (Conference of Platoon Commanders under Company Commanders 1400 hours daily.
(Conference of Company Commanders 1200 hours daily.

SPECIALISTS:-

	Signallers		Lewis Gunners		Scouts		Runners		N.C.O.s	Other Classes under training.
	Trained	Under Trng.	T.	U.T.	T.	U.T.	T.	U.T.	under training	
Abancourt	13	4	104	53	7	7			17	Transport 10
Martin Eglise		13		26	7	5			6	Shoemakers 3
										Tailors 2
Qualified to instruct	1 Off. 2 O.R.s		2 Off. 12 O.R.		1 Off.					Carpenters 4
										Musicians 20

11.7.1919

(signed) T. W. Prismall.
Capt. & A/Adjt. for Lieut-Colonel,
Commg. 9th. (N.H.) Battn. Northumberland Fusiliers.

9th (Northumberland Hussars) Battn NORTHUMBERLAND FUSILIERS.

TRAINING PROGRAMME for week ending July 12th 1919.

DAY.	MONDAY.	TUESDAY.	WEDNESDAY.	THURSDAY.	FRIDAY.	SATURDAY.
Units under training.	2 Companies and 2 Platoons	2 Companies and 2 Platoons	2 Companies and 2 Platoons	2 Companies and 2 Platoons	2 Companies and 2 Platoons	2 Companies and 2 Platoons
Period.						
0900-0950 hrs	Physical Training	Rifle Training	Route March with 1st.Line Transport. Route:- Arques- St.Nicolas.	Physical Training.	Rifle Training.	Commanding Officer's Kit Inspection.
0945-1050 hrs	Attack formation	Platoon Drill		Company Drill	Ceremonial Drill	
1045-1130 hrs	Fire positions	Guards & Sentries.		Rapid Loading etc.	Recognition of Targets.	
1130-1245	----Education----			----Education----		

Remarks. (Conference of Platoon Commanders under Company Commanders 1400 hours daily.
(Conference of Company Commanders 1200 hours daily.

SPECIALISTS:-	Signallers.		Lewis Gunners.		Scouts.		Runners.		N.C.Os. under training.	Other Classes under training.
	Trained.	Under Tng.	T.	U.T.	T.	U.T.	T.	U.T.		
	13.	17.	104.	31 Battn Class 48 Coy Classes	7.	12.	8.	-	23.	Transport Shoemakers Tailors Carpenters Musicians.

Qualified to instruct.	1 officer 2 O.Rs.	2 Officers 12 O.Rs.	1 officer

9th. (Northumberland Hussars) Battn. NORTHUMBERLAND FUSILIERS.

TRAINING PROGRAMME for week ending July 5th. 1919.

Day	Training	Place	Remarks.
MONDAY	0900-0930 hours Physical Training 1 Platoon Boxing 0945-1030 " Guards Drill 1030-1230 " Educ. as per Programme remainder of Battn. Miniature Range.	Football Field -do-	"C" Coy will find all Guards and Duties for the week.
TUESDAY	0900-0930 hours Rifle Training 1 Platoon Boxing 0945-1030 hours Platoon & Company Drill 1030-1230 hours Educ. as per programme remainder of Battn. Musketry Exam of all Sub. Officers in Chap. V. F.S.R. paras 75-89	Football Field -do- Off. Mess. Classroom	All officers will make themselves thoroughly acquainted with Camp VI paras. 90-03 F.S.R. All specialists will parade with the Bn. till 1030 hours they will "Fall Out" & be marched away for special instruction by their instructors. The classes under instruction are:- Signallers, Lewis Gunners, Band & N.C.O.s All men for Educ. Classes will be marched away in time for their various classes i.e. ½ hour before before the time scheduled to begin. Mon-Tues. & Friday afternoons from 1430-1600 hrs. are devoted to organized Recreational Training, Dancing and Singing in the evenings.
WEDNESDAY	0900-1230 hours Route March (Full marching order) 1st. line Transport		
THURSDAY	0900-0930 hours Physical Training 1 Platoon Boxing 0945-1045 hours Battalion Drill (Veremonial) 1100-1230 hours Educ. as per Programme remainder of Battn. Musketry	Football Field -do-	
FRIDAY	0900-0930 hours Physical Training 1 Platoon Boxing 0945-1030 hours Company in Attack 1030-1230 hours Education as per programme remainder of Battn. Musketry.	Football Field	
SATURDAY	0930 hours Company Commanders Kit Inspection. Education as per programme.		

27.6.1919.

(signed) T. W. Prismall,
Captain & Adjutant,
9th. (N.H.) Battn. Northumberland Fusiliers.

9th. (Northumberland Hussars) Battn. NORTHUMBERLAND FUSILIERS.

EDUCATIONAL PROGRAMME for week ending August 2nd, 1919.

DAY	1045-1145 hours	1145-1245 hours	Special subjects 1045/1245 hrs:
MONDAY	English French Shorthand History	Arithmetic French Shorthand Book-keeping	Carpentry Shoemaking
TUESDAY	As for Monday	As for Monday	
WEDNESDAY	English French Shorthand History	Arithmetic French Shorthand Book-keeping	Carpentry Shoemaking
THURSDAY	As for Wednesday	As for Wednesday	
FRIDAY	English French Shorthand History	Arithmetic French Shorthand Book-keeping	Carpentry Shoemaking
SATURDAY	As for Friday	As for Friday	

(signed) T. W. Prismall
Captain & A/Adjutant.
for Lieut-Colonel,
Commg. 9th (N.H.) Battn Northumberland Fusiliers.

26.7.1919.

9th. (N.F.) Battn.) NORTHUMBERLAND FUSILIERS.

EDUCATIONAL PROGRAMME for week ending July 26th, 1919.

	1015-1145 hours	1145-1245 hours	Special Subjects 1045-1245 hours.
MONDAY	English French Shorthand History	Arithmetic French Shorthand Book-keeping.	Carpentry Shoemaking
TUESDAY	As for Monday	As for Monday	As for Monday.
WEDNESDAY	English French Shorthand History	Arithmetic French Shorthand Book-keeping.	Carpentry Carpentry
THURSDAY	As for Wednesday	As for Wednesday	As for Wednesday
FRIDAY	English French Shorthand History	Arithmetic French Shorthand Book-keeping.	Carpentry Shoemaking
SATURDAY	As for Friday	As for Friday	Half day Friday

(signed) T: W. Prismall,
Capt. & A/Adjt. 9th(N.F.)Battn.Colonel,
Comdg. 9th. (N.F.) Battn. Northumberland Fusiliers.

20.7.1919.

9th. (Northumberland Hussars) Battn. NORTHUMBERLAND FUSILIERS.

EDUCATIONAL PROGRAMME for week ending July 19th, 1919.

DAY	1045-1145 hours.	1145-1245 hours	Special Subjects 1045-1245 hours:
MONDAY.	------------------HOLIDAY------------------		
TUESDAY	English French Shorthand History	Arithmetic French Shorthand Book-keeping	Carpentry Shoemaking
WEDNESDAY	English French Shorthand History	Arithmetic French Shorthand Book-keeping	Carpentry Shoemaking
FRIDAY	English French Shorthand History	Arithmetic French Shorthand Book-keeping	Carpentry Shoemaking
SATURDAY	------------------HOLIDAY------------------		

(signed) T.S. Pigrall,
Captain & A/Adjutant,
for Lieut-Colonel,
Comdg. 9th. (N.H.) Battn. Northumberland Fusiliers.

12.7.1919.

9th (Northumberland Hussars) Batn NORTHUMBERLAND FUSILIERS.

EDUCATIONAL PROGRAMME for week ending July 12th 1919.

DAY.	1045-1145	1145-1245	Special Subjects	Special Subjects.	Remarks.
MONDAY.	Shorthand A.& B. Geography English French	Book-keeping Arithmetic A.& B. French B. Typewriting Shorthand	Carpentry 1045 Cobbling to Tailoring 1245 Class {1045-1130 {1130-1215 {1230-1315	Reading Class 1800-1900 Officers Dunet Class 1800-1870 hours Dancing Class 1800-1900	Officers Classes may be arranged more frequently in the course of the week
TUESDAY.	Shorthand A.M.B. Geography French English	Book-keeping Arithmetic A.& B. French B Engineering C.O's Art Class	Ditto	Officers Book-keeping Class. Dancing Class	It is not yet certain upon which day the Education Officer and Staff Captain 189 Brigade will give their lectures.
WEDNESDAY.	Shorthand A.& B. History French English	Book-keeping Arithmetic A.& B. French Engineering	Ditto	Reading Class 1845-1930	
THURSDAY.	Shorthand A.& B. English History	Book-keeping Arithmetic A.& B. French B. C.O's Art Class	Ditto	Dancing Class 1800-1900	
FRIDAY.	Geography French English	Book-keeping Arithmetic A.& B. French B. C.O's Art Class	Ditto	Reading Class 1800-1900	
SATURDAY.	Shorthand A.& B. History French English	Book-keeping Arithmetic A.& B. French B.	Ditto		

(Signed) T.W.Prismall
Captain & A/Adjutant.
for Lieut-Colonel.
Comdg. 9th (N.H.) Batn Northumberland Fusiliers.

4/7/19.

9th (Northumberland Hussars) Battn NORTHUMBERLAND FUSILIERS.

EDUCATIONAL PROGRAMME for week ending July 5th 1919.

Day.	1045-1145	1145-1245	Special Subjects.	Special Subjects.	Remarks.
MONDAY.	Shorthand A.&.B. History English French	Book-keeping Arithmetic A.&.B. French B. Engineering	Carpentry) 1045 Cobbling) to Tailoring) 1245 Piano (1045-1130 (1130-1215 (1330-1415	Reading Class 1800-1900 hrs. Officers French Class 1600-1800 hours. Dancing Class 1800-1900 hrs.	Officers Classes may be arranged more frequently in the course of the week.
TUESDAY.	Shorthand A.&.B. History French English	Book-keeping Arithmetic A.&.B. French B. Engineering C.O's. Art Class	Ditto	Officers Book-keeping Class. Dancing Class	
THURSDAY.	Shorthand A.&.B. History French English	Book-keeping Arithmetic A.&.B. French Engineering	Ditto	Reading Class 1800-1900 hrs Dancing Class 1800-1900 "	
FRIDAY.	Shorthand A.&.B. History French A. English	Book-keeping Arithmetic A.&.B. French B. C.O's. Art Class	Ditto	Dancing Class 1800-1900 hrs.	
SATURDAY.	Shorthand A.&.B. History French English	Book-keeping Arithmetic A.&.B. French B.	Ditto		

29/6/19.

(Signed) T. W. Prismall.
Captain & A/Adjutant.
for Lieut-Colonel.
Commdg. 9th (N.H.) Battn Northumberland Fusiliers.

Comm'g Officer.

Army Form C. 2118.

WAR DIARY
or
INTELLIGENCE SUMMARY.
(Erase heading not required.)

AUGUST 1919

46⁰

Place	Date	Hour	Summary of Events and Information	Remarks and references to Appendices
			9th. (NORTHUMBERLAND HUSSARS) BATTN. NORTHUMBERLAND FUSILIERS.	
			Appendix "A" Education Programme.	
			Appendix "A" Training Programme.	

A5834 Wt.W4973/M687 750,000 8/16 D. D. & L. Ltd. Forms/C.2118/13.

Army Form C. 2118.

WAR DIARY
or
INTELLIGENCE SUMMARY

(Erase heading not required.)

Instructions regarding War Diaries and Intelligence Summaries are contained in F.S. Regs., Part II. and the Staff Manual respectively. Title pages will be prepared in manuscript.

August 1919

Place	Date	Hour	Summary of Events and Information	Remarks and references to Appendices
Martin Eglise	1st.		Training as per Programme Lieut-Colonel S.Boyle M.C. proceeded to Command 2/6th. Battn. Royal Warwick Regt.	
	2nd.		Training as per Programme.	
	3rd.		Church Parade.	
	4th.		August Bank Holiday.	
	5th.		Training as per Programme. Major A. Read-Kellett, D.S.O.M.C. South Wales Borderers joined Battalion as 2nd. in Command.	
	6th.		Training as per Programme.	
	7th.		Training as per Programme.	
	8th.		Training as per Programme.	
	9th.		Training as per Programme.	
	10th.		Church Parade.	
	11th.		Training as per Programme.	
	12th.		Training as per Programme.	
	13th.		Training as per Programme.	
	14th.		Training as per Programme.	
	15th.		Training as per Programme.	
	16th.		Training as per Programme.	

A5834 Wt.W4973/M687 730,000 8/16 D. D. & L. Ltd. Forms/C.2118/13.

Army Form C. 2118.

WAR DIARY
or
INTELLIGENCE SUMMARY.
(Erase heading not required.)

AUGUST 1919.

Instructions regarding War Diaries and Intelligence Summaries are contained in F. S. Regs., Part II. and the Staff Manual respectively. Title pages will be prepared in manuscript.

Place	Date	Hour	Summary of Events and Information	Remarks and references to Appendices
Martin Eglise	17th.		Church Parade.	
	18th.		Training as per Programme. Lecture to Officers by G.S.O 61st Division on "Aids to Civil Power"	
	19th.		Training as per Programme.	
	20th.		Training as per Programme.	
	21st.		Training as per Programme.	
	22nd.		Training as per Programme. 27 O.R.s who enlisted under the "Derby Scheme" proceeded for demobilization.	
	23rd.		Training as per Programme. 38 O.R.s who enlisted under the "Derby Scheme" proceeded for demobilization.	
	24th.		Church Parade.	
	25th.		Training as per Programme.	
	26th.		Training as per Programme. 8 O.R.s who enlisted under the "Derby Scheme" proceeded for demobilization.	
	27th.		Training as per Programme.	
	28th.		Training as per Programme. 13 O.R.s who enlisted under the "Derby Scheme" proceeded for demobilization.	
	29th.		Training as per Programme. 3 O.R.s who enlisted under the "Derby Scheme" proceeded for demobilization.	
	30th.		Training as per Programme. Lecture on "Through the Russian Revolution" by Rev. Courtier Forster.	
	31st.		Church Parade. 4 O.R.s who enlisted under the "Derby Scheme Proceeded for demobilization.	

Lieut-Colonel.
Commdg. 9th. (N.H.) Battn. Northumberland Fusiliers.

9th. (Northumberland Hussars) Battn. NORTHUMBERLAND FUSILIERS.

TRAINING PROGRAMME for week ending 30th August 1919.

DAY	MONDAY	TUESDAY	WEDNESDAY	THURSDAY	FRIDAY	SATURDAY
Units under training	2 Platoons	2 Platoons	2 Platoons	2 Platoons	2 Platoons	2 Platoon
PERIOD						
0900-0930 hours	Physical Training	Rifle Training	ROUTE MARCH	Physical Training	Rifle Training	Cmndg. Officer's Inspection of Camp
0945-1030 "	Platoon Drill	Guards and Sentries Drill	Arques } St.Nicholas } }	Extended Order Drill	Guards and Sentries Drill	
1045-1130 "	Guards and Sentries Drill	Musketry Tests		Platoon Drill	Musketry Tests	
1145-1245 "	Education	Education			Education	

Remarks (Conference of Company Commanders 1400 hours daily
(Conference of Platoon Commanders under Company Commanders 1430 hours daily

SPECIALISTS:-	Signallers		Lewis Gunners		Scouts		Runners		N.C.O.s	Other Classes
	Trained	Under Trng	T.	U.T.	T.	U.T.	T.	U.T.	under training	
Abancourt	6	4	64	53		7		17		Transport 10
Martin Eglise	7	12	50	26	7	5		6		Shoemakers 3
										Tailors 2
Qualified to instruct	1 Off. 2 O.R.s		2 Offs. 12 O.R.s		1 Officer					Carpenters 2
										Musicians 9

21.8.19.

(signed) T. W. Prismell
Captain & Adjutant
for Lieut-Colonel
Cmndg. 9th (N.H.) Battn. Northumberland Fusiliers.

9th.(Northumberland Hussars)Battn.Northumberland Fusiliers.

TRAINING PROGRAMME for week ending 23rd, August 1919

DAY	MONDAY	TUESDAY	WEDNESDAY	THURSDAY	FRIDAY	SATURDAY
Units under training	2 Platoons	2 Platoons	2 Platoons	2 Platoons	2 Platoons	2 Platoons
PERIOD						
0900-0935 hours	Rifle Training	Physical Training	ROUTE MARCH	Rifle training	Physical training	Commdg. officer's
0945-1030 "	Guards and Sentries drill	(Street (Fighting (Scheme	Dieppe Le Puits Croques	Squad Drill Extended Order drill	)Street)Fighting)Scheme	Kit Inspection.
1045-1120 "						
1145-1245 "	Education				Education	

Remarks (Conference of Company Commanders 1400 hours daily.
        (Conference of Platoon Commanders under Company Commanders 1430 hours daily.

Specialists.	Signallers	Lewis gunners	Scouts	Runners	N.C.O.'s under training
	Trained Under Trng.	T. U.T.	T. U.T.	T. U.T.	Other classes U.T.
Abancourt	6 4	64 53		7	Transport 10
Martin Eglise	7 12	50 26	7 5		Shoemakers 3
					Tailors 2
Qualified to instruct.	1 off. 2 O.R.s	2 off. 10 O.R.s		1off	Carpenters 2
					Musicians 9

14.8.19.

(signed) R.A.Fraser.

Lieut.& A/Adjt. for Lieut-Colonel.

Commdg. 9th.(N.H.)Battn. Northumberland Fusiliers.

9th. (Northumberland Hussars)Battn.Northumberland Fusiliers.

TRAINING PROGRAMME for week ending 16th. August 1919.

DAY	Monday	Tuesday	Wednesday	Thursday	Friday	Saturday
Units under Training	2 Platoons	2 Platoons	2 Platoons	2 Platoons	2 Platoons	2 Platoons
PERIOD						
0900-0930 hours	Physical Training	Rifle Training	ROUTE MARCH	Physical Training	Rifle Training	Company Commdrs.
0945-1030 "	Squad Drill	} Scheme	Arques	Squad Drill	Platoon Drill	Kit Inspection.
1045-1130 "	Practice Scheme	}	&	Guards and Sentries Drill	Extended Order Drill	Commdg. Officers Inspection of Camp
1145-1245 "	}}}}}}---Education---		St.Nicholas	-----------	Education	

Remarks (Conference of Company Commanders 1400 hours daily
        (Conference of Platoon Commanders under Company Commanders 1430 hours daily.

SPECIALISTS	Signallers		Lewis Gunners			Scouts		Runners		M.G.O.s	Other classes
	Trained	Under Trng.	T.	U.T.		T.	U.T.	T.	U.T.		under training under training
Abancourt	6	4	64	53			7				Transport 10
Martin Eglise	7	12	50	26			5				Shoemakers 6
											Tailors 2
Qualified to Instruct	4 Off. 2 O.R.s		2 Off.	12 O.R.s		1 Officer					Carpenters 2
											Musicians 9

(signed) E.A. Fraser.

Lieut:& A/Adjt. 9th Battn.Northumberland Fusiliers.

Commdg. 9th.(N.H.)Battn.Northumberland Fusiliers.

7.8.19.

9th. (Northumberland Hussars) Battn. NORTHUMBERLAND FUSILIERS.

TRAINING PROGRAMME for week ending 9th. August, 1919.

DAY	MONDAY	TUESDAY	WEDNESDAY	THURSDAY	FRIDAY	SATURDAY
Units under training	3 Platoons	3 Platoons	3 Platoons	3 Platoons	3 Platoons	3 Platoons
PERIOD						
0900-0930 hours	AUGUST	Physical Training	Rifle Training	Physical Training	Rifle Training	Commanding
0945-1050 "	BANK	Platoon Drill	Guards & Sentries Drill	Extended Order Drill	Platoon Drill	Officer's
1045-1130 "	HOLIDAY	Rapid Loading	Fire Positions	Recognition of Targets	Judging Distance	KIT INSPECTION
1145-1245 "			EDUCATION		EDUCATION	

Remarks (Conference of Company Commanders 1200 hours daily
        (Conference of Platoon Commanders under Company Commanders 1400 hours daily.

SPECIALISTS:-	Snipers		Lewis Gunners		Scouts		Runners		N.C.O.s	Other classes
	Trained	Under Trng.	T.	U.T.	T.	U.T.	T.	U.T.	Under training	under training
Acancourt		4		53		7		7	17	Transport 10
Martin Eglise	13	12	104	26	7	5			6	Shoemakers 3
										Tailors 2
Qualified to instruct	1 Off. 2 O.R.		2 Off. 12 O.R.s		1 Officer					Carpenters 4
										Musicians 20

(signed) T. W. Prismall,
Captain & Adjutant,
for Lieut-Colonel
Comdg. 9th. (N.H.) Battn. Northumberland Fusiliers.

31.7.1919.

9th. (Northumberland Hussars) Battn. Northumberland Fusiliers.

EDUCATIONAL PROGRAMME for week ending August 30th. 1919.

DAY	1045-1145 hours	1145-1245 hours	Special Subjects 1045-1245 hours
MONDAY	English French A & B. Shorthand.	Arithmetic French A&B Shorthand Book keeping	Carpentry Shoemaking Piano
TUESDAY	As for Monday	As for Monday	As for Monday C.O.S Art Class 1400
WEDNESDAY	ROUTE MARCH.		
THURSDAY	As for Monday	As for Monday	As for Monday
FRIDAY	As for Monday	As for Monday	As for Monday C.O.s Art Class 1400
SATURDAY	Lecture to Battn. by the Rev. R.Courtier Forster	As for Monday	

(Signed) T.W.Prismall.
Captain and Adjutant.
9th. (N.H.)Battn. Northumberland Fusiliers.

24.8.19.

9th. (Northumberland Hussars) Battn. NORTHUMBERLAND FUSILIERS.

EDUCATIONAL PROGRAMME for week ending August 23rd 1919.

DAY	1045-1145 hours	1145-1245 hours	Special Subjects 1045-1245 hours.
MONDAY	English French A & B. Shorthand	Arithmetic French A & B Shorthand Book-keeping	Carpentry Shoemaking Piano
TUESDAY	Lecture to Battn. by D.C.Holmes Esq, on the Peace Treaty.	Arithmetic Shorthand Book-keeping French A & B	Carpentry Shoemaking Piano C.O.s Art Class 1400 hours
WEDNESDAY	ROUTE	MARCH	
THURSDAY	As for Monday	As for Monday	As for Monday
FRIDAY	As for Monday	As for Monday	As for Monday C.O.s Art Class 1400 Hours
SATURDAY	As for Monday	As for Monday	As for Monday

(signed) R.A. Fraser
Lieut & A/Adjutant
for Lieut-Colonel
Cmmdg. 9th (N.H.) Battn Northumberland Fusiliers.

16.8.19

9th. (Northumberland Hussars) Battn. NORTHUMBERLAND FUSILIERS.

EDUCATIONAL PROGRAMME for week ending August 16th 1919.

DAY	1045-1145 hours	1145-1245 hours	Special Subjects 1045-1245 hours
MONDAY	English French Shorthand History	Arithmetic French Shorthand Book-keeping	Carpentry Shoemaking
TUESDAY	As for Monday	As for Monday.	As for Monday.
WEDNESDAY	English French Shorthand History	Arithmetic French Shorthand Book-keeping	Carpentry Shoemaking
THURSDAY	As for Wednesday	As for Wednesday	As for Wednesday
FRIDAY	English French Shorthand History	Arithmetic French Shorthand Book-keeping	Carpentry Shoemaking
SATURDAY	As for Friday	As for Friday.	As for Friday.

(Signed) R.A. Fraser
Lieut. & A/Adjutant
for Lieut-Colonel
Cmmdg 9th (N.H.) Battn Northumberland Fusiliers.

11.8.19.

9th. (Northumberland Hussars) Batn. NORTHUMBRIAN FUSILIERS.

EDUCATIONAL TIMETABLE for week ending August 9th, 1919.

DAY	1045-1145 hours	1145-1245 hours	Special subjects 1345/1545 hours
MONDAY	Holiday	Holiday	Holiday
TUESDAY	English French Shorthand History	Arithmetic French Shorthand Book-keeping	Carpentry Shoemaking
WEDNESDAY	As for Tuesday	As for Tuesday	As for Tuesday
THURSDAY	English French Shorthand History	Arithmetic French Shorthand Book-keeping	Carpentry Shoemaking
FRIDAY	As for Thursday	As for Thursday	As for Thursday
SATURDAY	English French Shorthand History	Arithmetic French Shorthand Book-keeping	Carpentry Shoemaking

(signed) T. T. Tylsmall,
Captain & Adjutant,
for Lieut-Colonel,
Comdg. 9th. (N.H.) Batn. Northumberland Fusiliers.

8.8.1919.

Army Form C. 2118

WAR DIARY
INTELLIGENCE SUMMARY
(Erase heading not required.)

SEPTEMBER, 1919.

Instructions regarding War Diaries and Intelligence Summaries are contained in F.S. Regs., Part II. and the Staff Manual respectively. Title Pages will be prepared in manuscript.

Place	Date	Hour	Summary of Events and Information	Remarks and references to Appendices
MARTIN EGLISE.	1st		Training as per programme. 1 Officer and 5 O.R. proceeded to England for demobilization.	
	2nd.		Training as per programme. Lecture by Colonel Lynden Bell on "Lessons from Roman and Venitian History".	
	3rd.		Training as per programme.	
	4th.		Training as per programme. 21 O.Rs. proceeded to England for demobilization.	
	5th.		Training as per programme.	
	6th.		Training as per programme. 11 O.Rs. proceeded to England for demobilization.	
	7th.		Church Parade.	
	8th.		Training as per programme. 12 O.Rs. proceeded to England for demobilization.	
	9th.		Training as per programme. 1 O.R. proceeded to England for demobilization.	
	10th.		Training as per programme. 1 O.R. proceeded to England for demobilization.	
	11th.		Training as per programme. 4 O.Rs. proceeded to England for demobilization.	
	12th.		Training as per programme.	
	13th.		Training as per programme.	
	14th.		Church Parade.	
	15th.		Training as per programme. 4 Officers and 4 O.Rs. proceeded to England for demobilization.	
	16th.		Battalion moved from Martin Eglise to Rouxmesnil. 3 Officers proceeded to England for dem	

Army Form C. 2118

WAR DIARY
INTELLIGENCE SUMMARY

SEPTEMBER 1919.

(Erase heading not required.)

Instructions regarding War Diaries and Intelligence Summaries are contained in F. S. Regs, Part II. and the Staff Manual respectively. Title Pages will be prepared in manuscript.

Place	Date	Hour	Summary of Events and Information	Remarks and references to Appendices
ROUXMESNIL	17th		Training as per programme. 1 Officer and 2 O.Rs. proceeded to England for demobilization	
	18th		Training as per programme. 34 O.Rs. proceeded to England for demobilization.	
	19th		Training as per programme. 24 O.Rs. proceeded to England for demobilization.	
	20th		Training as per programme. 3 Officers 2/6th.R.Warwickshire Regt, joined the Battalion. 40 O.Rs. proceeded to England for demobilization.	
	21st		Church Parade. 28 O.Rs. proceeded to England for demobilization.	
	22nd		Training as per programme. 36 O.Rs. proceeded to England for demobilization.	
	23rd		Training as per programme. 35 O.Rs. proceeded to England for demobilization.	
	24th		Training as per programme. 1 Officer 2/6th.R.Warwickshire Regt.joined the Battalion. 85 O.Rs. proceeded to England for demobilization.	
	25th		Training as per programme. 51 O.Rs. proceeded to England for demobilization.	
	26th		Training as per programme. All leave and demobilization cancelled owing to the Railway Strike in England.	
	27th		Training as per programme.	
	28th		Church Parade.	
	29th		Training as per programme.	
	30th		Training as per programme.	

Lieut-Colonel
Commdg. 9th.(N.H.)Battn. Northumberland Fusiliers.

Army Form C. 2118

WAR DIARY
INTELLIGENCE SUMMARY

(Erase heading not required)

1st (NH) Battn ~~Middlesex~~ Fusiliers

October 1919

Instructions regarding War Diaries and Intelligence Summaries are contained in F. S. Regs., Part II. and the Staff Manual respectively. Title Pages will be prepared in manuscript.

Place	Date	Hour	Summary of Events and Information	Remarks and references to Appendices
	1st		Training	
	2nd		Training	
	"		Draft of 3 officers and 40 O.Rs of the 17th Battn Worcester Regt arrived for attachment to the Battn	
	3rd		Training	
	"		Draft of 2 officers and 40 O.Rs of the 17th Battn.Worcester Regt arrived for attachment to the Battn	
	4th		Training	
	5th		Church Parade.	
	D="		Draft of 3 officers and 40 O.Rs of the 17th Battn. Worcester Regt arrived for Attachment to the Battn	
	6th		Training	
	7th		Training	
	8th		Training	
	9th		Training	
	10th		Training	
	11th		Training	
	"		2 Officers and 63 O.Rs Demobilised.	
	12th		Church Parade	
	"		2 Officers and 80 O.Rs Demobilised.	
	13th		Training	
	"		65 O.Rs Demobilised.	
	14th		Training	
	"		10 O.Rs Demobilised.	
	15th		Training	
	"		11 O.Rs Demobilised.	
	16th		Training	
	"		Draft of 21 O.Rs of the 17th Battn.Worcester Regt arrived for attachment to the Battalion.	
	17th		Training.	
	18th		Training.	
	19th		Church Parade.	
	"		12 O.Rs Demobilised.	
	20th		Draft of 16 O.Rs of the 17th Battn Worcester Regt arrived for attachment to the Battalion.	
	21st		Training and Education.	
	"		1 O.R. demobilised.	
	22nd		Training and Education.	
	"		14 Officers and 1 Q.R. demobilised.	

Army Form C. 2118.

WAR DIARY
or
INTELLIGENCE SUMMARY.
(Erase heading not required.)

October 1919

Instructions regarding War Diaries and Intelligence Summaries are contained in F.S. Regs., Part II. and the Staff Manual respectively. Title pages will be prepared in manuscript.

Place	Date	Hour	Summary of Events and Information	Remarks and references to Appendices
	23rd		Training and Education.	
	"		5 officers demobilised.	
	"		Draft of 60 O.Rs of the 17th Battn. Worcester Regt arrived for attachment to the Battalion.	
	24th		Training suspended.	
	"		Orders received to reduce the Battalion to Equipment Guard by 1/11/1919.	
	"		16 O.Rs demobilised.	
	25th		Day spent in cleaning up the camp.	
	26th		Church Parade.	
	2"		6 O.Rs demobilised.	
	27th		129 O.Rs demobilised.	
	28th		52 O.Rs demobilised.	
	29th		78 O.Rs demobilised.	
	30th		100 O.Rs demobilised.	
	31st		Battalion Orders issued for the last time.	
			Special Order of the Day issued by the Commanding Officer as follows:-	
			The Commanding Officer wishes to express to all ranks his sincerest thanks for their co-operation and loyalty during the time he has been in command of the Battalion. This copy of the Battalion Orders is the last that will be issued by the Battalion as on the 1st of November the Battalion will have ceased to exist.	
			The Battalion, which has always had a good name, has upheld it to the last, and has added fresh lustre to the glorious traditions of the "FIGHTING FIFTH".	
			On your return to civil life or other Units the Commanding Officer wishes you all the very best of luck and prosperity.	
			Lieut W. Hutton proceeded to England with the King's Colour to hand the same into the Depot, Newcastle.	
			69 O.Rs demobilised.	
Rouxmesnil. 3/11/1919.				

[signature]
Lieut-Colonel.
Comdg. 9th (N.H.) Battn. Northumberland Fusiliers.

[ORDERLY ROOM stamp 4 NOV 1919]